To Bella,

with very best wishes,

Philip

Conscience, Dissent and Reform in Soviet Russia

There was an ethical paradigm shift in the Soviet Union in the decades after Stalin's death; Leninist ethics were rejected, and religious and secular thinkers alike promoted respect for human rights, non-violence, truth-telling, repentance and conscience.

Conscience, Dissent and Reform in Soviet Russia examines this ethical change, focussing specifically on the idea of 'conscience' and the diverse ways in which dissidents and party reformers of the late Soviet era understood it. It explores the history of the idea of conscience before the revolution and in the early decades of Bolshevik rule, as well as under Khrushchev. It then examines the ethics of the human rights movement and the way in which dissident ethics were shaped by experiences of imprisonment and interrogation. This valuable study also explores the idea of conscience in late Soviet literature and philosophy, the enduring influence of Russian Orthodox spirituality in Soviet life, the ethics of party leaders such as Gorbachev and Yakovlev and the moral concerns of the intelligentsia and the emerging democratic movement.

An important and original contribution to research on Soviet history, this book contains many new insights and will be of interest to academics, historians and students of the Soviet era.

Philip Boobbyer is a Senior Lecturer in modern European history at the University of Kent. He specialises in Russian history, and his previous publications include *S. L. Frank: The Life and Work of a Russian Philosopher, 1877–1950* (Ohio University Press, 1995) and *The Stalin Era* (Routledge, 2000).

BASEES/Routledge series on Russian and East European studies

This series is published on behalf of BASEES (the British Association for Slavonic and East European Studies). The series comprises original, high-quality, research-level work by both new and established scholars on all aspects of Russian, Soviet, post-Soviet and East European Studies in humanities and social science subjects.

1 **Ukraine's Foreign and Security Policy, 1991–2000**
Roman Wolczuk

2 **Political Parties in the Russian Regions**
Derek S. Hutcheson

3 **Local Communities and Post-Communist Transformation**
Edited by Simon Smith

4 **Repression and Resistance in Communist Europe**
J.C. Sharman

5 **Political Elites and the New Russia**
Anton Steen

6 **Dostoevsky and the Idea of Russianness**
Sarah Hudspith

7 **Performing Russia – Folk Revival and Russian Identity**
Laura J. Olson

8 **Russian Transformations**
Edited by Leo McCann

9 **Soviet Music and Society under Lenin and Stalin**
The baton and sickle
Edited by Neil Edmunds

10 **State Building in Ukraine**
The Ukranian parliament, 1990–2003
Sarah Whitmore

11 **Defending Human Rights in Russia**
Sergei Kovalyov, dissident and Human Rights Commissioner, 1969–2003
Emma Gilligan

12 **Small-Town Russia**
Postcommunist livelihoods and identities: A portrait of the intelligentsia in Achit, Bednodemyanovsk and Zubtsov, 1999–2000
Anne White

13 **Russian Society and the Orthodox Church**
Religion in Russia after Communism
Zoe Knox

14 **Russian Literary Culture in the Camera Age**
The word as image
Stephen Hutchings

15 **Between Stalin and Hitler**
Class war and race war on the Dvina, 1940–46
Geoffrey Swain

16 **Literature in Post-Communist Russia and Eastern Europe**
The Russian, Czech and Slovak fiction of the changes 1988–98
Rajendra A. Chitnis

17 **The Legacy of Social Dissidents**
Dissidents, democratisation and radical nationalism in Russia
Robert Horvath

18 **Russian and Soviet Film Adaptations of Literature, 1900–2001**
Screening the word
Edited by Stephen Hutchings and Anat Vernitski

19 **Russia as a Great Power**
Dimensions of security under Putin
Edited by Jakob Hedenskog, Vilhelm Konnander, Bertil Nygren, Ingmar Oldberg and Christer Pursiainen

20 **Katyn and the Soviet Massacre of 1940**
Truth, justice and memory
George Sanford

21 **Conscience, Dissent and Reform in Soviet Russia**
Philip Boobbyer

22 **The Limits of Russian Democratisation**
Emergency powers and states of emergency
Alexander N. Domrin

23 **The Dilemmas of Destalinisation**
A social and cultural history of reform in the Khrushchev era
Edited by Polly Jones

Conscience, Dissent and Reform in Soviet Russia

Philip Boobbyer

LONDON AND NEW YORK

First published 2005
by Routledge
2 Park Square, Milton Park, Abingdon, Oxon OX14 4RN

Simultaneously published in the USA and Canada
by Routledge
270 Madison Ave, New York, NY 10016

Routledge is an imprint of the Taylor & Francis Group

Typeset in Times by Wearset Ltd, Boldon, Tyne and Wear
Printed and bound in Great Britain by MPG Books Ltd, Bodmin

British Library Cataloguing in Publication Data
A catalogue record for this book is available from the British Library

Library of Congress Cataloging in Publication Data
A catalog record for this book has been requested

ISBN 0-415-33186-2

To my parents

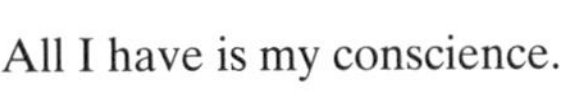

All I have is my conscience.

Svetlana Alliluyeva

Contents

Acknowledgements

I first had the idea of writing a book on this theme in early 1995, and later in that year I got a permanent post at the University of Kent. I owe a large debt of gratitude to my colleagues in the School of History at Kent for their support and advice over these years. The research culture of the School has shaped and sharpened my thinking in all sorts of ways. Among others, I would like to thank David Birmingham, Christine Bolt, Anthony Copley, William Fortescue, Ulf Schmidt and David Welch for conversations and support. I am also grateful to the colleagues from Kent University and elsewhere who read and commented on part or all of the manuscript: Hugh Cunningham, Geoffrey Hosking, Michael Hughes, Brian Kelly, Richard Sakwa and Charlotte Sleigh.

There are many friends and acquaintances that have contributed to this project in different ways. I would particularly like to thank Aleksei Bodrov, Vladimir Bukovskii, Patrick Colquhoun, Bryan Hamlin, Andrei Kirilenkov, Vera Lashkova, Andrei Mironov, Sergei Podbolotov, Irina Ratushinskaya, Peter Thwaites and Aleksandr Tsipko for their help. The ideas of Tat'yana Bakhmin, archivist at the Memorial Society, were important, and I am also grateful for the assistance of Malcolm Walker at the Keston Institute library. Thanks too are due to Irene Glazov and Anastasia Stepanova for their work in transcribing interviews. In addition, I would like to say a special word of thanks to Leif Hovelsen for his support; he was one of the chief inspirers of this project, and I am much indebted to him.

I am grateful too for financial assistance in various forms. Grants in 1996 from the Humanities Research Fund at Kent University and the Anglo-Nordic Productions Trust enabled me to buy the recording equipment that I used for my interviews. Funding from the British Council enabled me to do a three-week research visit to St Petersburg and Moscow in Spring 1996. More recently, in 2003, I was awarded a four-month research fellowship from the Leverhulme Trust that, in combination with a term's study leave from Kent University in late 2002, freed up most of an academic year to pursue the research and writing.

Finally, I would like to dedicate this book to my parents, who have been a permanent source of support and ideas over the years.

Canterbury
November 2004

Notes on the text

This book contains information, ideas and quotations from interviews that I conducted over a ten-year period from 1994–2003. These interviews, many of them with prominent Soviet dissidents or party reformers, were mostly about the moral dilemmas of late Soviet Russia and issues of conscience. The interviews were semi-structured, and revolved around two questions: how the moral and spiritual world-view of the interviewee was formed, and how the interviewee dealt with the moral dilemmas of Soviet life. I found the interviews very helpful. Oral history helped me to understand in a profounder and more personal way the dilemmas and struggles that people faced. This was important, because the book is partly an attempt to offer a portrait of the inner spiritual world of people in late Soviet Russia. For obvious reasons, interviews made a more intimate picture of life possible. However, interviews are not the main source of evidence for this book. Rather, they provide information that supplements what is already to be found in published sources.

Some of the material from the interviews appeared in two earlier articles: 'Religious Experiences of the Soviet Dissidents', *Religion, State and Society*, 27, 3/4, 1999, pp. 373–390; and 'Truth-telling, Conscience and Dissent in Late Soviet Russia: Evidence from Oral Histories', *European History Quarterly*, 30, 4, 2000, pp. 553–585. In the notes, wherever quotations from interviews first appeared in these articles, I have cited the articles rather than the interviews themselves.

A list of the interviews is given at the end of the book in the Appendix.

A note on transliteration

Throughout the book, I have used a modified form of the Library of Congress system of transliteration. The letters 'ia' and 'iu' have been transliterated as 'ya' and 'yu'. In addition, some Russian names have been anglicised.

Introduction

The Soviet Union's journey from crisis to collapse in 1985–1991 can be interpreted in various ways. At one level, the origins of the process can be read in terms of power politics: economic decline and geopolitical isolation forced the party leadership into embarking on radical reform.[1] Reforms then unleashed democratic and nationalist forces that proved impossible to manage. From another angle, however, what happened was rooted in longer-term social change: since Stalin's death, 'modernisation' in various forms had changed the social structure of the country and this in turn brought about a transformation in the country's political system.[2] Personalities mattered: Gorbachev and Yeltsin, for example, brought particular qualities to Soviet politics, which determined in no small measure how events unfolded. There was also an ideological and cultural shift: perestroika can be seen as an intellectual revolution brought about by a small, westernising elite.[3] All these approaches have their place, and contain important truths. However, the aim of this book is to consider a theme that, although it is partly assumed by other perspectives, has not yet received sufficient attention: the ethical dimension. There was a moral failure. One commentator recently wrote of the 'moral, intellectual and cultural defeat of the Soviet system'.[4] It proved impossible to resolve the contradictions that were inherent in the Bolshevik ideal. A sense of stagnation and corruption set in during the last decades of Soviet rule, and the regime lost its moral legitimacy. At the same time, alongside failure or decadence, there was also recovery and renewal. In the last decades of Soviet rule there emerged an alternative moral and spiritual culture that undermined the Soviet system and ideology. It is particularly with this alternative culture that this study is concerned.

Alongside a general focus on ethics, this book explores the meaning and influence of the idea of 'conscience' in late Soviet Russia. 'Conscience' was constantly emphasised during the perestroika era, and was generally used in two ways. By the mid-1980s, many intellectuals and politicians had come to believe that Soviet life was in need of moral regeneration. References to 'conscience' often reflected a belief that in its methods of building communism, the Soviet regime had infringed against some kind of universal moral order. In this connection, there was a search for a stronger moral foundation for society. At the same time, the word 'conscience' was used in relation to liberty; there was a lot of talk of 'freedom of conscience'. Some who emphasised moral absolutes were uneasy about aspects of liberal democracy and, conversely, some liberals and socialists were suspicious of conservative moral ideas. Yet moral opposition to communism was often rooted in a combination of these two tendencies.

Soviet dissidents and party reformers are the central focus of this study. The Soviet dissident movement emerged in the late 1960s primarily as a response to the authoritarianism of the Brezhnev regime. Although the movement was in some ways political in that it challenged the regime's authoritarianism, it gained much of its unity from its commitment to certain moral ideals. Most dissidents were committed to the defence of human rights and the principle of non-violence, and they often stressed the need for people to speak out against injustice. In addition, dissidents often called on people to live according to the truth or conscience. Aleksandr Solzhenitsyn's programmatic essay of 1974, 'Live Not by the Lie', gave expression to a wider aspiration in the intelligentsia to avoid lying, and to overcome a sense of inner spiritual dislocation.[5]

Although the dissident movement manifested itself in specific ways, it is not easy to define 'dissent' in the Soviet context. Some people spoke out boldly against the Soviet regime, while others discreetly tried to reform it from within. Yet the differences between such people were often blurred. The political scientist, Aleksandr Shtromas, who interpreted dissent simply to mean 'the refusal to assent to an established or imposed set of ideas', noted that in the Soviet case the boundaries between those who sought to change the Soviet system from within and those who opposed it from without, were not always clear.[6] There were certainly plenty of people who had doubts about the regime that they rarely expressed. Gorbachev and his team are best described as 'reformers'. Their initial aspiration was to try to reform the system rather than to dismantle it. Yet, as with the dissidents, there was an important moral component in their thinking. Those who initiated perestroika made repeated references to conscience and calls for national moral renewal. For example, in his book *Perestroika* (1987), Gorbachev suggested that the ideas of perestroika were prompted not just by pragmatic considerations, but also by a 'troubled conscience'.[7] In 1988, Politburo member Aleksandr Yakovlev stated that the 'moral aspects of the Socialist renewal' were 'the beginning and the end of the perestroika concept'.[8]

The fact that both dissidents and party reformers had moral concerns does not of course mean that they understood words like 'morality' and 'conscience' in the same way. A word can have many meanings. The moral philosophy of some intellectuals in the Brezhnev period was a self-defence mechanism: they saw the Soviet state as alien and predatory, and wanted to keep their inner selves free from being corrupted by it. On the other hand, during perestroika, party reformers often used the language of morality to mobilise the population to achieve social and political tasks; and they also used a discourse of conscience to try to legitimise their power and policies. Thus, the power context in which dissidents and party reformers talked of conscience, and the differing kinds of relations that these groups had with the country's power structures, shaped their diverse moral visions. On the other hand, it is all too easy to reduce issues of morality to questions of power. Although acting from different layers of society, there was sometimes common ground between dissidents and party reformers. In their upbringing and schooling, they had all been exposed to the diverse traditions that gave Russians their moral identities, even if in different ways. In this sense, the moral thinking of dissident and party intellectuals can be treated as part of the same cultural phenomenon. Moreover, the two groups were never completely isolated from one another; internal cultural transfer could take place, thus making it possible for the dissidents to influence perestroika at an intellectual and cultural level.[9]

An ethical history is necessarily an intellectual and cultural history. The thinking of both dissidents and party reformers was shaped by Soviet Russian culture. The Soviet project was from its inception a moral one; it sought to create a new society on the basis of a radical transformation of values. Indeed, the global appeal of Soviet communism, especially in its earlier decades, was due to the fact that it could project itself as a superior moral alternative to Western capitalism and liberal democracy. Dissidents and party reformers alike were shaped by an ethic of moral seriousness that pervaded Soviet political and social institutions, as well as literary culture. At the same time, the culture of the late Soviet era was rooted in traditions that went back far beyond 1917. 'Conscience' itself was a concept embedded in nineteenth-century Russian literature and Russian Orthodox thought, and in a longer-term sense understandings of it were shaped by the Byzantine heritage of the country. Beyond that even, the idea of conscience was rooted in Graeco-Roman and Judaeo-Christian culture more generally. The 'rebirth of conscience'[10] after Stalin's death can thus be viewed as a kind of restoration of older local and global patterns of moral thinking. At the same time, to speak in terms of restoration alone is misleading; some of these older traditions were in surprising ways present in the fabric even of Stalinist culture.

The rebirth of conscience thus grew out of long-term traditions, as well as being shaped by the particularities of Soviet culture and society. At the same time, the historian should not lose sight of the individual dimension; personal experience rarely coincides exactly with the periodisations that historians impose on the past. 'Each man has his secret personal world', wrote Yevgenii Yevtushenko in one of his poems.[11] This is important because biographical factors clearly influenced the intellectual and political culture of the late Soviet era. The historian of conscience must remain aware of the uniqueness of each person's moral and intellectual journey. Ethical motivations are also notoriously hard to pin down. People are constantly changing. What in one situation may be a form of truth-telling or courageous protest against injustice can in the next be a case of conformity or egocentrism. This precludes easy generalisations.

The focus of this book, then, is the moral and spiritual ideas and experiences of Soviet dissidents and party reformers, and the broader culture of which they were a part.

The Russian understanding of spiritual life and culture (*dukhovnaya kul'tura*) is less narrowly defined than its English equivalent.[12] In Russian, the concept of 'spirituality' can relate not only to the religious life itself, but also to the broader moral and intellectual qualities of man in his relation to God, nature and people.[13] It is with this broader understanding of spirituality that the book is concerned. Terminology can be problematic. Since human speech is so value-laden, it can be difficult to distinguish moral ideas from non-moral ones. If Douglas Cole and Isaiah Berlin were right to treat political theory as a branch of moral philosophy,[14] then almost everything that relates to thought and culture overlaps with morality; in that case intellectual and ethical history turn out to be very similar if not the same thing. Focussing on morality and conscience is thus justified not because the moral sphere can be isolated from others, but because it has not been sufficiently emphasised.

The word 'conscience' itself can have a variety of meanings. In the ancient Greek form, *synedeisis*, it originally had two meanings: one roughly referring to a state of consciousness, and the other meaning something like a feeling of moral unease or guilt.[15] In modern English, the word 'consciousness' itself has taken on the role of the first meaning, leaving 'conscience' to embrace the second.[16] However, the word 'conscience' itself has come to embrace a variety of interrelated meanings. A contributor to a recent encyclopaedia suggests that conscience is used to refer to four different things: (1) the moral convictions people actually hold to and judge themselves by; (2) the faculty by which people come to know moral truths; (3) the activity of moral self-examination; and (4) the experience of guilt – a 'bad conscience'.[17]

In modern Russia, the corresponding terms for consciousness and conscience are *soznanie* and *soznatel'nost'*, on the one hand, and *sovest'*, on the other. It should be noted, however, that in certain situations the meanings of these terms can overlap. Oleg Kharkhordin, writing about the Bolshevik use of the concept of conscience, noted that in the minds of some Bolsheviks *soznatel'nost'* came to play the role of the word *sovest'* in that it was understood to reflect 'an individual, yet undifferentiated, capacity of moral and factual judgement'.[18] Certainly, the Bolsheviks did not wholeheartedly embrace the term *sovest'* because of its religious associations, emphasising the more rational and secular *soznatel'nost'* instead. At the same time, *soznatel'nost'* never acquired the moral and spiritual connotations of *sovest'*, and it is primarily with 'conscience' in the sense of *sovest'* that this study is concerned.

Philosophers and theologians have understood conscience in a variety of ways. Cicero, a believer in natural law, described 'true law' as 'right reason in agreement with nature', and believed that knowledge of right and wrong could be found in human consciousness. This he called *conscientia*, which was the Latin equivalent of *synedeisis*.[19] Aquinas used two words for the idea: *synderesis* and *conscientia*. In his usage, *synderesis* related to the first principles of action, 'the universal principles of natural law', while *conscientia* involved the application of knowledge to a particular act. Conscience, he once stated, 'is the practical judgement of dictate or reason, by which we judge what here and now is to be done as being good, or avoided as evil'.[20] Luther broke with the Thomist tradition, rejecting the rationalistic basis of ethics, and declaring the primacy of the individual conscience over law. Although assuming a Christian world-view, he nevertheless introduced a strongly individualistic emphasis to the debate.[21] Kant argued that conscience is inherent in everyone from birth; in his writings, the rational and judgemental nature of conscience acquired a more juridical quality, and conscience came to be more directly associated with the voice of God. Marx interpreted conscience in class terms, seeing its origin in the struggle for goods. Nietzsche emphasised the will to power.[22] Freud, who saw the origin of conscience in the Oedipus crime, interpreted conscience not as the voice of God, but as the socially constructed ego rooted in the wider social conventions of the time, the superego.[23]

The ultimate origin of morality is not something that historians are likely to agree on. At the same time, it is worth observing that in histories of the USSR, a variety of understandings of ethics and spiritual life are evident. Some historians link ethics with class. In her study of Soviet literature in the 1930s and 1940s, *In Stalin's Time*, Vera Dunham suggested that the retreat from cultural radicalism during Stalin's rule was driven from below by a rising middle class that wanted to consolidate its gains. The concept 'middle class', as Dunham deployed it, was used to connote 'an attachment to specific values', to a 'way of life' that partly cut across differences of position and which was 'difficult to anchor in any one sharply defined social group'.[24] Some historians see ethical values in the context of 'progressive' and 'reactionary' ideas. For example, Trotskii's description of Stalin's cultural policies of the 1930s as a 'Thermidorian' retreat or reaction to the progressive policies of the 1920s was replicated in Richard Stites' analysis of the women's revolutionary movement in Russia; the Soviet sexual Thermidor, Stites suggested, was 'reactionary'.[25] Another approach, associated with the French philosopher Michel Foucault, is to suggest that moral ideas are best understood as belonging to particular discourses, and that these discourses are in turn rooted in social and political power struggles. Using this kind of methodology in *From Darkness to*

Light: Class, Consciousness and Salvation in Revolutionary Russia, Igal Halfin takes the view that poetics hold the key to Soviet history. He suggests that Soviet power was rooted in the underlying narratives deployed by the regime, and argues that the structures of Marxist and Bolshevik discourse were similar to those of traditional spiritual discourses.[26]

There are also historians who imply the existence of a more universal moral order. Martin Malia's *The Soviet Tragedy* uses the model of Greek tragedy, as articulated in Aeschylus's *Oresteia*, to illustrate the way in which violence and crime escalated under Soviet rule: 'The burden of [Aeschylus's] *Oresteia* is that crime begets crime, and violence violence, until the first crime in the chain, the original sin in the genus, is expiated through accumulated suffering.' Malia likens Dostoevskii's religious world-view to that of Aeschylus: 'The burden of Dostoevskii is the somewhat Aeschylean one that "the hubris of modern reason leads to moral sickness and murderous crime".'[27] Leonard Schapiro, writing in 1977 about the way violence became endemic in the Soviet system, also implied the existence of a kind of moral law:

> There are many examples in the history of the last fifty years alone to show that where a minority seeks to impose its will, in the profound conviction that it alone has possession of the truth, and the historic right to enforce it in defiance of all the legal and moral rights over which it rules, the amount of violence which it employs will steadily increase.[28]

Robert Service, also writing about violence in the USSR, observed that prior to Stalin's consolidation of power 'important moral thresholds had been crossed'.[29] What might be called 'moral realism' is tacitly accepted by many.[30]

There are clearly different methodologies and ethical assumptions present in the work of historians. In practice, historians do not always analyse their underlying moral philosophies, and they sometimes assume different interpretations of the nature of ethics in the same work. This is no bad thing since human experience is so varied, and each person and situation is different. There is an intellectual, social and cultural history of conscience, and indeed the late Soviet conscience is impossible to comprehend without a detailed examination of its historical context. At the same time, the tendency to reduce the moral and spiritual world to impersonal social, economic or cultural forces, and thereby to deny its real existence, is something to be avoided.

1 Russian moral traditions before 1917

It is impossible to understand the moral and spiritual culture of late Soviet Russia without considering some of the ideas and practices that were important in Russia before 1917. Certain things need to be highlighted if what happened in the late twentieth century is to be put into context, and some of the longer-term continuities in Russian spiritual culture adequately established. Russians were always drawn to ethical ideals, but by the late nineteenth century at least two major ascetic traditions had established themselves and were in various ways permeating Russian life: the monastic 'hesychast' tradition with its roots in Byzantine Orthodoxy and beyond, and the secular moralism of the Russian intelligentsia, which originated with certain trends in the Enlightenment. In addition to these two intellectual tendencies, Russian literature started to play a defining role in the moral formation of intellectuals. Political, economic and social factors must also be taken into account.

Language and religion played a vital role in the formation of Russian attitudes to conscience. Etymology is important, because the central conveyor of the idea of conscience in Russia was the Russian language itself. It is important to remember that the Bolsheviks criticised Russian tsarism while at the same time deploying the Russian language itself. The dissident poet, Yosif Brodskii, whose trial in 1964 was an important moment in the growth of the dissident movement, stated in one of his essays: 'Because civilizations are finite, in the life of each of them comes a moment when centers cease to hold. What keeps them at such times from disintegration is not legions but languages.'[1] The moral vocabulary of Russian civilisation continued to operate during the Soviet era, and the mentalities of the dissidents and party reformers owed much to it.

Russia owed its moral and religious vocabulary to Byzantine Orthodox culture and more generally to the Graeco-Roman civilisation that it grew out of. The Russian word for conscience '*sovest*'' was borrowed from Church Slavonic, and was a translation of the Greek word *synedeisis*.[2] The Byzantine understanding of conscience was partly derived from the Stoic conception of natural law. This found expression in Justinian's law code of 534 AD, which became the foundation of the Byzantine legal tradition.

Cicero, who helped to formulate these ideas, described *conscientia* as 'a "knowing with" . . . a moral awareness or capacity for judgment, a knowing in company with oneself'.[3] The Russian word for 'conscience' – *sovest'* has the same associations. The prefix *so*, meaning 'with', and the suffix *vest'*, signifying knowledge, come together to mean something like 'knowledge with'.

As well as 'conscience', the words for truth, *istina* and *pravda*, have always had a powerful resonance in Russian. As the Russian religious philosopher Pavel Florenskii observed, *istina* is related to the adjectives for true, authentic and real, *istyi, istinnyi* and *istovyi*. Florenskii also suggested that *istina* is connected to the Russian verb 'to be', *est'*, and thereby has ontological associations, although this remains unproven.[4] The other Russian word for truth, *pravda*, also contains a range of associations. In his essay in *Landmarks* (1909), the philosopher Nikolai Berdyaev juxtaposed philosophical truth, *filosofskaya istina*, with the intelligentsia's truth, *intelligentskaya pravda*, thereby suggesting that *pravda* carried more practical associations. Berdyaev believed that the intelligentsia lacked a respect for *istina*, subordinating it to utilitarian considerations. At the same time, Berdyaev suggested that the Russian intelligentsia needed to unify the philosophical and practical dimensions of the word *pravda*; it was important that the intelligentsia found a way of combining its commitments to philosophical truth, *pravda-istina*, and truth as justice, *pravda-spravedlivost'*, so as to bring theory and practice together.[5] Although the Bolsheviks attempted to take control of the word *pravda* by using it as the title of their party newspaper, the word retained its own broader religious and philosophical appeal throughout Soviet history. Solzhenitsyn used the word when in 1974 he paid tribute to people who continued to 'live in the truth' ('*zhivet po pravde*').[6]

There are two words in the Russian moral lexicon for a lie: *lozh'* and *vran'e*. Although there is overlap in the meaning of the words, *lozh'* is used for lies of a more substantial and serious nature. When Solzhenitsyn issued 'Live Not by the Lie', it was this word that he used; and generally in late Soviet Russia, when people attacked the pervasive dishonesty of the country, it was this kind of lie that they had in mind. *Vran'e*, on the other hand, was traditionally regarded as a less important matter. Before the First World War in an essay, 'Pan-Russian *vran'e*', the writer Leonid Andreev argued that Russians have no talent for lying of the *lozh'* kind, but that *vran'e* is as widespread as the aspen tree: 'It pops up uninvited everywhere and chokes other varieties.'[7] Dostoevskii also noted the prevalence of *vran'e*, stating in 1873 that there could hardly be any educated Russian who was not addicted to lying, often for the sake of hospitality or good social relations. Lying, he said, was so pervasive that people hardly noticed they were doing it; the truth was habitually considered prosaic and banal. In his view, the habit of never being really honest about oneself in public had been developing over a period of two hundred years.[8]

There are also two words for morality in Russian: *moral'* and *nravstvennost'*. In the Soviet era, some writers used *moral'* to refer to the subjectively moral dimension, and *nravstvennost'* to the objective sphere, while others used them in the reverse sense. In the end, the difference between the two words is not clear, and in practice, most writers used the terms interchangeably. One writer suggests that the two words reflect quite closely the difference in German between *Moralität* and *Sittlichkeit*, as described by Hegel.[9]

Religion as well as language was vital in the formation of Russian moral attitudes. Following the moment when Prince Vladimir embraced Eastern Christianity in 988, Russian culture developed within an Orthodox framework. Certain themes are particularly important in Russian spiritual culture. One of these is the positive role of suffering in the life of the religious believer. Belief in the therapeutic role of suffering has a long heritage in Russian thought. One particularly Russian feature of the spirituality that developed in the early centuries of Russian Christianity was the idea of non-resistance to evil. Already at that time, there were accounts of suffering being welcomed by the sufferer; in 1015 the Princes Boris and Gleb apparently refused to struggle against murder by their elder brother Svyatopolk, and even invited murder upon themselves.[10] According to the religious philosopher Georgii Fedotov, there then emerged a distinctive view of the Christian way of salvation; it was a spiritual tendency that involved an imitation of Christ's self-humiliation and voluntary sacrificial death.[11]

Russian spirituality always had a powerful other-worldly and monastic dimension. Although early Russian Christianity had strongly social tendencies, from the fourteenth century onwards there was a divergence between the mystical and social dimensions. In Orthodox countries the hesychast debates of the thirteenth and fourteenth centuries saw the victory of those who promoted a contemplative spirituality. Hesychasm had its roots in the Eastern monasticism of the fourth century, in which monks who lived in solitude rather than in community were known as hesychasts. It emphasised the use of breathing techniques, 'prayer of the mind' and thc 'Jesus prayer'.[12] Hesychasts believed that a direct, mystical knowledge of God was possible, and they downplayed secular concerns. In particular, a monk from Mount Athos, Grigorii Palamas (1296–1359) played an important part in defending hesychasm and making it central to an emerging pan-Orthodox world-view.[13] Following the influence of St Sergius in Russia, hesychasm became central to the lives of the mystics of Russia's northern forests, who cultivated poverty, silence and prayer.[14] It has been suggested that the focus on personal piety and the possibility of direct access to God in the hesychast tradition involved an 'Eastern anticipation of protestantism'.[15]

In the early sixteenth century, the Russian Orthodox Church split into two groups: the 'possessors', whose religious ideals were practical and social and who came to be associated with St Joseph Volotskii, and the 'non-possessors', backers of St Nilus Sorskii, who embraced the hesychast traditions of the church. The divisions between the groups were intertwined with the struggles of the Russian state under Ivan III and Vasilii III for greater control over monastic lands. The Josephites were victorious, and the followers of Nilus were condemned as heretics. The hesychast movement then went underground for about two centuries, before re-emerging again in the eighteenth century. Its re-emergence was associated with the publication of *The Philokalia* in Russian. This was an anthology of ascetical and mystical texts initially compiled by Nikodemos the Hagiorite and Makarios of Corinth. A Slavonic version of this was published in 1793 by the Ukrainian monk, Paissii Velichkovskii, and it was subsequently followed by two Russian translations in 1857 and 1883, edited by the monk, Theophan the Recluse.[16]

The idea of 'conscience' was central in the texts of *The Philokalia*. According to Stephen Thomas, *syneidisis* (conscience) is understood in *The Philokalia* as part of the broader concept of *nipsis*, which means 'watchfulness'. *Syneidisis* does not infallibly discern God's voice in terms of right and wrong, as it does in the Western religious writings of Hutcheson, Butler or Newman, but is nevertheless 'part of a conceptual system to describe *ascesis*, the spiritual struggle necessary for fellowship with God'. At the same time, it does not represent a secular autonomous faculty for the discernment of justice. Within the context of the call to fellowship with God, conscience condemns people when they experience a tension between the way things are and the way they ought to be; people thus sometimes experience a 'pricking of conscience' (*katanixis*).[17]

Conscience as *syneidisis* was used in a variety of ways in *The Philokalia*. St Philotheus of Sinai, for example, describes it as the 'heart's purity' and the 'soul's mirror', and St Peter of Damascus calls it 'the natural knowledge given us by God'.[18] St Mark the Ascetic suggests that conscience is 'nature's book', and that 'a good conscience is found through prayer, and pure prayer through the conscience'.[19] Some ascetic thinkers believed that people could not act against their conscience without experiencing punishment; St Isaiah the Solitary declared: 'If we do not obey our conscience, it will abandon us and we shall fall into the hands of our enemies, who will never let us go.'[20]

Dorotheus of Gaza suggested that when God created man, he breathed into him a divine spark that could illuminate the difference between right and wrong, but that since the fall that spark had become buried. However, he stated that divine revelation had through the law and the prophets, and the resurrection of Christ, given people the power to renew their consciences, if they were obedient to its promptings. According to Stephen Thomas, Dorotheus's teaching encapsulates the basic elements of the Eastern Orthodox interpretation of conscience:

> [In Dorotheus' view] conscience is an originally innate capacity to judge of good and evil which in the context of fallen human nature has been obscured and which requires the divine *Logos* to uncover it. Even after the acceptance of faith, *syneidisis* can become opaque again, so that the life of faith is a continual fall-redemption-death-resurrection drama rather than a definable moment.'[21]

The victory of the Josephites in the early sixteenth century coincided with the spread of messianic ideas in Russia. The idea of Moscow as the Third Rome was likely first suggested in the reign of Ivan III (1462–1505), and marked the beginning of a strong messianic tradition, which particularly influenced Muscovite ideology. This tradition was also powerfully at work in the seventeenth century when, following his election as Patriarch in 1652, Metropolitan Nikon of Novgorod sought to reform various aspects of church ritual; notably congregations were informed that they should bow to the waist rather than to the ground, and to make the sign of the cross with three fingers rather than two. The reforms were introduced with little consultation. Furthermore, the fact that Nikon was trying to adapt Russian rituals to contemporary Greek forms was controversial, and there was widespread suspicion that westernising influences were at work.

The schism that resulted had a major effect on religious attitudes in Russia. Those who refused to accept the reforms – the Old Believers – found themselves in opposition to the church and the state. Large numbers of conservative and patriotic Russians were driven into opposition and decided to try to live their lives outside the framework of church and state.[22] For many, to compromise with either church or state meant to compromise with evil; loyalty to conscience and opposition to the state or church became intertwined. The autobiography of Archpriest Avvakum is a good example of the robust spirituality of the early Old Believers. Avvakum depicts Nikon's reforms as the work of the anti-Christ, and concludes by encouraging his readers to 'speak without fear' and to 'keep a firm conscience'.[23]

The moral vocabulary of the late Soviet era certainly had origins in Stoic and Orthodox traditions. At the same time, for many intellectuals the medium for their moral formation was Russian literature. The modern Russian literary tradition emerged later than its Western counterparts, and from the beginning it contained a distinctive ethical dimension. Indeed, the education of the soul, moral enlightenment, and the influence upon the conscience were to become central interests of nineteenth-century Russian literature.[24]

Aleksandr Pushkin helped to create the vision of the writer as a prophet inspired by God. In his poem 'The Prophet' (1826), Pushkin depicted himself as a corpse lying in the desert, visited by the voice of God calling him to be a prophet: 'Arise, O prophet, see and hear, be filled with

My will, go forth over land and sea, and set the hearts of men on fire with your Word.'[25] Although Pushkin's personal life did not match up to the moral purity normally demanded of a biblical prophet, subsequent writers, notably Gogol, Lermontov, Dostoevskii and Vladimir Solov'ev, constructed versions of his life that consolidated his prophetic status.[26] Partly under this influence, the idea of the writer as prophet became established in Russian literary culture. At the same time, literature also acquired a prophetic social function because there was no public political opposition in the country, and it could offer an alternative forum for debate.

Pushkin had a lasting influence on Russian literary culture in other ways. Friendship was important in his world-view. In his poem '19 October 1825' (1825), Pushkin declared: 'My friends, our union is an excellent thing';[27] and the ideal of friendship was much valued in the Russian and Soviet intelligentsia. He also helped to consolidate the importance of conscience as a literary theme. In the main character of the play *Boris Godunov* (1825), he depicted a ruler in moral turmoil: 'Ah! Now I feel it; nothing can give us peace / Mid worldly cares, nothing save only conscience!. . . / Oh, pity him whose conscience is unclean!'[28] In another of his plays, *The Miserly Knight* (1830), conscience is described as a 'sharp-taloned beast, clawing the heart. . ., / an uninvited guest, an annoying interlocuter, / a rude creditor, and a witch / which dims the moon and graves'.[29]

Many of Russia's greatest writers were influenced by Orthodox values. Gogol, Dostoevskii and Tolstoi all sought inspiration at the famous Russian monastery at Optina Pustyn in the Kaluga guberniya, and through it were exposed to the Russian hesychast tradition. Gogol read the writings of the seventh-century hermit, John of Sinai, as he worked on *Dead Souls*, and he saw the writing of the novel as a mission from God.[30] Dostoevskii used to consult the *starets*, Father Amvrosii, and Father Amvrosii was the model for Father Zosima in his novel *The Brothers Karamazov* (1880); through Zosima, Soviet Russian readers could immerse themselves in a nineteenth-century version of hesychasm. Tolstoi too was increasingly religious, although he became very sceptical about the Russian Orthodox Church. Indeed, his views became so radical that Lenin later claimed him as a proto-Bolshevik.[31]

Dostoevskii's writings played a central role in making spiritual questions a central literary concern. He was always particularly interested in the nature of criminality, and in what happened to people who crossed moral boundaries. He was arrested in 1849 for his involvement in a socialist opposition group, and he spent the next four years in prison in Siberia. In *Notes from the House of the Dead* (1862), which grew out of his prison experience, he suggested that even the most hardened criminals retained an element of goodness in their hearts.[32] In *Crime and Punishment* (1866), he examined the spiritual life of a student, Raskolnikov, who kills an old pawnbroker to see what will happen if he disobeys the moral law. Again, in *The Devils*, in the character of Stavrogin, he explored the psychology of a man who shows contempt for traditional morality.[33]

Tolstoi too was interested in the nature of moral law. His work can conveniently be divided into the period before his religious conversion, when he wrote *War and Peace* and *Anna Karenina*, and the period after, when he wrote *Confession, the Death of Ivan Ilych* and his last major novel, *Resurrection*. Yet both before and after his conversion, he adhered to the classical doctrine of natural law.[34] In *Anna Karenina*, for example, the reader can contrast the fate of Anna, whose affair with Vronskii leads eventually to her suicide, with the life of Levin, who takes the spiritual questions of life seriously and whose life generally goes in the right direction. The biblical quotation with which the novel begins, 'Vengeance is Mine, I will Repay', suggests a world where evil punishes itself.[35] Similarly, *Resurrection* is the story of a landowner who during a legal case against a prostitute recognises a woman whom he himself had corrupted, and whom he subsequently attempts to rescue. It shows the consequences of departing from the moral law, although it differs from *Anna Karenina* in that it openly espouses certain kinds of Christian moral teaching.

The issue of crossing of moral borders interested another writer with religious concerns, Nikolai Leskov. In Leskov's story, 'Lady Macbeth of Mtsensk', a bored merchant's wife, Katerina L'vovna Izmailova, takes a young lover named Sergei, and the two of them then murder Katerina's husband and nephew. The story is a study of the moral disintegration of Katerina and Sergei, and their eventual estrangement in exile as Sergei takes new lovers. Accused in front of Katerina of having no conscience, Sergei replies: 'Why should I have any conscience [*sovestit'sia*] about her? I don't think I ever loved her anyway.'[36]

Painters as well as writers explored spiritual themes. Nikolai Ge (1831–1894), who was greatly influenced by Tolstoi, is a good example. In his painting, 'What is Truth?' (1890), Ge portrayed Christ before Pilate. Pontius Pilate intrigued certain Soviet writers, and notably made an appearance in Mikhail Bulgakov's *Master and Margerita*; Ge's painting suggests that this interest was not just a phenomenon of the Soviet era. Ge's painting of Judas, 'Conscience. Judas.' (1891), suggests that Judas's betrayal of Jesus led him into a state of profound isolation.

The fascination with the breaking of moral laws in the works of nineteenth-century Russian writers points to a society that was quite uncertain about its moral convictions. Gogol, Dostoevskii and Tolstoi themselves were often deeply troubled over their failures to live up to their ideals. Indeed, for all the religious intensity of nineteenth-century Russian literature, there is much evidence to suggest that the country was not very religious in practice. Tolstoi suggested in *Confession* that in reality religious doctrines were 'far from life and independent of it', and that most believers were dull, cruel and immoral people whereas honesty, straightforwardness, good-naturedness and morality were qualities to be found in non-believers.[37] Writing some decades later, the Russian liberal Aleksandr Izgoev, depicted contemporary students as corrupted by sensuality and lacking any kind of sound moral vision.[38] Increasingly for the people in the emerging intelligentsia, spiritual crisis led them away from faith. The Russian religious philosopher, Sergei Bulgakov, recalled that he lost his faith without a struggle while he was in his teens: 'I was helpless in the face of unbelief, and in my naivity thought . . . that it was the only possible and sound form of worldview for "clever" people.'[39]

The search for values by Russian writers led them not only in the direction of Orthodoxy, but also in the direction of the peasantry. Radishchev's *Journey from St Petersburg to Moscow* (1790) offered a Rousseauian description of peasant life in which innocent peasants were made to suffer by corrupt masters. Karamzin's story 'Poor Liza' (1792) was written according to 'sentimental-pastoral' conventions.[40] This idealisation of the Russian peasant became an important theme in the middle of the nineteenth century when the peasant emerged as a 'new heroic type' in Russian literature. Notably, the appearance of Dmitrii Grigorovich's *The Village* in 1846 and Turgenev's *A Sportsman's Sketches*, which started to come out the following year, presented a powerful image of an uncorrupted peasantry.[41] The idea of the inherent goodness of the peasant was a strong theme in Tolstoi's great novels. The peasant, he believed, had a more direct and authentic experience of life than the modern intellectual. Dostoevskii too was suspicious of certain features of modernity; on his return from Siberia he got involved with a group of writers known as *pochvenniki* who sought to penetrate the artificial exterior life to embrace the soil (*pochva*) and people.[42]

The idealisation of the peasant did not last, and it eventually gave way to the realism of writers like Chekhov, Gor'kii and Bunin. Many Russian writers, indeed, became sceptical about utopian ideas. Dostoevskii's *Notes from the Underground* (1864), for example, was a strong attack on the idea of the inherent rationality and goodness of man. In his story 'The idealist carp' (1884), the satirist M.E. Saltykov-Shchedrin depicted the naivity of utopian ideas: the stupidity of a carp that believes in the primacy of goodness is exposed when it is eaten by a pike.[43] Yet the romantic vision of the people, soil and countryside was to retain its allure, and the anti-modern mood would return in the village prose of the Brezhnev era.

One of the weaknesses of nineteenth-century Russian Orthodoxy was that it rarely appealed to people with radical social and political instincts. Faithfulness to conscience, as interpreted by *The Philokalia*, involved great interior discipline. It offered believers the possibility of establishing a direct relationship with God, and a sense of overall purpose for life. Yet, to a country facing major upheaval and the challenge of modernisation, it said little about politics, social change or justice, and thus left the way open for secular alternatives. Indeed, the Russian religious thinker S.A.

Askol'dov even suggested in 1918 that 'in its role as the *conscience* of the social organism of Russia the Orthodox Church had been inactive since the time of Peter I'.[44]

The rise of the Russian intelligentsia can be traced back to the Napoleonic wars. Soldiers stationed in Europe returned to Russia after 1815 much enamoured by French revolutionary ideas. The Decembrist revolt of 1825 was the first attempt by a new generation of soldier intellectuals to press for radical reform. The failure of the Decembrists' revolt led in the reign of Nicholas I to a widening of the gap between the state and the emerging intellectual class, and the appearance of a post-Decembrist generation of dissidents.[45] The appearance of the intelligentsia also partly reflected the expansion of both secondary and university education in the first part of the nineteenth century. There were roughly 62,000 pupils at secondary schools at the end of the eighteenth century, but this had jumped to 450,000 in 1856. Universities doubled their intake between 1836 and 1848.

In spite of government hostility and a strong regime of censorship, the reign of Nicholas I saw the appearance of certain instruments of self-expression that were to be of long-term importance. The 'thick journal' emerged as a central focus of intellectual culture. In addition, the 'circle' (*kruzhok*) became a central feature of intellectual self-organisation. 'Circles' were small groups of intellectuals who met privately for discussion and debate. The absence of open mechanisms for criticising the government forced people into these close-knit communities. It is estimated that around 400 different private circles existed in Russia between 1801 and 1855. It was partly the close-knit and intense atmosphere of these groups that shaped intellectuals' sense of their particular identity and calling. Moreover, until Alexander II's local government reforms in the early 1860s, there was little opportunity for students to engage in social activism, and even after that almost no opportunity for legitimate political engagement. Indeed, the government saw the universities as a means of training bureaucrats, and had little patience with free debate. Consequently, ideas took on an abstract theoretical character. These processes were evident in the literature of the period. In a story of 1851, Turgenev talked of 'superfluous men', and this phrase came to be applied to the new generation of well-educated but alienated intellectuals.[46]

A key area of debate in Nicholas I's reign was the question of Russian national identity. In 1836 the nobleman, Petr Chaadaev, lamented in a 'philosophical letter' that Russia had contributed nothing positive to the world: 'We have not contributed in any way to the progress of the human spirit, and whatever has come to us from that progress we have disfigured.'[47] Chaadaev's letter helped to provoke a vigorous debate between so-called 'Slavophiles' and 'Westernisers': Slavophiles were adherents of Orthodoxy who believed that there were elements of pre-Petrine Russia that gave Russian culture certain unique qualities;

Westernisers saw Russia's future in terms of a Western pattern of development. In practice, these groups contained figures with diverse opinions, and both in their own way were unhappy with the status quo. The Russian intelligentsia, which became a source of radical political opposition to the regime, originated primarily with the Westernisers. It is noteworthy that at the time when intellectuals became most enamoured of Western ideas, Western philosophy and social thought were particularly influenced by utilitarian and materialist ideas. The world-view of the revolutionary intelligentsia owed much to German and English positivism and French rationalism and materialism.

Although the emerging intelligentsia was generally anti-religious, it nevertheless derived its moral vocabulary from the same Russian language as did the Orthodox Church, and in this sense there was inevitably common ground between the religious and secular traditions. Moreover it could also be argued that the self-denying habits of mind that informed the thinking of committed Orthodox Christians were the same as those of the secular intelligentsia. This was a point made by Berdyaev in his comments on the influential literary critic of the 1850s, Nikolai Dobrolyubov. Berdyaev suggested that the sort of soul in which revolutionary and nihilist ideas were born was 'the kind of soul from which saints are made'. 'The cast of [Dobrolyubov's] soul', according to Berdyaev, 'was ascetic'; he had a 'strong sense of sin' and was 'very devout'. But then, Berdyaev noted, 'this devout ascetic soul, serious to the degree of harshness, lost his faith, appalled by the evil, the injustice, and the suffering of life'.[48] Berdyaev painted a picture of a man whose Orthodox asceticism was the foundation of his nihilism; the outward trappings of belief were different but the essential cast of mind remained the same. If Berdyaev was right, then the ethics of the Russian intelligentsia were the product of the mixing of two traditions: the practices of the monastery and the Enlightenment traditions of the West.

For all that, it is important to remember that the self-denying ethics of the emerging intelligentsia were not religious; indeed, they were generally anti-religious. Divine grace was no longer considered essential to the project of improving humanity. Moreover, in the eyes of the emerging intelligentsia, the church itself was one of the oppressive structures which mankind needed liberation from. The poetics of the two outlooks were in some features similar, but the reality of religious experience was in the second denied.

One of the early shapers of the Russian intelligentsia, Vissarion Belinskii, was strongly hostile to religion. Atheism was a central feature of his outlook; Berdyaev even suggests that in him 'Russian revolutionary socialism was combined emotionally with atheism'.[49] Belinskii assumed that the advancement of religion and the advancement of civilisation were incompatible. In 1847 in correspondence with Gogol, whose views on politics and religion were very conservative, Belinskii declared that Russia saw her salvation 'not in mysticism, asceticism or pietism, but in the advances of civilization, enlightenment and humanism'.[50] Belinskii's moral outlook combined passionate moralism, hatred of injustice and atheism in a way that foreshadowed certain Bolshevik attitudes. Indeed, his revolutionary maximalism was evident in a letter of 1841 in which he wrote: 'I am beginning to love humanity *à la* Marat: to make the least part of it happy, I believe I could destroy the rest of it with fire and sword.'[51]

Aleksandr Herzen, another formative influence on the intelligentsia, was also sceptical about religion. Herzen was a radical apostle of freedom. He came to hate all abstract attempts to answer the world's problems. He rejected the eighteenth-century idea that there might be a single body of knowledge that could interpret the world, believing instead, in the words of Isaiah Berlin, that 'nature obeys no plan', 'history follows no libretto', 'no formula can, in principle, solve the problems of individuals or societies' and that liberty is 'an absolute value'.[52] He believed that the idea of absolute morality was essentially a theoretical idea, unrelated to real life; in his view, 'there are several moralities, and they are all very relative, that is historical'. There was dawning a new day, he declared in his memoirs, 'revealing the glaring incompatibility of faith and knowledge, of Church and science, of law and conscience'.[53]

Alongside this libertarian streak, Herzen was a passionate moralist. Unlike the hesychasts, however, who believed that the origins of social evil lay in personal sin, Herzen saw the cause of corruption as the Russian autocracy. He hated all kinds of oppression, had a deep concern for social justice and equality and throughout his life sought to expose the repressive activities of the Russian state. In 1852, he set up the Free Russian Press in London, and his newspaper *The Bell* (*Kolokol*) was avidly read by radical intellectuals throughout the Russian empire. Herzen, for example, was one of many intellectuals who felt that the Emancipation Edict of 1861, which required peasants to buy their land over a period of forty-nine years, was unjust to the peasant community.

Herzen came to believe that there was something false about the Russian state itself; it was an artificial non-Russian imposition on the vital forces of the people.[54] Influenced by Herzen, and also by the anarchist Mikhail Bakunin, young intellectuals became attracted to the idea of devoting their lives to the struggle against state oppression; indeed the battle *against* the state was an important feature of the new secular asceticism. Many intellectuals came to assume that the state and the people were by their very nature enemies. Although a Westerniser, Herzen also popularised the idea, initially conceived by the Slavophiles, that the peasant commune or *mir* could become the basis for a Russian and socialist form of social development. Herzen's influence was so considerable that he was widely described as the 'conscience' of the Russian intelligentsia.[55]

Another figure whose life came to represent an ascetic ideal for young revolutionaries was Nikolai Chernyshevskii. A man much admired for his personal integrity, Chernyshevskii was committed to a version of historical materialism that left room for the influence of individuals. He believed that people of strong will and character could help Russia bypass capitalism and progress towards socialism on the basis of the peasant commune. His novel, *What Is to be Done?* (1861), was a portrait of the 'men of the sixties', the emerging group of radical socialists dedicated to improving the lot of the people, and ready to sacrifice their own comforts to do so. Noteworthy, in particular, was the hero of the novel Rakhmetov, a man dedicated to the common cause whose self-denying principles have forged within him a superior moral nature. Rakhmetov stands for a denial rather than a realisation of self.[56] As the narrator states at one point, he is a cold realist, committed to the truth at all costs: '[Rakhmetov] spoke so calmly, without any trace of personality, like a historian who judges things coldly, not with an intent to offend anyone, but to serve the truth.'[57] Chernyshevskii's depiction in Rakhmetov of a secularised, revolutionary form of sanctity became a model of self-sacrifice for a whole generation of revolutionaries. Most famously, Lenin was inspired by him, and consciously named his own revolutionary catechism, *What Is to be Done?* (1902), after Chernyshevskii's novel.

An influential figure in popularising this moral vision was Petr Lavrov. Lavrov believed that individuals with a commitment to justice and a desire to realise it could change the world. He wrote in 1860:

> The recognition of the injustice of what had seemed just is the first step ... This recognition gradually spreads, preparing the ground for individuals who are not only conscious of the principle, but are endowed with the determination to actualize it. These are the true heroes of humanity.[58]

Lavrov's thinking gave expression to a longing for self-sacrifice, and also to the desire of many to pay their debts towards the people. His *Historical Letters* (1869) in particular helped to mobilise students to try to serve and educate the people. Most famously, in 1874, the desire to heal social division spurred a group of young students into a mission to the villages – the so-called 'going-to-the-people' – to preach enlightenment and civilisation to the peasantry. Unfortunately, it was a very unsuccessful episode; the peasants showed a marked lack of interest in the young student revolutionaries, and there was a huge gulf caused by lack of understanding between the two sides.

The desire to pay off debts was undoubtedly an important factor in the formation of populism, and more generally of the world-view of the intelligentsia. Writing about the 1874 episode, the main historian of the populist movement noted: 'Renunciation of all privileges, the determination to be freed at last from the "debt" to the people, the desire for liberty – these were the real forces that drove the students into the country.'[59]

In the 1880s Marxism began to compete with populism for the minds of young Russian revolutionaries. It became increasingly clear that Russia could not avoid following a path of industrial development that was similar to that of the West. Marxism appealed to those who sought a scientific rather than a romantic approach to revolutionary struggle. At a political level, the two doctrines were very different: populists placed their hope in the peasantry as the revolutionary class; Marxists saw the industrial proletariat as the vanguard of the revolution. Yet, in terms of their ethical assumptions, the two doctrines had a lot in common. Both of them contained materialist and egalitarian assumptions, and preached a revolutionary transformation of society.

The revolutionary intelligentsia has often been blamed for the mixture of utopianism and violence that characterised the Soviet regime at certain points.[60] The idea that the intelligentsia's ideas were fundamentally flawed was central to *Landmarks*, a collection of essays that provoked widespread debate when it appeared in 1909. The contributors, a number of them former Marxists, were Berdyaev, Izgoev, Sergei Bulgakov, Semyon Frank, Mikhail Gershenzon, Bogdan Kistyakovskii and Petr Struve. In his essay, 'In Defense of Law', Kistyakovskii, a Ukrainian legal theorist, declared that there was a lack of respect for law in the Russian intelligentsia and that Russians made an insufficient distinction between law and ethics.[61] In 'Heroism and Asceticism: Reflections on the Religious Nature of the Russian Intelligentsia', Bulgakov suggested that the intelligentsia had turned away from the traditional Christian form of asceticism to embrace a secular, 'maximalist' heroism that was very dangerous.[62] In another essay, the Russian philosopher, Semyon Frank, saw in the revolutionary mentality 'nihilistic moralism': the denial of objective values in combination with a demand that people devote their whole lives to improving the lot of the people. This world-view, according to Frank, was derived from populism.[63]

Frank concluded his essay by stating: 'We must pass from unproductive, anti-cultural *nihilistic moralism* to the creative and constructive culture of *religious humanism*.'[64] The idea that religion and humanism need not conflict reflected the outlook of a number of the contributors to *Landmarks*, and can be seen as an appeal for a reconciliation of the different moral traditions of nineteenth-century Russia. However, it was very difficult to affect this kind of synthesis in late tsarist Russia because the country was so deeply polarised politically, socially and intellectually.

The autocracy was inclined to see conscience in an instrumental sense. Appeals to Orthodoxy and traditional morality were made by the autocracy to justify its own policies. The state itself sought to appropriate 'conscience' for its own ends. In the 1832 volume of the 'Collected Laws of the Russian Empire', it was written, in a formula dating to the reign of Peter the Great: 'The Emperor of All the Russias is an autocratic and unlimited monarch; God himself ordains that all must bow to his supreme power, not only out of fear, but out of conscience.'[65] At the same time, attempts were also made to limit the sphere of life to which the faculty of conscience could be applied. Too strong a reference to the individual conscience might prove destabilising. An educational text of 1848 stated: 'Conscience is necessary to man in his personal domestic life, but in service and in civic relations it is replaced by the higher authority.'[66] Of course, individual Russian tsars had different moral attitudes. For example, under the rule of Nicholas I, the government aligned itself with a conservative ideology known as Official Nationality, built on the principles of Orthodoxy, autocracy and nationality. Yet, the world-view of Nicholas II was slightly different. He was committed to ideas of hierarchy and duty, but also embraced a mystical and passive providentialism that was his own.

The nobility too had its own culture and ethics. The nobility had been granted privileged status in the second half of the eighteenth century. In 1762, they had been made exempt from the obligation to do state service, and in 1785 were given a charter that gave them their own associations in each region and district. Noble status could only be taken away from people following a trial by other nobles, and they were thus the first estate to possess legally guaranteed corporate rights. At the same time, the absence of such rights for serfs remained a problem.[67] The Emancipation Edict had long-term repercussions for Russia. The nobility were required to begin competing with the peasantry on equal terms. Furthermore, the source of their wealth was threatened. Tsarism itself lost its main social base. Stolypin's agricultural reforms of 1906–1910 were an attempt to create a property-owning rural middle class that would provide an alternative source of social support, but they came very late.

In regard to the origins of the late Soviet conscience, the ethics of the nobility should not be forgotten. Some of those involved in the human rights movement were greatly influenced by aristocratic as well as intelligentsia values. For example, the prominent activist Tat'yana Khodorovich, who was born in 1922, was brought up by her grandmother, a sister of the artist Mikhail Vrubel', and her second husband, a German aristocrat, Aleksandr von Biberstein. From the family she absorbed religious and noble traditions, as well as the thinking of the intelligentsia:

> It was an intelligentsia family ... Moreover, it was a family that did not hide their views, their convictions, their religiosity from their kids – it was accepted to hide things by that time ... [at] the end of the 20s, the beginning of the 30s. So from their lips, their day-to-day life and from my contact with other people, I absorbed pre-revolutionary Russia ... Our friends were generally from these families – the remnants of the old noble families and their children ... Late in the evenings, grandfather used to gather the family ... and read the Gospel aloud to us.[68]

The peasant world was very different. The basic unit of production in pre-revolutionary peasant communities was the family. It was a patriarchal system, in which the idea of individual rights did not play an important role. In extended peasant families, grandmothers had an important role in moral education. Things like avoiding unnecessary risks, minimising labour, telling falsehoods as a means of self-defence and manipulating official myths were all widely practised. The myth of the good tsar or the rebel hero was also prevalent.[69] Peasant moral attitudes were eclectic. Peasants attended church festivals while at the same time carrying out pagan or folk rituals. They attended Orthodox services on Easter day, but took food to the graves of their deceased ancestors during the pagan festival of *Radunitsa* in the second week after Easter.[70] Their attitudes were made up of a 'natural dionysism and a Christian asceticism'.[71] They were also rooted in a kind of magical world-view: illness was explained by a certain kind of cosmology; small rituals and charms were vital for carrying out everyday tasks.[72]

The practice of the commune was not to own land, but for the best strips to be regularly redistributed among peasants. This doubtless contributed to the development of the kind of strongly egalitarian attitudes that were evident during the revolutions. In the Russian countryside, communities were held together by a system called *krugovaya poruka*, or 'joint responsibility'. This involved paying taxes and supplying recruits for the army as a collective. If one family failed to fulfil its obligations, then the others suffered. In such a context, loyalty to communities was greatly emphasised, and also rigorously enforced. The method of judging other members of the commune in a *samosud*, by which peasants dispensed arbitrary justice, was well established and sometimes gave rise to great cruelties. Related to this, patronage networks were also important. Communities came to depend on local landlords, who offered their protection in return for finance. Social mobility thus came to depend on the maintenance of healthy patron–client relationships. The key to success was to please those further up in the social hierarchy.

There was no independent system of justice to which peasants could turn. Illegality and informal practices flourished. As Catherine the Great observed: 'Justice is sold to the highest bidder, and no use is made of the laws except when they benefit the most powerful.'[73] Such cynicism about the law pervaded popular culture: one nineteenth-century proverb stated that a lawyer (*ablakat*) was 'a hired conscience'.[74] The legal reforms introduced under Alexander II in 1864 introduced a more formalised system of justice, but they did not bring about an immediate change in attitudes to law.[75] Patronage networks continued to exist in the Soviet era. Rising political figures depended to a considerable extent on attaching themselves to party bosses who were doing well; in return for their loyalty, they could expect advancement.

In his account of collectivisation, *Red Bread*, the journalist Maurice Hindus declared that the Bolsheviks did not need to be alarmed by the stability of the ancient holidays, for the revolution was 'fast gnawing away at their roots and draining them of their vitality'.[76] According to this view, the traditions of the village did not have deep foundations. It is hard to agree with Hindus. It is true that aspects of rural religious life did disappear with collectivisation, but this was partly due to the forcible destruction of the churches, as well as because of the attractiveness of the new 'modernity' offered by the Bolsheviks. However, there were continuities; indeed, it is not possible to understand peasant society under Lenin and Stalin without taking into account traditional peasant political culture.[77] At the same time, the values of the older rural culture also influenced some of those who were involved in the human rights movement. Vera Lashkova, one of the defendants in the 'trial of the four' in 1968, came from a Belorussian peasant family that was fiercely independent and had strong religious convictions. She recalled: 'My father was fiercely anti-Soviet. He very well remembered what life was like before [the revolution]. They had a *khutor* [farmstead]. Father, mother, three strong sons . . . the family was strictly Orthodox.'[78]

The ethics of state and class before 1917, as well as language and ideas, helped to shape patterns of dissent and reform in late Soviet Russia. People encounter moralities in particular social and political contexts, and not just in the form of disembodied ideas. The experiences of Khodorovich and Lashkova illustrate the way in which older noble and peasant traditions survived and found expression in the dissident community.

2 Tension and change in revolutionary ethics

It is impossible to understand the moral opposition to communism in the late Soviet era without examining the moral vision of the early Soviet leaders and some of the practices that became a feature of the Soviet system. These were not exactly the same. As they sought to overthrow tsarism and establish their power, the early Bolsheviks emphasised revolutionary values. However, with the consolidation and defence of the new order, the emphasis began to change in the direction of a more conservative outlook; Stalinism emerged as a peculiar amalgam of revolutionary and conservative values. At the same time, throughout the early decades of Soviet history, there remained a common hostility to moral absolutes or the sanctity of the individual whenever the power of the state was perceived to be at stake.

There is considerable debate as to whether the Bolsheviks offered a new departure in Russian history, or whether the Soviet Union was simply Russian history under another name. Good arguments can be put forward for both sides. In terms of ethics, there is no doubt that Lenin espoused a different moral system to that of his predecessors. The tsars based their ideology on a certain reading of the Judaeo-Christian tradition; they had a providential and hierarchical view of the world. Lenin, by contrast, rejected Christian or traditional morality in favour of a revolutionary ethics that were supposed to serve the interests of the proletariat. Of course, the fact that tsarism and Bolshevism assumed different ethical positions does not mean that their habits of government were always different; the theory of continuity rests not on commonality of ideas but of practices.

The exact ethical nature of socialism and Marxism was a matter of considerable debate before the First World War. Both Engels and the German Social Democrat Karl Kautsky took the view that Marxian socialism should be a science and that it should contain no metaphysical dimension. Kautsky embraced the evolutionary idea of a genealogy of morals, as suggested by Darwin. By contrast, the French socialist leader Jean Jaurès advocated an idealistic variant of socialism that drew inspiration from Luther, Kant, Fichte and Hegel. Bernstein's advocacy of 'evolutionary socialism' also reflected a desire for a more idealistic variant of socialist thought. In Russia the 'legal Marxists' faced the same tension: Berdyaev, Bulgakov, Frank and Struve had all been Marxists and were drawn away from Marxism by neo-Kantian thinkers like Simmel, Rickert and Windelband. This tension between materialism or realism and idealism was to be a constant problem for Soviet ethicists; Soviet philosophers would state that morality was a social and historical construction, while at the same time making absolute and idealistic claims about their own vision of progress and history. It was a tension that never went away, and the fact that it was never resolved was ultimately a destabilising factor in the later decades of Soviet power.[1]

If the legal Marxists were drawn towards idealism before the revolution, some of the more orthodox Marxists also distanced themselves from extreme moral relativism. Notably, Plekhanov and Akselrod argued that there were simple laws of morality and right that had universal validity, and that were binding on the proletariat as well as on everyone else.[2] The Russian Social Democrats were clearly very divided on ethical questions. Indeed, in terms of ends and means, some members of the revolutionary intelligentsia were closer to their opponents in 1917 than it first appeared. Semyon Frank suggested that it was wrong to see the conflict between liberals and socialists as the primary issue of the period; what was more important was to examine real attitudes to law, freedom and the value of the individual. In spite of their words, he said, liberals like Milyukov and Guchkov were in practice not so different from Kerenskii and Plekhanov; the real cleavage lay between Bolsheviks and moderate socialists because they maintained such different attitudes to violence and tyranny.[3]

Although Bolshevism was not fully formed by October 1917, the habits of mind that the Bolsheviks brought into power with them inclined them to a particular way of responding to situations. In regard to violence, they had long assumed that violence would be a precondition of building a better society. The main Bolshevik theoreticians all took the view that the ends justified the means. History was thus divided into two time-periods: the present, or the time of transition, where terror and violence could not be avoided, and the future, where people would live together in peace and harmony. It was an overtly dualistic system: ends and means could be detached from one another; while moral absolutes or eternal values were regarded as inapplicable to the present time, people were concurrently encouraged to devote their lives to building a perfect, future society. In this scheme, the absolute ideal was not so much rejected as postponed. Lenin articulated the strategy clearly in *State and Revolution* (1917), when, on the one hand, he stated that the substitution of the proletarian state for the bourgeois state was impossible without a violent revolution, while at the same time envisaging a world where class antagonisms had been abolished and thus there was no need for violence.[4]

The potential liberation of mankind justified contemporary sacrifices. In *The ABC of Communism* (1919), one of the canonical texts of early Bolshevism, Nikolai Bukharin and Yevgenii Preobrazhenskii rejected the idea that Bolshevism offered a form of 'Hottentot' morality that could be summed up in the form of the statement, 'When I steal my neighbour's wife, it is good; when he steals my wife, it is bad.' This interpretation of Bolshevik ethics, they wrote, failed to take into account the fact that the proletariat was an enormous class that was fighting for the liberation of all mankind, whereas the bourgeoisie was a small group that was seeking the maintenance of oppression, war and exploitation.[5] These authors took the view that the new society was just around the corner. They operated on the assumption of an immediate realisation of the moral ideal; hence, it has been suggested, it would be wrong in a strict sense to describe them as 'moral nihilists'.[6]

The thinking of Bolshevik leaders on violence was shaped by many factors. At a certain level, it had its origins in Russian political history. For centuries, coercion had played a central role in Russian political culture. More recently, the First World War had contributed to processes of brutalisation. However, justifications of violence also had intellectual origins. Bolshevik attitudes were rooted in the maximalist aspirations of the Russian intelligentsia. More specifically, they were influenced by the idea in Marxian dialectics that history involves a permanent struggle between opposing forces; war and conflict are constant features of the world and a necessary condition of progress. Nietzsche too played a major role in creating justifications for violence. According to a recent study, he reinforced Promethean aspects of Marxism, and contributed to the admiration in Russian revolutionaries for the qualities of hardness, daring and will.[7] Certainly, well before 1914 Bolshevik intellectuals were defending violence: Gor'kii proclaimed that life was based on cruelty, horror and force, and that for reconstruction 'cold, rational cruelty' was necessary; Lunacharskii envisaged the possibility that a humane way of life would only be reached by 'rivers of blood'.[8]

Lenin himself played the central role in formulating Bolshevik political ethics. Occasionally, his writings suggest a man with considerable idealism. In *What is to Be Done?*, Lenin quoted a passage from the writings of the Russian nihilist of the 1860s, D. Pisarev, in which Pisarev stated that there was no harm in being a dreamer, 'if only a person dreaming believes seriously in his dream', '[if] he works conscientiously for the achievement of his phantasies' and 'if there is some connection between dreams and life'. Lenin then lamented that there was too little of this kind of dreaming in the social democratic movement.[9] Yet, this idealistic tone was unusual for Lenin. He had a deep suspicion of all forms of sentimentality, and the idealist in him usually gave way to the realist.

Lenin rejected universal moral values. In a speech to the Third All-Union Congress of the Komsomol in 1919, Lenin referred to 'elementary forms of community'.[10] However, this was unusual. Lenin generally saw morality in functional, class and historical terms. This was most famously evident in his speech to the All-Russian Congress of the Russian Komsomol on 2 October 1920. On this occasion, Lenin repudiated all morality drawn from 'non-human and non-class concepts'. Instead of deriving morality from the commandments of God, he said, communist morality was derived from the 'interests of the class struggle of the proletariat'; the basis of communist morality was the 'struggle for the consolidation of Communism'.[11] Lenin assumed that since the interests of the proletariat evolved with the march of history, there could be no one morality that would suit all situations. Instead, there would be a dynamic and flexible revolutionary morality designed to serve the proletariat's changing interests.

Lenin's revolutionary ethics were probably partly shaped by Machiavelli. Referring to Machiavelli in a letter to the Politburo of March 1922, he wrote:

> One wise writer on matters of statecraft rightly said that if it is necessary to resort to certain brutalities for the sake of realizing a certain political goal, they must be carried out in the most energetic fashion and in the briefest possible time because the masses will not tolerate prolonged application of brutality.[12]

Lenin's thinking about the concept of 'conscience' itself was ambiguous, partly because there is very little to go on. In an essay of December 1913, 'On Worker Unity', directed against the Menshevik leaders Tsereteli and Gegechkori, Lenin called for worker unity on the basis of conscience: 'Unity is essential for the working class. Unity is established by one organisation alone, the decisions of which are made by all conscious workers on the basis not of fear but of conscience.'[13] Although this statement could be read as endorsing the existence of an autonomous moral faculty in man, it is still notable that conscience was located here in a class context. Lenin's attitude to the individual conscience was possibly similar to his approach to artistic creativity as he once explained it to the artist, Yurii Annenkov, after the revolution. 'Art', he said, 'is like an intellectual blind gut, and when its propaganda value – which is essential for us – has been played out – we will – tsik tsik! – cut it out. Because it won't be needed anymore.'[14]

The Bolsheviks sought to exploit people's consciences and loyalties. A central feature of Lenin's system of rule was the use of hostage-taking (*zalozhnichestvo*), a form of coercion that exploited people's mutual dependencies and in that sense had much in common with the system of 'mutual responsibility' (*krugovaya poruka*) that had operated in peasant communities. Hostage-taking began to be systematically applied in the summer of 1918 in response to the grain crisis, and during the Red Terror, following the attempt on Lenin's life by Dora Kaplan on 30 August 1918. On 10 August 1918, Lenin drafted a decree, stating that in every grain-producing district twenty-five to thirty hostages should be selected from among the wealthy inhabitants, and that they should be killed if the necessary amount of grain was not delivered.[15] The method was replicated in another way in the 1930s, when the Stalin regime ensured that relatives of enemies of the people would themselves become subject to repression.[16] While people were sometimes willing to risk their personal security to oppose the regime, it was a different matter to risk the safety of family and close friends.

When talking about 'conscience' itself, the Bolsheviks endorsed what they called the 'revolutionary conscience'; Decree No. 1 on 7 December 1917 stated that the old laws should be observed only insofar as they had not been repealed by the 'Revolution' and did not contradict 'the revolutionary conscience and the revolutionary concept of justice'.[17] The Bolsheviks thus sought to imbue the idea of conscience with revolutionary content. As with all moral phenomena, they sought to historicise it. This was reflected some decades later in the entry on 'conscience' in the second edition of the *Great Soviet Encyclopaedia*: 'Conscience is a social, concretely-historical category which arises out of the relationships between people in the process of their historical development.'[18]

In general, the Bolsheviks emphasised 'consciousness' as much as 'conscience'. Lenin's works contained a strong emphasis on 'consciousness'. Notably, in *What Is to be Done?*, Lenin explored the relationship between consciousness (*soznatel'nost'*) and spontaneity (*stikhiinost'*), stating that the working class could develop a 'trade union consciousness' (*soznanie*) on its own, but that it needed the guidance of the revolutionary socialist intelligentsia to develop a mature Social Democratic consciousness.[19] People with a high level of 'consciousness' were highly esteemed after 1917. A resolution of the Ninth Party Conference in 1920, establishing the Central Control Commission, emphasised that party members should be distinguished by their 'consciousness [*soznatel'nost'*], dedication, endurance, political maturity, and readiness to sacrifice themselves'.[20] Addressing family relationships in a speech of 1924, the party ethicist, Emelyan Yaroslavskii stated that communists were obliged to invest into these relations 'maximum consciousness'.[21]

Lenin's rejection of a universal morality was connected with his hostility towards religion. At one level, Lenin defended religious freedom: he advocated the separation of church and state, and this was enshrined in the Constitution of 1918. At the same time, he also took the traditional Marxist view that religion was an instrument of oppression. In *Socialism and Religion* (1905), he stated that religion was an instrument by which the exploiting class kept the proletariat in a passive state in which they could continue to be exploited.[22] In 1909 he wrote that 'a Marxist must be a materialist, i.e. an enemy of religion', adding that his struggle against religion had to be 'based on class struggle'. Yet Lenin's hostility to religion was not only a principled intellectual opposition to it, but also an emotional hatred. He once said to Gor'kii that 'any religious idea, any idea of God at all, any flirtation even with a god ... is the most dangerous foulness, the most shameful "infection"'.[23] At the same time, there is also evidence to suggest that Lenin came to believe that religious ritual could be used to consolidate political control. He reportedly once discussed with Kalinin the need to give the masses a substitute for religion, and he welcomed Bolshevik attempts to create secular Soviet rituals as a substitute for religious ceremonies.[24] It was typical of him, however, to view religion purely in terms of political power.

Hatred of religion was a defining feature of Lenin's outlook. However, it should not be seen in isolation from the wider cluster of hatreds that were present in his mind; tsarism, capitalism, the bourgeoisie, etc., were all objects of his ire. Indeed, aggression characterised his attitude to politics. In his polemics, his aim was always as much to destroy the other person as his argument. In 1906, he attacked the Mensheviks, describing them as enemies of the working class and traitors. Before a jury of the Social Democratic Party, he stated openly that his aim was to 'evoke in the reader hatred' and that his form of argumentation was designed 'not to convince, but to break the ranks of the opponent'.[25]

Yet there were some complexities in Lenin's ethics. At least, according to the Soviet ethicist, Abdusalam Guseinov, Lenin's speech to the Komsomol of 1920 can be interpreted not only as an expression of the formula that the 'end justifies the means', but, rather differently, as a tacit recognition on Lenin's part that only morality could actually serve the work of communism. Indeed, Guseinov argues that the bloody 'bacchanalia' of the Civil War drove the Bolsheviks back in the direction of more traditional norms of morality.[26] Elsewhere, Lenin was keen to argue that violence was only necessary because of the Civil War situation. Violence was presented as a *defensive* response to the onslaughts of exploiters and oppressors; in a reference to the Civil War at the All-Union Central Executive Committee on 2 February 1920, Lenin stated:

> We were forced to use terror because of the terror practised by the Entente ... We say that the application of violence flows out of the decision to smother the exploiters, the big landowners and the capitalists; as soon as this was accomplished we gave up the use of all extraordinary methods.[27]

According to Lenin, then, the Bolsheviks were forced by others into using violence, and in this sense were not themselves the initiators of violence at all. Even if these opinions are interpreted as simply tactical ones, they still contain a recognition that a violent society is not desirable.

There was in Lenin, as with many of the nineteenth-century Russian revolutionaries, an outlook that combined moral asceticism with a principled denial of the very idea of objective moral laws.[28] Indeed, when it came to personal morality, Lenin was relatively conventional. For example, he was not at ease with the libertarian sexual morality associated with Aleksandra Kollontai. He took a strict view of personal morality and expected courteous behaviour from party members. In his Testament (1922), he was critical of Trotskii's 'self-assurance', and warned that Stalin was 'too crude', recommending that he be replaced by someone more tolerant, loyal and polite.[29] Of course, the Soviet system depended for its survival on the exercise of moral responsibility, and so once in power the Bolsheviks could not afford to be too cynical about traditional morality.

Lenin's moral philosophy was shared by his closest colleagues. Like Lenin, Trotskii had an uninhibited attitude to revolutionary violence. In *Terrorism and Communism* (1920), he strongly defended the use of terror during the Civil War. Later, in his 'Their Morals and Ours' (1938), he stated that morality was one of the 'ideological functions' in the class struggle. Rules of conduct, he said, were to be derived from 'the laws of the development of society, thus primarily from the class struggle'. He said that violence and lies would be necessary in revolutionary situations: '[Civil war] is unthinkable not only without violence against tertiary figures but, under contemporary technique, without murdering old men, old women and children ... Without lies war would be unimaginable as a machine without oil.'[30] Trotskii's relativism, however, was not absolute. He stated that 'elementary moral precepts exist', although he also argued that their action was 'extremely limited and unstable'. He was evidently aware of the dangers that his doctrine posed. The end, he declared, is justified only 'if it leads to increasing the power of man over nature and to the abolition of the power of man over man'; whatever '*really* leads to the liberation of mankind' is permissible.[31] There was clearly a tautology here; Trotskii rejected moral absolutes while still putting some conditions on the means that might be employed.[32] Trotskii was particularly anxious to avoid the potentially religious connotations of endorsing moral absolutes:

> The theory of eternal morals can in nowise survive without God ... Supra-class morality inevitably leads to the acknowledgements of a special substance, of a 'moral sense', 'conscience', some kind of absolute which is nothing more than the philosophical-cowardly pseudonym for God.

To the charge that Stalinism was an expression of Bolshevik amoralism, Trotskii suggested that it was not the fruit of Bolshevik amorality but the 'product of a concrete social struggle', 'the struggle of a new aristocracy against the masses'.[33]

The early Bolshevik leaders assumed that those who practised terror and dissimulation would not themselves be affected by it. There could be no possibility of Bolsheviks themselves being corrupted by the methods that they used. A person's actual behaviour could thus be altogether separated from his or her core personality. Bolshevik ethics were also very vague. As well as containing theoretical tensions, there were a host of practical issues that were problematic. Although lying to opponents could be justified, lying to the party was of course forbidden. Yet what should be done if those party members were in fact enemies in disguise? Violence was necessary at times of civil war, but if class war was a feature of all social life, when in the end was violence ever inappropriate? It is perhaps easy with hindsight to pick holes in Leninist ethics. Indeed, Bolshevik morality is really best understood as a means to an end: a way of justifying the Bolshevik seizure of power. Yet, the flexibility of the Soviet moral system became one of its determining features. It allowed the leadership to find moral justifications for any action it chose. At the same time, it opened the door to any kind of unscrupulous behaviour, and in the long run to the possibility that the party would lose altogether its moral legitimacy.

The threat posed to the regime by its own ethics is exemplified by attitudes to lying. In his memoirs, Viktor Kravchenko, a defector who had been one of the top industrial executives in the USSR, stated that no properly indoctrinated communist felt that professing one set of beliefs in public and another in private involved lying.[34] The very meaning and nature of lying had in effect been re-interpreted to suit party interests. This new attitude to lying is illustrated by an occasion described by the Italian communist Ignazio Silone in *The God that Failed* (1950). Silone recalled a meeting of the Comintern Executive in the mid-1920s at which the Russian delegate suggested that for tactical reasons the British trades unions should publicly agree to the decision of their Executive not to support the communists, but in practice do the opposite. An English communist objected on the grounds that this would be a lie. This objection, Silone recalled, was met with widespread mirth:

> Loud laughter greeted this ingenuous objection, frank, cordial, interminable laughter, the like of which the gloomy offices of the Communist International had perhaps never heard before. The joke quickly spread all over Moscow, for the Englishman's entertaining and incredible reply was telephoned at once to Stalin and then to the most important offices of State, provoking new waves of mirth everywhere.[35]

Once again, however, a doctrine developed for the consolidation of power was a potential threat to the party itself. It was assumed that dissimulation was to be practised on others, and that it was possible for party members to compartmentalise their lives and display a different set of moral attributes towards enemies than towards friends. However, since enemies were continually being found within the party itself, the practice of lying could just as easily become entrenched within it, as without it. Stalin was clearly ready to use any methods necessary to outmanoeuvre his party opponents. His opponents too, it seems, assumed the necessity of lying. The author of the 'Letter of an Old Bolshevik' (1936), sometimes thought to have been Bukharin, noted that in pre-revolutionary Russia, political oppositionists had a definite moral code in their relations with government, whereby it was not acceptable to petition for clemency, and people refused to promise not to try to escape. He suggested that a new morality had established itself in the party in the 1930s, which permitted one to 'accept any conditions, to sign any undertakings, with the premeditated intention not to observe them'. He declared that the borderline between what was and what was not admissible had been 'completely obliterated'; and he also noted that the widespread acceptance of this moral doctrine among the older generation of party members lent weight to those who opposed *rapprochement* with former Oppositionists on the grounds that they in principle recognised the permissibility of telling lies.[36]

With the consolidation of the Soviet state, an institutionalisation of Soviet life took place that had a significant effect on Soviet ethics. One area where this took place was in the sphere of law. According to Marxist theory, a state's legal framework was part of the 'superstructure' that was the product of society's social and economic base. In the transition to socialism, while the class struggle was still going on, it was permissible for revolutionaries to break the law since the laws were only bourgeois laws. Yet having established themselves in power, the situation changed. In the middle of the 1930s, Vyshinskii spearheaded moves to introduce a more clearly defined body of law.[37] The Bolsheviks wanted to exercise power through arbitrary rule, without making themselves accountable to law, yet at the same time to institute a new and fixed system of law that could lead to a healthy and functioning political system. Indeed, it has been rightly noted that the regime never overcame 'the irreconcilable conflict between an arbitrary personal despotism and the regulatory order needed by the bureaucratic administration of modern states'.[38] Respect and contempt for law were combined. A similar ambivalence was also present in official attitudes to the individual conscience. The 1936 Constitution enshrined the separation of church and state in order to guarantee 'freedom of conscience' for Soviet citizens.[39] However, this guarantee of freedom of conscience was given in the context of the larger task of constructing socialism, and for this reason the individual conscience was often set aside in favour of the interests of the collective as defined by the party.

Some of the same dilemmas were evident in Soviet attitudes to the family. From 1917 onwards, there were two tendencies in Soviet family policy. On the one hand, the Bolsheviks embraced the Marxist interpretation of the family, believing that in a bourgeois state the family was a patriarchal institution instituted for the management of property, in which women were treated as commodities. Following this approach, the Bolsheviks understood themselves to be liberators of women, and more libertarian attitudes to sexual morality were encouraged. On the other hand, there was also a more traditional attitude to sexuality, in which the virtues of self-restraint and fidelity were praised. Kollontai came to be the standard-bearer of the former attitude. However, even in her thought there was an ambiguity. In an article of 1923, 'Make Way for the Winged Eros!', she condemned bourgeois marriage for being too centred on personal love, while at the same time suggesting that relationships in a proletarian state should honour the collective: 'Bourgeois morality demanded all for the loved one. The morality of the proletariat demands all for the collective.'[40] Kollontai's thought implicitly contained the idea of self-sacrifice for the sake of the collective. She was effectively proposing another form of asceticism. Indeed, the idea of self-sacrifice, which was so important in the Russian revolutionary tradition, was widely promoted by the regime in the 1920s.[41]

The combination of libertarianism and collectivism that made up Kollontai's vision was in reality contradictory and vague. The same tensions were evident in Soviet attitudes to the family more generally. The regime's suspicion of the family was most evident in the cult of Pavlik Morozov. Pavlik Morozov was a boy from Siberia who supposedly denounced his father to the authorities in 1930 for having kulak sympathies. He quickly became an iconic figure in the Soviet media. His readiness to sacrifice private loyalties for the sake of the state was heralded as an example of model behaviour, and over subsequent decades hundreds of artistic works were produced in celebration of his action. For young people growing up in the 1930s, Pavlik Morozov was presented as a person who acted according to his conscience.[42] Yet, in 1936, the regime re-introduced stricter divorce laws, prohibited abortions, and started to promote the 'spiritual side of marriage'.[43] The cult of Pavlik Morozov suddenly did not sit easily with this renewed emphasis on the family.

In terms of the formation of conscience, the rehabilitation of marriage in the middle of the 1930s was an important moment, for the family was to be a very influential institution in terms of moral education. In recalling the factors that shaped their moral attitudes, future dissidents and party reformers often emphasised family influences. Asked where he got his sense of conscience from, Gorbachev's ideology chief Aleksandr Yakovlev said it was from his mother; it was she who introduced him to words that expressed a sense of moral doubt like 'uneasy' (*nelovko*), 'uncomfortable' (*neudobno*) and 'shameful' (*stydno*).[44] Grandparents were also important. The future dissident Ludmilla Alekseeva stated that her spiritual outlook was to a considerable degree shaped by the Protestant work ethic of an Estonian grandmother.[45] Gorbachev's Interior Minister from 1988–1990, Vadim Bakatin was also influenced by a grandmother: 'My grandmother brought me up in the right way [*pravil'no*]: to work hard, not to be deceitful and to wash my hands.'[46] Gorbachev's grandparents introduced him to a synthesis of communist and Orthodox values. In his grandfather's house, there was in one corner an icon and an icon-lamp – Gorbachev's grandmother was very religious – while under the icon there were portraits of Lenin and Stalin. According to Gorbachev, 'this peaceful co-existence did not bother Grandfather in the least'.[47]

The rehabilitation of the family contributed to the growing emphasis on traditional moral values. For the family to survive, it had to impart a certain set of values. The dissident Russian poet, Irina Ratushinskaya, observed: 'Just to survive and be in control, you have to teach your children to be honest, not to steal ... You have to tell them what is right and what is wrong. And the very structure of life dictates its own laws.'[48] This point, reflecting an understanding of the world based on natural law, ultimately pertains to the state itself; the very structures that the Soviet regime established began to impart a more traditional morality. The point, indeed, might be made in relation to all social institutions; the Pioneers, Komsomol, school, party, church, to the extent that they commanded any loyalty, were all productive of the idea of personal responsibility. With the institutionalisation of Soviet life, accountability, responsibility and honesty were encouraged. At the same time, although the family was in a sense a stabilising institution as far as the regime was concerned, it also posed a threat to the state. For many people, family connections were a means of discovering an alternative view of Russian and Soviet history; many parents and grandparents could remember pre-revolutionary Russia, and thus could inculcate a non-Soviet view of the world. With more and more women working, grandparents came to play an important role in bringing up children.

The growing emphasis on traditional values was reinforced by changes in education policy in the 1930s. In August 1931, the Central Committee broke with the experimental educational tradition that had been influential in the 1920s, and called for a fixed curriculum and the transmission of a clearly defined body of knowledge from teachers to pupils. Hierarchy and obedience, rather than independence, were to be stressed. In history teaching, there was a new emphasis on the role of personalities in history, and consequently on heroic behaviour. Makarenko's *Book for Parents* (1937) reflected the new conservatism: it stressed respect for authority, punctuality, disciplined sexual relations and the avoidance of swearing.[49] Importantly, Makarenko also emphasised the training of the will. This was an important dimension of Stalinist moral education; chess, for example, was promoted as a discipline that fostered the formation of the will.[50] The 1930s also saw a stress on *kul'turnost'*, a quality associated with personal hygiene, civilised behaviour and the avoidance of dirty language.[51] The idea of honour, *chest'*, a much admired quality in traditional Russian culture, was often emphasised, defined in terms of the social honour bestowed by the state on those who had completed their allotted tasks. It was nevertheless a kind of honour that had little to do with a personal sense of honour or pride.[52] In schools the rules for pupils that were instituted in 1943 emphasised punctuality, hard work, cleanliness and respect for authority.[53]

Critical thinking was also taught in the classroom. At one level, attitudes to science were illustrated by the rise of T.D. Lysenko, and the attempt to subject the field of biology to an ideological strait-jacket. On the other hand, the regime declared that its ideology was based on a scientific account of the world. This had its subversive side as well. Yulii Shreider, a mathematician from a Jewish background who eventually became a leading Russian Catholic in the 1990s, stated: 'Science itself teaches values . . . that truth proves itself [*istina dokazyvaet'sya*]. Science is in a certain sense a teacher of morality . . . The honest pursuit of science is already something.'[54] In time, this emphasis on science and scholarship could only endanger the regime itself, since it could mean that it too would become the subject of analysis. Even the teaching of Marxism posed the same problem, for Marx taught his readers to subject the world to rigorous criticism. Gorbachev noted in his memoirs that the first authors to sow seeds of doubt in his mind about the official truths presented by the system were Marx, Engels and Lenin; their works, containing 'a detailed criticism of their opponents' theses, a system of counter-arguments and theoretically-sustained conclusions' were in sharp contrast to the Stalinist system of debating.[55]

Prominent socialist writers taught people the importance of honesty and conscience. In Gor'kii's *My Universities* (1921), the good-hearted peasant, Kukushkin, observes to a colleague: 'I can see you don't believe in conscience, Antonych, but you can't get by without it, no matter how clever you are!'[56] In Sholokhov's *Virgin Soil Upturned*, a novel about collectivisation that started appearing in 1932, there was a reference to conscience in relation to membership of the Communist Party. One of the characters, the collective farm-worker and former Cossack, Kondrat Maidannikov, states that 'his conscience won't let [him] join the Party just now', because he still has hankerings after private property. The party secretary, Makara Nagulnov, endorses Kondrat's decision, observing that 'you have to come into the Party when you're clean all through'.[57]

The values promoted by the policy of socialist realism in the arts, launched in 1934, strengthened this tendency. The socialist realist tradition had in common with nineteenth-century Russian realism a desire to educate and elevate readers; in a sense, it continued to portray a world in which there was a battle between good and evil. Socialist realist novels promoted party-mindedness, *partiinost'*, a commitment to the party and its values, and set up conflicts between honest loyal servants of the party, and selfish, egotistical careerists. There was a hagiographical dimension to the literature that emerged since it became the function of the Soviet novel to become a 'repository of state myths'.[58] Biographies played the same role. Notably, Gor'kii launched a series entitled 'Lives of Remarkable People', in which suitable biographies were presented to the public.[59]

The growing conservatism of Stalinist ethics was combined with the increasing emphasis on patriotic values. During the first Five-Year Plan, Stalin sought to mobilise patriotic opinion to achieve its industrial targets. In 1934, there was a move away from the Marxist historiography associated with historian Mikhail Pokrovskii towards an emphasis on the role of personalities in history. There emerged an interest in certain pre-revolutionary Russian tsars. Already in 1930, Aleksei Tolstoi published the first two parts of a novel on Peter the Great. Eisenstein's film *Alexander Nevsky* (1938) was a celebration of Russian nationalistic and military values. During the Second World War, a cult of Ivan the Terrible appeared.[60] Indeed, both before and during the war, state ideology turned into a form of national Bolshevism.[61] New patriotic values meant new role models. In a speech of 1937, Soviet President Mikhail Kalinin drew attention to the contribution of Russians to world culture; and in the same year, the centenary of Pushkin's death was the occasion of widespread public rejoicing.[62] Indeed, according to one critic, Pushkin was elevated to a kind of 'sainthood' in Soviet society.[63] During the war, iconographic portrayals of devotion to the motherland were widely disseminated.

An important role model for young people in the war and post-war years was Zoya Kosmodem'yanskaya. Zoya was an icon of anti-fascist struggle. As a young woman, she was taken prisoner by the Nazis in November 1941 and, in spite of terrible tortures, refused to betray her comrades or reveal her name. She was subsequently turned into an icon of loyalty to the socialist homeland and devotion to the communist cause.[64] A contemporary account of the life of Zoya and her brother Shura presented the two of them as icons of youthful virtue. According to her teacher, Zoya was a 'very straight, honest girl', committed to 'fair play', 'determined' and 'strict with herself, too'. Her mother described her as 'surprisingly exact and conscientious about the carrying out of her duties'.[65] Zoya's life unfolds as it ought to: she admires Pushkin, Chernyshevskii and the children's writer Arkadii Gaidar, joins the Pioneers and the Komsomol, and eventually sacrifices her life in the struggle against fascism. After she embarks for the front, Zoya's mother discovers her notebook, which is filled with quotations from favourite authors that suggest a person of high integrity and moral seriousness. It includes patriotic references to the 'Russian earth' and the 'Red Army', and quotations from a range of authors including Chekhov, Mayakovskii, Tolstoi and Gor'kii. She knows world literature too. She writes that '*Othello* expresses the struggle of man for the high ideals of truth, moral purity and sincerity', and that 'the death of a hero in Shakespeare's work is always accompanied by the triumph of a high moral principle'. She notes too that 'Don Quixote is will, self-sacrifice, intelligence'.[66]

This Zoya is of course an ideological construct, a woman reflecting all the appropriate communist virtues of the later Stalin era. There is incarnated in her a synthesis of Russian and Soviet values, and the heritage of both Russian and world literature. She is also a martyr. At the same time, the discreet threat of coercion is discernible in the teachings of Zoya's teacher, Lydia Nikolaevna:

> If someone owns up then it means he has understood his fault, and there is no point in punishing him severely. But if he denies his guilt, that means he doesn't understand anything and will go and do the same thing again, and that means he ought to be punished.[67]

Guilt, here, is something to be decided by the collective, and thus truth-telling is placed firmly in the context of the needs of the party. The tension between universal moral values and Soviet ethics remained.

The Soviet moral system contained unresolved tensions that were evident in many areas of social and cultural policy. While certain moral absolutes or conservative values were in theory rejected, the institutionalisation of Soviet power pushed the regime into re-embracing a more traditional set of practices. In the long run these practices were potentially dangerous to the regime for they would instil in people the capacity to subject the regime itself to moral and critical scrutiny. It was always highly likely that in the post-Stalin era these tensions would be exposed and the moral foundations of the Soviet state brought into question. The renewal of interest in ethical questions that accompanied Khrushchev's 'thaw' was partly engendered by the regime itself.

For all its suspicion of the individual conscience, the Soviet regime kept on appealing to it. In addition, in spite of the party's hostility to Christianity, its approach to guilt and redemption sometimes suggested the influence of a religious ethic. In his study of the trials of Oppositionists in Tomsk in 1928, Igal Halfin notes that the party kept focussing on the moral condition of a person's true self. Oppositionists were encouraged to go through a process of 'correction' (*ispravlenie*) or 'healing' (*ozdorovlenie*) where their doubts were 'revealed' (*vyyavleny*) and murky thoughts 'cleared up' (*priyasnyatsya*). Here communist and Christian poetics had much in common.[68] A similar argument can be made about Soviet rituals of public penitence. Oleg Kharkhordin suggests that unlike in the West, where private confession became the norm, public penance was much used in Eastern Orthodoxy. It was the same in the Soviet Union, the difference being that Bolshevik public penance was a requirement for everybody, rather than just for those volunteering for it or for those who had previously been cast out by a community. The practice of *oblichenie* – public criticism and self-criticism – which became so common in the USSR, was widely used by Orthodox teachers down the centuries.[69]

Comparisons between Christian and communist poetics can be overdone. There were major differences between the two systems. For all its concern with personal motivation, the Bolsheviks were always more interested in controlling exterior behaviour than internal feelings and attitudes.[70] Moreover, they left no place for God Himself. As Halfin himself notes, Christian ethical teaching emphasised that it was for God alone to reveal the 'purposes of the heart', and communists did not endorse that kind of moral scepticism.[71]

Public self-criticism became institutionalised during the purges. The show trials of the first Five-Year Plan and of the years 1936–1938 had a certain function in terms of moral education; they were designed to establish in the minds of observers what the regime regarded as good and bad, and to establish a set of procedures for recantation and the punishment of wrong-doing. The rhetoric of the show trials was very moralistic. In the summing up of the case for the prosecution at the end of the third show trial in March 1938, Vyshinkii sought primarily to emphasise the immorality of the defendants rather than to offer a detailed legal case. He referred to 'the chain of shameful, unparalleled, monstrous crimes' committed by the accused, and said that the trial had shown 'the whole of our people and all honest people throughout the world' the 'bestial countenance' of the defendants.[72] The show trials, however, were not isolated phenomena, but visible examples of a wider phenomenon. *Prorabotki*, public occasions in which the ideological vigilance of party members was scrutinised, were widely instituted. In her memoirs, Evgeniya Ginzburg described how, during the Great Terror, 'great concert and leisure halls were turned into public confessionals' and that people 'did penance' for a wide range of crimes, such as misunderstanding the theory of permanent revolution and failing to purge themselves of great-power chauvinism.[73]

Of course, the truth-telling required by these occasions took place within a framework defined by the party. *Prorabotki* did not take place in the privacy of the confessional, and thus they served a different function from religious confession. It would have been much too dangerous for the regime to emphasise one-to-one moral accountability, for in private conversations it might turn out that both parties did not agree with the official line. In his memoirs the medievalist Dmitrii Likhachev emphasised the cynicism of *prorabotki*, declaring that they represented 'the pinnacle of the informer's art', and 'a mass spiritual sickness which gradually tightened its grip on the whole country'. The prosecutor, Andrei Vyshinskii played an important role in establishing these procedures. He developed a theory to describe it – 'the theory of the self-sufficiency of public acknowledgement of one's guilt' – although, according to Likhachev, this was really just an acknowledgement of what already existed in practice.[74]

By emphasising truth-telling, the Soviet regime effectively acknowledged the idea of truth and the moral nature of personality, and hence hinted at the existence of some kind of over-arching moral system and the rights of the individual. At the same time, the politicised nature of truth-telling had the converse effect of undermining the very idea of personal honesty. Once again, this reflected the dualism and contradictory nature of the Soviet moral system; by emphasising truth-telling in the way that it did, the regime undermined the very idea of truth-telling. Hannah Arendt observed that 'totalitarian terror achieved its most terrible triumph when it succeeded in cutting the moral person off from the individualist escape and in making the decisions of conscience absolutely questionable and equivocal'.[75] This is an important key to the way the Soviet regime worked. The politicisation of truth-telling, guilt and redemption put into question the very idea of guilt and responsibility in absolute terms. In addition, it became difficult to distinguish between the rhetorical articulation of penitence and a genuine expression of contrition. The very idea of truth-telling, as distinct from pure rhetoric, was undermined.[76]

The politicised nature of morality meant that Soviet ethics placed considerable burdens on people. According to Soviet ideology, the dialectical nature of history meant that the truth was continually changing. This reflected a radical moral relativism. Ironically, however, this actually made Soviet moral standards very demanding. The world was divided into friends and enemies of the revolution, but since the criteria for defining friends and enemies was vague and dependent on political circumstances, it was a considerable burden on people to measure how they were doing.

Stalin himself used the word 'conscience' in various ways. For example, in a letter to the American Catholic priest Stanislaus Orlemanski in 1944, he stated that he supported 'freedom of conscience and ... worship'.[77] Here his use of the term reflected the wider contemporary emphasis in Soviet propaganda on the regime's tolerance of religion. Also during the war Stalin described the Nazis as a 'people without conscience ... with the morality of animals'.[78] There was here an implicitly Manichaean view of the world; the Soviet regime had morality on its side, while the enemy lacked all sense of conscience. This Manichaean quality was also evident in the successor to the *ABC of Communism*, the *Short Course: A History of the Communist Party of the Soviet Union/Bolsheviks* (1938), which Stalin helped to edit. In the *Short Course*, good and evil were everywhere externalised so that the struggle between different political factions was presented as a historically necessary battle between good and evil.

A Manichaean-type understanding of ethics was inherent in Soviet communism, since classes rather than individuals were understood to be incarnations of progressive and reactionary forces. Yet Manichaean attitudes were prevalent at certain times more than others. During the Great Purge of 1935–1938, Halfin notes, the idea that evil acts reflected inherently wicked traits in individuals rather than free moral choices, became widely accepted. Moreover, during the Great Purge, the borderline between mistakes and treason was erased.[79] Of course, the emphasis on an externalised conflict between good and evil conflicted with the idea that there existed in party members an internal struggle. The Manichaean-type approach easily slipped into a more traditional poetics when moral changes were called for in people who were not labelled as enemies.

The fact that the Soviet system held to a traditional poetics of repentance and moral recovery while at the same time advocating class or group moralities in which individual guilt played little role, reflected the essentially dualistic nature of the Bolshevik project. In effect, two views of the world that were incompatible were being advocated at the same time. While personal sincerity was sometimes emphasised, an ethical world-view that advocated a lack of respect for the individual was propagated to the country. At different times, perhaps, one or another of the approaches was deployed to a greater extent. However, the two continued to exist in tension with one another. The instability of holding these contradictory ideas together at the same time was at the heart of the whole system. The party denied the authority of the individual conscience while at the same time appealing to it.

3 Moral experience under Stalin

Before exploring the moral dimensions of dissent under Stalin, it is important to note that there was a significant amount of support for Stalinism. There were many who benefited from the Stalinist programme of modernisation, and who consequently were grateful to the Stalin regime. Furthermore, Stalin himself was popular in many ways, as the mass outpouring of grief at his death testified. The affection for him was of course a complex phenomenon because it was so mixed up with fear; nevertheless, it certainly existed at some level. It is also easy to assume that people living under Stalin understood the Soviet or at least the Stalinist regime to be an alien reality artificially imposed on an otherwise natural order. Yet some people undoubtedly accepted or endorsed the framework. Stepan Podlyubnyi, a man from a dekulakised Ukrainian family, whose diary of the 1930s has been a focus of study by the German historian Jochen Hellbeck, sought to refashion himself in line with the values and demands of the Stalinist system. He wrote: 'I have noticeably redirected myself from careerism to a system that is as necessary as food.'[1] Podlyubnyi saw the Stalinist system as the normal measure of things. The novelist, Vasilii Aksenov, whose novels gave expression to the aspirations of young Russians after 1956, later noted a similar attitude in his reaction to the post-war *zhdanovshchina*, which included the suppression of the writers Mikhail Zoshchenko and Anna Akhmatova: 'Even as we giggled over Zoshchenko's little monkey and wrote out Akhmatova's verses for girls, even then deep down – yes, deep down – we were convinced of the normality of Zhdanov's world and of the abnormality, sickliness and shamefulness of Zoshchenko's.'[2]

This belief in, or at least acceptance of Stalinism, was widely shared even among those who later opposed the regime in various ways. Yulii Shreider commented that it was 'not pleasant' for him to recall his attitudes in Stalin's time; at that time he 'did not recognise the way things were'.[3] Sometimes this support for the regime had a powerful moral component; people supported Stalinist policies out of a sense of conviction or conscience. A Soviet NKVD official who worked under Yezhov, Semyon Prygov, was reported to have had a faith in the Stalinist system 'founded on conviction that it fully accorded with the demands of reason and conscience ... He was convinced of the logical and ethical correctness of his Marxist principles.'[4]

Certainly, state propaganda was sometimes very successful at shaping or reshaping people's moral convictions. In *Red Bread*, Maurice Hindus reported a conversation that he had had with a peasant who had accepted collectivisation on something like ethical grounds. Threatened with dekulakisation, the peasant began to feel a sense of moral unease at retaining his wealth, as well as fear of the consequences of not letting go of it. The peasant's account of his decision to surrender his property to the state is a good example of a story of 'self-overcoming' that conforms to an orthodox Stalinist narrative. Furthermore, it contains many of the ingredients of a traditional spiritual narrative, containing a period of struggle and inner conflict, a moment of decision, and a sense of peace when the right decision has been made.

> When the injustice of inequality in material enjoyment is hammered at you all the time, it sinks in, and makes you uneasy. It bothers not only your mind but your conscience. Well, I decided it was time to act...
>
> ...finally [the family] agreed that we would give up the old way of living and join a *kolkhoz* ... We decided we'd not only give up our land but everything. 'We must tear up the old books', I said to the family, 'and burn the old records. We must start life all over again as though we were newly born' ... And we did ... And do you know after we had made our decisions we felt happy, regenerated, free of fears, suspicions, premonitions. We gave up everything we owned, but we gained peace of mind and reconciliation with our own inner selves.[5]

Yet enthusiasm for the regime was not always straightforward. Some people had to force themselves to believe in the regime's policies. In 1928, the prominent Soviet leader and member of the Left Opposition, Georgii Pyatakov, decided to return to supporting Stalin. In conversation with the old Bolshevik, N. Valentinov, Pyatakov noted that self-coercion was sometimes necessary when it came to embracing new opinions:

> We are a party consisting of people who make the impossible possible; imbued with the idea of violence, we direct *it against ourselves* and if the party demands it, if it is necessary or important, we can in an act of the will in twenty-four hours exclude certain ideas from our brains which we have held for years.[6]

In addition, some of the general enthusiasm for Stalinism seems to have involved a strained form of zeal. Gosplan chairman G.M. Krzhizhanovskii wrote to his wife in May 1929, stating that a speech he had given on the

Five-Year Plan was greeted by thunderous applause, and that there were instances of hysterics. He noted too that he often took some time to recover from such speeches.[7] This kind of strained enthusiasm was in fact a feature of all the European inter-war dictatorships.

The moral commitment of some of the perpetrators of terror can also be hard to interpret. Just before he was executed, Yezhov announced: 'I have always been a conscientious Leninist! Tell Stalin that I will die with his name on my lips.'[8] Others of course did not see it in the same way. The writer Andrei Sinyavskii once said that the Soviet regime was successful in its attempt to remake human nature because it 'created a person who could denounce and kill a man without the slightest twinge of conscience'.[9]

Alongside support for Stalin, there were plenty of signs of dissent. Most notably of course, collectivisation provoked peasant uprisings that threatened the regime itself. At a political level, the last manifestation of serious political opposition to Stalin occurred in 1932, when the so-called 'Ryutin Group', which included former members of the Right Opposition and some academics, circulated in the Central Committee a document that called for Stalin's overthrow, and a return to party democracy. The members of the group were arrested and exiled. Within the Politburo itself, it can be argued that 'Sergo' Ordzhonikidze, the People's Commissar for Heavy Industry, represented a moderate opposition to Stalin's purges, and that his death in February 1937 paved the way for the unleashing of the terror on the whole country.[10]

From the earliest times, there were people within the system who were worried about the ethical implications of the doctrines being espoused. Angelica Balabanova, an admirer of Lenin who became the first Secretary to the Communist International in 1919, finally left the movement after concluding that Lenin's moral philosophy was ultimately counter-productive: 'Lenin's tragic error consisted in having used and suggested methods which could not fail to produce deleterious effects on the movement to which he dedicated his entire life.'[11] Stalin, according to Balabanova, simply deepened what was already there:

> [Stalin's] contribution to the moral deterioration of the Soviet regime was merely quantitative. He introduced no new element, but multiplied the misdeeds and annihilated by his example the last remnants of scruple that still lingered in Russia ... Yet he merely hastened the moral débâcle of the regime, using the methods introduced by Lenin.[12]

At the same time, in spite of the fact that some party members were concerned about the implications of Bolshevik morality, the party was still able to retain the commitment of people who had a reputation for integrity. The novelist Yurii Trifonov recalled the case of Aron Sol'ts, known in his time as the 'conscience of the party', who worked in the Procurator's office in the 1930s. In a case against Trifonov's father, Sol'ts asked for evidence to back up the charge, suggesting that Vyshinskii was lying over the matter, and then publicly called for an investigation into Vyshinskii's activity.[13] Sol'ts was eventually dismissed and confined to a psychiatric hospital.

The very fact that the epithet 'conscience of the party' was used about people itself illustrates the fact that party members understood the revolutionary project to have a serious moral purpose, and also the way in which they sought to appropriate the word 'conscience' for their purposes. Sol'ts himself evidently retained the respect of people in the wider intelligentsia. Yaroslavskii, a high-level party member and campaigner against religion, was another person who was called 'the conscience of the party'. At the same time, he was not universally admired. During the purges the young communist Evgeniya Ginzburg, who was charged with failing to denounce counterrevolutionary ideas in an article by a party intellectual in Kazan, discovered that Yaroslavskii was one of her accusers. She confronted Yaroslavskii with the fact that he himself was responsible for publishing the offending article, and shouted at him: 'I am a young member of the party while you are its "conscience" [*partiinaya sovest'*]. Why must I be torn to pieces and you left sitting behind that desk?' It was to no avail; Ginzburg went to prison for two years before being sent to the camps in Siberia.[14]

Ginzburg recalled that she suffered 'torment of the soul' (*dushevnuyu muku*) over whether to maintain relations with a good friend who had been arrested.[15] Clearly some party members were morally troubled about how to respond to the purges. The existence of moral unease was something the regime had to deal with, and it developed ways of helping people override any sense of guilt they may have felt about their involvement in certain practices. For example, the widespread Soviet emphasis on theory created a culture that allowed people to isolate themselves from the world of facts.[16] Balabanova noted that the Bolsheviks created a 'cynical dichotomy between words and deeds'.[17] Some decades later, in his essay 'The Power of the Powerless', Vaclav Havel argued that in the socialist system, ideology performed the role of enabling people 'to deceive their conscience'.[18]

Such things as the ban on factions in the party, the promise of a future communist ideal and the idea that the end justifies the means all played a role in helping people to set aside their scruples. It was emphasised that moral resistance was old-fashioned. Nadezhda Mandelstam reported that in the 1920s the idea of intellectual, moral or spiritual resistance came to be regarded as old-fashioned and a mark of backwardness. One could not, it was argued, hold out against the inevitable march of history: '[People's] inner voices ... had been stilled by the victory of the "new".'[19] Traditional moral virtues lost ground. Dmitrii Panin recalled that after 1917 the very word 'honesty' came to be regarded as unfashionable.[20] Subtly, the concept of sin and the concurrent idea of personal moral responsibility for evil actions were replaced by the idea that errors occurred through 'mistakes' and lack of information. The literary critic and writer, Yurii Karyakin, an outspoken critic of Stalinism in the 1980s and 1990s, asserted that 'one of the spiritual crimes of communism ... was that it wholly replaced the concepts of "sin" and "vice" with the concepts of "mistakes" and "deficiencies"'.[21]

Threat of physical coercion was of course a vital means of enforcing Soviet power. Yet fear and torture alone are not enough to explain the mechanisms of Soviet moral control. As well as emphasising certain general ideas that could help people to block out their scruples, agents of the regime also adopted individualised strategies. In interrogations, as well as using physical coercion, investigators grew practised in discovering and exploiting a prisoner's sense of guilt. The records of the interrogations of the writer Isaac Babel illustrate the way the regime could exploit a person's desire to do something useful with his life. Babel, author of *Red Cavalry* (1920), was arrested on 16 May 1939 and charged with anti-Soviet activities. During a series of interrogations, he confessed to being a spy and being involved in anti-Soviet Trotskyite activities. Desperate to try to secure his release, Babel wrote to Beria on 11 September, declaring his willingness to devote his future literary work to the state, and concluding: 'I burn with the desire to work, to repent and to condemn a life wrongly and criminally wasted.' The evidence of the letter, if it is taken at face value, suggests that Babel's investigators were able to exploit a sense of guilt in Babel that he had failed in his career to realise his full literary potential and make a positive contribution to society. There was, however, another sense of guilt at work. Babel started to take back his testimony, declaring that he had lied and falsely implicated a number of people during his interrogations. He wrote three letters to the USSR Procurator's General Office, taking back aspects of his testimony, and expressing remorse for falsely accusing other writers of anti-Soviet behaviour, stating in the third of them that his slander was prompted by 'faint-hearted behaviour during the cross-examination'.[22] Another sense of guilt thus came into play. It thus seems that in Babel there were at least two competing moral claims: the first involved a desire to be useful to Soviet society, and the second was rooted in a wish to be truthful and not to slander innocent people.

Interrogators were doubtless aware of the competing moral demands within people, and where possible they countered a person's doubts about certain actions by mobilising or exploiting a sense of guilt about something else. This was clearly deliberate policy. In a state memorandum on interrogation techniques of 17 July 1947, the then head of the MGB, V.S. Abakumov, observed that, among other things, investigators might confront an arrested person with 'compromising data', or draw his attention to 'particular intimate details from his personal life, vices which he conceals from his associates and others'.[23] The exploitation of guilt was not only a strategy of interrogation, but it was also a means of ensuring the loyalty of the investigators themselves. M.P. Frinovskii, who was Yezhov's deputy in the NKVD at the height of the Great Terror, recalled that Yezhov instructed him to exploit the moral weaknesses of his own investigators:

> Yezhov demanded that I select investigators who would be completely bound to him, who had some sins in their pasts and who would know that they had these sins in their pasts, and then that I, on the basis of these sins, kept them completely in line.[24]

A similar approach had been applied to the clergy. A document originating in the Secret Department of the Cheka in 1921 suggested that the Cheka should aim to turn each of its agents among the Orthodox clergy into an 'eternal slave' of the Cheka who was fearful that his collaboration with the organs would be exposed.[25]

Even at the very highest level, it seems, the regime sought to exploit feelings of guilt in order to enforce compliance. In terms of complicity in the criminality of the regime, members of the Stalinist elite were all fully involved. Molotov, Mikoyan, Malenkov and Beria all signed lists of those to be executed. Khrushchev recalled that when an investigation was over, Stalin would sometimes sign it and then pass it to the rest of those at the meeting to sign it also: 'We would sign it without reading it, as if we all knew about it from the information Stalin gave, the views he stated. And thereby, it was already, so to speak, a kind of collective sentence.'[26] At the highest levels, there was silence about the violence and terror that was being inflicted on the country. However, the silencing of moral protest in the party elite was probably something that took place over time. Dmitrii Volkogonov suggested that the 'slide into coercion as a universal method went through various stages ... If lies are repeated often enough they come to seem like the truth.' No one, in the Central Committee, according to Volkogonov, attempted to 'exercise their conscience' when they had the chance.[27]

Perhaps in some cases a sense of guilt drove people to even greater protestations of loyalty. In his last letter to Stalin of 10 December 1937, Bukharin wrote that he believed he was 'suffering retribution' for the years in which he really had waged a campaign against Stalin. Specifically, he declared himself 'oppressed' by the fact that in 1928 he had schemed against Stalin, stating that he was paying for this misdemeanour with his honour and his life and asking Stalin for forgiveness.[28]

In her study of the peasantry under Stalin, Sheila Fitzpatrick observes that alongside the regime's suppression of the population, the historian can in certain episodes discern a 'process of negotiation' between state and society. For example, the fact that, following collectivisation, the state permitted peasants to maintain private plots, albeit relatively small ones, indicates that peasant opposition to collectivisation had itself influenced the regime; there was discreet kind of deal between the regime and the peasantry.[29] In another study, Stephen Kotkin draws attention to the widespread use of survival strategies; in his study of working-class culture in Magnitogorsk in the 1930s, Kotkin argues that there emerged a set of 'rules of urban life' in which learning how to 'speak Bolshevik' became of crucial importance. Furthermore, Kotkin suggests that the set of practices associated with this behaviour involved a kind of resistance, in particular for couples: 'It might even be said that a kind of unacknowledged "private sphere" re-emerged, a pocket of structural resistance based on the couple, playing the game according to the rules and yet constantly violating them.'[30]

The development of survival tactics was certainly a feature of Stalinist culture. This points to a population that was made up not so much of enthusiastic Stalinists and heroic dissidents, but of pragmatists who would do whatever it was necessary to do in order to survive. Doubtless, the party itself was full of careerists and survivors. In his memoirs, the religious philosopher and dissident Grigorii Pomerants described a person who exhibited this kind of pragmatism, Aleksandr Egolin. Pomerants attended Egolin's class on nineteenth-century Russian literature in 1939 when Egolin was Professor in the Faculty of Russian Literature at Moscow University. Pomerants recalled that he gave an anti-Marxist presentation in his exam, and that in his subsequent oral exam, he described Chernyshevskii's *What Is to be Done?* as boring, and praised Ivan Goncharov's less radical nineteenth-century novel, *Oblomov*. Pomerants' comments were a sign of considerable independence, but Egolin still gave him a '4' and the top mark '5' for the exams. Egolin's career flourished. He later became a member of the Central Committee Propaganda Administration and as editor-in-chief of *Zvezda* in 1946 masterminded the attacks on Akhmatova. However, according to Pomerants, Egolin was no ideologue; he was playing the system:

> Egolin fulfilled this task wholeheartedly, earning tens of thousands along the way, and eventually burned out ... In another regime he would have been a bath-house attendant or a waiter in an inn and would have led a moderately honest life ... Egolin did not *seem* to be good-natured, he really was good-natured.[31]

Pomerants's story is worth recounting for two reasons. First, his own readiness to express independent views in 1939 indicates that restrictions on freedom of thought and expression were not always absolute, even before the war. Second, Egolin's tolerant attitude as an examiner illustrates Kotkin's argument that men whose motivations were primarily pragmatic rather than ideological were able to use the Stalinist regime to their own advantage.

Clearly, to play by the 'rules of the game' was not necessarily the same thing as to engage in some kind of moral resistance. As one historian has rightly observed, 'the emergent cynical subject was not tantamount to the rebirth of liberal man'.[32] However, living by tactics did not preclude a person from attempting small acts of moral protest. Some people seem to have tried to do a kind of deal with the state, through which they bought time for themselves and which gave them space to make coded criticisms. The film-maker Sergei Eisenstein was one who seems to have tried to cut a secret deal, or something like it. All of Eisenstein's works were political, and they contained little if any independent criticism of the Soviet or Stalinist regime. The exception, however, was *Ivan the Terrible*, Part 2 (1946). The cult of Ivan the Terrible during the Second World War reflected Stalin's desire to legitimise his own power and find historical precedents for some of his policies. The first part of Eisenstein's film was a very effective contribution to that. However, Part 2, which presented Ivan as a dark figure struggling with his conscience, was different, and it was banned. This alternative presentation of Stalin was apparently a deliberate attempt by Eisenstein to make a moral point about the system. Asked by a friend as to whether his film reflected the tradition of Pushkin's *Boris Godunov*, Eisenstein replied:

> Of course it's Boris Godunov: 'Five years I have governed in peace, but my soul is troubled...' I couldn't make a film like that without Russian tradition ... the tradition of conscience. Violence can be explained, legalised, validated, but it cannot be justified. If you are a human being it must be atoned.[33]

Eisenstein, then, finally got to make a film that contained a serious moral commentary on the system. Even then, it would be wrong to describe the work as the creation of a dissident, for there was much that was positive about Stalin that could be read from the film too. Indeed, such ambiguity was a typical feature of this kind of dissent. Writers and artists became accomplished at producing works that could be read on different levels.

One of the most famous examples of this was Shostakovich's Fifth Sympathy, first performed in November 1937. The symphony, which was written in response to criticism of Shostakovich's opera *Lady Macbeth of Mtsensk*, ended with an apparently triumphant and upbeat finale, and satisfied the censors as to Shostakovich's political loyalty. However, many years later Shostakovich declared that the ending depicted an enforced celebration and thus had a very different meaning.[34] By 1979, it was perhaps in Shostakovich's interests to depict himself as a man who had always harboured dissident convictions, and indeed it is important to be cautious about memoir accounts in which people discovered dissident attitudes in their past activities. In the end, it is not exactly clear what Shostakovich was trying to say. He was a complex personality. In a piece made in the mid-1970s, the dissident sculptor Ernst Neizvestnyi depicted him as a tortured and divided person.[35] Doubtless, there were many people like him.

There are a number of examples of people who went along with the system up to a certain point, and then felt they could go no further. V.G. Sorin, who was for a time Assistant Director of the Marx-Engels-Lenin Institute, was very willing to supply Stalin with documents and quotations to support his policies. However, according to Viktor Kravchenko, he 'drew the line at *inventing* texts and *falsifying* quotations' and was arrested as 'an enemy of the people' in 1939, dying in a labour camp or prison in 1944.[36] Sorin, according to this evidence, was thus prepared to support the Stalinist regime to a certain degree, but then drew a moral line beyond which he would not go.

Sometimes there was a hidden history of moral doubt that preceded an act of moral resistance. Some kind of 'torment of the soul' would suddenly find public expression. Tat'yana Khodorovich recalled that as a teacher of Russian language and literature in 1948–1951 she was horrified at the propagandistic nature of what she was doing: the grammatical exercises were all constructed to praise the Soviet state; official poets, like Vasilii Lebedev-Kumach, were required reading. She sometimes referred to poets like Pushkin and Tsvetaeva in a subversive way, emphasising to the pupils that they should not tell anyone about it. However, she was forced to present the official line for the sake of the pupils:

> I understood that I was lying to them, telling them to study the verse of, say, Lebedev-Kumach . . . What would they answer in the exams to these academic institutions, if I told them that these were bad verses, if I told them the truth?

Fed up with what she was doing, Khodorovich left the job.[37] Khodorovich tried all sorts of options for dealing with her unease before she finally acted on it.

Khodorovich was looking back from the vantage-point of the 1990s. A useful account of the period, that also reflected an ethical opposition to communism, was Kravchenko's *I Chose Freedom* (1948). Kravchenko defected during the Second World War while on secondment to the USA with the Soviet Purchasing Commission. Although the memoirs were doubtless shaped to meet the interests of a Western audience, they are very illuminating.

I Chose Freedom was in many ways a moral confession, an account of the evolution of Kravchenko's conscience. In his youth, Kravchenko had what he called a 'Comsomol conscience', and he entered the party honestly and without misgivings or doubts. Participation in the process of collectivisation in Ukraine was a particular shock to him. He noted that to avoid sinking into despair about what was happening, people had to 'avert [their] eyes from the village and contemplate other parts of the picture'. It was a point that he made about his later life as a top industrial executive: 'I learned at last to blot out disturbing knowledge. It's not an easy art to acquire, but only those who master it can survive as industrial executives in the USSR.'[38]

The concept of conscience came up repeatedly in Kravchenko's account. He noted that when he was a party activist during the horrors of collectivisation, his 'conscious mind reached out desperately for alibis, for compromises with conscience'. He also recalled that his participation in the Stalinist project led to a breach with his father, who had been a committed and idealistic socialist. He justified his actions to his father by saying that he was a small cog in a big machine, and that he did not have the time or strength to worry about first principles. Their differences, he suggested, were rooted in unresolved inner tensions of his own: 'My father had become for me conscience incarnate. The misunderstanding was not so much with him as with myself. When I should be reconciled with my conscience, I would be reconciled with him.' Kravchenko appeared to have understood conscience in terms of moral or natural law, although without a metaphysical or religious dimension. Although he noted that his mother believed that her prayers were responsible for saving his life during the great purges, in general he did not link his moral awakening to a religious one. On the other hand, he clearly understood his experience in 'spiritual' terms, stating: 'If the years seem so empty, despite their clamorous events, it is because I lived in a spiritual void.'[39]

Kravchenko stated that the idealism of his father and the religious faith of his mother remained in the core of his being, and that they therefore played a part in his decision to defect. At the same time, he could not pinpoint the moment when he decided to defect: 'It was the result of feelings that had matured within me slowly and inevitably.' He chose 'a precarious freedom as against a comfortable enslavement'. His book, he said, was an appeal to the 'democratic conscience' of America and the world. He also referred to the '*moral disarmament*' of the Russian people in the years before the war, and described Russians as 'morally and politically maimed'.[40]

Kravchenko was apparently not unusual in seeking for ways to 'blot out' disturbing knowledge. Other memoirists testified to the same thing. The future dissident Petr Grigorenko, who participated in the process of collectivisation and later became a general, observed in his memoirs: 'We were deceived because we wanted to be deceived. We believed so strongly in communism that we were ready to accept any crime if it was glossed over with the least little bit of communist phraseology.'[41] Similarly, another future dissident, Lev Kopelev, one of the twenty-five-thousanders during collectivisation, recalled: 'Some sort of rationalistic fanaticism overcame my doubts, my pangs of conscience, and simple feelings of pity and shame.'[42]

The difficulty of writing an accurate account of the 'blocking out' of uncomfortable information is that people are continually revising their life histories. The thinking of some of the Soviet dissidents was sometimes shaped by particular experiences – a traumatic encounter with the regime, for example, or an important political development – that prompted them to reconsider their previous views of the regime. Following that, a new narrative of the past would emerge to take account of the new information. The fact that Kravchenko, Grigorenko and Kopelev recalled pangs of conscience that they then suppressed seems to have depended on later decisions that led to a revising of memories. Yet this should not be taken to mean that the doubts of these men only really existed with hindsight. Doubts were evidently very real at the time. G.A. Tokaev, a high-level member of the Moscow Air Academy who defected to the British in 1945, recalled in his memoirs that, under the influence of his brother, Andrei, who was critical of certain aspects of the revolution, he had begun to entertain doubts about the direction of the revolution in the 1920s. Moreover, he insisted that these doubts were very genuine:

> Looking back on that time, I observe that a first embryonic doubt was even implanted by Andrei, however heavily it was overlaid by other influences. I say *observe* advisedly, because though I was so little conscious of it, I am convinced that I have not invented this doubt nor thought it into my past.[43]

These memoirists clearly assumed that their original doubts represented their true convictions, and that their support for the regime involved a turning away from their true selves. Writing about post-war Poland in *The Captive Mind* (1950), Czeslaw Milosz made a similar point. He noted that, as intellectuals developed elaborate theoretical and moral explanations to justify complicity with a regime about which they had doubts, the life of pretence that they adopted changed their moral identities. As they played public roles that they did not in fact believe in, their personalities changed:

> After long acquaintance with his role, a man grows into it so closely that he can no longer differentiate his true self from the self he simulates, so that even the most intimate of individuals speak to each other in Party slogans.[44]

Milosz's statement is a challenging one. He assumes that there is such a thing as a real self and that it can be distorted. If he is right, discourse analysis becomes very hard. It may be, as Halfin observes, that people can mean what they say even when their language is 'ideological through and through'.[45] However, if Milosz is right, people can also become trapped in ways of thinking that they only think they believe in.

The origins of dissent are sometimes to be found in ordinary human conflicts. Svetlana Alliluyeva described in her memoirs how her love affair with the Jewish intellectual Aleksei Kapler contributed to her growing estrangement from her father; Stalin's hostility to Kapler and abusive attitude to his daughter's emotions poisoned their relationship. She recalled: 'I was never again the beloved daughter I had once been.'[46] Generational conflict was clearly a factor here too. What began, however, as a simple human conflict between father and daughter grew to a point where Svetlana came to associate herself with the dissident movement of the 1960s, and expressed her hostility to the Soviet regime in strongly moral terms.

The wartime period was very important in terms of the development of Soviet dissent. Hannah Arendt was surely right in suggesting that 'totalitarian' regimes flourish by exploiting loneliness. A regime can exploit a population much more easily when people are isolated from one another. Totalitarian domination, Arendt noted, 'bases itself on loneliness, on the experience of not belonging to the world at all, which is among the most radical and desperate experiences of man'.[47] One of the distinctive features of the war period, however, was the development of a strong sense of national identity. This sometimes worked in favour of the system. The non-conformist Russian novelist, Viktor Nekrasov, recalled that the war created a 'powerful patriotic feeling' which led him and his friends to forgive Stalin for all the atrocities of the regime: 'And we, lads from intelligentsia families, became soldiers and believed the whole myth with a clear conscience. With open hearts we joined the party of Lenin and Stalin.'[48]

At the same time, the war created a strong sense of freedom. One soldier, Vyacheslav Kondrat'ev, noted that during the war people felt freer than in peacetime; the war gave soldiers at the front line a real sense of responsibility to the extent that they felt that they even had Russia's fate in their hands: 'It was a real genuine feeling of being citizens, responsible for the Fatherland.'[49] People had experiences of social involvement that were not architected by the state. A good example of this was during the siege of Leningrad; in her diary of the siege, Vera Inber recalled that the entire population of the city came out to clean the streets. One 11-year-old observed: 'Nobody ordered us to clean up the courtyard, we did it of our own free will.'[50] People were brought together spontaneously by adversity. Nadezhda Mandelstam recalled that 'for a brief moment the war brought people together again', and that 'it was this momentarily restored sense of community that prepared the ground for the events of the fifties and the ferment in the minds of the younger generation that followed'.[51]

There is no doubt that wartime experiences of adversity did contribute to a new sense of solidarity; the war fostered communal experiences that gave rise to new emotions and feelings of responsibility. Adversity caused by Stalinist terror also gave rise to new forms of community and alternative ethical ideas. Notably, the origins of dissident moral attitudes were often to be found in the experiences of life in prison or labour camp. The camps fostered a variety of moral experiences. For many, the criminal community in the camps was influential. In *Kolyma Tales*, Varlaam

Shalamov argued that hundreds of thousands of people were permanently seduced by the ideology of the labour camp criminals, and that the camps were 'in every way schools of the negative'. In the camps, convicts learned 'flattery, lying, petty acts and major villainies'; returning to civilian life, the convict discovered that moral barriers had somehow been 'pushed aside'.[52] Shalamov highlighted the importance of the cult of motherhood in the criminal community of the camps, suggesting that devotion to motherhood was in fact a 'camouflage, a means of deceit – at best, a more or less bright expression of sentimentality in prison'; it was 'the sentimentality of a person who bandages the wound of some small bird and who, an hour later, is capable of tearing this bird to shreds'.[53] Words sometimes acquired new meanings in the camps. For example, in labour camp jargon, the adjective 'conscientious' (*sovestlivyi*) was sometimes used as an ironic reference to men who had been convicted for small-scale robbery.[54]

The question of whether people's characters were enhanced or corrupted by their experiences in the camps is a contentious one. Shalamov saw the camps as an instrument of dehumanisation, and he was not unique in his pessimism. In a short article, 'While conscience exists' (1994), the Ukrainian poet and camp veteran Boris Chichibabin stated that although some people survived spiritually, they were very few in number.[55] Yet, some memoirists took a different view. Evgeniya Ginzburg found that imprisonment provided her with space to reflect on the meaning of life. It brought out the best in her: 'Never before or since was the better side of me so strongly brought out.' While in the camps she was 'kinder, more intelligent and perceptive than at any other time in her life'.[56]

In *The Gulag Archipelago* Solzhenitsyn, too, expressed his gratitude to the camps for what they had taught him. Indeed, he wrote: '*Bless you, prison*, for having been in my life', declaring that 'Tolstoi was right when he *dreamed* of being put in prison'.[57] In the chapter entitled 'The Ascent', Solzhenitsyn stated that the experience of the camps could help a person resist the wrong kind of repentance and embrace the true form of it. The official purpose of imprisonment, he noted, was to give the criminal time to think about his crime so that he would become 'conscience-stricken (*terzalsia*), repent and gradually reform'. However, in that corrective sense, he declared, most of the inmates of the Gulag were in reality innocent, and thus the labour camps '[*knew*] *no pangs of conscience*'. In fact, he stated, the opposite process occurred; not only do you not repent, but 'your clean conscience, like a clear mountain lake, shines in your eyes'. Moreover, you learn spiritual discernment: 'Your eyes, purified by suffering, infallibly perceive the least haze in other eyes; for example they infallibly pick out stool pigeons.' At the same time, Solzhenitsyn suggested that in another way imprisonment did bring a person face to face with his own misdemeanours. He recounts how he came to see good and evil inside himself, and thus broke with the world-view that assumed good and evil to be attributes of states, classes or political parties; he embraced instead the idea that the dividing line between good and evil passed 'through every human heart'.[58] The camp, Solzhenitsyn stated in another chapter, made him face the truth about himself, and it helped him to develop his character:

> The day when I deliberately let myself sink to the bottom and felt it firm under my feet – the hard, rocky bottom, which is the same for all – was the beginning of the most important years in my life, the years which put the finishing touches to my character. From then onwards there seem to have been no upheavals in my life.[59]

The Gulag Archipelago contains an underlying religious vision. Religious motifs were not infrequent in labour camp memoirs. Some memoirists refer to experiences through which they came to entrust their lives to God. For example, the medievalist Dmitrii Likhachev, who had a religious experience while he was a prisoner in the labour camp on Solovki in 1929, recalled that a transformation took place in him that led him to believe that 'every day was a gift of God', that he had to live 'day by day'. Likhachev's religious feelings were also stimulated by the landscape and culture – by 'the change of seasons . . . the variety of landscapes . . . [and] the shrines and chapels'.[60]

There is something similar in Panin's *The Notebooks of Sologdin*. Panin, who was the model for the character of Sologdin in Solzhenitsyn's novel *The First Circle*, had a remarkable experience of healing from a severe case of diarrhoea while he was in a camp. As in many religious narratives, Panin, who became a Catholic, described it as a consequence of a kind of spiritual leap forward and a new dedication of himself to God:

> In some way not understood by me, I had long been prepared to make such a vow. At the moment of self-dedication I experienced a feeling of confidence that has not abandoned me to this present day. I knew with certainty and conviction that God would save my life.

Alongside this religious experience, however, Panin also developed a moral philosophy that he summed up in ten precepts that were far from fully Christian. The precepts were: 1. Wipe out the stool pigeons. 2. Repay a blow with a blow. 3 Help the deserving. 4 Keep your nose out of your neighbour's business. 5 Don't look for trouble. 6. Remember that your bread ration belongs to you alone. 7. A slave morality is for Chekists to live by. 8. Your friends are like your family. 9. Be a slave without but a warrior within. 10. Save your soul, and you'll save your body too.[61]

A non-Soviet religious account of life in Soviet prisons that emphasised the theme of 'acceptance' and 'letting go' was Father Walter Ciszek's account of his time in the Lubyanka in the 1940s, *He Leadeth Me*. Ciszek interpreted his ordeals in the light of the Jesuit system of spiritual discernment, and emphasised God's providential involvement in his life.[62]

Although the religious experiences of men like Likhachev, Panin and Solzhenitsyn were not mediated by the church, they were still shaped by a cultural environment that was influenced by Orthodoxy. Religious culture was clearly an important, if discreet, formative influence for many Soviet citizens. It is important not to underestimate the power of the regime's attack on the church, but even in 1937 the census was reported to have stated that 57 per cent of the population were still believers. The main religious persecutions were comparatively recent. Anyone coming to the towns from the villages would have been brought up with some Orthodox moral convictions. At a domestic level, young people were often brought up by parents and grandparents whose moral values had been shaped by Orthodoxy. Children were sometimes baptised on the quiet, and the very act of having a child baptised was understood to be a secret act of non-conformity.[63]

The Russian Orthodox Church was, of course, in a very difficult situation. Like so many individuals, it too made its deals with the regime in order to survive. It came to emphasise obedience to the state as a moral duty. In his declaration of support for the Soviet regime in 1927, Metropolitan Sergei quoted St Paul to the effect that Orthodox Christians should support their rulers not from fear, but from conscience.[64] Obedience to the state and obedience to the church were now synonymous. Sergei's eventual successor as Patriarch, Aleksei, stated that serving the Russian Orthodox church was inseparable from serving the Fatherland. At the same time, after the Nazi invasion the Russian Orthodox Church also went along with the official propaganda that the war was a battle for freedom of conscience; in a Declaration of Russian clergy of November 1941, it was announced that the war effort was a 'struggle for Christian civilisation, for freedom of conscience and faith'.[65]

Alongside the church's increasing statism, other mystical and more personalised religious traditions continued to exist. Notably, the hesychast practices associated with Optina Pustyn remained alive, if hidden from view. People continued to go to confession. The Orthodox priest Father Aleksandr Men', for example, who was influential during perestroika, made his first confession to a priest named Father Serafim Batyukov in 1942 when he was 7 years old. Men' and his family owed a lot to Father Serafim's spirituality. Father Serafim belonged at that time to the Catacomb church, a branch of Russian Orthodoxy that refused to accept the policies of Metropolitan Sergei in the late 1920s and re-entered the established Church after 1945. Before the revolution, Father Serafim had been under the direction of one of the *startsy* of the monastery of Optina Pustyn, and he developed a very strict but differentiated system of spiritual direction. He treated each person differently. He once stated: 'Every bird has its own flight. An eagle flies in the clouds, while the nightingale sits on the branch, but each of them glorifies God. And there is no need for a nightingale to be an eagle.'[66] Following Father Serafim's death in

1942, and the exile of other priests associated with him, the young Men' and his mother, Elena, became linked to a community of nuns in Zagorsk under the direction of the higumena, Mother Maria. Mother Maria, Men' recalled, had qualities that were typical of the Optina *startsy* – 'openness to people, their problems and their searchings, an openness to the world'.[67]

Of course, like the Catacomb Church, non-Orthodox religious groups were often hostile to the Soviet regime, and this also gave rise to ethical forms of dissent. For example, some Baptists and Evangelicals refused to do military service. When a Seventh Day Adventist student from Dnepropetrovsk refused to serve in the Red Army, six fellow students wrote a petition calling for his release, stating that for each person military service should be a matter of 'his own conscience'.[68]

Camps and underground churches fostered forms of community and social interaction that were not planned by the state. The direction of a person's conscience owes much to personal decisions and individual moral and spiritual experience. At the same time, since moral choices are influenced by social processes, it is not surprising that ethical opposition to the Soviet regime or simply moral non-conformism was sometimes the outcome of people belonging to these excluded or more isolated social networks.

4 The rebirth of conscience under Khrushchev

Stalin's death in March 1953 was a turning point in Soviet history. However, changes were already afoot even before 1953. A recent overview of twentieth-century Russia has divided Soviet history into the pre- and post-1945 periods, thereby emphasising that the war changed the USSR in important ways, and that some of the reformist currents of later decades were rooted in the experience of defeating Nazism.[1] Certainly, the wartime period saw a greater element of personal freedom and social solidarity than existed before it. At the same time, the tradition of the activist political underground can be traced back even to the 1930s.[2]

Dissent often originated with small informal groups of intellectuals. While at school in the 1930s, the future dissident Larisa Bogoraz was so convinced by Stalinism that when her father was sent to the labour camps in Vorkuta as an enemy of the people, she refused to write to him.[3] However, when Bogoraz went to university in 1946, she became part of a small group of people who read poetry together, which included the writer Yulii Daniel, whom she later married. She then visited her father in Vorkuta, taking the view that the labour camp inmates were 'in no way enemies of the people'.[4] The change of mind was doubtless partly the result of growing up, but it was also caused by contact with a new community of people. Another future human rights activist, Viktor Krasin, was a member of a circle of Moscow intellectuals who from 1946 met weekly to discuss literature and philosophy. Used-book stores in Moscow were scoured for interesting reading material, and the group was able to get hold of works by Nietzsche, Dostoevskii and Schopenhauer, and material on Indian philosophy. Eventually, in January 1949, Krasin and seven other members of the group were arrested.[5] Krasin was sent to the camps, and spent four years in Kolyma.

Of course, not all participants in such circles became dissidents. In 1949, the sculptor Ernst Neizvestnyi, who was forced into emigration in 1976, formed a small circle with three other friends. Neizvestnyi was then studying at the Academy of Arts and in the Faculty of Philosophy of Moscow University, and was deeply disillusioned by the politicised nature of the curriculum. He and his friends wanted to create a 'catacomb culture'; and they even managed to translate and distribute some of George Orwell's work. Some of the participants in the circle, Neizvestnyi recalled, became important party functionaries.[6]

The death of Stalin, then, did not suddenly bring society to life. In some cases it gave impetus to circles of independent activity that were already in place. Ludmilla Alekseeva recalled that in 1953 she was part of a small group that met regularly in the smoking room of the basement of the Lenin Library. On Wednesdays, when *Literaturnaya gazeta* came out, the numbers swelled, and on the days when *Novyi mir* came out, crowds would gather. By the late 1950s, these small communities or circles (*kompanii*) had started to become quite substantial. Alekseeva recalled that a typical Moscow circle numbered forty to fifty 'close friends'. The circles were themselves divided into smaller subgroups, but all members would meet together for larger social occasions. Such groups were central to the spread of ideas under Khrushchev. They broke down divisions between intellectual and social life, and also over subsequent decades provided the setting for the spread of the music of singers like Bulat Okudzhava, Vladimir Vysotskii and Aleksandr Galich, who articulated some of the emotional passion of subversive opinion. The human rights movement of the late 1960s in part originated with these social networks.

In some ways, these micro-communities were simply networks of friends. Yet friendship itself could easily prove subversive in Soviet life, for it represented a zone of private loyalty that the state could not always reach. Simply living in a flat with someone could turn out to be productive of subversive sentiments. Fedor Burlatskii, one of Gorbachev's political advisers during perestroika, recalled that when he was at university in Moscow in the late 1940s and early 1950s, he lived with an old communist friend of his family who knew the history of the party well, and who had an apartment full of forbidden Soviet books and old party documents. He recalled that he would 'sit by candlelight at night and read the real history of the party' and that he consequently developed clear anti-Stalinist convictions before 1956.[7] People's moral attitudes were often shaped by personal encounters. The dissident activist Aleksandr Ginzburg recalled that Pasternak's character, as well as his writings, influenced him considerably. Pasternak's first reaction to things, Ginzburg said, was 'deeply moral', and 'deeply linked to conscience'. Lev Kruglyi, a popular Moscow actor of the 1960s and 1970s, recalled that he was deeply impressed by Vera Pashennaya, a well-known stage and film actress who won a Lenin Prize in 1961. Peshennaya's reactions, he stated, were human rather than professional: 'She would react to a character in a certain way and this nudged my inner life in a particular direction.'[8]

Circles as a feature of independent activity, and in embryo as a basis for civil society, were part of a broader and very important facet of Soviet life: informal networks. This partly had its root in the economic system that was created by Stalin, in which to avoid the inefficiencies of central planning, factory directors had to set up alternative sources of supply. Eventually, the whole economic system was so riddled with inefficiency that informal networks became a vital element of the way it functioned. People resorted to 'blat', the personalised systems of exchange that flourished and were intimately linked to people's social circles.[9] These informal networks clearly helped to shape people's moral ideas and habits.

In their own way, academic institutes came to function as intellectual circles. For example, in spite of Lysenkoism, some scientific subjects remained relatively un-politicised by comparison with other subjects. Furthermore, scientists were a privileged group in the USSR; the state's global ambitions depended on their successes, and they thus had a certain bargaining power that others did not. One historian noted that scientists were often 'intelligent, sceptical, better informed and better educated than most Soviet citizens'; furthermore because of their importance to the regime, they were sometimes able to question the party's monopoly on things.[10] Scientific research institutes, then, were often pockets of independent thinking; and sometimes the scientists were quite independent. It was from this milieu that Andrei Sakharov emerged when in July 1961 he suggested to Khrushchev that there was no need to resume nuclear testing.[11] The prevalence of scientists, particularly of physicists, in the dissident movement was remarkable. Furthermore, their political, humanistic, artistic and sometimes religious concerns suggest that in the USSR there did not exist the polarity between arts and sciences that C.P. Snow saw in the West and described in his book, *The Two Cultures*.[12] One reason for this was that science often attracted honest people. The Ukrainian dissident, Leonid Plyushch observed: 'Conscientious teachers prefer to teach natural science because it requires less lying than literature or the social sciences.'[13]

Brodskii once suggested that consciousness itself has a moral dimension: 'The history of consciousness starts with one's first lie.'[14] The reverse process surely also happens: the birth of moral conviction is often connected with the awakening of consciousness. If this is so, the spread of information itself was productive of moral awareness. Circles clearly facilitated the spreading of information. Social mobility was also vital. In this respect, the mass releases from the labour camps were very significant. Access to independent or foreign forms of media was also vital for the raising of consciousness. Aleksandr Ginzburg recalled that at home in Moscow his family listened to Western radio from 1949 onwards.[15] The Leningrad-based dissident, Boris Pustintsev, grew up in Vladivostok, and from listening to foreign radio transmissions on the Korean War and meeting soldiers who had been wounded in the fighting, he concluded that the Soviet official explanations of the war were not reliable.[16] Burlatskii's access to his friend's private library, and Krasin's experience of finding books in Moscow indicate that second-hand bookshops and personal collections of books were also important sources of suspect literature.

The key medium for the spread of information, however, was the system of independent publishing, known as samizdat. There was an element of samizdat even in the late Stalin era.[17] However, in the late 1950s and especially in the middle of the 1960s, it became an important cultural phenomenon. The human rights movement partly had its roots in samizdat networks. Initially, samizdat started as a literary phenomenon and only grew later into something of social and political significance. The dissident, Mikhail Meerson-Aksenov, interpreted this to suggest that dissident social and political thought had spiritual origins: the fact that social samizdat came after literary samizdat indicated the 'spiritual source' of dissident thought.[18] He also stated that the emergence of a new creative intelligentsia at the beginning of the 1960s had involved a growing 'individualisation of the social consciousness', and that *Doctor Zhivago*'s emphasis on the individual personality, and Solzhenitsyn's stress on ethical personhood, had played an important role in this.[19] Certainly, existential questions often preceded political opposition in the evolution of dissident thought, and throughout these decades, literature was a central vehicle for discussion and polemic. During the 1960s, samizdat became the central medium for spreading news about the trials of writers and human rights activists, but its origins were to be found in the previous decade.

To some extent the literary and political break with Stalinism that took place in the 1950s reflected the aspirations of people who had been silent under Stalin, and finally had the opportunity to say what they were thinking. However, during the 1950s there also began to emerge a new generation of figures who were to play a central role in the dissident movement itself. The late 1950s saw the beginnings of a youth movement in the USSR. The poetry readings that started at the Mayakovskii Square in July 1958 played a formative role in this; people gathered to read poetry and to talk about philosophy and politics. After a few months the crowds were not permitted to assemble. Also in the late 1950s, Aleksandr Ginzburg, who knew many of the organisers of the Mayakovskii Square readings, organised some exhibitions of work by young artists, and then produced a type-written samizdat journal, *Syntax*. *Syntax*, which printed only poetry, and expressed a somewhat 'pessimistic, disheartened mood', included work by such figures as Bella Akhmadulina, Brodskii and Okudzhava.[20] It came out three times in 1959–1960 before Ginzburg was arrested and sentenced to two years in normal-regime labour camps. Others who were associated with the Mayakovskii Square readings also produced magazines: Vladimir Osipov brought out one issue of a magazine called *Boomerang*, and Yurii Galanskov put together *Phoenix-61*.

An important participant in the Mayakovskii Square readings was Vladimir Bukovskii. Bukovskii, who has been described as the 'pioneering practitioner' of *glasnost'*,[21] became politicised at a young age. He was born in 1942, and was brought up to be a convinced Stalinist. Yet Stalin's death was a great shock to him, because it made him realise that Stalin was mortal. 'Hadn't God died', he asked, 'without whom nothing was supposed to take place?'[22] As a 10-year-old, he resigned as chairman of his class Pioneer group, following an experience when he was required to reprimand one of his classmates for some misdemeanour. It was in some ways an impulsive decision; in his memoirs he reports that he would not have been able to fully explain why he had resigned. In his early teens, he read some of the works of Lenin and the nineteenth-century Russian revolutionary thinkers. At 14, he refused to join the Komsomol. Following the Soviet invasion of Hungary in 1956, he joined some classmates in a secretive organisation; in one way it was a youthful game, but members were instructed in how to behave under interrogation, and how to lose a KGB 'tail'. He and his schoolmates found that only 'cynicism struck [them] as sincere'. Still at school, he was brought before the Moscow City Committee for his uncooperative behaviour.[23]

Bukovskii became interested in organising alternative political and cultural events. In September 1960, he and a couple of friends decided to try to revive the Mayakovskii Square readings. One of the works that was most frequently read in the square was Galanskov's *The Manifesto of Man*, a provocative poem in which the author declared: 'This is me / calling to truth and revolt, / willing no more to serve, / I break your black tethers woven of lies.'[24] There was a large demonstration on 14 April 1961, at which there were a number of arrests. Many of those involved in the readings were either under arrest or being interrogated regularly, and Bukovskii was himself interrogated twice in Spring 1961, and thrown out of university that year.[25] Also in the early 1960s, Bukovskii came under the influence of Aleksandr Yesenin-Vol'pin, the 'father of the human rights movement'. Yesenin-Vol'pin, who was the son of the poet Sergei Yesenin, was born in 1925 and belonged to an older generation of activists. Yesenin-Vol'pin conceived the idea that the Soviet government should be held accountable to its own laws. Indeed, during his stay in the mental hospital, he defended himself by pleading that the doctors and the KGB were themselves breaking Soviet laws by confining him.[26]

Yesenin-Vol'pin was not a moralist. Although a mathematician who thought in extremely rationalistic terms, Yesenin-Vol'pin resisted all attempts to define his ideas in terms of a system, and was very anti-dogmatic in outlook. Liberty was central to his vision. In a poem of 1946, he wrote 'one goal alone is crystal clear, / The irrational goal of liberty!'[27] In 'A Free Philosophical Treatise' (1959), he stated that he did not regard 'good' and 'evil' as philosophical categories, and believed that it was of primary importance that choices between representations of good and evil should be made without compulsion. Indeed he regretted that the Russian word for 'freely' (*dobrovol'no*) included within it the word for 'good' (*dobro*) and thereby set a certain limitation on the category of freedom. At the same time, he also recognised that the search for truth, whether truth existed or not, was part of the process of thinking, and noted the apparent conflict between life and thought: '1. As a living being I place life above thought. II. As a thinking being I place thought above life.'[28]

In his political thought, Yesenin-Vol'pin believed that in formally emphasising the need for legality, the Soviet regime had given the opposition an opportunity. Opponents of the regime could claim that the government itself was refusing to abide by its own laws, and that they were the true defenders of the state. Yesenin-Vol'pin also emphasised the idea of *glasnost'*, believing that legality could only be protected by *glasnost'* in the judicial process.[29] He also argued that it would be wrong to try to fight the system by breaking the law or by using violence and lies. He believed that people should see themselves as citizens of the Soviet state, and take personal responsibility for their lives. According to Bukovskii, this was an inspired approach because it challenged the internal excuses by which people justified their complicity in the regime's crimes: 'It presupposed a small core of freedom in each individual, his "subjective sense of right" . . . In other words, a consciousness of personal responsibility. Which meant, in effect, inner freedom.'[30] Initially, Yesenin-Vol'pin's ideas met with scepticism. However, in February 1962, on the final day of the trial of three men who had been involved with the Mayakovksii Square readings, Osipov, Il'ya Bakstein and Eduard Kuznetsov, Yesenin-Vol'pin managed to gain entry to the courtroom by showing the guards a copy of the Criminal Code. The incident, according to Bukovskii, was the beginning of the human or civil rights movement.[31]

The fact that the Soviet regime became increasingly conservative and cautious under Stalin reflected the interests of a government that wanted social reconciliation. However, in spite of the shift away from revolutionary ethics in Stalinist cultural policy, the underlying morality did not change fundamentally. There was still a compartmentalisation of ethics: one system of values for the present, and another for the future; one for party members and another for the rest. This continued to be the case under Khrushchev, although the growing move towards the articulation of universal values continued.

Khrushchev's Secret Speech was an important moment in Soviet history. Khrushchev talked about the Stalinist terror and the cult of personality in a way that had not happened before. In a community of people who had learned not to take risks, this was remarkable. It played a role in awakening an individual sense of conscience.[32] Yet Khrushchev's speech was also very selective. Khrushchev owed his own power to Stalin and to the system that he had created, and thus the criticisms that he made of the Stalin cult were in part self-serving; he did nothing to try to change the system fundamentally. Furthermore, there is no substantial evidence to suggest that the speech was prompted by moral considerations as opposed to pragmatic ones. Volkogonov, at least, suggests that it was not 'the call of heart and conscience' that prompted him, so much as the large number of letters coming into the Central Committee from gulag inmates and their relatives.[33]

Khrushchev endorsed the Leninist moral position that there should be one system of ethics for a time of revolutionary transition, and another after the enemy has been defeated. In this respect he referred supportively to Lenin's speech of 2 February 1920, in which Lenin had stated that revolutionary violence was 'necessitated by the resistance of the exploiting classes', and that as soon as the nation's political situation had improved in early 1920, he had instructed Dzerzhinskii to stop the terror and to abolish the death penalty. However, according to Khrushchev, Stalin had departed from the Leninist approach:

> Stalin deviated from these clear and plain precepts of Lenin. Stalin put the Party and the NKVD up to the use of mass terror when the exploiting classes had been liquidated in our country and when there were no serious reasons for the use of extraordinary mass terror.[34]

Khrushchev also depicted Lenin as a man who always sought to deal with his political opponents with argument and education. He did not impose his views on his co-workers by force. He kept in close touch with people who had shown 'indecision or temporary nonconformity with the Party line', and sought to draw them back onto the correct path by persuasion. Stalin, on the other hand, discarded the Leninist method of using persuasion and education and instead resorted to the use of administrative violence, mass repressions, and terror. Stalin, Khrushchev noted, violated all 'existing norms of morality and of Soviet laws'. Khrushchev also attacked the formulation 'enemy of the people', lamenting the fact that 'many honest communists' had been repressed; and he also condemned the trial system in which the only proof of guilt was the confession of the accused.[35]

There was in these statements an implicit call for universal values: honesty, persuasion, legality, and norms of morality were all praised. On the other hand, Khrushchev defended 'honest Communists', rather than honesty itself, and thereby sought to mobilise universal morality only to the extent that it served the party's interests. He complained of the repressive methods used against party members in the 1930s, but mentioned the fact that exploiting classes had been 'liquidated' without concern.[36] This was the speech of a man who sought a turn to universal values while rejecting them at the same time. These ambiguities indicate that it would be a mistake to see the Secret Speech as a straightforward exercise in truth-telling and a signal to political elites that the past could now be examined openly. Certainly, there is no doubt that the speech helped to create a climate of optimism about the possibilities of reform in the USSR. For example, it engaged the idealism of many younger members of the party. To future supporters of perestroika like Nail' Bikennin, editor of the journal *Kommunist* under Gorbachev, it made a more liberal variant of communism seem much more viable.[37] More generally, it led many party members and intellectuals to reappraise their commitment to the Soviet model of socialism; it was a key factor, according to two *émigré* Russian historians, in the cultural thaw that paved the way for a 'spiritual renewal' in Soviet society.[38]

On the other hand, according to the scholar Ronald Hingley, the relaxation of controls under Khrushchev released 'a torrent of *vran'e* which had been damned up for decades'.[39] From this perspective, Khrushchev's speech did not open the door to a process of truth-telling, but rather provided a new model for the evasion of the truth. It can also be argued that Khrushchev's modest reforms in a certain sense delayed the final reckoning with Bolshevism that one day would have to come. The Soviet philosopher Aleksandr Tsipko argued that at a certain level de-Stalinisation helped to maintain the Soviet system because the new moral thinking was formulated within the framework of the official consciousness and ideology; instead of breaking up the Soviet system, the thaw 'prolonged it'.[40] Intellectuals were mobilised to fight for the new humanist and non-Stalinist version of communism. Certainly, the ideology of the Khrushchev era involved a 'neo-communist romanticism' that brought the party and the intelligentsia into a temporary alliance.[41]

The tensions in Soviet ethical thinking continued to be evident after 1956. The new Party Programme that Khrushchev presented to the 22nd Party Congress in 1961 announced that socialism had been achieved and thus that antagonistic classes were therefore abolished. Implicitly the context in which the suspension of universal moral principles was to be justified no longer existed. Indeed, the Programme announced that communist morality included the 'fundamental all-human moral norms' that had been worked out by the popular masses over thousands of years.[42] On the other hand, the emphasis of Soviet ethics remained very much on the rights of the collective over the individual. In 1963, Khrushchev suggested that the advocates of greater liberalism were in fact promoters of anarchy. In a talk on 8 March 1963, he said that the advocates of freedom for the individual were advocates of some kind of 'absolute freedom', and declared that under communism the will of one person should submit to the will of the collective; 'unless that is so', he said, 'anarchic self-will will sow dissension and disorganize the life of society'. Lenin, Khrushchev observed, had rejected any belief in 'absolutes'.[43]

These ambiguities were also evident in the twelve-point 'Moral Code of the Builder of Communism', which was included in the 1961 Party Programme:

> The Party holds that *the moral code of the builder of communism* should comprise the following principles:
>
> 1 devotion to the communist cause; love of the socialist motherland and of the other socialist countries;

2 conscientious labour for the good of society – he who does not work, neither shall he eat;
3 concern on the part of everyone for the preservation and growth of public wealth;
4 a high sense of public duty; intolerance of actions harmful to the public interest;
5 collectivism and comradely mutual assistance; one for all and all for one;
6 humane relations and mutual respect between individuals – man is to man a friend, comrade, and brother;
7 honesty and truthfulness, moral purity, modesty, and unpretentiousness in social and private life;
8 mutual respect in the family, and concern for the upbringing of children;
9 an uncompromising attitude to injustice, parasitism, dishonesty, careerism, and money grabbing;
10 friendship and brotherhood among all the people of the USSR; intolerance of national and racial hatred;
11 an uncompromising attitude to the enemies of communism, peace, and the freedom of nations;
12 fraternal solidarity with the working people of all countries, and with all peoples.[44]

The 1961 Party Programme suggested that in the course of the transition to communism, moral principles would become increasingly important. This arguably indicated that an effort was being made to make moral persuasion rather than legal coercion the chief regulator of behaviour in Soviet society.[45] In this sense, the Moral Code belonged to the hesitant process of de-Stalinisation that took place under Khrushchev. The Code certainly reflected a move away from class-based to universal morality. At the same time, the Code was also very vague, and contained little of a liberal nature. It prioritised collective over individual concerns, and interpreted morality in functional terms, as something reinforcing the power of the state.[46] It has also been noted that there was another tension in the regime's value system: the code's enthusiasm for simplicity and modesty contrasted with the promotion of consumerist attitudes that reflected a 'destabilisation of asceticism'.[47] Indeed, in some sense the regime was beginning to encounter the dilemma facing Western consumer societies: how to respect individual preferences while protecting the interests of the whole.

The reference in the Moral Code to 'conscientious labour' is an indication of the way the principle of conscience and hard work for the collective were sometimes associated. This was certainly evident in some of Khrushchev's speeches. In a book in 1959, Khruschshev declared: 'There should be no bargains [*sdelki*] with one's conscience. Such bargains with one's conscience can only bring harm to our communist construction work.'[48] At the 22nd Party Congress in 1962, he declared that 'to approach one's work with a good conscience [*dobrosovestno*], and to do everything on time and well, means in practice to be concerned for one's comrades – who are also working for everyone else, including "for you".'[49] Contemporary role models reinforced the link between conscience and integrity in the workplace. In January 1962, *Izvestiya* printed an article entitled 'An Incorruptible Conscience', which recounted the story of a communist worker whose conscience did not permit him to exploit his position at work to his advantage, even under pressure from his wife and mother.[50]

The party remained keen to associate itself with the principle of conscience. At the 22nd Party Congress, it was stated: 'The party is the mind, honour and conscience of our age, of the Soviet people as it performs great revolutionary transformations.'[51] The phrase, 'the party is the mind, honour and conscience of our age' established itself as an official catchphrase, and was later used in a poster by Nikolai Babin that was published under Brezhnev and Gorbachev.[52] Propaganda continually stressed that obedience to the state was a matter of conscience. Even in the labour camps it was emphasised. On the door out of Butyrki Prison there was a sign that read 'To Freedom, with a Clear Conscience'[53], and the camp motto at one of the camps in Mordovia in the 1980s was 'Back to work, with a clear conscience'.[54]

The ambiguous signals that Khrushchev sent out in the Secret Speech were replicated by certain features of his rule. It is notable, for example, that after 1956 execution ceased to be the main method of dealing with opposition. After the deaths of Beria and Abakumov, which Khrushchev himself was involved with, elimination ceased to be a main method of removing political rivals. At the same time, the tension that existed under Stalin between the desire for a legal state and the habit of arbitrary rule continued: a new Criminal Code was introduced in 1958 that sought to establish basic rules and procedures for law courts; on the other hand, there were a large number of economic trials in cities across the USSR between November 1962 and July 1963, which led to a number of death sentences.[55] The same tension was to be seen in foreign policy. The doctrine of peaceful co-existence and non-interference in the internal affairs of other countries that became policy in the 1950s was in stark contrast to the vision of global conflict articulated by Stalin in his *Economic Problems of Socialism* (1952). Yet Soviet global ambitions had not really been scaled down, as the Cuban missile crisis illustrated. Repression of the church was also a major feature of Khrushchev's rule. In November 1954, the regime condemned 'administrative measures' against the church, and the number of functioning churches remained relatively stable until 1958. However, after the defeat of the 'anti-party' group in 1957, there was a renewed campaign to close churches; 44 per cent of the churches open in 1958 were closed by 1966. Khrushchev himself declared at the 22nd Party Congress that it was important to free the Soviet people from the 'dreadful power' of religious prejudice and superstition.[56]

In his headstone for Khrushchev's grave at the Novodevichii Cemetery in Moscow, Neizvestnyi juxtaposed blocks of black and white stone in a way that suggested that Khrushchev was a deeply divided person.[57] Khrushchev was clearly a man of contradictions. It seems that he came to be troubled by his past. Once, in a conversation with the playwright Mikhail Shatrov, he noted that his arms were 'up to the elbow' in blood, and stated: 'That is the most terrible thing that lies in my soul.'[58] In his memoirs, which were written in the late 1960s, Khrushchev recalled that in the years 1953–1956, the Soviet leadership had been unable to free itself from the legacy of the Stalinist past:

> It was as though we were enchained by our own activities under Stalin's leadership and couldn't free ourselves from his control even after he was dead. Not until 1956 could we rid ourselves of the psychological after-effects of the hysteria which had gripped us during the hunt for enemies of the people.[59]

The word 'enchained' is important here, for it suggests that with hindsight Khrushchev saw certain inner constraints on his own actions that prevented him making a full appraisal of the nature of Stalinism at an earlier period. It is hard to imagine Khrushchev saying this so openly while he was still in power, and it suggests that his own moral outlook altered after 1964. Certainly, after 1964 he had contact with social networks with which he had no link before. In his memoirs, Bukovskii recalled being present during a telephone conversation between his dissident colleague Petr Yakir and Khrushchev following the news that Solzhenitsyn had received the Nobel Prize in 1970. Khrushchev noted that he got all his news from the BBC, and said: 'They don't give Nobel Prizes for nothing.'[60]

Khrushchev's interest in universal values, even if ambiguous, reflected a wider tendency. Indeed, after 1953 there was something of a general offensive by intellectuals against class morality in support of universal and to some extent Christian values in order to prevent the population sinking into moral degradation.[61] A 'rebirth of conscience' took place in the cultural sphere.[62] Literature was at the forefront of the campaign for a change of moral direction, and the literature of the period is a good guide to the underlying ethical debates that existed within the country at the time. Just a few weeks after Stalin's death, the writer Olga Berggol'ts published an article in *Literaturnaya gazeta* calling for a greater emphasis on personal feeling in lyric poetry.[63] In November 1953 in *Novyi mir*, Vladimir Pomerantsev published an article, 'On Sincerity in Literature', in which he accused official Soviet writers of producing formulaic works that distorted reality. He noted that, historically, writers of literature had sought to produce 'the confession, and not only the sermon'; and he called for the kind of sincerity that embraced 'reason, conscience, and inclination' (*sklonnost'*).[64] Pomerantsev's article struck an important chord with young intellectuals; Ludmilla Alekseeva recalled that of those in the Lenin Library discussion circle, she and everyone else in the group agreed with all of Pomerantsev's points.[65]

Pomerantsev's call for sincerity highlighted a potential problem for the proponents of the doctrine of socialist realism; there was a tension between the stress on socialism and the emphasis on realism. As a framework for unifying some of the diverse elements in Soviet ideology, socialist realism had its advantages. However, an appeal to its realist component could easily become a discreet way of attacking the regime itself. In another article in *Novyi mir* in 1954, Fedor Abramov, who became an important contributor to the school of Soviet 'rural' prose, declared:

> Only the truth [*pravda*] – straightforward and impartial, a passionate party-minded [*partiinoe*] penetration into the deep processes of our life, the formulation of the essential questions of the construction of communism, the depiction of the genuine spiritual life of the Soviet people: only these things are worthy of a Soviet writer.[66]

At one level, this was a thoroughly orthodox statement. At the same time it could also be read as a discreet call for less censorship. The idea of truth, which the Bolsheviks had used in their struggle against tsarism, could easily be turned against them.

Novyi mir was the central vehicle for literary dissent in the middle of the 1950s. Its editor from 1950–1954, and then in 1958–1970 was Andrei Tvardovskii. His publication of Pomerantsev's article and other daring pieces aroused considerable opposition in the party, and he was replaced in 1954 by Konstantin Simonov, who had edited the journal in 1946–1950. However, Simonov, in a very moderate way, was also ready to support calls for greater realism. In an article entitled 'Literary Notes' published at the end of 1956, Simonov lamented that too many Soviet writers had shied away from a real depiction of Soviet life, and called for a genuine socialist realism based on the 'full, unconditional truth', and founded on 'a depiction of real life with all its light and dark elements'. The problem, he said, was not so much insincerity, although he recognised that cynicism was also a factor, but rather a lack of 'moral intelligence' (*ideinosti*).[67]

The dissent that was articulated in *Novyi mir* following Khrushchev's Secret Speech has been described as 'moral humanist'; the full dimension of the human personality, including in its moral and creative dimensions, was its main concern.[68] Vladimir Dudintsev's novel, *Not by Bread Alone*, which was serialised in 1956 in the August, September and October issues of *Novyi mir*, expressed the 'moral humanist' tendency very well. It traced the attempts of a corrupt bureaucracy to obstruct the efforts of an inventor, Lopatkin, to get a design for a new system for pipe-casting accepted and implemented. At one level, it was a typical socialist realist novel, involving a struggle between clearly identifiable forces of good and evil, in which greater productivity and true communism were held up as high ideals. However, the communism that it promoted was of a highly modified form. Lopatkin looks to a 'true communism' rather than the coarse materialism of 'vulgar communism', and in a biblical allusion declares that 'Man lives not by bread alone, if he is honest'.[69] Freedom of thought is promoted; defending himself to the Public Prosecutor, Lopatkin states that 'it is impossible to destroy those who think differently – they are needed, just as a conscience is needed'. Russian literary culture has a part. The Russian symbolist poet, Valerii Bryussov, is quoted by one of Lopatkin's colleagues as saying, 'We shall carry our lighted torches into the catacombs, the deserts, the caves.'[70]

Dudintsev's novel was effectively an attempt to detach the universalist dimension of Soviet communism from its revolutionary component and to combine it with certain Christian, liberal and patriotic features. Not surprisingly, the book, which was published as a whole in 1957 in an edition of 30,000 copies, caused considerable controversy. Defending himself in the Western edition of the book, Dudintsev suggested something of the ethical purpose of the novel; he invited the reader to share his countrymen's 'great love of humanity and faith in the inevitable victory of the forces of reason and justice, as well as hatred of evil'.[71]

If Dudintsev accepted the framework of socialist realism, Pasternak's *Doctor Zhivago*, which was first published in Italian in 1957 was altogether different; it proposed a paradigm shift of larger proportions. Indeed, *Novyi mir* rejected *Doctor Zhivago* in September 1956, at the very moment it was publishing Dudintsev's novel. Pasternak's novel was completely at odds with Soviet ideology and culture. Pasternak's own outlook had been formed by pre-revolutionary Russian culture, and his novel was both a lament for the passing of that culture, and a call for its restoration. Pasternak's characters did not divide easily into good and evil as did Dudintsev's; indeed Strelnikov, the revolutionary leader and estranged husband of the main heroine of the novel, Lara, is portrayed with considerable sympathy. At the same time, certain of the characters were clearly vehicles for Pasternak's own ideas, ideas that together made up a form of Christian personalism. Yurii Zhivago's uncle, Nikolai Nikolaevich, laments the 'mediocrity in people when they herd together', and states that 'truth is only sought by individuals'. He declares that 'everything necessary has been given us in the Gospels', and that the two concepts that make up modern man are 'the ideas of free personality and of life regarded as sacrifice'.[72] Sacrifice and resurrection were central ideas in the novel. Using metaphors from nature, Pasternak hints that Russia's rich spiritual heritage and culture could come alive again:

> At first the snow melted quietly and secretly from the inside. But by the time half the gigantic work of melting was done, it could not be hidden any longer and the miracle became visible. Waters came rushing out from below, singing loudly. The forest stirred in its impenetrable depths, and everything in it awoke.

One of the poems at the end of the novel, 'Holy Week', touches on the same subject; Easter day dawns with the promise of new life: 'But at midnight beasts and men fall silent, / Hearing the spring rumour / That as soon as the weather changes / Death can be vanquished / Through the travail of the Resurrection.'[73]

The novel reflected a dual commitment to freedom and morality. Lara states: 'The great misfortune, the root of all the evil to come, was the loss of faith in the value of personal opinions. People imagined that it was out of date to follow their own moral sense.' Yet this commitment to freedom did not involve a call to radical individualism. Implicit in Pasternak's thinking was the idea that freedom could only be true freedom if it was rooted in an underlying moral and spiritual order. Strelnikov, the representative of the revolutionary ethic at its best, lacks an understanding of the moral and spiritual realities of life. His character is described as a 'finished product of the will', and his attitudes are artificial, rather than genuine. Strelnikov's suicide is in part the result of his losing Lara, but in the context of the novel as a whole, it is a judgement on an unsustainable world-view. In regard to violence, the novel contained some very direct criticisms of revolutionary ethics. Zhivago, for example, states: 'I used to be quite revolutionary-minded, but now I think that nothing can be gained by violence. People must be drawn to good by goodness'.[74]

It is not surprising, then, that the regime was worried about *Doctor Zhivago* and made systematic attempts to prevent its publication in the West. The novel was a challenge to the moral foundations of the regime in every way. According to James Billington, Pasternak 'presented in Zhivago a challenge to the moral superiority of the imitative activist who has externalized and materialized life', and an 'alternative to the two-dimensional "new Soviet man"'.[75] In its stress on the personal dimension, *Doctor Zhivago* was not alone. Mikhail Kalatozov's film *The Cranes Are Flying* (1957), a romance set against the background of the Second World War, also involved an intimate exploration of emotion, and contained almost no ideological content. Yet *Doctor Zhivago's* spiritual message was unusual for its time, and not only for the USSR. In a broader sense, the novel was critical of modern secular civilisation in general.[76] Its spiritual vision was also different from some of the mainstream literature coming from the West, which was more sceptical and individualistic.

Khrushchev's attack on Stalin led to an alliance between the party and the intelligentsia. The message of the Secret Speech was a kind of strategic half-way house: the regime admitted that mistakes had been made; the intelligentsia accepted that this was as far as things could go for the present. The problem with this for the Soviet regime was that having initiated a certain kind of *glasnost'*, it had either to continue with it or retreat. Pasternak's novel offered the regime an avenue for a more open discussion of things, but the regime refused to follow the logic of the discussion further. Indeed, the Soviet regime made every effort to prevent the publication of *Doctor Zhivago* abroad, and Pasternak was pressured into declining the Nobel Prize for Literature. The clampdown on Pasternak had important consequences. It brought the alliance between the party and the intelligentsia to an end, and it gave impetus to the growth of samizdat.

The poet Yevgenii Yevtushenko was another figure who articulated the more liberal spirit of the time. In an interview published in the late 1980s, Yevtushenko suggested that the origins of perestroika were to be found in the poetry readings of the 1950s: 'The poetry of our generation was the cradle of *glasnost'*', he said. He stated that 'hidden *glasnost'* had always existed in Russian literature' and that Russian literature was the 'literature of conscience'; Russia's writers and poets 'protected ideals and conscience'.[77] Yevtushenko was a complex figure. He gained a reputation for bending with the party line; he was 'selflessly devoted to a shifting morality', one poet sarcastically remarked. Yevtushenko protested that his approach to opposition was tactical.[78] His work certainly contributed to the culture of de-Stalinisation. In his poem 'Heirs of Stalin' (1962), he observed of Stalin: 'Believing in a great goal, he forgot / that the means must be worthy / of the goal's greatness'; and in his poem 'Fears' (1962), he warned that although fear was losing its power in Russia, people should not lose 'the fear / of condemning someone without trial, / the fear of debasing ideas with untruths'.[79]

Although literature was an important forum for intellectual debate under Khrushchev, many writers still accepted the 'rules of the game' of the period. This is illustrated by the reactions of certain literary figures to the clampdown on literature that took place in 1963. On 8 March 1963, at a meeting with prominent representatives of the arts, Khrushchev stated that he welcomed the appearance of certain works which offered a truthful account of life during the period of the personality cult; and he cited approvingly Tvardovskii's *Distant Horizons*, Solzhenitsyn's *One Day in the Life of Ivan Denisovich*, some of Yevtushenko's poems, and Grigorii Chukhrai's painting *Clear Skies*. At the same time, he expressed concern at the one-sided attention that was being devoted to 'lawlessness, arbitrary reprisals and abuse of power'. He noted that 'art belongs to the sphere of ideology' and declared that the people and party would never tolerate those who advocated the 'peaceful coexistence of ideologies'. Furthermore, he called on those still mistaken 'to reflect, to analyze their errors, to understand their nature and sources, [and] to overcome their mistakes'.[80]

Pressure was put on many writers to recant or admit that they had made mistakes in some way. There followed a variety of recantations, most of them distinctly ambiguous. At the meeting in March 1963, the poet Andrei Voznesenskii stated: 'Here at the plenary session I have been told that I must not forget Nikita Sergeevich's stern and severe words. I will never forget them.' Yevtushenko said that the ideology of communism was the basis of his life, and that his autobiography contained much immodesty: 'I feel heavy guilt on my shoulders . . . I want to assure the writers' collective that I fully understand and realize my error, and that I will try to correct it by all my future work.'[81] Neizvestnyi stated in *Pravda* that he had been thinking a great deal about 'the responsibility of the artist to society', and that the Marxist-Leninist world-view was the 'most comprehensive of all those existing in the world'.

Vasilii Aksenov also admitted past mistakes. In an article in *Pravda* on 3 April he stated that he was thinking deeply about the responsibility of artists 'to the people, to the Soviet land, to the Communist Party'. 'The conscience of the artist', he said, 'must become a part of the common conscience of the people'. Aksenov also disassociated himself from an interview he had given for the Workers' News Service of Poland the previous autumn. On rereading the interview, he declared that he had to 'reject' some of the words in it:

> Some of the names I mentioned were dropped from the interview for some reason, and other names I had not mentioned appeared in it . . . I cannot justify my thoughtlessness. I am ashamed to recall the circumstances in which this interview was given . . . Of course, Poland is a socialist country, and readers there can figure out what is going on, but the bourgeois hacks are watching the socialist press like hawks.[82]

Although this was a very public recantation, Aksenov was in fact not very specific about what exactly he was repenting of it. Yet for the regime, this elusiveness probably did not matter. The most important thing was not whether these artists had really recanted, but whether they were ready to give the impression that they had recanted. The readiness of Aksenov and others to give the impression of penitence was a victory for the regime. More generally the recantations indicate that when people's careers were at stake, survival tactics were still brought into operation; this was in spite of the fact that the immediate threat of being shot as an enemy of the people had been removed. The tactics themselves were evolving.

Perhaps the most sensational literary event of the early 1960s was the publication of Solzhenitsyn's novel, *One Day in the Life of Ivan Denisevich*. This short work was a grim account of a day in the life of a labour camp inmate. It appeared in *Novyi mir* in November 1962, primarily due to the determination of Tvardovskii and some of his staff. At the same time, the relationship between Solzhenitysn and Tvardovskii was not easy, and is illustrative of the tensions that existed between writers who had different approaches to dealing with the system.

Tvardovskii had been supportive of Stalin before 1953, but then transferred his loyalties to Khrushchev. *Novyi mir* under his leadership kept to a moderate neo-Leninist position, holding that the revolution itself had been a great event that had then lost direction under Stalin.[83] In the summer of 1963, Tvardovskii was among a group of Russian and European writers, including Sholokhov, Fedin and Leonov, who visited Khrushchev in Gagra on the Black Sea coast. On Khrushchev's invitation, he recited his narrative poem 'Tyorkin in the Other World', which was a parody of the Soviet bureaucracy. In the poem, a young man Vasilii Tyorkin checks into the next world and discovers there a society that bears a remarkable resemblance to Stalinist Russia. The horrors of Stalinism are touched upon; Kolyma, Magadan, Vorkuta and Narym all get a mention. Liberty is stressed. The narrator concludes the poem by giving Tyorkin his freedom, noting that 'Where he chooses, / There he goes. / It's his right', and stating that 'Where there's life, / he's free, / untramelled'.[84] The poem was published in *Izvestiya* on 18 August.

Solzhenitsyn was very different from Tvardovskii. He was more hostile to communism, and less inclined to seek reconciliation with the system. This was doubtless partly due to his experiences in the labour camps; indeed, the stronger current of dissent that he represented to some extent emerged ready-made from the labour camps. At the same time, Solzhenitsyn's robuster attitudes to dealing with the regime were also forged by the very experience of struggling with Khrushchev's regime. In his memoir *The Oak and the Calf*, Solzhenitsyn devoted a lot of space to his struggles with the board at *Novyi mir*, and his personal spiritual discoveries. Solzhenitsyn recalled his 'newly-won strength' following the publication of *One Day in the Life of Ivan Denisevich*, but stated that the force of inertia kept him 'cautious and secretive'.[85] He felt distinctly uncomfortable about his story 'For the Good of the Cause', which was published in *Novyi mir* in Spring 1963. He believed that he had given way to a certain pragmatism in writing the story, and the fact that the editors at *Novyi mir* were delighted with the story, worried him. He suspected he was becoming a pawn in *Novyi mir*'s struggles with the state, and he turned down an offer to be part of a Soviet delegation to a symposium in the West. He wrote in *The Oak and the Calf*: 'The most terrible danger of all is that you may do violence to your conscience, sully your honour. No threat of physical destruction can compare with it.' Solzhenitsyn was afraid of being spiritually compromised by his dealings with the state, and increasingly wanted to work with it on his own terms or not at all.[86]

Solzhenitsyn, although he benefited from the patronage of Tvardovskii, concluded in his memoirs that *Novyi mir* 'came nowhere near the limits of the possible'. Tvardovskii, he came to believe, was a man who could not extract himself from the system at a psychological level:

> Lapses and recoveries, blackouts and illuminations, the struggle between the dossier and his soul, made up his tormented life. He was not one of those who fear everything, nor yet one of those who crash boldly through all the obstacles. His was the hardest path of all.

Tvardovskii, Solzhenitsyn stated, was like the 'soft-centred' people who could not bring themselves to 'say no abruptly'; he 'needed the fireproof firmness to which the zeks on the Archipelago are trained'. Describing one episode of state pressure on Tvardovskii in 1969, Solzhenitsyn suggested that he found it very hard 'to escape the maze in which decades of office holding . . . had ensnared him'.[87]

Solzhenitsyn was not alone in believing that *Novyi mir* had only a limited influence. The writer, Feliks Svetov, who worked for the journal in the 1960s, later commented that *Novyi mir* 'never went beyond the framework of the options offered by the 20th [Party] Congress, and was an incarnation of the same naïve demagogy'.[88] However, the tone of *The Oak and the Calf* was harsher than in some of Solzhenitysn's previous work. Reviewing the book in 1980, the Lithuanian poet Thomas Venclova regretted that there was a merciless quality in some of Solzhenitsyn's criticisms, although he still thought it a great book.[89] Solzhenitsyn's comments about Tvardovskii certainly provoked a hostile response from one of Tvardovskii's former colleagues at *Novyi mir*, Vladimir Lakshin. Solzhenitsyn, Lakshin suggested, had 'insulted the memory of Tvardovskii' and 'exaggerated, invented, and blown up Tvardovskii's weaknesses out of all proportion'. He concentrated on Tvardovskii's failings, for example, while omitting to mention that the publication of *Ivan Denisovich* had been a major act of personal courage. He had also offered a selective account of *Novyi mir*'s relations with the Soviet authorities. Lakshin was instead sympathetic towards Tvardovskii's ideological evolution; he noted that he had continued to believe in certain aspects of the communist ideal and that into that ideal he had incorporated 'everything that was best in the social and moral experience of mankind'. Solzhenitsyn, Lakshin stated, in his 'fanatical intolerance' saw 'the mark of Cain' on Tvardovskii because he was a party member; he chose to see humanity purely in terms of religious believers and unbelievers, whereas history had shown that doctrinal affiliation was not in itself a guide to virtue.[90]

The Oak and the Calf can be read as a guide to the literary politics of the Khrushchev era. It can also be seen as representative of the kind of dissident memoir literature that structured Soviet history in moral terms. It was certainly an uncompromising document. However, Lakshin was not really correct in portraying Solzhenitsyn as having a Manichaean-type attitude in which the party itself was an evil. Although Solzhenitsyn did have a tendency to divide people into allies and enemies, he never saw good and evil in purely external terms. Possibly there was an element of self-defence in Lakshin's criticisms. The issue at stake was whether or not people like Tvardovskii and he had compromised with evil in following the career path they had chosen. Such a question was bound to engender a lot of emotion.

5 The ethics of the human rights movement

The Soviet dissidents are not easy to define. The Soviet regime itself happily labelled its opponents 'dissidents' because the word had anti-social and extremist connotations. Partly for this reason, oppositionists generally did not like the term 'dissident'. The dissidents sometimes preferred to describe themselves as '*inakomyslyashchie*', literally, 'people who think differently', because it was a less loaded term. *Inakomyslie*, meaning something like 'non-conformist thought', is the Russian equivalent of the English word 'dissent'.[1] Yet *inakomyslie* fails to embrace the fact that the dissidents sought to *articulate* their opposition to the regime; '*inakoslovie*', meaning 'speaking differently', could be considered a more accurate term.[2] At the same time, the idea that dissidents were engaged in something that was essentially different, subversive or iconoclastic is also controversial. Another angle is to suggest that the dissidents were characterised not so much by thinking differently as thinking freely; it has been suggested that 'free thought' (*svobodomyslie*) is a more accurate description of the dissident tendency.[3] Dissidents have also sometimes been termed 'non-conformists', but that epithet fails to embrace the social activism of many dissidents. Pavel Litvinov, grandson of the former foreign minister, argued that the 'human rights movement' was the best term to embrace the dissident activities of the late 1960s and early 1970s because the movement was essentially 'non-political' in character. Its alternatives, in his opinion, were inadequate: the word *inakomyslyashchie* in his view did not sit easily with Russians; and the phrase 'the democratic movement' suggested that dissident activity was a larger phenomenon than in fact it was. Moreover, all regimes describe themselves as democratic.[4]

The 'human rights movement' has the advantage that it is more historically specific. There was much 'dissent' under Khrushchev, but little in the way of formal human rights activity. The human rights movement was essentially a phenomenon of the Brezhnev era. In this connection, it should be noted that there was a difference between the Khrushchev and Brezhnev eras in terms of mentality. The dissident intellectual, Andrei Amalrik, who was sentenced to three years in labour camps in 1970 for 'anti-Soviet fabrications', argued that there were two generations of oppositionists, if 'generation' is understood in a philosophical rather than chronological sense: the 'generation of 1956' was particularly influenced by the process of de-Stalinisation whereas the 'generation of 1966' was formed under the influence of the Sinyavskii–Daniel trial of 1966 and the experiences of the Czech reform movement in 1967–1968.[5]

Like Litvinov, many dissidents endorsed the view that their activities were non-political. Indeed, most of them understood dissent as a moral phenomenon. For some, the 'moral' dimension of the movement was rooted in the fact that many people had to undergo a process of self-overcoming in order to participate in the movement; they had to conquer their fear. A dissident, according to Sinyavskii, was a person who had developed a certain 'moral resistance' or 'strength of conscience' in relation to the regime.[6] Aleksandr Ginzburg stated that of the roughly 2,000 people he had known who had been involved in dissident activities, 80 per cent of them had primarily moral objectives; in this connection, he defined a moral person as one who had to fight against something inside himself. At the same time, Ginzburg excluded both Sakharov and himself from this group, suggesting that Sakharov never had an alternative to what he did, i.e. he never really went through a process of self-overcoming: 'Sakharov was never in a situation where he could go back. It is a special case. And my situation is close to that.' Nevertheless, it seems that Sakharov and Ginzburg were exceptions; most dissidents passed through times of considerable personal turmoil in order to do what they were doing.

The physicist and human rights activist Sergei Kovalev also saw dissident activity in moral terms. In an interview in 1990 Kovalev stated:

> Act according to your conscience. That was the basis of the human rights movements of the 1960s-1980s. It was not a political platform – there was no such thing then. Only naïve people thought that we were engaged in politics. Political platforms were not the basis of our behaviour, but rather moral incompatibility.[7]

In this case, Kovalev used the term 'moral' not so much in reference to a process of self-overcoming, but to describe the legal struggle for human rights. Kovalev divided dissidents into *zakonniki* and *politiki*, those who simply sought to make the USSR accountable to basic law, and those who had political objectives.[8] Kovalev recalled the 'absence of political manoeuvre' in the dissident movement and suggested that it was this that led to the movement's central interest in law.[9] Larisa Bogoraz also stated that the struggle for human rights was 'non-political'; writing in 1991, she stated that the emphasis on fundamental human rights had 'predetermined the non-political nature of the human rights movement'.[10]

This distinction between morality and law, on the one hand, and politics, on the other, is revealing; many dissidents considered politics by its very nature to be something manipulative and morally dubious. Indeed, according to the human rights activist, Vyacheslav Bakhmin, most dissidents assumed that politics was by definition a 'dirty thing' (*veshch' gryaznaya*).[11] It could be that the utopian hostility to the state and to politics that characterised some of Russia's nineteenth-century thinkers continued to be present in the human rights movement. Yet the hostility to politics was also specific to the time. After Khrushchev's Secret Speech, intellectuals were relatively optimistic about the power of politics to change things. Yet in the mid to late 1960s that optimism became much weaker.

In reality, the language of moral and legal opposition was sometimes used to gloss over what was clearly a political struggle at a certain level. The Soviet regime maintained itself by emphasising collective rather than individual rights, and thus to emphasise human rights could only be perceived as a political challenge by the state. Andrei Amalrik divided dissidents into 'politicals' and 'moralists', but noted that the division between the two was arbitrary and that both elements were reflected in most people.[12]

In his essay, 'Will the Soviet Union Survive until 1984?' (1970), Amalrik suggested that there were three different ideological tendencies in the opposition movement: genuine Marxist-Leninism, Christian ideology, and liberal ideology. He stated that the 'democratic movement' could be seen either as a synthesis of the three perspectives or as something that was based on what was common in all three. His own preference was to see it as the latter. He stated that all supporters of the movement had one common aim: 'the rule of law, founded on respect for the basic rights of man'.[13] There is much to be said for Amalrik's interpretation; the emphasis on the rule of law in the human rights movement brought together intellectuals and activists with very diverse beliefs. At the same time, other moral principles were important too. There was also a widespread commitment to non-violence, and to truth-telling and not lying.[14]

The human rights movement was partly a response to the succession of highly publicised show trials of intellectuals that took place from the middle of the 1960s onwards. The trial of Brodskii in March 1964 was an important milestone in this process. A verbatim account of the trial was circulated in the West, and dissidents became increasingly aware of the possibility of mobilising Western opinion to support their claims.[15] However, it was the trial in February 1966 of Andrei Sinyavskii and Yulii Daniel that brought the Soviet legal system into the international spotlight. Sinyavskii and Daniel were charged under Article 70 of the constitution with 'anti-Soviet agitation and propaganda'.

Sinyavskii, who worked at the Gor'kii Institute of World Literature and taught courses at Moscow University, was a specialist on Pasternak. Indeed, he and Daniel had been pall-bearers at Pasternak's funeral in May 1960 – something which was in itself a gesture of defiance of the regime. From 1959 onwards, Sinyavskii published a series of books in the West under the pseudonym, Abram Tertz, including the novellas, *The Trial Begins* (1960) which was a portrait of the corruption and anti-Semitism of the late Stalin years, *The Makepiece Experiment* (1965) which was in part a satire on political demagogy, and the essay, *On Socialist Realism* (1960). He also wrote articles for *Novyi mir* that were very critical of conservative and neo-Stalinist writers.[16] Sinyavskii was a not unusual example of a man who remained committed to the principles of the revolution, yet who questioned the methods by which communism had been built. Yet the trial proceedings forced him to declare publicly what he thought about certain features of the regime and effectively turned him into a dissident. He stated that he did not reject communism. He said that communism was 'the only goal that can be put forward by the modern mind', and even declared that the Stalin period had its 'legitimate place in history', noting that Western ideas about the renunciation of force did not appeal to him.[17] On the other hand, while rejecting Western accusations of brutality, he also observed that 'brutalities and inhuman methods' were used under Stalin. In his essay *On Socialist Realism*, he had suggested that communism had itself been sacrificed for the sake of communism: 'So that prisons should vanish forever, we built new prisons ... So that not one drop of blood be shed any more, we killed and killed and killed.'[18] It was a robust attack on some of Stalin's crimes, and it was evidence used by the judge in the trial to try to portray Sinyavskii as anti-Soviet.[19]

Yulii Daniel was a less-known figure who, with Sinyavskii's help, had also published a series of stories abroad. One of them, 'This is Moscow Speaking', was an account of an imaginary Public Murder Day in which a government ordered its people to kill one another; another story, 'Atonement', recounted the experiences of a man who becomes a social outcast after being falsely accused of having informed on people under Stalin. The stories were widely admired; indeed, the dissident philosopher Boris Shragin suggested that 'Atonement' marked the birth of the idea of the rights of man in the Soviet context.[20]

The crime of Sinyavskii and Daniel was to confront awkward questions in print, and to be independent and publish abroad. They denied that their actions were anti-Soviet, and pleaded not guilty to the charges. This was significant in itself. If in 1963 some of the most prominent liberal writers had publicly recanted and given the impression that they had recognised their errors, then the Sinyavskii–Daniel trial broke new ground. One commentator observed that, by refusing to plead guilty, Sinyavskii and Daniel exposed the 'artificial character' of the consensus that was imposed by the regime, and they thus broke the 'magic spell' of the show trials of 1936–1938.[21] Nevertheless, Sinyavskii was sentenced to seven years in the camps, and Daniel to five.

From the regime's point of view, the trial created a lot of problems. In particular, fierce international protests drew attention to Soviet methods of dealing with opposition. At the same time, unlike in the 1930s trials, systematic torture and the threat of execution were no longer a central element in the preparation of witnesses, so it was harder for the regime to enforce the right kind of messages. Moreover, Yesenin-Vol'pin's legalist strategy was beginning to gain some popular backing. In December 1965, two hundred people assembled in Pushkin Square, demanding that the regime respect its own constitution and calling for a public trial of Sinyavskii and Daniel. The regime reacted. Bukovskii, who was one of the organisers of the demonstration, was arrested three days before it took place, and during the demonstration itself some of the protesters themselves were also detained. During the trial itself, the wives of the defendants, Maria Sinyavskaya and Larisa Bogoraz, recorded the proceedings, and subsequently a partial transcript was assembled that was eventually published in the West.

The trial provoked a number of letters of protest. Notably, following the trial, there was a letter to the Presidiums of the 23rd Congress of the CPSU and the Supreme Soviets of the USSR and RSFSR from sixty-three Moscow writers, all of them members of the Union of Writers. The signatories stated that although Sinyavskii and Daniel were wrong to publish their work abroad, they were not anti-Soviet, and that there was a need for 'freedom for intellectual and artistic experiment in the country'.[22] Solzhenitsyn, Yevtushenko and Voznesenskii and the physicists, Sakharov, Igor Tamm and Petr Kapitsa were all signatories to other letters. On the other side, Mikhail Sholokhov, who received the Nobel Prize for literature in 1966, suggested that the government had been too lenient with Sinyavskii and Daniel, and described them as 'rascals with black consciences'. As a precaution against future demonstrations, the government added Articles 190–1 and 190–3 to the criminal code, prohibiting the violation of public order.[23]

Further trials followed in 1967 and 1968. In January 1967, Galanskov, Aleksei Dobrovolskii, Aleksandr Ginzburg and Vera Lashkova were arrested for their involvement in samizdat, and brought to court a year later in what became known as the 'trial of the four'. After a demonstration in Pushkin Square protesting their arrest, Bukovskii and two of his fellow demonstrators, Vadim Delone and Yevgenii Kushev, were themselves arrested and put on trial. In prison, Bukovskii successfully threatened a hunger strike unless the regime gave him a copy of the criminal code, and during the trial itself strongly attacked the regime's failure to adhere to its own constitution.[24] He was sentenced to three years. Delone and Kushev pleaded guilty, although in their final summing up they refused to acknowledge their guilt, and received one-year suspended sentences in normal regime labour camps.[25] The 'trial of the four' provoked protest at home and abroad, and played an important role in the formation of the human rights movement. The KGB managed to compromise Dobrovolskii and he denounced the other three defendants; he received two years hard labour. Lashkova admitted her guilt and received a year.

Galanskov initially incriminated himself for some of Dobrovolskii's crimes, but then tried to change his testimony and disputed his guilt; he received seven years. Ginzburg also disputed his guilt and received five years.[26] A substantial letter-writing campaign of protest accompanied the trial.[27] The records of the two trials were assembled by Pavel Litvinov, and first published in the samizdat journal, *A Chronicle of Current Events*.[28]

In terms of their moral philosophy at this time, many dissidents assumed a liberal belief in human rights and civil society. This is illustrated by the use of the term 'conscience' in the open letters of Anatolii Marchenko. In 1961, Marchenko, born in 1938, was sentenced to six years in labour camps and prisons for high treason. In 1967, he completed *My Testimony*, the first account of the post-Stalin prisons to circulate unofficially in Moscow.[29] Marchenko was concerned about the abuse of human rights in the camps. In March 1968, he wrote to Aleksandr Chakovskii, editor of *Literaturnaya gazeta*, suggesting that since he claimed to have a 'civic conscience', he should make a determined effort to discover the truth about conditions in the labour camps. Then, in April 1968, in an open letter to the Chairman of the Soviet Red Cross and others, Marchenko declared that the Soviet camps had not improved since the death of Stalin and complained about optimistic newspaper articles that were designed to 'lull the public conscience'. He appealed for investigation into the situation of political prisoners, and stated that 'it is our civic duty, the duty of our human conscience, to put a stop to crimes against humanity'.[30] Marchenko's use of the word 'conscience' reflected the widespread use of the word in the human rights movement; it did not necessarily carry metaphysical implications, but was used more in connection with the development of a humane civil society, and the defence of human rights.

Marchenko, however, was clearly not just interested in individual liberty. He also pointed to the necessity of a moral struggle against criminality. Protests over the 'trial of the four' also contained a moral as well as a liberal component. Bogoraz and Litvinov wrote a letter, 'To World Public Opinion', in which they drew international attention to the way the court was trying to manipulate Dobrovolskii to give false evidence against Galanskov and Ginzburg. They appealed to 'everyone in whom conscience is alive' to condemn the trial, and declared that the trial was a 'stain on the honour of our state and on the conscience of everyone of us'.[31]

Marchenko's biography was important for another reason. According to Aleksandr Daniel, the period 1966–1968 saw the appearance of a single 'informational field' among dissident intellectuals. By 1968, a particular set of dissident 'rules of the game' had appeared that could be considered their own 'culture-forming factor'. An important feature of the emerging dissident culture was the emergence of the dissident biography, a form of biography that differed from other contemporary biographies in that it was rooted in a 'specific dialogue with power' and a certain 'paradigm of protest'. The aim of the dialogue, from the point of view both of dissidents and the regime, was not to convince the opponent. In the case of the dissidents, it was really a dialogue with a third party – public opinion – both at home and abroad.[32] Marchenko's memoirs clearly played a role in this process. Marchenko was later rearrested and spent more years in prison, before he was sent into internal exile in 1971. He then married Bogoraz, who had by then separated from Daniel.

In the late 1960s letter-writing became a central strategy of dissident activity. Meerson-Aksenov suggested that letters fulfilled the same function as the press in free societies in that they gave expression to independent opinion. However, they differed from the Western press in that they were signed and therefore personal; as such they were an expression of the author's 'moral consciousness' and an appeal to the 'moral consciousness' of the addressee. At the same time, the letter-writing campaigns were important in another way; they presented potential signatories with the choice of whether or not they would sign; whether they would thereby challenge the 'rules of the game'. A moment of self-overcoming was needed if a letter was to be written or signed. There was often a lot of inner turmoil over whether to sign letters.[33]

Some people promoted the letter-writing campaigns as part of a strategy to mobilise people to act upon their convictions. The potential costs were clear. For example, Sakharov wrote to Brezhnev in support of the defendants at the 'trial of the four' in 1968, and subsequently lost his post as head of department at the secret nuclear research establishment in the Urals where he worked. Whether signatories to letters thought that their actions would influence the government is not fully clear. In his memoirs Sergei Kovalev recalled that he had no sense that letters would necessarily affect the fate of those who had been condemned. Rather, he interpreted his involvement in the letter-writing campaigns as indicative of a growing sense of 'civic responsibility'; it was the 'first step' along a road that changed his life.[34] At the same time, signing letters reflected fashion as well as moral conviction. According to Sakharov, many people signed letters in the 1967 campaign because it was fashionable and cost them nothing; things had changed significantly by the early 1970s.[35] There was also peer pressure to sign letters. Asked in 1967 to sign a letter calling for the Galanskov–Ginzburg trial to be an open one, Amalrik was sceptical about the likely outcome of the letter and uncertain about collective protest, yet also anxious not to give the impression that he was afraid or that he was unconcerned about the people in prison. Amalrik subsequently came to believe that the letter-writing campaign had restrained the process of de-Stalinisation and that signing letters did encourage processes of 'self-liberation'.[36]

The moral dimension of dissent was particularly evident in the thinking of some of the seven demonstrators who on 25 August 1968 gathered in Red Square to protest against the Soviet invasion of Czechoslovakia.

Those who demonstrated were Bogoraz, Delone, Litvinov, Konstantin Babitskii, Vladimir Dremlyuga, Viktor Feinberg and Natal'ya Gorbanevskaya. A former student, Tat'yana Baeva, also attended the demonstration. The demonstration was immediately broken up. Babitskii, Bogoraz, Delone, Dremlyuga and Litvinov went on trial in October. Gorbanevskaya was arrested later in December 1969 and spent nearly two years in a psychiatric hospital; Feinberg was confined in Leningrad Psychiatric Prison; and Baeva, although allowed to go free, was expelled from her Institute.

At one level, the demonstration was simply about liberty. One of the banners at the demonstration was entitled 'For your freedom and ours'. This slogan had been used by Polish insurgents fighting against the Russian empire in the nineteenth century, and its use here indicated that the demonstrators saw their action as part of a long-term tradition of protest. However, other factors were involved too. Bogoraz recalled that Gorbanevskaya wept over the phone as she recounted that Soviet tanks had entered Prague. Bogoraz and Delone both recalled experiencing feelings of shame at the time.[37] This feeling of shame was apparently not uncommon among intellectuals. Kovalev recalled that one of his colleagues, the biologist Aleksandr Neifakh, 'experienced our national disgrace in Czechoslovakia as his own'; and he added that this response reflected the moral basis of dissident activity, 'You answer for everything that your country does.'[38] In her final plea at her trial, Bogoraz declared that she could not say silent because that would have meant sharing in the general approval of actions that she could not endorse. She believed that speaking out was a way of taking responsibility:

> Had I not done this, I would have considered myself responsible for these actions of the government, just as all adult citizens bear the responsibility for all the actions of our government, just as our whole people bear the responsibility for the Stalin-Beria camps, the death sentences . . . I decided that it was not a matter of effectiveness in so far as I was concerned, but of my responsibility.[39]

Bogoraz, then, believed that it was only through public articulation of her protest that she would be freed from complicity in the regime's actions. Her actions were intended to bring about a form of self-liberation. Yet, there was also another element here: the assumption that the wider population was responsible for the actions of the government. It was a point also made by Gorbanevskaya in her compilation of materials relating to the trial, *Red Square at Noon*. Gorbanevskaya observed that people had demonstrated for a variety of reasons. For herself, she lamented that the nations who made up the USSR had become 'accomplices in this crime', and that the purpose of the demonstration had been 'not merely to give expression to our own remorse, but also to redeem a fraction of our people's guilt before history'. In this, she said, the purpose of the demonstration 'was fulfilled'.[40] Later she commented:

> The very demonstration was an act of protest and participation in that it was founded on individual moral impulse, on a feeling of personal responsibility – I am not afraid of grand words – for history. For the history of our country.

She also argued that it was a deliberately unselfish act in the sense that the demonstrators were sacrificing their freedom in defence of others.[41]

The decision to demonstrate was not widely supported. The legal specialist Valerii Chalidze spent the night before the demonstration trying to dissuade the protestors from participating.[42] In particular, there was a lot of scepticism as to whether the demonstration could have any positive effect. People were also afraid of the consequences of demonstrating. The physicist Yurii Orlov, then a Professor in the Armenian Academy of Sciences, was impressed by the demonstration, but held back from expressing his views about the invasion in order to protect his job: 'To open my mouth meant to be expelled from the science I loved.'[43] Attitudes to the event began to change over time. At the time Amalrik believed that the demonstration was a 'tactical mistake' and that it would have been better for the democratic movement to focus on domestic problems; later, however, he stated that he had been wrong and that to say 'an emphatic No to Russian imperialism' was more important than tactical considerations.[44]

The demonstration entered the mythology of the dissident movement. As Gorbanevskaya noted later, it was a 'legend' that gained in importance over time.[45] Arguably, *Red Square at Noon* played a part in creating the legend too. Like the compilations of documents on the Sinyavskii–Daniel trial and the 'trial of the four', Gorbanevskaya's text contributed to the creation of a tradition of protest. Moreover, in this case it was very consciously a *moral* tradition of protest. Gorbanevskaya included in the collection a letter by Anatolii Yakobson, later an editor of the *Chronicle of Current Events*, in which Yakobson suggested that demonstrations of this type could not be measured by the yardstick of ordinary politics where actions had to produce an immediate result or a material advantage. He said: 'The 25 August demonstration was not the manifestation of a political struggle ... but the manifestation of a *moral* struggle ... One must begin by postulating that truth is needed for its own sake and for no other reason.'[46]

By including Yakobson's letter in *Red Square at Noon*, Gorbanevskaya sought to reinforce the idea that the demonstration was a moral act. In this she contributed to a wider cultural process. A form of 'canonisation' of some of the dissidents took place in these years, even if it was 'independently of the wishes of the participants of the movement'. The dissident 'stars' sometimes attracted great interest. There was, for example, an occasion when policemen ran to take a look at Yakir, Litvinov and Grigorenko.[47] One samizdat writer, who suspected that the democratic movement was insufficiently critical of socialism, nevertheless heralded the 'moral example' of such 'martyrs' of the movement as Galanskov and Bukovskii.[48]

According to legend, then, the protest was an act of courage. In his 'Petersburg Romance', written in Dubno on 23 August before the demonstration and almost immediately circulated in Moscow, Aleksandr Galich cited the history of protests against tyranny, and asked: 'Can you go out onto the square / Do you dare go onto the square / At the appointed time?!'[49] In 1983, Gorbanevskaya used Galich's lines as the title for an article commemorating the fifteenth anniversary of the demonstration.[50]

Certainly the demonstrators did show courage. At the same time, their motives were often complex and very personal. Bogoraz later told one journalist that she participated in the demonstration in order to be an example to her own son, Aleksandr Daniel: 'I assumed that for the formation of his personality the example of opposition to evil was necessary.'[51] At his trial, Delone stated: 'I understood that *I could pay off years of non-freedom with five minutes of freedom on Red Square*.'[52] By demonstrating, Delone was trying to overcome a sense of inner enslavement. A process of self-fashioning was at work. Peter Vail' and Aleksandr Genis, in their account of Soviet life in the 1960s, stressed the importance of friendship as a unifying factor in the dissident movement: 'To be friends with clever, talented and courageous people was itself an achievement and an honour.' In their view, friendship and a desire not to appear worse than others were among some of the reasons for the protest: '[Delone and Kushev] went to the demonstration not because they felt an individual obligation to do so, but rather because it was "uncomfortable to refuse", "uncomfortable to be unfaithful to one's given word".'[53]

During the winter of 1967–1968, Gorbanevskaya had decided to start the *Chronicle of Current Events*. The first issue, which came out on 30 April 1968, contained a strong emphasis on human rights. On the front page there was a reference to Article 19 of the United Nations Universal Declaration on Human Rights, which stated that everyone had the right to freedom of opinion and expression, and the bulk of the issue focussed on the aftermath of the Galanskov–Ginzburg trial. The journal, which became the central organ of the human rights movement, disseminated information rather than ideas, and was edited with a strongly dispassionate tone. It declared that it was 'in no sense an illegal publication'.[54] Articles were unsigned. After Gorbanevskaya was arrested in 1969, the *Chronicle* continued to appear under other editors.

Gorbanevskaya represented an important dimension of the human rights movement. In pre-revolutionary Russia, Orthodox and Enlightenment ideas were often in conflict. However, Gorbanevskaya combined religious belief with a commitment to human rights. Gorbanevskaya had originally been arrested by the KGB in 1957 when she was still at university. At the time, she had been outwitted by the KGB into giving information about the activities and views of two of her friends with suspect opinions, and this had led to both of them receiving jail terms; and she also expressed certain pro-Soviet opinions in the course of the interrogations that differed strongly from what she really believed. She felt guilty about these things and, according to a later interview, it was not until she was baptised in 1967 that she had some sense of freedom about the matter. She recalled: 'All my open activities, when I signed letters and did things, all this occurred after the autumn of 1967, after I was baptised, i.e. after that sin had been taken away from me. I don't think I recognised that at the time. It is only now with a certain hindsight that I say this.'[55] There was a religious or metaphysical element in Bogoraz's thinking too. She recalled later that she had started to move closer to Christianity at this time, not in the sense of being drawn to the Church, but from an 'inner, world-view [*mirovozzrencheskom*]' perspective.[56]

The *Chronicle* brought together people of high moral quality. It also played an important role in unifying the human rights movement. In this, as Peter Reddaway noted, it had no forebears in Russian history. It had something in common with Petr Struve's journal *Liberation* of 1902–1905, which also sought to unify different sides of the political opposition, but it was more successful.[57] The focus on law and human rights, in particular, allowed people with Marxist-Leninist, Christian and liberal views to work together. The *Chronicle*'s unifying influence was increased by the fact that in its early days the dissident movement was generally relatively united; the division of the movement into categories of dissidents came later.[58]

The importance of 'self-overcoming' to the human rights movement is illustrated by an episode relating to the *Chronicle*. In early 1972, the regime took steps to try to suppress the *Chronicle*, and there were searches and arrests of activists all across the USSR, among them Viktor Krasin and Petr Yakir. Both Krasin and Yakir had played an important role in the Initiative Group for the Defence of Human Rights that had been set up in May 1969 following the arrest of the former general Petr Grigorenko. Gorbanevskaya, Kovalev, Yakobson, Tat'yana Khodorovich, Tat'yana Velikanova, and the Ukrainian Leonid Plyushch were among the others who signed the Group's initial petition, which was an appeal to the United Nations to defend human rights in the USSR.[59] Following their arrests, both Krasin and Yakir gave way under interrogation and divulged a lot of information about the *Chronicle* and about samizdat more generally. At their trial in August 1973 for 'anti-Soviet agitation and propaganda', both men pleaded guilty and recanted. It was a difficult moment for the human rights movement, and the *Chronicle* ceased to appear for a few months.[60] In May 1974, at a press conference held in the flat of Andrei Sakharov, Khodorovich, Kovalev and Velikanova released three new issues of the *Chronicle*, declaring once again that they did not consider it to be an illegal or libellous publication. Kovalev was arrested at the end of the year and at his trial in December 1975 sentenced to seven years in a labour camp, and three in internal exile.

In attempting to intimidate the editors of the *Chronicle*, the authorities used the Leninist tactic of 'hostage-taking'; they sought to exploit fear for the fate of others in their attacks on the *Chronicle*. In this case, the regime stated that whenever an issue of the *Chronicle* appeared, arrests would be made of people not directly involved. Responding to the threat in January 1974, Khodorovich, Kovalev and Velikanova issued a strongly worded open letter in which they described how the authorities had tried to get them to moderate their activities in return for an improvement in the conditions of some of those who were in prison. To accept the deal offered, they declared, was to commit spiritual suicide; it was an attempt by the regime to load onto the dissidents guilt for actions for which it itself was responsible, and they would have none of it:

> We are presented with an unendurably difficult choice – a precisely and cruelly considered blackmail. We know that we cannot judge anyone who would do this deal – such a step is made with compassion and love.
> But to sacrifice one's spirit – this is suicide, and another's – murder. In a spiritual sense.
> We will not do this.
> And to those who put us in this position, we say only one thing: NO.
> Your deeds, your conscience, your sin – these are on your account.
> Do you want to take hostages?
> We will not assist you.[61]

In his memoirs, Kovalev stated that to reject hostage-taking meant to reject the system of '*krugovaya poruka*' (mutual responsibility): 'An ultimatum from the KGB cannot be accepted, and responsibility for resulting repressions lies not with us, but with the regime.' Indeed, he even declared that 'hostage-taking generally was the foundation of the Soviet system starting with the shootings of 1918–1921'. Velikanova, a mathematician who was married to Babitskii, was effectively the main organiser of the *Chronicle* in the 1970s and was known as its 'Director'.[62] She also had strong views on the matter. Commenting on the question years later, she declared: 'I was always disgusted by it . . . Is it necessary to go into these compromises and collusions? My view was "never".'[63]

Velikanova was greatly admired in the dissident movement; according to one commentator, only Sakharov among the dissidents had greater moral authority than she did.[64] Sakharov himself paid tribute to her integrity, stating that she embodied the 'moral inspiration', 'purity' and 'force' of the human rights movement.[65] The future librarian at the Memorial Society, Boris Belenken, recalled that people like Sakharov and Velikanova were his 'idols'.[66] Velikanova's arrest in November 1979 provoked a number of letters of protest to the authorities; one open letter was signed by 350 people. The letters are indicative of some of the qualities that were particularly admired among dissidents. Velikanova's children wrote a letter referring to 'her conscience, her responsiveness to another's pain, her readiness to help with a word, her high sense of honour and sacrificial love for her neighbour'. In a letter published abroad, Viktor Sokirko, Viktor Sorokin and Valerii Abramkin, all involved with the publication of the underground journal *Poiski*, stated that she was an 'almost unattainable ideal of fearlessness and firmness, hard work and humility'. The dissident writer Viktor Nekipelov noted that she was 'far from what might be called politics, and was never engaged in it'.[67]

The number of capable women in the dissident movement is noteworthy. One reason for this was probably that women had less to lose from a career point of view by being involved in the movement. The religious historian Andrei Zubov, recalling the small circle to which he belonged in the late 1960s at the Moscow State Institute of International Relations (MGIMO), noted that 'there were people, especially women, who naturally had less to lose, who did not want to play by the rules of the game'.[68] Women were often involved in organising the infrastructure of the dissident movement.[69] Some perhaps were looking for an opportunity to play a constructive part in society. Ironically, party and dissident activism were sometimes appealing for the same reasons. Ludmilla Alekseeva, who lost her party membership in 1968 because of her involvement in the human rights movement, recalled that she had been originally drawn into the party for the same reasons that she was later attracted by the dissidents: she was attracted by the opportunity to exercise a sense of social responsibility.[70] Yet the prominence of women among the dissidents was not a new phenomenon historically; even in the nineteenth century, there were many prominent women in the revolutionary intelligentsia.

The 'Initiative Group' was not the only group dedicated to the defence of human rights. In 1970, Sakharov, Chalidze and Andrei Tverdokhlebov founded the Moscow Human Rights Committee. The Committee adopted a legalist strategy, declaring that it was a 'creative association acting in accordance with the laws of the land'. The Committee, which was deliberately cautious and un-revolutionary in its formal objectives, soon established an impressive record. It devoted particular attention to the question of psychiatric abuse, the need for adequate defence rights, and the right of Tatars to return to Crimea.[71] In October 1973, the physicist Valentin Turchin set up the Soviet Amnesty International Group; the main practical side of its work was organised by Tverdokhlebov, and it included scientists and writers from Moscow, Leningrad, Kiev and Tbilisi.

In May 1976, the Public Group to Support Compliance with the Helsinki Accords in the USSR was founded. The original idea for the group came from the young Jewish activist Anatolii Shcharanskii. It was led by Yurii Orlov, and included Shcharanskii, Ginzburg, Grigorenko, Turchin, Alekseeva, Sakharov's wife, Elena Bonner, and the geologist Mal'va Landa. Like its predecessors, the group saw its objectives as monitoring the regime's compliance with its own legal commitments. The practices that the group condemned included 'compulsory psychiatric treatment aimed at altering a person's ideas, conscience, religion and beliefs'.[72] The Moscow Group, which soon spawned similar committees in other parts of the USSR, proved extremely effective at highlighting abuses, but with the arrests of Orlov, Ginzburg and Shcharanskii in the first three months of 1977, and the exile of Alekseeva abroad, it went into a decline.[73] Like the *Chronicle*, the Moscow Helsinki Group brought together an impressive cross-section of people. Shcharanskii's involvement reflected the fact that nationalist aspirations played a big role in the human rights movement. The question of Jewish emigration was particularly controversial, in part because the US Congress had in 1974 added the Jackson-Vanik Amendment to a trade bill, which specifically linked US trade relations with the USSR with Jewish emigration rights.

Orlov himself endorsed a form of ethical universalism that was typical of the more secular members of the human rights movement. In a letter to Brezhnev in September 1973, Orlov wrote that the state and the people ought to profess 'certain moral principles drawn up long ago in human experience: love for one's native land, and human conscience'. He referred to 'ethics common to all humanity' noting that they were 'created and preached by the best representatives of all generations.' He went on to say that 'human ethics – conscience – exists', and that it 'springs up in a person together with imagination, and thanks to a capacity to feel pain not just from actual but even from imagined sufferings'.[74]

The setting-up of the Helsinki Group caused controversy among dissidents. The problem centred round how far it was possible to work with the authorities without being compromised. Khodorovich refused to join the group because she felt that the Helsinki Act was only useful to the regime itself and she did not like the idea of supporting the regime in any way. Orlov believed that the Helsinki accords were political accords and that political levers could be used to defend human rights. Khodorovich disagreed and believed that they would be outmanoeuvred. Orlov suggested that Khodorovich believed that nothing could be changed in the USSR at the time, and that this was another reason why she rejected political tactics. Mal'va Landa, who eventually joined the group, was also worried by the implication that the regime was being supported in some way.[75] According to Orlov, a suspicion of 'politics' was also at the root of the criticism: 'Landa and Khodorovich didn't like my game playing when I was naming the group. They thought that anything that has the appearance of politics had to be deplored and avoided, but I thought the element of political game playing was essential.'[76]

The human rights movement was political in the sense that it threatened the foundations of Soviet power. Furthermore, activists like Bukovskii, Krasin and Orlov clearly had political instincts. At the same time, the emphasis on human rights rather than on political programmes meant that the human rights movement was able to unify a very diverse collection of intellectuals and activists. For this reason, dissidents who stressed the non-political nature of the movement were right to do so. A common political programme would have been impossible. People would have fallen out over the details.

Solzhenitsyn's short essay, 'Live Not by the Lie' offered the kind of moral programme that could appeal to people with very different political views. Solzhenitsyn was not directly involved in the human rights movement itself and disliked the term 'dissident'. Yet his thinking was influential both in dissident circles and among the wider reformist intelligentsia. In 'Live Not by the Lie', which was released into samizdat just before Solzhenitsyn's deportation to the West in February 1974, Solzhenitysn stated that people should stop blaming others for their predicament: 'It is not "they" who are guilty – it is we ourselves, only we.' People had to begin with themselves. The power of the state and its employment of violence depended on the willingness of individuals to bow before lies. However, according to Solzhenitsyn, people had the freedom not to be dishonest. He stated: 'Our path is not to support the lie consciously in anything.' Among a range of proposals, he challenged people not to include phrases that distorted the truth in their conversation, writings or artistic works; not to vote for people whom they did not support; not to hold up slogans promoting opinions that they did not share; not to be present at occasions when other people promoted lies; and not to subscribe to or buy newspapers or journals that distorted the truth. This would not be an easy path, he observed; it was 'a difficult choice for the body, but the only one for the soul'.[77] In another essay in which he made similar points, Solzhenitsyn replied to the question, 'What is a Lie?', by saying, 'Decide *yourself*, as *your* conscience dictates.'[78]

'Live Not by the Lie' was certainly a radical document; it was also one of the most universal documents of the dissident movement in the USSR and Eastern Europe. It was both simple and revolutionary. It was 'apophatic' in the sense that it stressed what should not be done rather than what should be done; and because it was moral rather than political in emphasis it appealed to people across the political spectrum. It also focussed for people the small ways in which their behaviour buttressed the regime, and offered them somewhere to begin. At the same time, the political implications were enormous, for in the language of 'social contract' Solzhenitsysn wanted people to withdraw their consent from the mechanisms of Soviet ideological control. This message had an appeal across Eastern Europe. In 'The Power of the Powerless', Vaclav Havel imagined a greengrocer who suddenly rejected the 'ritual' and broke the 'rules of the game', noting that 'his revolt [was] an attempt to *live within the truth*'.[79] Ideologically, Havel was a Kantian rather than a Christian, but his strategy of moral opposition was similar to Solzhenitsyn's. People could interpret Solzhenitsyn's thinking in different ways. Amalrik observed that since he was a leader of '*moral* opposition' to communism, 'everyone saw in him what that person believed'.[80]

'Live Not by the Lie' generated heated discussion in dissident and wider intelligentsia circles. Pavel Litvinov published an open letter to Solzhenitsyn in the Parisian religious journal *Vestnik RSKhD* in which he stated that Solzhenitsyn was proposing a closed system of normative ethics that failed to embrace those who did not have the strength to live by them, and which did not recognise the possibility of scepticism about moral principles in general. Indeed, he declared that in any case people made their choices on the basis of experience rather than directives. Solzhenitsyn's principles, he suggested, lacked the compassion that was evident in his novels. He was calling for the kind of destructive moral heroism that Sergei Bulgakov had condemned in his essay in *Landmarks*.[81] Solzhenitsyn replied by stating that Bulgakov had not rejected a Christian form of heroism and self-limitation at all, and that he was not trying to propose a normative system of ethics. At the same time he argued that to refuse to lie was 'a minimal, but also optimal' strategy because the regime was helpless in the face of 'staunch human spirit'.[82]

'Live Not by the Lie' also provoked three short collections of essays in samizdat, edited by K. Burzhuademov. In his own essay, 'Think Actively, Work Effectively, Live Boldly', Burzhuademov suggested that Solzhenitsyn did not himself live by his own moral code. He noted that in *The Gulag Archipelago*, Solzhenitsyn had observed that before 1961, the murder of stool pigeons in the labour camps had been an effective method of isolating camp administrators from prisoners; further, that a useful later method of resistance had been to steal and spoil possessions belonging to stool pigeons. If murder and stealing were permitted in one circumstance, Burzhuademov wrote, then surely lies could not be considered so bad. Furthermore, Burzhuademov endorsed what he saw as Solzhenitsyn's own pragmatic readiness to evade the truth while fighting the system: '[Solzhenitsyn's] whole life was a fulfilment of the testament "Live Not by the Lie"; but daily silences and even the minor lie were [for him] insignificant tactical retreats'. Burzhuademov warned that 'moral rigorism' had its limits, and proposed instead ethical egoism and an economic programme based on self-interest: 'The better it is for you and those around you, the better it will be for society and its future.'[83] In another response, Pomerants also took issue with 'rigorism', suggesting that it led to cruelty, rigidity and pharisaism. He said: '[Solzhenitsyn] does not want, and maybe is not able to think himself into the context of an alien discourse [*chuzhoi rechi*].'[84]

The impact of Solzhenitsyn's essay was arguably greater on the wider intelligentsia than on the dissident milieu itself.[85] Indeed, there was another important moral tradition in dissident ethics. In his letter in *Red Square at Noon*, Yakobson referred to some lines of Tolstoi, in which Tolstoi had argued that the consequences of people's actions should not be the ultimate guide for their behaviour, but that conscience was a superior arbiter: 'Man is endowed with another and incontrovertible guidance – the guidance of his conscience, by following which he is certain that what he does is what he should be doing.' This, Yakobson noted, led on to the moral principle summed up in the expression 'I cannot keep silent'.[86] 'I cannot keep silent' was the title of a 1908 essay by Tolstoi that was critical of the death penalty. Tolstoi's maxim reflected dissident ethics very well. Indeed, according to Aleksandr Daniel, the Tolstoian formula fitted the dissident mentality exactly, whereas Solzhenitsyn's formula was vaguer, and for all its apparent radicalism 'softer'.[87] Many dissidents certainly emphasised the necessity of speaking out. Sakharov, for example, said to a Western reporter in 1973: '[A man] may hope for nothing, but nevertheless speak because he cannot, simply cannot remain silent.'[88]

There was, of course, a Russian spiritual tradition that emphasised the importance of silence. The nineteenth-century poet Fedor Tyutchev famously wrote: 'Be silent, hide yourself, and conceal your feelings and your dreams.'[89] Yet this was never a central principle in the intelligentsia. The dissidents were suspicious of too much silence. Indeed, it has been argued that they destroyed the 'law of silence' in Russia.[90] There was the worry that silence meant complicity. In his poem 'The Prospector's Waltz' (1963), Galich played on the idea that 'silence is golden', noting that the silent (*molchal'niki*) easily turned into bosses (*nachal'niki*), and might easily become executioners (*palachi*) too. The message was that it was necessary to speak out simply in order to avoid turning into a monstrous person. In 'Petersburg Romance', Galich noted: 'We pay for our participation with silence.'[91]

In a response to Burzhuademov's essay on 'Live Not by the Lie', Velikanova suggested that in their personal behaviour people should be guided by reality and not by models, and suggested that Burzhuademov was drawn to models of behaviour; furthermore, she declared that it was not worth looking for a way out of the contemporary situation through a 'rational reconstruction of the economy'. She also rejected opposition to the regime for its own sake, declaring that it was necessary to oppose it when it was the source of evil.[92] Velikanova was very hostile to dogmatic moral attitudes. Aleksandr Daniel once recalled an occasion in 1974 following the recantations of Krasin and Yakir, when she said to some friends that she wanted to go to visit Yakir in exile. This wish to visit a disgraced man was unexpected, and it met with protests from Daniel and others. However, Velikanova replied that she would go anyway. 'She was a free person', Daniel recalled with admiration: free in the sense that she was not dogmatic in her judgements.[93]

Krasin, although not a typical case, was once described as a 'Bolshevik in reverse'.[94] There is no doubt that the dissidents were sometimes dogmatic in their attitudes. Tat'yana Khodorovich once stated that the 'inner freedom' that characterised certain figures in the dissident movement sometimes attracted people who lacked deep convictions, and who sought to be involved in the opposition for purely emotional reasons.[95] In his memoirs Kovalev recalled that he was very uncomfortable with the idea, which a number of dissidents held, that dissidents should be an example to others. Pressured by some of his own scientific colleagues to leave his work – for the sake of their jobs and work – he eventually concluded that the purpose of dissident activity was 'not a demonstration of [their] own boldness and sense of principle, but the spreading of information', and he decided to leave. Maintaining a moral reputation was not the primary purpose. Kovalev agreed with the philosopher Boris Shragin that acts of self-liberation, although existential by nature, could easily turn into a profession.[96]

Just as some party members eventually regretted their subservience to the regime, so also some dissidents came to believe that the motives behind their dissident activities had been mixed. Tat'yana Trusova, a human rights activist of the early 1980s who helped with *Chronicle* and the dissident journal *Bulletin V*, later commented that like many neophytes, she had been hard in her judgements,[97] and she regretted that there had been too much 'exultation' in her dissident activities: '[There was] an indecent enthusiasm for the struggle . . . for those moments I am ashamed.'[98] Some went further than that, to regret more generally their anti-Soviet attitudes. In a letter of the early 1980s entitled 'The Truth and Misfortune of the Dissidents', Sokirko stated that the human rights movement, under the influence of Bogoraz and Daniel, had became too strongly anti-Soviet and too dependent on the West for help, and he himself expressed regret that he had signed the letter of protest about Velikanova.[99]

Another person who became critical of dissident ethics was the writer Vladimir Voinovich. In his *Portrait against the Background of a Myth* (2002), Voinovich recalled that, following an occasion in 1973, one outspoken young monarchist woman, suspicious of the fact that Voinovich had a Zhiguli car of his own, asked him: 'How much did the car cost your conscience?'[100] On another occasion, in July 1970, he was asked by a zealous dissident woman activist to sign a letter of protest. He refused on the grounds that he needed to protect his mother who was facing medical treatment, but felt ashamed as he tried to explain this to her. However, with hindsight he saw his sense of shame in a different light: 'I am ashamed that I was ashamed, ashamed both for myself and my deceased mother that I did not seize the fiery girl by the collar and take her down the stairs.' Voinovich also suggested that the dissidents manifested some of the same extremist tendencies of the populist groups, the *narodovol'tsy*, of the nineteenth century. Voinovich was particularly critical of Solzhenitsyn. He satirised him in his novel, *Moscow 2042* (1987) and in *Portrait against the Background of a Myth* suggested that he had become a cult figure of whom miracles were expected whereas in fact he was a destructive figure.[101]

Dissident ethics were, of course, shaped by a particular set of problems. Their main focus was on relations with the state. It is interesting to note that there is little reference in dissident thought to property or to stealing. Dissidents who stressed the 'no compromise' message regarding the regime did not necessarily exercise the same strictness when it came to stealing or illegally utilising state property, or making use of 'blat'. This is not surprising since, unlike in the West, the dissident conscience was not shaped by the experience of property ownership. That being said, many dissidents were very honest with money. Gorbanevskaya, for example, generally paid for her bus tickets. Ironically, she was once criticised for it: 'I punched my ticket, and suddenly a woman rushed up to me and said: "You have committed a civil act! No one of your age pays for their ticket."'[102]

It is hard to measure the success or failure of the human rights movement. At one level, it clearly failed. By the end of the 1970s most of the activists were in prison or abroad. Arguably, the dissidents were better at speaking out than creating an effective movement of reform. In his diaries in 1981, the poet David Samoilov compared them unfavourably with the Decembrists, stating that they had a tendency to be too critical of Russia, and that they were 'people of the word' rather than 'people of the deed'.[103] Yet, it is important not to underestimate the social pressures that the dissidents were under. Furthermore, it is worth asking what the essential purposes of the movement were. Vail' and Genis stated that the aim was not so much victory as 'free behaviour, the creation of a precedent, the formation of public opinion'.[104] Similarly, Aleksandr Daniel suggests that dissidents were 'playing the game of [*igrali*] civil society'.[105] If these were the aims, then the dissident project must be regarded as relatively successful. Certainly, human rights activists contributed greatly to the Soviet regime's loss of moral legitimacy, and the formation of an alternative moral and civic tradition.

6 In search of inner freedom

'Inner freedom' was a popular theme among dissidents. Gorbanevskaya once said: 'It is possible to become free at that moment when you lose your freedom and go to jail.'[1] Amalrik, in a letter of 1969 to the writer and defector, Anatolii Kuznetsov, wrote: 'You constantly speak of freedom, but of external freedom. You say nothing of inner freedom ... Such freedom and the responsibility attributed to it is a necessary prerequisite of external freedom.'[2] The greatness of the dissidents, Amalrik said elsewhere, was that 'in an unfree country, they behaved like free men'.[3]

The emphasis on inner freedom partly grew out of the wider dissident hostility to the Soviet state and to politics in general. The Soviet state was understood to be predatory by nature. This is illustrated by a well-known samizdat article by Dmitrii Nelidov (pseudonym), 'Ideocratic Consciousness and Personality' (1973). Nelidov argued that Soviet culture had produced a 'system of conditioned reflexes' in the population that had become inseparable from personality. Doublethink was the normal pattern of life: 'Doublethink is a voluntary submission to the given mannequin, becoming accustomed to it, correcting oneself according to the mechanics of the reflexes elaborated in it and to the censorship prescribed by it.' According to Nelidov, people had learned to present a form of themselves 'in the formal ideological display window' which differed from how they were in actuality; this resulted, he said, in 'a perversion of human nature, a derogation of humanity'. The significance of the democratic movement, he suggested, lay in the fact that it challenged this. It was a form of 'expressing the humane in an environment where human nature was suppressed and perverted'. It was a 'struggle for the liberation of the spirit', for 'only spirit makes [man] a personality'.[4]

Nelidov's thinking was representative of a wider tendency. People were very conscious of the presence of non-freedom inside themselves. Yulii Daniel's story 'Atonement' contained the statement:

> It makes no difference whether we are in prison or the prison's within us ... We have to cut the camp out of ourselves ... Do you think it was the Cheka, the NKVD, or the KGB that had imprisoned us? No, we did it to ourselves.[5]

In this context, much dissident thinking was focussed on how to survive those moments when the war with the state was at its height: investigation, interrogation and imprisonment. There was such concern about how to act during these times that it led to an attempt by Vladimir Al'brekht, for a time acting secretary of the Moscow Amnesty International Group in the mid-1970s, to approach the subject in a systematic way. In the mid-1970s, Al'brekht produced two manuals of advice to potential dissidents that were circulated in samizdat before being published abroad. His *How to Behave During a House Search* contained a warning that people should avoid getting into conversations on the investigator's terms: 'Do not talk for long in their language. Let them get accustomed to yours.'[6] The other book, *How to Be A Witness*, contained a similar point. Al'brekht noted that people were easily drawn into dangerous conversations; starting politely, and with questions that were trivial, the investigator would entice the witness into speaking freely, and then lay traps for him. In trying to justify himself, the witness would reveal even more about himself. Consequently, Al'brekht stressed the vital importance of slowing the conversations, and refusing to hurry. As a solution for not falling into the traps, he offered witnesses a four-pronged defensive strategy (entitled 'PLOD'): first, witnesses should demand that all the details of the conversation should be written up into the interrogation protocol; second, witnesses should avoid questions that did not concern them personally; third, they should avoid questions which did not specifically relate to the matter under investigation; and fourth, they should permit themselves to express their moral convictions. They should also exploit the fact that investigation procedures were by law subject to certain rules.[7]

Al'brekht also stressed the importance of giving truthful answers. He declared nonetheless that it was an 'honest tactic' for witnesses to try to be cunning in their answers, and thereby to guide interrogations in directions of their own choosing. He also stressed the importance of witnesses being true to themselves, using the word 'conscience' here to refer to a person's essential identity or self:

> No one and nothing should limit your will, reader, your particular will to respond in the investigation as you like – neither unexpected developments or advice . . . Absolutely nothing: neither worries about those close to you, nor fear, nor the desire to find something out, nothing except your conscience. It is necessary simply to be yourself – that is the main advice.[8]

There was in Al'brekht's understanding of conscience an existential dimension. Conscience and personality were closely linked. This reflected a wider existential emphasis on conscience in dissident thought. Typically, Boris Shragin stated in his account of life in the USSR: 'The choice is between two ways of life. One consists of obeying one's conscience with all the suffering that is bound to ensue; the other of avoiding anxiety by renouncing one's freedom.'[9] Svetlana Alliluyeva, who in the 1960s associated herself with the emerging human rights movement, declared in her memoirs: 'All I have is my conscience.'[10] In these cases, the assumption was that conscience was at the centre of a person's true personality or self.

Al'brekht gave expression to tactics that were widely practised in dissident circles, and doubtless he reinforced some of them. The importance of slowing down conversations with investigators, for example, was widely recognised. Aleksei Yudin, a member of the semi-underground religious group 'Ecumen' in the 1980s, recalled how he tried to slow down his conversations with the KGB:

> Smoking helped. I smoked a pipe and gave some good long pauses. It was possible to drag things out. The pause is the main thing, because if you start to speak ... answer questions, that means that sooner or later they will draw you into their situation.[11]

There was in Al'brekht's texts a sense that the clashes with the authorities were a kind of game. Indeed it has even been suggested that the human rights movement owed some of its attractiveness to the 'temptation of the game' (*soblaznu igry*).[12] However, if it was a game for some, it was a dangerous one. Leonid Plyushch agreed at one point to be an informer, with the idea that he would be able to deceive the KGB; but he later concluded: 'It is impossible to play such games; because it draws you further in.'[13] Yurii Shikhanovich, an editor of *Chronicle* who was arrested under Article 70 in 1983, agreed to tell his interrogators the whereabouts of his library in order to soften his possible punishment, but found that this led on to his giving away the names of people as well.[14] Imprisonment sometimes affected people's personalities. Nina Komarova lamented that her husband, Viktor Nekipelov, returned from the camps a different and spiritually-broken man: 'Vitia did not return from the camp. He died, perhaps in Chistopol, perhaps in Vladimir, perhaps in the Perm camp.'[15]

A number of dissidents argued that everybody has a breaking point. Amalrik stated that coercion is possible wherever there is a readiness to submit to it, and that a person's capacity to resist is limited. During one interrogation, he himself said to his investigator that if he were hung up by his feet and beaten, he would tell him from whom he got his typewriter and papers. However, Amalrik also noted that 'once a person has reached a certain limit and passed through the crisis, he can find new strength in himself'.[16]

In practice, most defendants and witnesses developed their own defence tactics. Valerii Senderov, a member of the *émigré* political organisation National Labour Union (NTS), who was sentenced in the 1980s under Article 70 to seven years strict regime and five years of exile, decided that he would be silent during investigations. However, when the investigations took place, he concluded that it was 'possible and necessary' to give an account of his views and programme; indeed, interrogations provided him with a chance to pass on his ideas to his fellow-countrymen.[17] Ludmilla Alekseeva developed a strategy whereby she would begin an interrogation by stating two things: first, that she had a bad memory, and thus that there would be things she would simply not remember; and second, that for 'ethical reasons' she would refuse to give evidence where the matter concerned other people and not just herself. Sometimes, she recalled, it was a lie to say that she did not remember, but she had come to the conclusion that it was not wrong to lie when dealing with the party or the KGB, and there were a number of occasions during interrogations when she lied and her 'conscience was clean'. Not everyone was happy with such an approach; Alekseeva recalled that Chalidze, who had been brought up by a strict grandmother, did not feel comfortable with even very small lies. Alekseeva also refused to adopt the strategy that involved avoiding all communication with the interrogator; she was more at ease with herself using the approach she adopted. In such situations, she suggested, it was important that people acted 'according to their nature'.[18]

Others were more radical. Aleksandr Podrabinek, one of the most uncompromising of the dissidents, recalled that in one investigation he did not feel it necessary to stand up for his views, and instead ignored the investigation.[19] Here, in the context of interrogation, some of the dissidents were closer to the ethic that stressed silence rather than outspoken protest. Tat'yana Velikanova was often completely silent in answer to questions during interrogation.[20] The lawyer Sofiya Kallistratova, who defended Delone in the 1968 trial, adopted an ethical outlook based on three principles: 'Do not be afraid. Never collaborate. Do not tell untruths (*nepravdy*).' To protect herself in interrogations, she frequently resorted to the phrases, 'I will not give any evidence', and 'I refuse to answer that question'. Indeed, she repeatedly used the phrase 'I refuse to answer' when she was herself tried for her human rights activities in April 1982.[21] Her commitment to honesty was very strong; in publicising human rights violations, she refused to permit marginal distortions of the truth in favour of defendants.[22]

The writing of the memoirs of Soviet oppositionists was a complex phenomenon. The KGB defector to Britain, Oleg Gordievskii recalled that he had wished his memoir, *Next Stop Execution* (1995), to be more focussed on his life in the KGB, but that the English ghost-writer chose to structure his story in a more personal and traditional way.[23] It illustrates the fact that memoirs are not the purely personal account that they sometimes appear; they are the fruit of collaboration and teamwork and a range of influences goes into their creation. Gordievskii's memoirs, written in the West for a Western market, were subject to a range of influences that did not exist for memoirs that were written in Russia itself. The Russian memoir was not a new phenomenon. Soviet memoir literature had its roots as far back as the late eighteenth century in the so-called 'contemporaries' genre in which Russian observers penned accounts and reflections on their intellectual contemporaries. It was a genre that played a part in the formation of the Russian intelligentsia's self-understanding, and it helped to promote role models and cult figures. Solzhenitsyn's *The Oak and the Calf* and Nadezhda Mandelstam's *Hope Abandoned* can be seen as reflecting this tradition.[24]

There was also a strongly intimate and spiritual dimension to the memoirs of the late Soviet era. Leona Toker has noted that ethical as much as aesthetic factors were central to gulag memoirs. She observed that a 'Lenten' modal scheme often played an important role in the structure of these works: memoirists took inspiration from Jewish and Christian accounts of how suffering and self-denial could be made to work for good. The gulag accounts of Varlam Shalamov, Ekaterina Olitskaya, Evgeniya Ginzburg, Panin and Solzhenitsyn suggested that the demands of the moral self often outweighed biological need.[25] This narrative emphasis on self-denial and self-overcoming was also a central feature of the memoirs of some of the younger generation of dissidents who passed through the post-Stalin prisons and camps. It was by no means universal. The purpose of Marchenko's *My Testimony*, for example, was simply to introduce people to the hidden world of the post-Stalin camps, and it contained little subjective reflection. Sakharov's memoirs also had a similar purpose to inform, and did not offer an intimate portrait of the author. Indeed, Sakharov himself stated that his memoirs were not a confession, and that he had a dislike of self-flagellation and public soul-searching.[26] Nevertheless, there was a strongly confessional element in a lot of dissident memoir literature. This confessional literature was also specifically autobiographical in the sense that it addressed the genesis of personality.[27]

Bukovskii's *To Build a Castle* (1978) and Shcharankii's *Fear No Evil* (1988) are good examples of a certain type of autobiographical memoir or subjective history. Both were accounts of what might be called 'spiritual warfare' in a prison situation, although they proposed different philosophies of life. Both contained a strongly personal element, in that they recounted experiences of self-defence or self-overcoming. However, since both figures related how they had passed through their ordeals successfully, they were also designed to be programmatic texts, and thus went beyond autobiography into politics. They were effectively statements of political philosophy, representing secular or religious accounts of human nature and thus diverse philosophies of liberalism.

Much of *To Build a Castle* was about Bukovskii's struggle to preserve his integrity. During his interrogations in 1961, he tried to give the impression that he was a Soviet patriot, and he 'gave a completely false impression of himself'. This, he subsequently concluded, was a great mistake, for it gave the KGB the sense that he was a 'yielding, pliable sort of fellow'. He thought he had outwitted them. When he was re-arrested in 1963, he was found to have a copy of Milovan Djilas's critique of communism, *The New Class.* The KGB assumed he was subject to pressure and demanded that he either tell them who had given him the book, or go to jail. However, on this occasion, he 'refused pointblank to talk', and the only statement that he signed was one in which he declared that he would never allow the authorities to decide what he should and should not read. Eventually, the interrogations came to an end. These were vital experiences for Bukovskii, because he concluded that it was wrong to give way to the regime in any way; moreover, it was better to go on the attack fearlessly. Bukovskii concluded that 'giving way partially' was the 'commonest mistake'. Giving way even for the sake of others could be counterproductive. Referring to a hunger strike, he noted that 'when one weakened it got much worse for the rest'. On the other hand, a resolute approach was more effective: 'Citizens who had resolved to submit to their conscience instead of their Party card were beginning to force their own reality upon the state.'[28]

Bukovskii's ethics were uncompromising. In a later interview, he condemned tactical compromises: 'If you are strategically against the system but for tactical considerations . . . wish to work within it, then you will end either with an inevitable break with the system or you will repudiate your strategic goals.'[29] He also said that the refusal to give way was a new departure in the methods of Soviet dissent. The older generation had taught that people should admit to accusations of crimes, because otherwise they would be tortured. There was in this approach, he said, the assumption that 'it was normal to pretend to be a Soviet person'. The ethics of resistance only started to change in the 1960s. At the same time, Bukovskii acknowledged that most people had some kind of weakness. For example, using a variant of the 'hostage-taking' method, the system would often pressure potential dissenters by threatening their children. This, Bukovskii noted, was very difficult for people.[30] Certainly, the state's potential hold on Bukovskii himself was lessened by the fact that he did not have a wife and children.

Bukovskii's moral philosophy was derived more from experience than from books, so it is not easy to define it in theoretical terms. It contained the implicit idea that there are two selves, one which is real and to which a person should remain loyal, and another that is shaped by social pressure and ambitions and which is false. There are some similarities here with a Christian perspective, and Bukovskii himself acknowledged that there were Christian elements in his thinking, although he was not religious himself. He later declared that liberal ethics contained Christian elements, and that the actions of the dissidents were Christian to the extent that the dissidents were offering themselves as a sacrifice:

> I clearly understood we were in a certain sense offering ourselves as victims ... There was in this something of a Christian model ... In that we became an extreme sacrifice, we were expiating for the sin of those who did not go down that road. And it is almost mathematically so. For if these people had not gone down the conformist road, then we would not have had to pay such a high price. If you think about it arithmetically, that is the way it is. I have never been or become a religious person, but nevertheless these categories are universal. Our civilisation is nevertheless constructed around Christian ethics.[31]

Bukovskii's emphasis on self-sacrifice was shared by others. Gorbanevskaya once noted that the demonstration on Red Square of August 1968 was a way of saying that not everyone approved of the invasion of Czechoslovakia. She noted that 'the whole nation minus one' was no longer the whole nation. This, she said, was the 'arithmetic of atonement'.[32] The founder and editor of the *émigré* journal *Kontinent*, Vladimir Maksimov, stated in 1977 that many of the participants of the democratic movement, which he suggested was formally atheistic, were in practice imbued with a Christian spirit in that readiness for self-sacrifice was a central feature of their outlook.[33] Sacrifice' was also an important theme in the thinking of some of the East European dissidents.[34]

Shcharanskii was arrested in March 1977 for his part in the Moscow Helsinki Group and his involvement in the campaign to allow Jewish emigration. Convicted the following year of treason and espionage, he was given a sentence of three years in prisons and ten in labour camp, and was eventually released in 1986. His memoir, *Fear No Evil*, like *To Build a Castle*, emphasised self-liberation through speaking out.[35] It also conveyed the message that compromise with the system should not be countenanced. At the same time there were differences between Shcharanskii and Bukovskii. Bukovskii tried to make himself spiritually invulnerable. He said: 'Let the storm rage outside the castle – it can never tear off the roof, penetrate the thick walls or extinguish my fire.'[36] Shcharanskii found sustenance not so much in creating an inner wall against the system, as in opening up his spirit to positive forms of spiritual support. His experience of inner freedom was closely linked to a discovery of his national (Jewish) identity and to certain religious experiences.

Much of Shcharanskii's memoir addressed the question of how to deal with interrogation. At times, Shcharanskii played games with his KGB interrogators; he developed, for example, methods for working out whether the interrogators were lying to him or not.[37] However, like other dissidents he also warned that 'everyone who ventured to play games with the KGB invariably lost'. He got accustomed to praying before his interrogations, asking God for strength, power, intelligence, good fortune and patience to leave jail and reach Israel 'in an honest and worthy manner'. In addition, he developed certain mental strategies to cultivate an inner world independent of his conversations with his interrogators. Before his trial, he became concerned that he was coming to see his interrogators as human beings, worrying that this might be the first step towards betraying himself and collaborating with them; he wondered if this kind of thinking had been the undoing of Yakir and Krasin. Indeed, Krasin himself commented that the 'construction of cordial friendly relations' between him and the interrogators had helped to break down his resistance.[38] Shcharanskii concluded that he had to create an alternative mental environment to protect himself. So he adapted a relaxation technique recommended by one of his Jewish friends. Lying on his cot, he found that through reviewing events from his past life, he could stop his thoughts and refocus them on other things. In his mind he could dream of being with his friends and loved ones, and then when mentally returning to his cell, it no longer seemed so depressing or so frightening, and he no longer felt alone. At these times, his imagined communication with his wife Avital seemed closer than his prison reality:

> The world I re-created in my head turned out to be more powerful and more real than the world of Lefortovo Prison; my bond with Avital was stronger than my isolation, and my inner freedom more powerful than the external bondage.[39]

Shcharanskii found that he could return to this alternative environment any time he chose.

Shcharanskii's 'inner' communication was not only with Avital and others, but also with historical and literary figures. King David and his Psalms became particularly important to him, and provided him with a sympathetic example of what to do in difficult situations. He noted too that in Lefortovo, Socrates, Don Quixote, Ulysses, Gargantua, Oedipus and Hamlet had 'rushed to [his] aid', and that he had felt a 'spiritual bond with these figures'. Moreover, he also experienced a reverse process in which 'it was also important to *them*, who had been created so many centuries ago, to know how I was acting today'. In some sense, he could 'inspire or disenchant those who existed in the past as well as those who would come in the future'.[40]

The message of Shcharanski's account was that he needed to belong to a living social environment for his moral integrity to survive; and he asserted that people have it within their power to create their own inner spiritual environments, which are as real as external ones. Protection against evil in the labour camps, he declared, came either from the 'zeks' solidarity' or through the inner spiritual world that he could summon up 'through a mental effort'. He talked of the 'interconnection' and 'interdependence' of human souls, and of the way moral environments were preserved and transmitted through communication. He formulated for himself what he called 'the law of universal attraction, interconnection, and interdependence of human souls':

> In addition to Newton's law of universal gravitational pull of objects, there is also a universal gravitational pull of souls, of the bond between them and the influence of one soul on the other. With each word we speak and each step we take, we touch other souls and have an impact on them.[41]

Another memoir, Viktor Krasin's *The Trial* (1983), bore some similarity to the accounts of Bukovskii and Shcharanskii, but differed in that it was essentially a chronicle of failure rather than success. Following his trial and recantation in August 1973, Krasin was sent into internal exile, and then allowed to emigrate in 1975. *The Trial*, which was structured as a dialogue between Krasin and his wife, was an attempt to explain his 'fall' to the dissident intelligentsia. The book was a 'confession'.[42] It opened with a quotation from the Gospel of Matthew, that indicated a Christian poetics of redemption: 'Do not fear those who kill the body but cannot kill the soul; rather fear him who can destroy both body and soul in hell'; and it concluded with Krasin asking forgiveness of those he had wronged.[43] In the book, Krasin sought to take responsibility for his own actions. He noted that although the KGB had forced him to do certain things, he himself was responsible for them: 'I did them myself.'[44]

Krasin suggested that his breakdown in 1972–1973 had its roots in earlier compromises. At the end of 1970, he had been in exile in Siberia, and in the course of conversations with a KGB operative, he had indicated that he would be willing to give an assurance that he would not play a further part in the human rights movements if he was allowed to return to Moscow. With hindsight, Krasin suggested that the KGB had started to get a hold on him during these conversations; they started the process that led to his 'breakage' (*slom*) and 'surrender' (*sdachu*). Krasin thus linked his ultimate surrender to smaller compromises. Indeed, the link between the larger and the smaller compromise was an important theme of the book. Krasin was asked to say to whom he had given copies of Abdurakhman Avtorkhanov's *The Technology of Power*, a book that the KGB regarded as particularly dangerous. At first he gave the name of someone who had no involvement in the human rights movement, thinking that one name would be enough, but he eventually gave others away too.[45]

Two months into his interrogations, Krasin decided to surrender his collection of samizdat literature; and this, he concluded, had marked the beginning of his capitulation. Krasin recalled that in the process of giving up the literature, he drew his wife, Nadezhda Emelkina, who was then in exile in Eniseisk, into the process. During the interrogations, he asked her to reveal the whereabouts of their samizdat collection. This she did, and subsequently she herself started to give evidence to the KGB. Krasin stated to her in the book: 'I wanted to transfer responsibility for my decision onto you. And that is what happened. You took my sin upon yourself.' Krasin recalled that when he heard that she too was giving evidence, he became very angry, and demanded that she take back the evidence, but that this anger was not really genuine, and that he was soon reconciled to what had happened. He recalled that if he had been firmer, then even her surrender would not have moved him, and furthermore it might have given her the strength to resist as well. But, hearing of her surrender, he too 'immediately and without any struggle agreed to surrender'. With hindsight, he said to his wife, he had come to believe that he had really been trying to surrender all along and looking for an excuse for it.[46]

Krasin never recovered his reputation in the dissident community, and there was always the suspicion that his confession was in some ways artificial. At the same time, the very fact that he chose to structure his story in a traditional redemptive framework, employing an intimately confessional tone, was indicative of the values of the dissident intelligentsia of the early 1980s. He was adopting a narrative framework that was now widely established. His text also contained another assumption that reflected wider beliefs: Krasin assumed that a truthful account of his past was only possible if he had overcome those things within himself that prevented the possibility of such a true story; he believed or had come to believe that self-overcoming and truthful personal biography were connected.

Krasin, Bukovskii and Shcharanskii all warned of the dangers of little compromises. This was typical of dissident thinking. In another labour camp memoir, *Grey is the Colour of Hope* (1988), the Russian poet Irina Ratushinskaya recalled a moment when she had tried to engineer a meeting with her husband, Igor, through telling a little lie in a letter to the camp commandant. She had been taken over by the desire to see Igor, and at that moment nothing seemed to matter:

> Even now I cringe when I recall that incident. It's not as though I didn't know that lying to an adversary is tantamount to sanctioning his lies to you. I know that the difference between us lay in that we had moral standards and consciences! Where had my brains been, if not my conscience, in those moments?

The message was clear; small compromises lead to the corruption of the soul. Ratushinskaya was wary not only of lies, but also of hatred and fear. For example, she warned against allowing hatred to take root, for if allowed to flourish, it would ultimately 'corrode' and 'warp' the soul.[47]

The context was of course all-important for Ratushinskaya: the battle with the Soviet state was a matter of spiritual life and death. In other circumstances, certain dissidents were less strict with themselves. Bogoraz, for example, endorsed the traditional Russian distinction between *lozh'* and *vran'e*; she took the view that while a serious *lozh'* kind of lie was a 'heavy sin', the *vran'e* form of lie was a more trivial and forgivable offence that was acceptable in some circumstances.[48]

Many dissidents clearly emphasised the importance of struggle with oneself. In an interview about his spiritual journey in 1977, Vladimir Maksimov stated: 'The struggle with ourselves really makes us into people.' He also stated that a person had to suffer a great deal if he was to fathom his 'mystical origin' and his 'belonging to God'. In his own case, he noted that he had come from an atheistical family, and that, like David Copperfield, he had spent years in an orphanage. Coming to faith, he said, was not something logical, but rather a 'dawning' process (*ozarenie*). But he found that faith cleansed him from all that was 'dirty and dark' in his past.'[49]

Maksimov's belief in the positive role of suffering was shared by many religious dissidents. Another with a similar conviction was Zoya Krakhmal'nikova. Krakhmal'nikova and her husband Feliks Svetov were baptised by Father Dmitrii Dudko in the 1970s. Krakhmal'nikova then edited the samizdat religious journal, *Nadezhda*, and also wrote a number of religious novels.[50] She was arrested in August 1982, and sentenced in 1983 to a year in prison and five in internal exile.[51] In a subsequent memoir, *Listen, Prison!* (1993), Krakhmal'nikova interpreted imprisonment as God's providential instrument for liberating her from evil: 'As I paid my farthings, He stripped the world of its crust for me, layer by layer.' As with Shcharanskii, the Bible provided her with the vocabulary with which to interpret her experience. When the doors of her cell were first shut, her 'inner voice' said, quoting the Gospel of Matthew, 'Thou shalt by no means come out thence, till thou has paid the uttermost farthing.'[52] Krakhmal'nikova came to believe that what she was experiencing was occurring 'in history and in meta-history, "above" history'.[53] Her situation was ultimately a conflict between truth and lies in which the interrogator tempted her to declare 'truth to be a lie' and align herself with a kind of 'anti-logic'. In this wider context, Krakhmal'nikova saw what was happening to her in terms of a world-wide spiritual epidemic; it was part of a '*spiritual* problem', 'the problem of conscience and freedom'.[54] Krakhmal'nikova's assertion that her own spiritual struggles were representative of a global conflict reflected a widespread tendency among dissidents to universalise their experience.[55]

Krakhmal'nikova also interpreted her experience in the light of the teachings of the Church Fathers. She noted that during interrogations, people sometimes found themselves in a state of fear or 'mystical horror', which could be likened to what the Holy Fathers called a 'provocation', or what St Simeon the New Theologian called the 'onslaught of mental demons'. She also used the writings of Maximus the Confessor to explain the various ways in which God forsook his people, noting that all of them were 'salutary and imbued with Divine Grace and love for man'. Krakhmal'nikova's work indicates that the Orthodox tradition provided religious people with a way of interpreting their experience, both during and after interrogation. The fact that Krakhmal'nikova used the Christian tradition to explain her experience did not, however, mean that her prison strategies necessarily differed from those of more secular figures. Like many members of the human rights movement, she warned that it was best to avoid too much conversation with the investigator. In this respect, she noted that Jesus kept silent when he was interrogated by Pontius Pilate.[56]

Like Krakhmal'nikova, another Orthodox writer, Tat'yana Goricheva, saw in contemporary experience a revival of older forms of Orthodox spirituality. In *Talking about God is Dangerous* (1984) Tat'yana Goricheva wrote that in the camps the reality of the old Christian tradition had been rediscovered. Indeed, she noted that for her contemporaries it was found that the experience of the dissidents and ascetical experience coincided.[57] Goricheva was a member of a small circle of Leningrad Orthodox intellectuals in the late 1970s and 1980s. In her view, her contemporaries differed from the previous generation of dissidents in that they had no roots to turn to; traditional values of culture, religion and morality had been 'deliberately and successfully eradicated'. Goricheva highlighted the role of existentialism in the lives of her contemporaries, noting that existentialism was the vehicle by which she and her colleagues travelled to Christianity: 'For us existentialism was the first taste of freedom, the first public discussion that was not forbidden ... Our liberation began with the discovery of Western free thought.' Goricheva saw in this fascination for European thought the same enthusiasm felt by the nineteenth-century Russian intelligentsia for European ideas. However, Goricheva also had a suspicion of Western intellectual culture, typical of the Slavophile tradition.[58] She distanced herself from the dissident movement. In her view, the dissident emphasis on the liberation of personality did not in the end satisfy people. There were dangers in heroism: 'love of self, theatricalism, egocentric self-confidence'. 'Merely heroic people', she noted, 'need an enemy', need a 'boundary situation'. In her view, the new Christians of her own circle had gone 'beyond the principle of resistance'.[59]

In the tradition of the Church Fathers, the desert was a place where a person could meet with God unencumbered by the distractions of the world. The Soviet prison camp was effectively interpreted as a desert by people like Krakhmal'nikova and Goricheva.[60] This reflected wider literary currents. Venclova noted the existence of Romantic topoi in some gulag literature; the prison in the books of Sinyavskii or Yurii Dombrovskii was interpreted as a kind of monastic cell or place of religious or poetic meditation.[61]

Krakhmal'nikova and Goricheva were influenced by the Bible, the Church Fathers, Russian literature and by European philosophy. However, they were also influenced by the dissident tradition itself. In discussing labour camp literature, Goricheva noted that in the writings of Solzhenitsyn, Panin and the Jewish writer, Abram Shifrin, there were descriptions of people who were saved 'in seemingly miraculous circumstances'.[62] In saying this, she was effectively promoting a certain body of labour camp literature as a basis for moral and spiritual formation. The memoirs of Goricheva, Krakhmal'nikova and Ratushinkaya were consciously or unconsciously written within this wider literary-religious tradition. Certainly, Solzhenitsyn's *The Gulag Archipelago*, had become the canonical labour camp text immediately following its publication in 1973–1974. People used it as a spiritual guide. For example, Lev Timofeev, editor of the human rights journal *Referendum* in the late 1980s, recalled that when he was in prison he had been sustained spiritually by the memory of certain parts of *Gulag* about the spiritual life of prisoners.[63]

The spirituality that emerged from the prisons and labour camps was very ecumenical. There were clearly some strongly Orthodox writers. However, Panin was a Catholic, Shcharanskii and Shifrin were Jewish, and Bukovskii was a more secular liberal. Indeed, in these years spirituality was sometimes universalised and secularised to the extent that it was not linked to particular traditions at all. To pray did not necessarily mean to belong to a particular church or religious community. Following a conversation with the KGB in 1984, Grigorii Pomerants felt himself on the brink of a psychological collapse. He resorted to prayer to deal with the problem:

> I knew that there was a method for stopping one's thought-process. And I began to pray: 'Lord, stop my thoughts.' . . . After a few minutes I felt strength flowing into me. I prayed continually for an hour and when the hour came to an end, I felt myself completely free from fear.[64]

Although Pomerants's prayer has the feel of something from the Jewish or Christian tradition, no religious institution was directly involved in the experience. His religious experience took place at home.

The universalist current in dissident spirituality was illustrated by an essay by Yugoslav writer and dissident Mikhailo Mikhailov, 'The Mystical Experience of the Loss of Freedom', which appeared in *Kontinent* in 1974. Mihailov observed that Solzhenitsyn's *The Gulag Archipelago*, Panin's *The Notebooks of Sologdin*, Shifrin's *In the Fourth Dimension*[65] and Andrei Sinyavskii's *A Voice from the Chorus*, although very different in perspective, all contained similar spiritual observations about how a person could survive the camps with integrity intact. Although each of these writers was very different, Mikhailov observed, they all had concluded that whoever tried to save his life at the expense of his soul would lose both; on the other hand, whoever listened to the voice of his soul, letting go of physical security or social approval, found that what he had given up was preserved and that his most secret wishes were in fact fulfilled.[66]

The providentialism that was evident in the ideas of Krakhmal'nikova and Mikhailov was not unusual. In his memoirs, Solzhenitsyn declared that his recovery from a bad case of cancer after his release from the camps was a 'divine miracle'. In his search for a publisher of his novel *Cancer Ward*, he found that 'God's appointed time had come', and that he had a 'presentiment' that he was being 'carried along a path where none could withstand [him]'.[67] In preserving one set of documents, he declared elsewhere, an 'inner voice' kept telling him to put them into a separate storage.[68] Providentialism, too, was evident in Evgeniya Ginzburg's memoirs. Unlike Solzhenitsyn, Ginzburg remained a loyal communist throughout her time in the camps, and declared that she was glad that 'the great Leninist truth' had prevailed during the Khrushchev era. At the same time, she also recalled that in the camps she was frequently 'helped by events which at first sight seemed accidental, but which were in reality manifestations of the Supreme Good which, in spite of everything, rules the world'.[69]

In his youth, Sinyavskii had been a convinced atheist, but by the mid-1960s he had become an Orthodox believer. His spiritual view of the world, as with that of some other dissidents, reflected the idea that there existed true and false selves. In *A Voice from the Chorus* (1973), Sinyavskii suggested that souls in hell would not scream with their own voice, just like an epileptic man screamed in a 'completely unrecognizable voice'. Moreover, Sinyavskii suggested, happiness and self-concern could not go together: 'A man is entirely happy when he forgets about himself and no longer belongs to himself.'[70] For Sinyavskii, letting-go of self was thus necessary for the finding of self. This was a typical religious perspective, and, indeed, Sinyavskii took the Pauline view that in man there are two natures. In *Unguarded Thoughts* (1965), Sinyavskii suggested that Christian feelings were 'mad' and 'unnatural' to the humanist but 'supernatural' to the Christian, and that 'we don't overcome our nature – it is replaced by some other, unfamiliar nature which teaches us how to be ill, suffer and die and relieves us of the obligation to fear and hate'.[71]

The spirituality of the dissident intelligentsia was shaped not only by the experience of prisons and labour camps, but also by the survival of older religious traditions. Although the Soviet regime instituted very public forms of penitence, more personalised traditions of spirituality continued to exist. Many dissident intellectuals at some point consulted *startsy* or spiritual directors.

There were a number of figures who performed the role of the *starets* in the post-Stalin era. One of those was Archimandrite Tavrion Batozskii (1898–1978). Father Tavrion had spent twenty years of his life in prisons and exile for his religious convictions. In 1969, he was sent to the Spaso-Preobrazhenskii hermitage near Elvaga in Latvia. Thousands of people from all parts of the USSR came to visit the hermitage while Tavrion was there, sometimes for extended visits. According to one account, the hermitage became 'one of the main spiritual centres of the Russian Orthodox

Church'. Visitors included many members of the intelligentsia, among them some dissidents.[72] Like other *startsy*, Tavrion believed in the uniqueness of each person. He saw his mission as the struggle for 'the image of man, personality and the renewal of Christianity'. Apparently, neither social background nor religious affiliation interfered with this focus on individuals; indeed, Lutherans and Catholics also came to consult with him, and he was consequently sometimes labelled a 'Catholic' or a 'renovationist'.[73]

Father Tavrion had certain ways of concealing the full range of his activities from the authorities. For example, places where people could stay were constructed in nearby buildings that were officially built for other purposes; thus, a network of '*skity*' was created around the hermitage. There were regular visits from local inspectors, sometimes in response to denunciations. Although Tavrion was very cautious in his dealings with the authorities, he did not see officials as enemies; he treated them warmly, gave them tea, and also envelopes of money for the road (*na dorozhku*). This way of buying off potential interference was generally successful, although Tavrion complained that some of the visitors misused the situation and came for the 'bait' (*k kormushke*) too often.[74]

Central to the work of the *starets* or spiritual father was the time of confession. In this connection, methods of conducting confession were an important aspect of Orthodox spirituality, and illustrative of prevailing understandings of conscience. If someone was troubled during a time of confession, one famous *starets*, Father Serafim Tyapochkin (1894–1982), from 1961 the abbot of the Svyato-Nikolskii church in the village of Rakitnoe in Belgorodskii oblast, would ask: 'Tell me, what is on your conscience?' Father Serafim also strongly emphasised the importance of community life, believing that people would get a better understanding of themselves through living for a time with other people; '[l]ive with us for a time', he would say. After a few days living in community, a person would be ready to hear the truth spoken about him, but this would not be possible immediately.[75]

Although not known as a *starets*, Father Aleksandr Men' was widely consulted as a spiritual director. According to one of his spiritual followers, Natal'ya Bolshakova, Men' was interested in the underlying causes of a person's behaviour; during confession he would ask a person why he had sinned. He was keen that people should themselves discover the roots of their problems.[76] Like others, Men' emphasised the uniqueness of the individual. He understood the Christian concept of calling to mean 'the realisation of the plan of the Creator for [each person] personally'. Each person had his own role in life.[77]

Clearly conscience for these men was understood within a defined system of moral and spiritual law. It was a key to determining the will of God. The *starets* Savva (1898–1980), who was based from 1955 at the Pskovo-Pecherskii monastery, stated that a peaceful conscience was a sign of God's approval: 'If on strict examination [of a proposed course of action] the conscience is peaceful, then you should carry out your intention.'[78]

Since certain *startsy* or spiritual directors were influential on the wider intelligentsia, it could be argued that the roots of the late Soviet conscience could partly be found in traditional practices of confession. There were evidently many uneasy consciences. Father Dmitrii Dudko published a description of some of his conversations in the confessional in 1961–1963. The range of cases cited included people who repented of registering as unbelievers, or of being party members. Drinking was much mentioned. One war veteran had a guilty conscience over the fact that during the war he had killed two hundred people in self-defence. Many of the people mentioned were women. One woman had a guilty conscience for her part in killing a child, and another for living an immoral life with different men. Abortion was frequently mentioned. One woman said that she had been harmed by a witch that was living in her house. An old woman confessed that she had burned down her house in order to get the insurance. One young girl had a general sense of sin, but could not be specific.[79]

Other traditional, Orthodox practices continued to be employed. For example, the practice of '*yurodstvo*' (behaving like a Holy Fool) continued to exist in some monasteries. Archimandrite Viktor Mamontov recalled that a man named Misha, renowned for his rudeness and readiness to confront people with their sins, lived at the Pyukhtitskii monastery in Estonia in the 1970s. The Pochaev monastery in Western Ukraine was also home to a number of holy fools.[80] Possibly, the quality of *yurodstvo* existed more widely. At least, Amalrik saw something of the quality in Galanskov; Galanskov, he said, either had little understanding of people or else felt that there was something good in everyone; and he said that there was something similar in Sakharov.[81]

The confessional effectively promoted the idea of conscience as a higher yet internal, moral arbiter. However, obedience to the church and the authorities was also commanded. The question of whether and to what extent it was necessary to obey the authorities was a dilemma for reform-minded priests. Men', for example, differed considerably from his friend Father Gleb Yakunin, who was more of a social activist, and who became the most prominent Orthodox critic of the Moscow Patriarchate. Men' and Yakunin had a different attitude to religious authority and to political involvement. In 1961 an administrative reform was introduced by the Synod of Bishops that weakened Episcopal authority over local parishes, and effectively handed control of parishes over to local authorities. It was a measure that made it easier for the state to pursue its campaign of church closures, and although the Orthodox leadership made no public protest, there was deep unease in ecclesiastical circles. In 1965, Men', Yakunin, Dudko and Father Nikolai Eshliman, who had been meeting together regularly since 1962,[82] considered writing to the Patriarch about it. However, they differed on strategy. Men' believed that a lengthy letter drafted by Eshliman and Yakunin was too aggressive, and he proposed a more moderate three-page alternative. Men' and Dudko instinctively differed from Eshliman and Yakunin in their attitudes to religious authority; they were cautious about writing letters without Episcopal blessing.[83]

Eshliman and Yakunin were more radically inclined, and went ahead on their own with open letters to the Patriarch and the President of the Presidium of the Supreme Soviet, protesting at what they perceived to be a wrongful subservience to the state by the church and illegal state inference in Church affairs. In their open letter to the Patriarch (November 1965), Eshliman and Yakunin suggested that the church had wrongfully come under the influence of the atheistic Council of Russian Orthodox Church Affairs, and contravened the apostolic command by 'compromising with this world'. Using arguments reminiscent of Luther, Eshliman and Yakunin stated that they had been forced by 'Christian conscience and pastoral duty' and the 'intractable demands of Christian conscience' to write the letter. There were also political implications in their wording. They called for 'an end to the intrusion of "Caesar" into the internal life of the Church'; and they suggested that 'the interests of the Church in the civil sphere coincide with the interests of a free and just government'. The letter and the liberal understanding of conscience suggested by it were perceived by the Patriarch as a challenge to ecclesiastic authority. In May 1966, Eshliman and Yakunin were suspended from working as priests, and in a letter to his bishops the Patriarch complained that the open letter violated church practice, and that people who wrote open addresses to their superiors were trying to sow distrust between the church authorities and the clergy and laity.[84]

Eshliman and Yakunin were not the only priests who were concerned about the situation of the church. Other churchmen raised similar concerns, but using more internal channels. In the summer of 1965, eight bishops handed the Patriarch a declaration expressing concern about the 1961 reforms. In 1966, attempts were made to disrupt the Moscow church of the well-known priest, Father Vsevolod Shpiller, St-Nicholas-in-Kuznetskii, through the appointment of a hostile churchwarden. Shpiller reacted by withdrawing his pastoral blessing from the warden and his assistant, and informing the Patriarch in detail how their actions had undermined the unity of the parish. One contemporary chronicler contrasted Shpiller's respect for the Patriarch with Eshliman and Yakunin's approach, noting that Shpiller considered the Orthodox Patriarch to be the living organ of the 'ever-present expression of the canonical conscience of the church'. Shpiller sought reform from within, and was anxious to avoid any possibility of schism within the church. He wrote in March 1966 to Metropolitan Nikodim of Leningrad and Ladoga that 'long-suffering and patience' were qualities that were needed in dealing with the authorities, expressing a conviction that the tendency to re-establish 'socialist legality' in the church was 'undeniable'. He also wrote to Archbishop Basil of Brussels in January 1967 that it was important to approach issues of parish organisation with 'sufficient self-control'.[85]

Metropolitan Nikodim himself was a man who understood this kind of language. He was a firm supporter of the view taken by Metropolitan Sergei in 1927 that compromise with the regime was necessary to ensure the survival of the church. Confronted with the suggestion that Orthodox bishops had got used to disseminating falsehoods in defence of their position, he once declared: 'We're used to this sort of thing in the Soviet Union, and we don't react.' He described himself as a man who preferred to take small side roads in getting to his destination rather than getting into trouble on the main route.[86]

Although he had many friends in the reform-minded intelligentsia, Shpiller was anxious to avoid any mixing of religion and politics. He caused controversy in February 1974 when he gave an interview for the Novosti Press Agency, in which he stated that it was a mistake to consider Solzhenitsyn a Christian writer. Solzhenitsyn, Shpiller stated, saw the world in moral terms, and was not able to fathom the deeper spiritual and metaphysical dimensions of reality. Solzhenitsyn, he said, had failed to understand that evil could only be overcome by a 'good spirit': 'A conception of the world, of man, and of life primarily through the prism of the evil in it – no, this is not a Christian outlook.' Shpiller warned that Solzhenitsyn wanted to create inside the church a Christian alternative to Soviet society as a whole, and that this threatened a schism. He stated that this meant a wrongful linkage of religion and politics: 'Solzhenitsyn has not understood that any political materialisation of religious energy, which is embraced by the Church, kills the Church, such that, subjecting itself to this materialisation, the Church stops being the Church.' One of Shpiller's associates, the former White Army officer, Yeromonakh Pavel Troitskii, wrote him an enthusiastic letter of support, endorsing the same point: 'A Christian is not a politician.'[87] It is notable that the suspicion of politics that pervaded the human rights movement was also present in the church.

Shpiller's approach to some extent reflected the prevailing survival strategy of the Orthodox Church; in the context of Soviet oppression, otherworldliness was the only option available.[88] Yet it was itself a controversial position to take. Too much compromise could and did alienate the intelligentsia. Moreover, it appeared that Shpiller's attack on Solzhenitsyn had proved helpful to the state; his interview was published in a distorted form in an English-language book aimed at destroying Solzhenitsyn's reputation.[89] Yakunin wrote to him stating that he did not doubt his sincerity, but saying that he had been unwise: 'You had to agree to sing in a choir that was unworthy of you, at a time not of your choosing, and furthermore your part was touched up by the bureaucratic conductor.' Also in a letter to Shpiller, the prominent religious thinker, Mikhail Agurskii, a Jewish convert to Orthodoxy, implied that Shpiller had in fact allowed himself to be drawn into politics: 'You have sometimes stressed that the Church must refuse to participate in political life, [and] although I do not agree with you, your personal non-participation in it would be the best line of behaviour in future.' Agurskii, however, in a letter to *Russian Thought* and *Vestnik RSKhD* in Paris, went beyond the question of Shpiller's judgement in giving the interview, to suggest that in fact Solzhenitsyn and Shpiller represented two forms of Orthodox spirituality; Solzhenitsyn represented the kind of believer who sought a sacrificial, active engagement with the world, while Shpiller preferred the ideal of a sacramental withdrawal from it.[90] In effect, he was suggesting that within Orthodoxy itself there were two different models of conscience.

In June 1980, Father Dmitrii Dudko made a public denial of some of his former activities. His 'recantation' illustrates some of the moral dilemmas that were faced by priests in the Soviet system. Dudko appeared on television on 20 June to make a confession and reject his former anti-Soviet views, and a statement was published the following day in *Izvestiya*. Dudko cited St Paul's maxim that all authority was from God, and asserted that much of his previous activity had broken this rule. He noted that it was the Patriarchs who had chosen the current direction of the Orthodox Church, and condemned himself for trying to persuade bishops to go against their authority. He recalled that he had been warned that his work had been too political, and stated that many of his views and statements had in fact been anti-Soviet: 'I have re-interpreted my battle with atheism as a battle with the Soviet regime.'[91] Dudko was clearly put under extreme pressure to make his recantation, and there must be some doubt as to whether he indeed wrote the whole article. At the same time, it is also clear that his interrogators had confronted Dudko with issues that were complicated ones for priests in the Orthodox church; it was a problem for free-thinking churchman to know how to fulfil the requirement to respect world authorities.[92]

The authorities certainly understood that religious figures could sometimes be tripped up by their scruples. In his labour camp in Perm, Shcharanskii shared a cell with Vladimir Poresh, an Orthodox believer and member of a religious-philosophical seminar founded by Aleksandr Ogorodnikov in 1974.[93] The KGB tried to undermine Vladimir Poresh by trying to impress upon him the idea that all authority emanated from God and therefore that it was sinful to oppose it. Poresh himself was in turmoil over how to discern the dividing line between struggle against evil and the beginning of pride. According to Shcharanskii, Poresh suffered because he realised that he was 'insufficiently prepared for his encounter with evil'.[94]

Agurskii's observation that Solzhenitysn and Shpiller represented two forms of Orthodox spirituality points to the fact that there existed in late Soviet Russia a competition to establish different models of sanctity. This was particularly evident during the process to re-establish the practice of canonisation. The practice of venerating saints was given impetus in

1946–1947 at the end of the war when a number of the relics of saints were returned to the church, including those of such luminary figures as Tikhon Zadonsk, Sergei Radonezhskii and Feodosii Chernigovskii.[95] From the 1960s onwards, there was also a renewed interest in canonisation. In 1964, the Russian Orthodox Church Abroad (ROCA) canonised John of Kronstadt. The Moscow Patriarchate followed by canonising Nikolai Yaponskii in 1970. In this way, 'one of the system-forming social conventions of Russian Orthodoxy was re-established'. It was the means by which the churches declared their own existence. Even more so could the canonisations at the time of the millennium celebrations in 1988 be understood in this way. One scholar calls these canonisations a kind of 'visiting card' for the church: a certain kind of advertising.[96]

The question of who would qualify for sainthood was fraught with problems for the Moscow Patriarchate because certain views of sanctity, articulated at home and abroad, were potentially a threat to its own power. In particular, the views of the rival, monarchist ROCA, were a challenge to its own. In May 1967, ROCA announced that it was naming Nicholas II 'the tsar-martyr', and in 1971, at the same time as the Moscow Patriarch was choosing Pimen Izvekov as its next Patriarchate, it announced that it was preparing for the canonisation of martyrs who had suffered for their faith in the USSR since 1917.

The view of Soviet history on which this initiative was based, of course appealed to radicals and dissidents. In 1975, Yakunin joined with the church historian Lev Regelson and the layman Viktor Kapitanchuk in a letter to Patriarch Pimen and the heads of the different Russian Orthodox churches overseas, calling for the commemoration of martyrs of the church of the communist period. Dudko was also consistently supportive of the idea of the canonisation of Nicholas II. Yet, radicals also had to wrestle with the matter of church authority. In 1979, Yakunin, Regelson, Kapitanchuk and Father Vasilii Fonchenkov in an open letter to all Orthodox Christians, expressed support for canonisation, but also argued that the issue could only be decided by the Orthodox Church as a whole.[97] Undeterred, in November 1981, ROCA canonised Nicholas II and his family along with all the other martyrs who had suffered under communism. Apart from the reference to the tsar's family, this event was distinctive in that it involved canonisation of the very phenomenon of martyrdom under communism; no list of names was provided, and the veneration of saints and the saying of prayers for the dead became intertwined. From that time onwards, ROCA made the canonisation of all martyrs under communism a condition for the reconciliation of their church with the Moscow Patriarchate. Clearly, the Moscow Patriarchate and ROCA drew inspiration from different periods of history. While ROCA saw suffering under communism as a mark of saintliness, the Moscow Patriarchate remained anxious not to displease the Soviet authorities, and looked to the pre-revolutionary period for inspiration.[98]

7 Dialogue and division in the dissident movement

The dissident movement was very divided ideologically, but sometimes the differences were not clearly visible, even to those concerned. This is illustrated by a dispute between Solzhenitsyn and Elena Chukovskaya, granddaughter of the writer, Kornei Chukovskii. Elena Chukovskaya did a lot of work for Solzhenitsyn in the late 1960s and early 1970s, and was for a time his closest collaborator in the practical side of his work. However, the two of them never discussed their views on the fundamental questions of life. In fact, their views of the world were very different; Solzhenitsyn was much more religious than Chukovskaya. According to Solzhenitsyn, the Chukovskii family was 'psychologically wedded to the non-religious traditions of the Russian nineteenth-century liberation movement with its special brand of populism'. Suddenly, in 1972, when Solzhenitsyn asked Chukovskaya to type out his 'Lenten Letter to Patriarch Pimen', she refused to help. Solzhenitsyn recalled: 'After more than six years of working together, it became apparent that we did not think alike.'[1]

The disagreement between Solzhenitsyn and Chukovskaya suggests that nineteenth-century divisions between Slavophiles and Westernisers continued to exist in dissident circles. However, resemblances between dissident and nineteenth-century debates could have been coincidental, and divisions were not always replicated exactly.[2] In addition, there was a dialogue of religious and secular traditions in the dissident intelligentsia that was new in Russian history. People of diverse persuasions often found that they could unite around a common commitment to certain absolute or universal values. This is evident in the speeches made at the funeral of the veteran communist Aleksei Kosterin in November 1968. Kosterin was one of a group of five people who in 1968 formed a circle of communists disillusioned with the regime, the others being Petr Grigorenko, Valerii Pavlinchuk, Sergei Pisarev and Ivan Yakhimovich. Kosterin and Grigorenko became particularly well known for their struggle for the rights of Crimean Tatars. A number of important figures in the democratic movement attended Kosterin's funeral, and speakers at the occasion often emphasised Kosterin's communist convictions. An occasion that was productive of an iconographic picture of Kosterin himself, it was also indicative of an underlying dissident search for a moral basis for socialism.

A eulogy read by Anatolii Yakobson, on behalf of a group of friends and co-workers, stressed Kosterin's commitment to Leninist ideals. Kosterin had been reprimanded by the party after he had protested against the invasion of Czechoslovakia, and he resigned from the party as a result. Yakobson commented that these actions showed that up until his death Kosterin had acted like a 'genuine Bolshevik-Leninist, like a fighter – thinking not about himself but about those who would remain after him', his friends and co-workers, Yakobson declared, would continue to be inspired by his commitment to democracy, the emancipation of humanity and humanism.[3] Petr Yakir also stressed Kosterin's Leninist convictions. He described the leaders of the USSR as either fanatics or philistines who had never read the works of the creators of Marxist-Leninism; and he compared them to those who shouted 'Crucify him' to Pontius Pilate during the trial of Christ. Kosterin, he declared, had believed that there was no such thing as a pure Marxist-Leninism which was correct in all ways; however, Stalinists, Khrushchevists and Brezhnevites had taken quotations from Marx, Engels and Lenin and used them out of context, and this had created the basis for Stalinism and neo-Stalinism. While setting aside the question of whether Kosterin's views were correct or not, Yakir stated that Kosterin was a man of 'crystal purity', 'enormous courage' and 'incredibly strong will'; he referred too to his 'clarity of thought and loyalty to ideals'.[4]

Yakir's version of communism was clearly ethical and undogmatic. The same was true of Grigorenko's. In his eulogy, Grigorenko emphasised Kosterin's 'civic valour', 'humanity', 'inexhaustible love for people, and his faith in them'. He declared that the central contemporary task was the development of a 'genuine *Leninist democracy*', and referred positively to Pushkin, Tolstoi, Pasternak and Solzhenitsyn.[5] In his report of the occasion, entitled 'Yet Another Mockery of Sacred Feelings', Grigorenko praised Kosterin's daughter, Nina, who had written a famous diary about her life in the 1930s that was published in *Novyi mir* in 1962; Nina Kosterina, he noted, had retained an 'uncorrupted sense of right and wrong' and had revealed through her diary an 'impeccable and honest soul'.[6]

Grigorenko's moral vision clearly involved a variety of components; it was a mixture of communist, humanist and possibly Christian elements, and it illustrated something of the way in which different ethical traditions were combined in the dissident movement. His views were certainly not typical of a Bolshevik. Subsequently, his opinions evolved further. In his memoirs, written from abroad after his Soviet citizenship was revoked in 1977 during a visit to the USA, he recalled: 'Things did not seem to "add up" in Lenin. But ... at the time I did not have the courage to understand this ... I began to "sort out" Lenin unconsciously, selecting to retain only that which suited my own views.'[7]

The ethical universalism evident in the speeches at Kosterin's funeral was also present in the eulogy of another unnamed person who attended the funeral, whom Grigorenko identified as 'The Christian'. The Christian suggested that Kosterin had been sent to them by God, saying, 'God recalls his existence to us through such people.' He stated that up until that day he had believed that his faith was incompatible with Marxist-Leninism, but that the funeral had led him to think that the problem lay not at a doctrinal level, but rather in people themselves:

> I want to say to you that the memory of a man like Aleksei Yevgrafovich [Kosterin] must unite all those who want to bar the way to evil, who want to give full scope to the *divine basis* in *human beings* – their intellect, their unhindered creativity – no matter what these people are called: communists, socialists, Christians, or simply people.[8]

It was effectively a declaration of a certain kind of religious and ethical universalism, and it once again reflected the way in which people who were doctrinally different could unite around certain common moral convictions.

The dialogue, if also the tension, between Christianity and humanism in the dissident intelligentsia was also evident in the correspondence between the Orthodox priest, Sergei Zheludkov, and the physicist and human rights activist, Kronid Lyubarskii. Lyubarskii was arrested in January 1972 for his involvement in the reproduction and distribution of samizdat, and in 1973 was sent to a camp in Mordovia. In 1974, Zheludkov, who first met Lyubarskii in 1971, initiated a correspondence with him about religious and ethical questions that lasted for almost three years. Zheludkov was attracted to the idea, articulated by the Catholic theologian, Karl Rahner, that many non-believers could be described as 'anonymous Christians' because their lives and values reflected a Christian spirit. Lyubarskii, however, was committed to an atheist stance, and rejected Zheludkov's arguments.

Zheludkov outlined some of his theories in an essay entitled 'The Church of Good Will or Christianity for All', in which he wrote of what he called 'Christianity of the will'. In his view, it was best when Christianity of the will coincided with the Christianity of faith, but he stated that 'any orientation of our will towards ideal humanness is an orientation towards Christ'. In the twentieth century, he saw in such figures as Gandhi and Schweitzer representatives of the non-Christian world who were nevertheless part of the Church of Christ.[9] Zheludkov was seeking common ground between the different intellectual traditions; he referred positively to 'Christian humanism', and suggested that there were analogous elements in the religious and scientific forms of knowledge.[10] Lyubarskii, on the other hand, declared that morality was shaped by the laws of nature: 'Natural morality, just like the natural law, is the sum of norms of behaviour that most contribute to the preservation of man as the biological species *Homo Sapiens*.'[11] He argued for a strong separation of morality and religion. He also believed religious ideas to be inherently totalitarian, and defended man as the highest value.[12]

Zheludkov attributed man's sense of guilt, the 'mysterious inner voice' and his 'unbribable conscience' to the religious nature of man.[13] Lyubarskii responded that 'conscience is conscience, love is love', and there was no need to find the roots of such concepts in God. According to Lyubarskii, conscience was something that only seemed to be spontaneous, beyond the control of reason, and of miraculous origin; on closer analysis, it turned out to be a mechanism that came into operation when people had to take quick decisions; it was an 'inbuilt mechanism for immediate decision-making, favouring altruistic actions, and suppressing temptations'. In discussing C.S. Lewis's *The Problem of Pain*, Lyubarskii rejected Lewis's statement that God's plans for people brought them greater happiness than their own by stating that to reject one's own autonomy for the sake of happiness was 'too high a price'.[14]

Another exchange that illustrated the dialogue of traditions that took place within the human rights movement was an exchange of letters between Tat'yana Khodorovich and Leonid Plyushch in *Kontinent* in 1976. Plyushch was arrested in January 1972, and a year later sentenced to confinement in a psychiatric hospital. He stayed there until in early 1976 he was permitted to emigrate to the West. The case provoked an international outcry, and Amnesty International sponsored an International Day for Leonid Plyushch in April 1975. Khodorovich was a central figure in the campaign to free Plyushch, and published a book, *The Case of Leonid Plyushch* in 1974.[15] However, Khodorovich, who was by now a committed Orthodox believer, was distressed to discover that in the West Plyushch let it be known that he was still a communist and that he thought the horrors of the Soviet system were basically distortions of what had been a good idea. This she articulated in an 'Open Letter to Leonid Plyushch', to which Plyushch replied.

Khodorovich stated that she had known all along that Plyushch was a Marxist, but that she had assumed that his Marxism was rather the result of inertia, an expression of youth or the reflection of his scientific need for an all-embracing view of the world, than a deeply held conviction. She was disappointed to discover that this was not so, and felt compelled to say that she considered his views 'evil'. She rejected the 'dialectics of good and evil' and the belief in the relativity or class character of those concepts; and she advocated instead non-violence. She saw the meaning of her own life in 'the rejection of evil, in charity, sympathy, compassion and help for those in need', and declared: 'I love spirituality, culture, freedom, and hold to charity and goodness (universal, all to all) and for this reason I do not accept anything that threatens these values, which are absolute for me.' She could find nothing in the writings of the early Marx or the later Lenin to disabuse her of the view that Soviet history was a logical outcome of the

Marxist vision; in her view, the ethical foundation of Marxism was the total non-acceptance of the 'individual-spiritual principle' in man. Khodorovich also warned Plyushch to be very careful about how his opinions might be interpreted in the West.[16]

In his reply, Plyushch said that, in spite of their differences, he and Khodorovich had certain beliefs in common. These were:

> truth is the best politics; man is not made for the sabbath, but the sabbath for man; anyone who describes an ideology based on evil and violence as a bright and pure ideal takes upon himself a worse sin than the evil itself; the propaganda of anti-Semitism is the moral corruption of people; the criteria of a healthy society are always the criteria of love and freedom, and of the complexity and depth of the human personality; those who have experienced totalitarianism are obliged to be especially sensitive to anything that concerns bright ideals; there must be a feeling of responsibility for one's own words.[17]

In his defence, Plyushch wrote that he saw in Stalinism not so much Marxism as a return to the methods of Peter the Great and Ivan the Terrible. Words and deeds needed to be distinguished; Soviet leaders, he wrote, used the terminology of Marxism, just like the Holy Father-Inquisitors used certain quotations from the Bible to justify themselves. Plyushch declared that he was not a doctrinaire Marxist, but that his thinking rested on certain of his principles, in particular his idea of freedom. He understood Marx's phrase, 'freedom is recognised necessity', to mean simply that a person could not be free without understanding the laws of the surrounding world; on the other hand, he believed that Hegel's more abstract thinking was much more dangerous because men such as Stalin could use his concept of 'necessity' to justify their destruction of millions of people. ''Recognised necessity', he stated, was not a recipe for determinism, for nature did contain elements of spontaneity. Moreover, he suggested that in Marxism there was room for the idea that a person could rise above the level of being; this could never be total, however, for even for Christ the will of God the Father, which for him was equivalent to history and being, was higher than his will. At the same time, Plyushch believed that Marxism needed to be constantly modified by practice. Furthermore, he was not happy with the interpretation of nationality in classical Marxism. This was not surprising since he was a Ukrainian nationalist.[18]

Plyushch agreed that class morality could be misused; with Lenin, he wrote, the idea of class morality had been vulgarised to the point where it meant that everything was moral that served the socialist revolution. On the other hand, while accepting the idea that it was impossible to build a humane society with immoral methods, Plyushch warned that absolute, eternal morality was 'metaphysical' and could lead to 'immoralism'. He said: 'There is not and cannot be one moral formula for all the situations of life.' He stated that the decision by England and France to go to war with Hitler involved the 'defence of a relative good with evil methods, with violence'. On a related point, Plyushch saw the individual as a historical being; the only real freedom, he suggested, was the freedom to choose between good and evil, but people only became free and truly themselves through the particularities of their culture.[19]

The debate between Khodorovich and Plyushch illustrated the common ground that existed within the dissident movement between people with religious and secular convictions; the list of points on which, according to Plyushch, he and Khodorovich agreed, was undoubtedly a firm foundation for joint activity in the context of Soviet life. Khodorovich and Plyushch saw in Marxism different things, and in practice they had more in common than at first appeared. At the same time, the common ground was easier to maintain when there was a common enemy.

Aside from differences over religious questions, a central area of disagreement among oppositionists was attitudes to Russian national identity. In 1970 *Vestnik RSKhD* published three samizdat articles under the title 'Metanoia', that addressed this issue. All the authors published under a pseudonym. In the introduction, 'NN' called on Russia to repent of its sins, and declared that communism, Great Power chauvinism and Orthodox pre-eminence represented various temptations which had beset the country. He also stated that more evil has been brought into the world by Russia than any other country.[20] In another essay, 'The Dual Consciousness of the Intelligentsia and Pseudo-Culture', O. Altaev stressed the similarities between the values of the Bolsheviks and the pre-revolutionary intelligentsia, and further argued that the history of the intelligentsia over the previous fifty years could be understood as a series of temptations, whereby the intelligentsia was drawn into believing that the regime had finally abandoned its essential inhumanity. These temptations, which Altaev described as the 'guiding factors of the perverted spirituality of the intelligentsia', were those of revolution, *smenovekhovism*,[21] socialism, war, the thaw and technocracy. The temptations were not wrong in themselves, he said; rather they became temptations when people sought in them a solution to complex problems.[22] In the third article, 'Russian Messianism and the New National Consciousness', V. Gorskii stated that the October Revolution, in spite of its anti-national and conspiratorial character, was 'linked to the deepest strata of the national soul', and that overcoming the 'national-messianic temptation' was Russia's 'first and foremost task'.[23] The revolution, even if destructive of Russian national values, was also a distorted version of them.

The authors of the 'Metanoia' symposium all saw Russian history in spiritual terms. Consciousness of Russia as a collective moral being was a widespread phenomenon. Indeed, it had been articulated to some degree at the time of the invasion of Czechoslovakia by Bogoraz and Gorbanevskaya. In addition, the view that Russia had succumbed to certain 'temptations' also seems to have been widely held. Nadezhda Mandelstam, for example, stated: 'Everything we have been through was the result of succumbing to the temptations of our era.'[24] Yet the collection provoked a storm of controversy, especially among nationalist or patriotic writers. The dissident G.M. Shimanov complained that it revealed a hatred of things Russian. The writer Leonid Borodin attacked it in the nationalist journal *Veche*, noting that many of the Bolsheviks were Jews.[25] Solzhenitsyn too was hostile. Writing in *From under the Rubble* (1974) about the Gorskii article, he suggested that it was a perversion of history to focus on messianism at the expense of other national characteristics: 'With the obsessive thoroughness of hate, our whole history is arbitrarily distorted for some never quite graspable purpose – and all this is presented as an act of *repentance*.' Solzhenitsyn also said of 'NN' and Gorskii: 'Nowhere do we feel that the authors think of themselves and their readers as "we". Living among us, they call on us to repent, while they themselves remain unassailable and guiltless.' He was also critical of the idea that Bolshevism contained something Russian; in his view Russia was Orthodox, whereas Bolshevism's main content was atheism and class hatred.[26]

From under the Rubble was an attempt to articulate a new set of national values. Edited by Solzhenitsyn himself, it brought together authors with diverse patriotic and nationalist perspectives. In his essay 'Repentance and Self-Limitation in the Life of Nations', Solzhenitsyn sought to apply the lexicon of personal spirituality to social life. Unlike political parties, which he believed to be 'utterly inhuman formations', Solzhenitsyn declared that nations were 'vital formations, susceptible to all moral feelings, including ... repentance'. In a point also made in *The Gulag Archipelago*, Solzhenitsyn stressed that the boundary line separating good and evil ran through every human heart. However, in this case, he also suggested that this line '[oscillated] continuously in the consciousness of a nation'. All nations, he observed, had sinned at some point in their history, and it was a matter for special consideration in each particular case how much time had to elapse before a sin ceased to weigh on the national conscience. According to Solzhenitsyn, a nation was an integrated organism and thus the majority of a population could not but answer for the sins and mistakes of its political leaders. He said that the nation was 'mystically welded together in a community of guilt' and that its inescapable destiny was 'common repentance'. Occasionally, he argued, individuals could articulate the repentance of a nation, although it was only from a historical distance that people could judge whether they had really expressed a genuine national change of heart.[27]

While Solzhenitsyn declared that Russia had suffered more than any other country in the twentieth century, he said, '*We, all of us*, Russia herself, were the necessary accomplices', and that love for the nation should be combined with a frank assessment of its sins and vices. In terms of her neighbours, Solzhenitsyn commented that Russia was not always the perpetrator of wrongs; for example, while Russia had wronged Poland, Poland was not herself historically guiltless towards Russia. Nevertheless, wrongs needed to be put right, and this could only be done through concrete actions. This meant giving people in and beyond Russia's borders the freedom to decide their own future.[28]

Solzhenitsyn's essay reflected a political philosophy that had much in common with nineteenth-century *pochvennichestvo*. Attacking the Petrine form of Westernisation, Solzhenitsyn stated that while there were many examples of national repentance in Russian history, the whole Petersburg period of Russian history had drawn Russia away from the tradition of repentance. Positivism too was disputed: the reality of national spiritual life, Solzhenitsyn observed, was evident to people who consulted their intuitions, rather than 'the dictates of positive knowledge'. There was a call for 'self-limitation'. Solzhenitsyn differentiated this from the Western ideal of 'unlimited freedom', and stated that in Christian terms it was better understood as 'self-restriction'. There was also hostility to certain forms of modernisation. Solzhenitsyn called for Russia to withdraw from the global tasks that had left it 'tired', in order to concentrate on healing of soul, the education of children and putting its own house in order. In particular, he highlighted the development opportunities offered by the Russian North-east. The North-east was Russia's natural terrain of influence; it offered plenty of room to correct what Solzhenitsyn called the country's 'idiocies' in building towns, industrial enterprises, power stations and roads. The region, he said, could only be brought back to life by a free people: 'Only free people with a free understanding of our national mission can resurrect these great spaces, awaken them, heal them, beautify them with feats of engineering.'[29]

The idea of the nation as a spiritual being was explored in other essays in *From under the Rubble*. In 'Personality and National Awareness', the historian Vadim Borisov followed Dostoevskii in depicting the nation as 'the *spiritual reality* that binds all the concrete, historical and empirical manifestations of national life into a single whole';[30] and he also cited the opinion of the French historian Michelet that a nation was a 'moral personality'. At the same time, he distinguished between nationalism and national feeling; the former he regarded as a dangerous ideological force that failed to recognise the absoluteness of every national personality and replaced the idea of a supra-sociological Christian idea of personality with a naturalistic perception of it that emphasised blood and kinship.[31] In 'Russian Destinies' F. Korsakov offered a providentialist reading of Russian history, comparing Russia's experience during Soviet rule with the fate of Job in the Old Testament:

> Surely Job's fate can be seen as a prophetic analogy to the fate of Russia throughout her history ... The Lord knew and loved his servant Job, and marked him out by testing him. And Job repudiated

> what he had said and repented in dust and ashes. Can we still not see the finger of God pointing at us?[32]

Korsakov's understanding of Russia's spiritual journey contained a messianic tendency that was absent in the essays of Solzhenitsyn and Borisov. He endorsed the view of the Russian philosopher Petr Chaadaev, that Russia existed to provide some great object lesson for the world, and he likened the wounds of the Russian Orthodox Church under Soviet rule to those of Christ.[33] Suffering, he believed, had given Russia a special task. Another of the authors, Igor Shafarevich, also declared that communist rule had provided the country with a unique experience, suggesting that Russia's task was to lead mankind out of the 'blind alley' of contemporary civilisation and the ideology of progress. This was possible because of her sufferings: 'Russia has passed through death and may hear the voice of God.'[34] Shafarevich eventually became the spokesman for a more extreme right-wing position. In particular his book *Russofobiya* (1982) gave ammunition to a militant and anti-Semitic nationalism that was influential in the late 1980s and early 1990s, but the roots of this were not fully visible in the mid-1970s.[35]

From under the Rubble provoked a strong reaction. Solzhenitsyn's national liberalism differed from the messianic ideas of Korsakov and Shafarevich. It was also more moderate than the ideas promoted elsewhere by Vladimir Osipov, the editor of the journal *Veche*. Yet it worried those on the liberal-left. The stress on the spiritual life of the nation brought to the surface political differences between people in a way that the emphasis on personal conscience did not. The veteran communist Raissa Lert feared that Solzhenitysn's quiet nationalism might grow into a Stalinist form of nationalism.[36] It was not so much the conviction that nations might be understood from a spiritual point of view, as the potentially conservative political conclusions that could be drawn from it, that were disputed. Two collections of essays by dissident writers were published in response to it: *Self-Consciousness: Collected Articles* (1976) and *Democratic Alternatives: Collected Articles and Documents* (1976).[37] Both collections took issue with the idea that the revolutionary tradition itself was to blame for Russia's ills and with the view that the Bolshevik Revolution was a new departure in Russian history.

Self-Consciousness was liberal-democratic in orientation. In their introduction, its editors, Litvinov, Meerson-Aksenov and Shragin, noted that those fighting for liberal values in Russia had been much inspired by the works of Berdyaev, Bulgakov, Milyukov, Struve, Fedotov and Frank. From an earlier generation, Herzen, Saltykov-Schedrin and V.G. Korolenko were also mentioned. The authors noted that the sources of the religious renewal that was taking place within the liberal-democratic movement were not to be found in conservative Orthodoxy, but in the ideas of the 'religious renaissance',[38] which, they believed, were capable of answering the needs of modern man, and in the ecumenistic aspirations of a liberal minority in the Russian emigration. They also endorsed the UN Universal Declaration on the Rights of Man as the 'highest achievement of the democratic consciousness in the post-war world'. The authors lamented the lack of a developed liberal theory in Russia, although they also recognised the importance of Amalrik, Yesenin-Volpin, Pomerants, Sakharov, Tverdokhlebov, Turchin and Chalidze in developing this tendency.[39]

By endorsing both religion and the human rights tradition, the editors of *Self-Consciousness* were again seeking to find common ground between the Enlightenment and Christian traditions. This was the thrust of the first essay in the collection, 'The Truth of Humanism', by Yevgenii Barabanov, who in fact had himself contributed to *From under the Rubble*. Barbanov noted that the essence of humanism since the Renaissance had been to play down the distinctiveness of the Christian message and to separate religion from ethics, to make the individual conscience the final arbiter for distinguishing between good and evil. The religious wars and persecutions of early modern Europe had accentuated the divide between Christianity and humanism, and this had meant that the fate of humanism turned out to be tragic. There had been an attempt to turn man into a God: 'This was a false, inhuman religion.'[40] Yet while the split had proved damaging from the humanist point of view, it had also been a disaster for the church. The church had failed to recognise the truths of humanism: '[Humanism's] quest, initiative, conscience and truth turn out to be unnecessary to the Christian world'; 'in the modern world, the burden of the human conscience is carried by people who stand outside the walls of the church'. Historically, Barabanov said, Christianity had often lacked a respect for the freedom, personality and creativity of the individual: 'In striving to free man from the power of stagnation (*kosnosti*) and sin, the divine sources of man's freedom were often forgotten.' The result was that it was now people who stood outside the church who were courageously fighting for man and his dignity.[41]

Barabanov himself used the term 'anonymous Christians' to describe the new humanists, meaning that they articulated a Christian spirit while not being members of a church. Barabanov also argued that there was appearing a new more moderate humanism in Russia that was different from its early form. He stated that the attitude of some Christians to this phenomenon suggested a pharisaical attitude. Goodness, he declared, was indivisible, and attempts to limit God's goodness were ungodly; in any case the historical forms of Christianity were changeable.[42]

Similar themes were raised by Meerson-Aksenov in his article, 'The Birth of a New Intelligentsia'. Meerson-Aksenov disputed the widespread and negative view of the revolutionary intelligentsia popularised by *Landmarks*. He suggested that the identification of the Orthodox Church with tsarism had led the intelligentsia to take an anti-clerical position: 'Its sharp anthropocentrism was in its own way a response to the monophysite tone of Orthodox theocentrism'. However, there were Christian elements in certain intelligentsia attitudes; and moreover the February rather than the October Revolution reflected the true aspirations of the intelligentsia.[43] For the Soviet intelligentsia, however, 'the individual conscience gave way to the social conscience'. Contact with the West, however, had given intellectuals an awareness of the 'unity of human nature, indestructible by class distinctions', and they had lost their faith in the state ideology. According to Meerson-Aksenov, the collapse of communism as a world-view had been accompanied by the rise of ethical personalism, which had received its social expression in the human rights movement. Meerson-Akenov's concept of Christianity was a radical liberal one: 'Christianity liberates, since it does not recognise any external legislation over man, rejecting all legalism, postulating only the law of the heart and respect for the freedom of the other individual.' Inspired by G.P. Fedotov, Meerson-Aksenov envisaged the possibility of a new intellectual elite that could unite the Christian faith with the democratic traditions of the Russian intelligentsia.[44]

In his article, Litvinov attacked what he saw as a lack of respect for law and freedom in Solzhenitsyn's thought. In 'As Breathing and Consciousness Return', Solzhenitsyn had argued that intellectual freedom, while very desirable, was a gift of conditional rather than intrinsic worth, and best understood as a means by which people could attain another and higher goal.[45] This was not an unusual view for conservative Russian thinkers who were suspicious of Enlightenment thought; Semyon Frank, for example, argued in *The Spiritual Foundations of Society* (1930), that true democracy should best be understood in combination with man's innate calling to serve goodness.[46] Yet, Litvinov felt that this indicated authoritarian tendencies on Solzhenitsyn's part. He cited with approval Kistyakovskii's argument in *Landmarks* that Russia lacked a legal consciousness, and observed too that freedom was not in any way the same thing as anarchy.[47]

From under the Rubble provoked another collection of essays entitled *Democratic Alternatives* (1976) from a group of mainly *émigré* Russians who identified with a 'liberal-left' outlook. In his essay, the editor of the collection, Vadim Belotserkovskii, outlined the essential features of what he saw as a new left-wing world-view which was emerging in the USSR, especially among those in the scientific-technical and factory intelligentsia. Belotserkovskii declared that advocates of the new world-view rejected the Leninist idea that morality could be defined as what was in the interests of the proletariat. Instead, they believed that nothing could justify violence over the individual, and asserted the primacy of morality in all spheres of life: 'The immutability of moral principles, their unconditionality in all episodes of life, their primacy in politics, economics and ideology – this is the essential principle of the new left worldview in the USSR.'

Furthermore, he said, the new left derived its moral principles and norms from the 'basic, unchanging needs and qualities of human nature', and he stated that conscience and moral norms were immutable. He suggested that one of the constituent features of heroism was a 'clear conscience', declaring: 'Being cannot change moral norms, but it can hinder or help a person to live according to them.'[48] According to Belotserkovskii, the new left sought a synthesis between Westernisers and Slavopohiles, and between capitalism and communism. The idea of synthesis, he argued, was a 'third way' approach based on the thesis that what was in the interests of all would also be in the interests of each; it was rooted in a 'moral existence' that corresponded to the immanent needs of human nature. This process, he declared, would be a 'moral revolution'. Yet, he also stated, members of the new left differed from the old in that they were not 'boundless optimists'.[49]

Unbeknownst to Solzhenitsyn, the 'Gorskii' whom he criticised in *From under the Rubble* was Grigorii Pomerants. Solzhenitsyn and Pomerants repeatedly differed on many issues. As well as disagreeing about the relative dangers of Russian messianism, they also disagreed over the nature of peasant religiosity. Pomerants doubted the profundity of the peasants' system of devotion, whereas Solzhenitsyn was close to the Christian naturalism of the nineteenth-century *pochvenniki.* In 'The Smatterers', Solzhenitsyn strongly attacked Pomerants, Gorskii, Altaev and another pseudonymous samizdat writer, Sergei Telegin, for failing to respect Russian national and rural traditions and warned of the threats to Russia from too much internationalism.[50] Dostoevskii had suggested that the Russian people were a God-fearing people, and Solzhenitsyn's disputes with Pomerants were in part about the validity of that. However, the two men also seem to have differed in their interpretations of evil. Pomerants later suggested that Solzhenitsyn was attracted to struggling against a mature and well-established evil and had a tendency to associate global evil with communism itself, whereas he believed that in the depths of being itself there was no evil at all, and that, as Lao-Tse suggested, a powerful and well-established evil would soon disappear.[51] Fighting for the good was sometimes counterproductive, Pomerants believed. Commenting on Solzhenitsyn's ethics in another piece, Pomerants observed that 'insisting on good, we constantly sin against the good'.[52]

The two men thus differed on the extent to which it was necessary to actively oppose evil. Solzhenitsyn certainly saw himself as at war with the state. Although a fierce critic of the regime, Pomerants was less drawn to an overt confrontation. Pomerants himself was a religious universalist in the sense that, while his works contained a strong dose of Christianity, his writings contained references to all religious traditions, and he stressed the common foundations of the different faiths. He was also less critical of the Bolshevik Revolution itself. This was evident in a talk he gave at the Institute of Philosophy in December 1965, which was a sustained attack on Stalinism. Referring to the poetry of the dissident writer Naum Korzhavin, he rejected the idea that it was possible to be 'base of heart' and at the same time a contributor to social progress. He defended Marx, Engels and Lenin, by noting that although they had human failings, they were still people. Stalin, whom he described as a 'moral monster', was a different matter. For this, party members who had refused to take Lenin's warnings about Stalin seriously were to blame. In giving meaning only to ideological differences between party members, and ignoring 'petty' moral differences, they had eventually paid with their lives. The country, he argued, was in desperate need of moral improvement, and for that there had to be 'a renaissance of the most elementary virtue – fortitude'.[53]

The view, expressed by Litvinov in *Self-Consciousness*, that Solzhenitsyn lacked a respect for law, was shared by others. Shragin, for example, also complained that in *From under the Rubble* Solzhenitsyn over-emphasised the importance of the spiritual dimension at the expense of legal norms.[54] Certainly, Solzhenitysn disliked the Western human rights tradition, and instead endorsed a more conservative or statist form of liberalism. Stolypin was his model.[55] According to Sakharov, he sought a non-party, rather than a multiparty system.[56] Underlying this, he was opposed to pluralistic views of the world, and there was an overlap in his understandings of justice and conscience. This was evident in a letter to three students in 1967, in which he discussed the nature of conscience. Here he used the word 'conscience' in relation to a personal sense of conscience and to a wider concept of justice. He stated that a sense of justice was inherent in man, and that there was nothing relative about it. He wrote: 'Justice *is* conscience, not a personal conscience, but the conscience of the whole of humanity.' There was a link between the two concepts, he said; people who recognised the voice of their own consciences were generally able to recognise the voice of justice. Moreover he believed that in all social and historical situations, a spiritually-informed justice would find a way to act that was not in conflict with conscience. Solzhenitsyn rejected the idea that each person had a different concept of justice: 'Convictions based on conscience are as infallible as the internal rhythm of the heart.'[57]

Some of the 'legalists' of the human rights movement had a very different view of law from Solzhenitsyn. One of the key promoters of 'law', for example, Valerii Chalidze, had a more sceptical interpretation of human nature. Chalidze, who from 1968 onwards edited the samizdat journal *Social Problems* before he emigrated to the USA in November 1972, emphasised the element of self-interest in society, and believed that individuals had a 'natural subjective right' to manifest their wills.[58] Chalidze's strategy was based on the idea that a bad law was better than no law at all. The emphasis on law, however, he later declared, was not a tactic: 'We were sincere when we called for respect for the Soviet Constitution.'[59] He endorsed Kistyakovskii's point that Russians had failed to distinguish adequately between the norms of law and the norms of ethics. In reply to those who accused him of over-emphasising the legal objectives of his work, he lamented the lack of a legal consciousness in Russia, noting the widespread belief in the country that the emphasis on legality was a 'Western import' which Russians had no need of because of the 'special moral quality of the Russian soul'.[60]

Chalidze's scepticism highlights the fact that not all dissidents were idealists. Pessimism of various kinds was indeed widespread. Eduard Kuznetsov, a Jewish activist who was tried for his role in a plan to hijack a plane and fly to Sweden, wrote in his *Prison Diaries* (1975) that optimists were much more to be feared than sceptics. The optimist was sometimes so certain of his convictions that he would rush to build Utopia in his own lifetime: 'The more convinced and morally justified the monomaniac, the more he reeks of the blood of the innocent.' Kuznetsov was a passionate defender of individual freedom and he used the term 'conscience' in this connection. He described the mature dissident as a person capable of thinking for himself and of listening to the 'voice of conscience'. He was sceptical of the religious aspiration in man; he interpreted the Soviet regime and ideology as 'a mixture of pagan cults' and stated that every religion was characterised by violence at the dawn of its existence. In this connection, he interpreted Soviet ideology as a kind of religion.[61]

Another writer who was impatient with too much optimism was the philosopher Aleksandr Zinoviev. In *The Reality of Communism* (1981), Zinoviev distinguished between ideological and personal morality. He believed that all true morality presupposed personal freedom. However, ideological or collective morality denied it. The advantage of ideological morality was that it released people from 'internal self-restraint', and justified the crimes committed by a country's government. Such a morality was supportive of personal morality, but only to the degree that it presented no danger to the society's foundations and gave its support to them.[62] This hollow communist man was satirised in Zinoviev's *Homo Sovieticus* (1982). 'Homo Sovieticus' or 'Homosos' was described by Zinoviev as a 'new type of man' or 'new being'. He had no moral qualities at all, for he had lost his capacity to have any personal convictions: 'Convictions are something Western man has, not Soviet man.' He said that convictions were simply 'a compensation for not being able to understand a given phenomenon quickly', observing: '[They] merely beautify vanity, relieve unclear consciences and cover up stupidity.'[63] The Homosos's opinions were all 'plastic, supple and adaptive'; bad behaviour by a Homosos was not experienced as bad because it was experienced only as an element in a 'complex whole [block] which doesn't appear bad as a complete entity'.[64]

True morality, according to Zinoviev, lay in the voluntary decisions of individuals to limit themselves. However, self-limitation was rare under communism: 'People are brought up from birth under Communism in such a way that only a few people in their adulthood are capable of being moral beings and even then not all the time.' However, he cited a number of precepts or actions that he considered to be a source of morality:

> Do not coerce anyone and let nobody coerce you. Resist. Do not humble yourself. Do not be a lackey. Pay tribute to those who deserve it. Have nothing to do with bad people. Avoid their company. If there is no need to speak, be silent. Don't draw attention to yourself. Don't thrust yourself on anyone. Refuse undeserved honours. Keep your word. Do not preach at people. Do not gloat over the misfortunes of others. Take no part in power and do not cooperate with it.[65]

Zinoviev combined a universal ethic with radical individualism. His praise for honesty, discretion and unselfish attitudes suggested an older traditional morality. Yet dissent was also clearly encouraged. Zinoviev's moral philosophy was extremely hostile to the state in general, and in this sense it had something in common with the radical liberal traditions of the pre-revolutionary intelligentsia. At the same time, there was none of the 'love of the people' that was so central to populist ethics. The idea that rebellion and morality were connected was to be found in other dissident writers with an individualistic stamp. Brodskii wrote that the surest defence against Evil was 'extreme individualism'.[66] As well as emphasising the primacy of the individual moral conscience, Zinoviev seems to have believed in the existence of corporate moral identities. He stated, for example, that the behaviour of the Soviet Union on the world stage as a 'collective individual' was a classic example of 'immoral behaviour'.[67]

The question of how far it was right to actively oppose the Soviet system was a factor not only in Solzhenitsyn's disagreements with Pomerants, but also in his differences with Sakharov. Sakharov's doubts about the Soviet regime emerged relatively late. He first learned of the crimes of the Stalin period in 1966 through reading extracts of Roy Medvedev's manuscript, *Let History Judge*, and other samizdat texts, and he signed his first letter of protest against the enactment of Article 190–191 in the same year. He then came to prominence in 1968 when he published the essay, 'Progress, Co-Existence and Intellectual Freedom', in which he promoted the idea of the convergence of capitalist and socialist economic systems. Sakharov's father's highest value was 'moderation',[68] and it seems that Sakharov was similar. He was less suspicious of people than Solzhenitsyn. Sakharov regretted the fact that he had attacked Sergei Trapeznikov, head of the Central Committee's science department in his 'Progress' article, and he once said that it was wrong to criticise people for recanting: 'Human nature has its limitations, and there's a tendency to over-estimate one's staying power, particularly in the face of the unexpected.'[69] Solzhenitsyn, on the other hand, believed that Sakharov was naïve about the motives of some of the dissidents, and that he signed appeals and protests too often.[70] He was apparently very pleased when Sakharov joined Turchin and Roy Medvedev in signing a letter to Soviet leaders in 1970 calling for democracy and intellectual freedom, for that meant that he (Sakharov) had entered into clear-cut opposition to the regime. Tensions between the two men were accentuated by the fact that Solzhenitsyn was sceptical about the judgement of Sakharov's second wife, Elena Bonner.[71] There is no doubt that Sakharov had a gentler mentality. Following Solzhenitsyn, Amalrik took the view that Sakharov was a poor tactician. However, he declared that he was a 'great strategist', involving 'an infallible understanding of good and a constant readiness to oppose evil'.[72]

According to Kovalev, Sakharov's essay 'Progress, Coexistence and Intellectual Freedom' moved the debate about human rights out of the purely moral realm into the context of the struggle for the development of humanity as a whole.[73] Sakharov opened the essay by remarking that his views were formed in the 'milieu of the scientific and scientific-technical intelligentsia', and regretting that the scientific method of directing policy had not yet become a reality in the country. According to Sakharov, the scientific method involved 'unprejudiced, unfearing open discussion'. Sakharov also declared that he remained committed to the 'lofty moral ideals of socialism and labour'.[74] In general, Sakharov was committed to science, progress and human rights. Looking at the future of mankind in 1974, he predicted the appearance of flying cities, subterranean cities for sleep, artificial superfertile soil, genetics and selection and universal information systems; at the same time, he declared that mankind would find a 'rational solution' to the problem of realising the goal of human progress 'without losing the humaneness of man and the naturalness of nature'.[75]Although he never lost some of his socialist convictions, Sakharov became less convinced about them over time. He said in an interview of 1973 that he was 'sceptical about socialism in general', and in 1975 that, although 'socialism with a human face' was possible and that it represented a 'high form of social organization', it could only be achieved by 'extraordinary collective efforts'. He also said that the nationalisation of all means of production, the one-party system and the repression of honest convictions should all be avoided or totalitarianism would prevail.[76] Politically, he held to an ideology of human rights that was 'essentially pluralistic'.[77]

Sakharov used the word conscience itself in connection with the struggle for personal liberty as in 'freedom of conscience' and 'prisoners of conscience'.[78] He associated the term 'prisoner of conscience' with Amnesty International,[79] and undoubtedly the widespread use of this phrase in the human rights movement reflected the fact that dissidents borrowed some of their vocabulary from the West.[80] Sakharov also used the word 'conscience' to refer to the mechanism of internal moral judgement or opinion. Writing in September 1975 to the chairman of the Supreme Soviet about the case of Kovalev, he said that Kovalev had been tried for obeying the 'dictates of his conscience'. The dissident strategy, he said in another statement, was based on a 'total, principled, rejection of force or the advocacy of violence'.[81] One of the purposes of political reform in the USSR, he said in *My Country and the World* (1975), was to create a 'moral climate of freedom, happiness and good will'. Its aim was to restore to mankind values that had been lost.[82]

Sakharov appears to have had little interest in metaphysical questions. His world-view did not completely exclude a spiritual dimension, but it was not pronounced. Sakharov observed in his memoirs that while he did not believe in any dogma, he could not imagine a universe without 'a guiding principle', 'a source of spiritual "warmth" which [was] non-material', and that this outlook had something of a religious quality in it.[83] Sakharov signed the Humanist Manifesto that was produced by *The Humanist* magazine in 1973, but stipulated that he did not consider correct from a philosophical and ethical point of view the idea that religion was opposed to either humanism or scientific knowledge.[84] He once said to Tat'yana Khodorovich that he envied the fact she had a religious faith, but that he did not believe himself.[85] Elena Bonner rejected the idea that he was a man with religious convictions.[86]

Although Sakharov became more sceptical about socialism, he never lost his optimism about the possibilities of progress. Socialist optimism was certainly alive elsewhere in certain dissident circles, as the examples of Grigorenko, Kosterin and others indicated. Roy Medvedev was another dissident who remained committed to socialist principles. In *Let History Judge* (1972), the first substantial history of Stalinism to emerge from within the USSR, Medvedev took the view that the criminality of the Soviet system lay not in Leninism, but in Stalin's personality and system of government. In terms of ethics, Medvedev held to a Leninist position. He argued that such things as the shooting of the tsar's family, the sinking of the Black Sea Fleet and the Red Terror were justified, but that such methods were not always permissible and that the party had to decide according to each situation what was the right thing to do. It was Stalin, he believed, whose concept of ends and means had been flawed. He also cited – with evident approval – the views on evil and violence of Raissa Lert. Lert believed that the revolution could not have been accomplished without violence, and that the refusal to resist evil by force could itself help evil to triumph; however, she also said that although this evil was 'temporarily necessary', it was still an evil. She stated: 'In romanticizing violence, we gave it added life, we preserved it even when it became absolutely superfluous, when it became an absolute evil.'[87]

Medvedev's brother, Zhores, whose books on Soviet science were critical of the regime's lack of respect for intellectual freedom, and whose commitment to a mental hospital in 1970 provoked widespread international protest, was also a Marxist; he was impressed by Marxism's 'logic and scientific appeal'.[88] Indeed, Medvedev saw rationality and science as the primary measures of things. In 1971, he declared that independent states should gradually be replaced by 'the particular forms of the scientific organization of society', and suggested that the Second World War had taken place because the world had not been under the 'sum total of scientific intellect'.[89] As regards ethics, he saw things in terms of rationality and irrationality, rather than in terms of good and evil. In his view, 'absurd and irrational situations' arose when the state displayed 'common human vices', or when those vices became inherent in social, national or political groups.[90]

The dissident interest in ethics, and the practices of resistance that were provoked by the Soviet state encouraged a dialogue between different wings of the dissident intelligentsia. In terms of intellectual ferment, it was a productive and interesting exchange. On the other hand, the differences remained, and when a positive programme was called for, they came into the open. Furthermore, as with the nineteenth century, there was sometimes a disengaged feel about the debates. The ideas were the fruit of personal experiences and the discussions of the 'kitchen' rather than engagement with the practicalities of wider social, economic and political life.

8 Conscience in literature

Under Khrushchev, literature played an important role in expanding the boundaries of discussion. Through the works of writers like Dudintsev, Pasternak and Yevtushenko, there emerged an intense discussion about the moral dimensions of Stalinism and of Soviet communism generally. Subsequently, following the fall of Khrushchev, writers continued to play a central role in promoting reform and new ideas. Samizdat culture, and the trials of Brodskii, and Sinyavskii and Daniel, all played a part in shaping the emergence of the human rights movement. Theatre too was at the forefront of the struggle for free expression. Solzhenitsyn was fond of saying that a great writer was like 'a second government'.[1] Certainly, writers and artists were among the Soviet regime's most persistent critics.

The importance of literature was partly due to the fact that people were often isolated from one another. There was great emphasis in Soviet culture on the value of reading. However, people were attracted by reading partly because there were few public outlets for independent expression or debate, and they could at least explore the bigger questions of life by retreating into their books; reading reflected the 'internal emigration' that was a feature of late Soviet life. Authors and their characters became companions to people at a very intimate level. Brodskii commented: 'If we made ethical choices, they were based not so much on immediate reality as on moral standards derived from fiction'; and he suggested that his was 'the only generation of Russians . . . for whom Giotto and Mandelstam were more important than their own ethical choices'.[2] Likewise, the dissident writer and literary critic Grigorii Svirskii stated that his generation 'accepted the thoughts and feelings of Alexander Galich's heroes as their own'.[3]

Nineteenth-century Russian literature played an important role in shaping the moral outlook of the Soviet intelligentsia. The desire of the Stalin regime to identify itself with certain features of tsarism meant that the classics of Russian literature were widely disseminated. Whether this was wise, from the regime's point of view, is another matter. Amalrik argued that it might have been a mistake for the regime not to proscribe the nineteenth-century classics, for it was a literature 'passionate in its defence of the individual against the system'. Indeed Amalrik also suggested that Russian literature was a crucial influence in the rise of the phenomenon of dissidence, and that it played a role in the 'formation of every educated citizen'.[4] Certainly, many of the dissidents cited Russian literature as a central formative influence in their lives. German Andreev, a teacher at Moscow's School Number 2 in the 1960s, stated that he owed a lot to Tolstoi: 'Reading Tolstoi, I understood I was an enemy of that system ... My spiritual conscience [was formed] through Russian literature, but everyday conscience through father and mother.'[5] Yurii Orlov discovered with enthusiasm the works of Lenin and Tolstoi in the year before the war broke out. Over time his admiration for Lenin waned, but Tolstoi remained the 'love of [his] life'. He particularly liked the novel *Resurrection* and recalled that the teachings of Tolstoi about moral perfection and resurrection 'became part of [his] soul'.[6]

Even more than Tolstoi, Dostoevskii was a formative influence. Pomerants stated that Dostoevskii was his 'companion' (*sputnik*) over fifty years, and that Dostoevskii helped him to understand himself.[7] Gennadii Shimanov recalled that Dostoevskii became his spiritual guide while he was in the army: 'Like Dante's Virgil, he took me by the hand and descended with me into the hell of my own soul, and showed these endless circles, these senseless circles of life.'[8] The film director Andrei Tarkovskii suggested that the contradictory beliefs of Shatov in Dostoevskii's *The Devils* were an excellent illustration of the confused state of soul that was typical of modern man.[9] For these men, and many others, Dostoevskii's works were a repository of spiritual knowledge. Not everyone took this view. The novelist Vasilii Grossman thought Dostoevskii's mysticism was Byzantine in origin; it emphasised asceticism, negation of self, and withdrawal from the world, and he compared Dostoevskii's mentality with Lenin's.[10]

Sometimes writers became moral guides in a very personal way. Natal'ya Bolshakova, who wrote a dissertation on Chekhov at the Gor'kii Literary Institute of the Union of Writers in Moscow in the late 1970s, soon found that she was measuring her actions by what she believed Chekhov would have done. Tempted on one occasion to boast about something, she saw in her mind's eye a humorous expression on Chekhov's face saying that this was an ugly and indecent thing to do, and she desisted. More generally, she recalled, she was 'morally formed' by literature, particularly Russian literature, and that as a lonely child she found her 'companions' (*blizkikh*) there.[11]

As sources of inspiration, literary and political culture often overlapped. Pushkin's poem, 'From Piedmont' (1836), was an inspiration for those committed to human rights; Sergei Kovalev considered it one of the most remarkable human rights texts of the nineteenth century, and it was one of Sakharov's favourite poems.[12] Nina Komarova included in one of her letters to her husband in prison a poem by Marina Volkhonskaya, the wife of one of the Decembrists who had gone with her husband to Siberia.[13]

European culture as well as Russian literature was influential. Tarkovskii grew up in a household where Russian classics and albums of paintings by Leonardo and Michelangelo were available.[14] It was clearly not just potential dissident intellectuals who drew upon these resources. Aleksandr Yakovlev paid tribute to the 'whole richness of Western literature' and the 'powerful humanistic appeal of the Russian classics' that he absorbed in his youth.[15] Shevardnadze was stirred in his youth by a television production of Dickens's *David Copperfield*.[16] For gaining access to Russian and European literature, personal libraries were very important; indeed, they began to grow from the 1950s onwards.[17] Sakharov, who grew up in a Moscow apartment, recalled that every family in his house had a library – 'mainly of pre-revolutionary editions passed from generation to generation'; indeed, his own reading when he was young was remarkable for its variety.[18] At a later period, the defector to Britain Oleg Gordievskii built up a substantial personal library of dissident books published abroad, many of which he bought while he was stationed in Denmark.[19]

It seems that people were sometimes politicised by the process of reading itself. The future librarian at the Memorial Society, Boris Belenken, read Grossman's *Forever Flowing* in a type-written copy in the early 1970s. It was a difficult book to get hold of, and it affected his life. He recalled: 'Reading that book, one could say that I finally became an anti-Soviet element.'[20] However, it was not just the content of the books that was important; the way that books were read was sometimes influential too. By its very nature, reading samizdat consolidated a sense of opposition in people. Samizdat was passed around from individual to individual, but it was also consumed in larger groups. Tat'yana Velikanova recalled reading Solzhenitsyn's *Cancer Ward* in a room with a large number of people, reading each page separately and passing it on to the next person.[21] In this way, the reading of forbidden literature reinforced the sense of being part of a wider dissident collective. A positivist circle of the 1960s and 1970s was described as having the 'pathos of a religious order'[22]; samizdat networks were sometimes productive of the same mentality.

This sense of being part of an oppositional community was accentuated by the fact that samizdat spawned its own code-words and anecdotes. As Ludmilla Alekseeva noted, questions like, 'Have you finished the pie my wife gave you last night?', were in fact references to subversive literature.[23] Also, through samizdat networks, books sometimes linked reform-minded people across wide geographical areas. Natal'ya Eksler recalled that her family copy of the *Gulag Archipelago*, a gift from Amalrik in 1976, was taken to so many places that it was at different times reported to be in the Urals, the Baltic and the Ukraine. In the Baltic, there were so many people wishing to read it that a 'queue for the Book' was created.[24]

Many of the great writers of the early Soviet period were potentially subversive. For example, the poets Pasternak, Akhmatova and Osip Mandelstam were certainly advocates of non-communist values. However, as Sinyavskii observed, it would be wrong to classify these figures as dissidents because, although they were an inspiration for later dissident intellectuals, they were culturally formed in the pre-revolutionary era, whereas the dissidents were Soviet by mentality.[25] Another poet of that generation, Marina Tsvetaeva, in her short poem 'Hamlet's dialogue with conscience' (1923), depicted Hamlet wrestling with himself as to whether or not he really loved Ophelia.[26] Ultimately, Tsvetaeva and these other poets could not endorse the Soviet ideological vision because they saw the individual as a complex emotional and spiritual being.

Prose writers like Babel, Bulgakov, Zoshchenko, Yurii Olesha and Andrei Platonov were also sources of ideas that were dangerous to the state.[27] Admittedly the works of some of these authors were hard to get hold of, if they were officially published at all. However, their existence was indicative of a strand of twentieth-century literature that linked the nineteenth-century classics with the dissident generation. Bulgakov's *Master and Margerita*, which was published in restricted editions mainly for the foreign market, acquired cult status in the late Soviet era. Leonid Batkin, a prominent member of the democratic movement in the 1980s, recalled that Bulgakov's novel had an important impact on the mentality of people:

> The novel, pushing itself into reality like a peculiar wedge, and becoming a kind of part of it and within it one of the few permitted points of support, made existence somehow freer and more tolerable. Quotations from *The Master and Margerita* became signs of an innocent opposition.[28]

However, unlike Dostoevskii and Tolstoi, who in their ways suggested that the universe was built on a stable moral order, Bulgakov's vision was more ambiguous. *The Master and Margerita* depicted a world that was disintegrating. Bulgakov's account of the visit of a professor of black magic, Woland, to Moscow in the 1930s, pointed to a divided moral universe. At the beginning of the novel, the lines from Goethe's *Faust* were quoted in which Lucifer was described as 'That Power . . . / Which wills forever evil / Yet does forever good'.[29] In Bulgakov's world, there was a sense that people had become pawns in the hands of demonic powers. Woland plays chess against his cat, Behemoth, with live pieces, and at the end of the game the pieces run back into their box.[30] It was of course satire, but it contained a more pessimistic note.

Andrei Platonov was also pessimistic. In particular, his satire on collectivisation, *The Foundation Pit* (*Kotlovan*), which was written in the early 1930s and circulated in samizdat before it was first published abroad in 1973, was very influential in dissident circles. The novel was jointly about the disintegration of humanity and language. Platonov showed how words were used to distance people from reality. For example, the character Chiklin, after murdering someone, is reassured by another character: 'Don't worry, comrade Chiklin. It isn't you, it's that sledgehammer fist of yours.'[31] In Brodskii's words,

> Platonov speaks of a nation which in a sense has become the victim of its own language; or, to put it more accurately, he tells the story about this very language, which turns out to be capable of generating a fictitious world, and then falls into grammatical dependence on it.[32]

Platonov was worried that mankind was losing its spiritual direction. The narrator of his story, 'The Seventh Man', first published in 1966, declared: 'In our time wrongdoing can appear inspired and righteous', and 'Violence has instilled wickedness in man and squeezed out of him his ancient, sacred essence.'[33]

It was not just subversive writers who were interested in morality; ethical issues were also of great interest to most authors who were either approved of or tolerated by the authorities. This is not surprising. Socialist realism was itself a highly moral literary tradition. Moral seriousness, or 'civic-mindedness', as a particular feature of Russian culture,[34] was thus very much present in both establishment and dissident writers alike. In any case, it would be a mistake to divide all writers clearly into pro- or anti-Soviet categories. Writers whose work was published in the USSR in fact represented a variety of opinions and genres. Even those who adopted the standard features of socialist realism could sometimes use them to get round the censors and make relatively strong criticisms of state and society.[35] Official and dissident writers alike were constantly exploring moral issues. The ethical concerns of writers was well encapsulated by Mikhail Epstein in a 'periodic table' of Russian literature, in which he suggested that the predominant values of Russian literature between 1920 and 1990 were: 'Socialist sentimentalism. Sincerity. Confessional prose. The poetry of the bared "I". The freshness of feelings. Self-expression. "We aren't screws." Moral searching. "To live not by lies." Conscience. Guilt. Repentance.'[36]

Dudintsev's *Not by Bread Alone* was a good example of the way in which socialist realism could be used to criticise the regime itself. Another such work was Leonid Leonov's novel, *The Russian Forest* (1953). Leonov's work has been described as the 'art of compromise', and indeed in 1949 he wrote an article for Stalin's seventieth birthday in which he said that he could foresee a time when Stalin's birthday would be celebrated worldwide as a 'day of gratitude'. *The Russian Forest*, however, while formally written within the socialist realist framework, was in fact very critical of the values of the regime. The novel revolves around a dispute between two forestry specialists: Vikhrov, a defender of Russia's forests who represents the author's voice in the story; and Gratsyanskii, an opportunist figure who is willing to exploit the forests, and whose general cynicism suggests the attitudes of corrupt party officials.[37] Vikhrov advocates a universal morality and condemns revolutionary ethics. He is not satisfied with materialism alone: 'In [Vikhrov's] conviction, the October Revolution had been a battle not only for a fair distribution of material values, but perhaps, first and foremost, for the purity of human values.' He is very opposed to the doctrine that the end justifies the means. Gratsyanskii states that it is wrong to stand by and wait for social improvements to be brought about peacefully, and that 'every sacred cause is sealed by the blood of martyrs'; Vikhrov, on the other hand, considers this 'satanic' argument to be the 'lowest depth of depravity'. Furthermore, Vikhrov is described as a free-thinking person – a 'man with an extraordinary capacity for independent thought'.[38] Outwardly committed to Soviet communism, Leonov's hero believes in universal values and freedom of thought, and also has a respect for nature.

The Russian Forest was important because it reflected an emerging interest in the Russian countryside. Rural life and values were to become a central interest of late Soviet prose. Writers of 'village prose', as it came to be known, generally portrayed collectivisation and modernisation in negative terms, and suggested that respect for the Russian people, and a sense of closeness to nature had been lost. Aleksandr Yashin's 'The Levers' (1956), which appeared in *Literary Moscow* in 1956, was another early expression of the genre. According to one writer, 'The Levers' caused an impression like an 'exploding bomb' when it came out.[39] The story opened with a small group of peasants discussing their lives on a deprived and corrupt collective farm. One of the peasants states that it is necessary to trust peasants, for they have minds of their own; another that it is necessary to listen to them. The story ends with the statement that the peasants are 'people, and not levers'.[40] The message is clear: the peasants are themselves a repository of Russian values, and should not be treated as means to ends. Yashin himself was very interested in 'conscience'. In his collection of verse, *Conscience* (1961), he linked honour, conscience and happiness: 'Live honourably (*po chesti*), / In agreement with conscience!. . . – / [Mother] wanted her son to be happy. . .'[41]

Fedor Abramov, Viktor Astaf'ev, Vasilii Belov, Valentin Rasputin, Vladimir Tendryakov, Vasilii Shukshin, and Sergei Zalygin were among those who wrote important works about life in the village. These writers had diverse perspectives on morality and conscience. Vladimir Tendryakov, for example, had an objectivist moral vision that was akin to Tolstoi's. His novella *The Trial*, published in *Novyi mir* in 1961, is a good example of this. Tendryakov described a bear-hunt in the northern forests of Russia that concludes with the accidental and fatal shooting of a young man as well as a bear. The chief hunter Semyon Teterin discovers that the boss of a local construction combine, Dudyrev, fired the fatal bullet, rather than the initial suspect, a young medical orderly, named Mityagin. However, at the trial Teterin retracts the evidence to protect Dudyrev; and Dudyrev and Mityagin are jointly found guilty and released. The novella concludes with the line, 'Trial by one's own conscience is the harshest trial of all'; and indeed the exterior events of the novella run parallel to a deeper moral narrative. Teterin's failure to tell the full truth at the trial is presented as a serious moral defeat from which his character suffers.[42] Similarly Dudyrev, who himself suffers pangs of conscience over the whole affair, is shown to be a flawed character who uses the idea that both he and Mityagin are to blame as a way of avoiding the truth. The final message of the novella, as one critic observes, is that actions should be governed by absolute moral values, and that conscience and truth are 'objective and pre-eminent categories'.[43] At the same time, the personal moral trial of these men is also accompanied by a broader social one; the worlds that these two men represent are also on trial. The traditional village, associated with Teterin, is shown to be powerless in the face of industrialisation, while the machines at Dudyrev's construction combine are compared to 'iron-limbed monsters', and his construction combines disturb the 'the inborn peace of a man accustomed to the forest'.[44]

If Tendryakov saw things in terms of a universal moral law, Valentin Rasputin linked morality to nation, family and nature. Rasputin's acclaimed novel, *Farewell to Matyora* (1976), was about a Siberian village named Matyora that was doomed to disappear with the building of a new reservoir. The novel promotes a version of *pochvennichestvo*; the heroine, Darya, espouses an ethic that combines traditional Christian values with a respect for the soul and for ancestors. Darya laments the passing of the old rural culture, and the disappearance of what she calls 'conscience'. Darya notes that 'in the old days conscience was very important', and recalls that her father believed that the most important thing in life was 'to have a conscience and not to be bothered by it'. In the past, she said, you could see if anyone tried to live without conscience: 'Those who had it were conscientious, those without it were conscienceless. And now only the devil can tell, everything is mixed up in one pile.' Now, she suggests, conscience was 'not for asking questions of', but something that was 'just for show'; 'our conscience is getting old, it's an old woman, and no one looks at it anymore'.[45] For Darya, the disappearance of the village is tragic because she can no longer be buried alongside her father and mother. She says to her dead father: 'I'll have to die away from Matyora. I won't lie with you, it won't work . . . Don't be mad at me, it's not my fault. I am guilty, I am. I'm guilty because it fell on me.' Furthermore, she imagines that after death her forebears will judge her harshly for what she has done.[46] Darya laments the loss of Matyora because it means the loss of a connection with the past and her memory of it. The narrator here observes: 'Truth is in memory. The person without memory is without life.' There is here an implicitly patriotic emphasis. The tragedy of modernisation, according to *Farewell to Matyora*, is that it detaches people from their national traditions. Conscience, patriotism and environmental values are thus brought together.

References to 'conscience' did not imply religious conviction. Olesha, one of the chief characters in Vasilii Belov's 'Carpenter Yarns', an older man with 'calm and wise' eyes, states that he has stopped going to the priest to repent because 'there's no priest sterner than your own conscience'.[47] This is a humanist, peasant conscience. There was, however, an increasing interest in religious values among Soviet writers. This was expressed in Vasilii Shukshin's story, 'I Believe' (1971). The story focussed on the meeting between an unhappy man, Maksim, who wants to know why his soul is aching, and a priest with an unorthodox philosophy of life. The priest is not a religious believer in a conventional sense; he drinks heavily, believes in 'Life', and advocates a philosophy that embraces both good and evil. The story concludes with a frenzied, pagan dance of celebration by Maksim and the priest.[48] The priest's philosophy is not Christian, but a kind of 'Manichaean pantheism'. Possibly the priest is a satire on contemporary spirituality; indeed, unorthodox spiritualities flourished in the late Soviet period. At the same time, there might have been something of Shukshin's own outlook reflected in it.[49]

Moral issues were also central in the writings of Yurii Trifonov, an exponent of the 'urban prose' tradition who was very skilled at dissecting the moral compromises of daily Soviet life. According to two critics, his particular interest lay in 'examining the precise moment when a man takes a wrong turn in life, the moment of moral betrayal'.[50] His *The House on the Embankment* (1976) was very daring for its time, and it was remarkable that it passed the censor. The novel examines the conformist ethics of a respectable and well-to-do academic, Vadim Glebov. In 1948, Glebov gets drawn into a politically motivated attack on his supervisor, Professor Nikolai Ganchuk, with whose daughter, Sonia, Glebov is romantically involved. Following a public examination of the case, Ganchuk is removed from his post for ideological deficiencies, and Glebov's affair with Sonia collapses. Glebov is not pro-actively evil. Rather, he is a bystander. A man who will not confront issues directly, he does not openly support the attack on Ganchuk. Comparing Glebov to a knight at a crossroads in a fairy story, the narrator declares:

> Glebov belonged to a special breed of knight; he was prepared to hang around at the crossroads until the last possible moment, until that final split second . . . He was a knight who could temporise . . . ; one of those who never decided anything for themselves but leave the decisions to their horse.

Furthermore, the narrator suggests that Glebov's actions are rooted in unrecognised fears that are representative of the wider population: 'We see

[here] the bone-structure of our deeds, their skeletal pattern – and it is a pattern of *fear*.' To use one of Trifonov's central images, Glebov swims with the current; Glebov reflects that 'to try to save [Ganchuk] was like swimming against the current in a flood that carried everything before it'. The outcome of Glebov's moral weakness is in his own character. Years later, his memory does not function properly; he finds it painful to recall what really happened with Ganchuk and Sonia. Trying to recall a meeting where he had witnessed attacks on Ganchuk, the reader is told: 'Maybe it wasn't quite like that, because he was trying to forget it. Whatever one ceased to remember ceased to exist.' One of the novel's wider messages is that crossing moral boundaries can be dangerous. Ganchuk says: 'Today's Raskolnikovs did not murder old women moneylenders with an axe, but they were faced with the same agonising choice: to cross or not to cross the line.'[51]

Trifonov was a very popular writer, but also a pessimistic one. Shragin compared him to Yulii Daniel. Daniel was a unique figure, according to Shragin, because he was not taken over by the 'mutual bitterness' at everything which conceals an 'unclean conscience'. Trifonov's moral vision, he suggested, was like Daniel's, but his heroes were weaker than his and perhaps for this reason he had a wider readership: 'In Trifonov, people lost themselves; in Daniel, they were still trying to find themselves.'[52]

The literary emphasis on conscience and morality was reinforced by the writings of Solzhenitsyn. Solzhenitsyn saw the role of the artist in ethical terms. In his Nobel Prize lecture, 'One Word of Truth' (1970), he declared that the role of the arts was to give the human race a single system of evaluation for good and evil deeds. Art enabled people to appreciate the lives of others, and it facilitated the transfer of experience from one nation to another to the extent that it could sometimes prevent countries from taking the wrong path: 'Art can somewhat straighten the twisted paths of man's history.' Solzhenitsyn's vision for the artist was a religious one in that he presented the true artist as 'a common apprentice under God's heaven' rather than as a 'creator of an independent spiritual world'.[53]

Solzhenitsyn was not alone in stressing the ethical and prophetic calling of the writer or artist. Tarkovskii, who died in the West in 1986, had a similar view of art. In his posthumously published, *Sculpting in Time*, Tarkovskii attacked modern art for assuming that any personalised action was of intrinsic value simply as a display of self-will. Instead, he argued that a 'true affirmation of self' could only be expressed in 'sacrifice'.[54] 'The artist', he wrote, 'is always a servant', and art had the capacity to give expression to the spiritual dimension of things: 'The idea of infinity cannot be expressed in words or even described, but it can be apprehended through art, which makes infinity tangible.' He stated that the aim of art was 'to prepare a person for death, to plough and harrow his soul, rendering it capable of turning to good'.[55]

Solzhenitsyn and Tarkovskii believed that the purpose of the artist was to inculcate the deepest moral and spiritual truths. Their vision of the arts sat more easily with the Victorian novel, or with the artistic vision of Dante and Milton, than with twentieth-century modernism. It was alien to the scepticism of the twentieth-century West. Not all Russians shared it either. In her essay, *Art in the Light of Conscience*, Marina Tsvetaeva suggested that conscience and artistry were not compatible.[56] Solzhenitsyn, Tarkovskii and many of their contemporaries took the view that artistic and moral truth could be combined.

Solzhenitsyn's own stories and novels reflected his ideas about the moral purposes of literature. For example, his story, 'Matryona's House' (1962) was a portrait of a selfless but ordinary peasant woman who represented the best of traditional Russian rural values. At one level, the story was a eulogy to a lost, pre-modern Russian past that belonged in the genre of village prose. At the same time, Matryona's kindness was not presented as typical of the Russian countryside. She stands out from her peers as a moral example; she is, the narrator says, one of those people 'without whom ... no village can stand'. The narrator draws attention to her face, noting that 'people who are at ease with their consciences always have nice faces'.[57] It is thus also a tale about individual moral virtue. It was certainly very influential; Pomerants wrote in samizdat that 'for a million people Christianity began with reading "Matryona's House"'.[58] Yet the religious message was not doctrinal. Solzhenitsyn's literary work was more phenomenological and experiential than theological in character.[59]

Solzhenitsyn's *The First Circle*, which was completed in 1958 but did not appear until it was published abroad a decade later, had a definite educative function. The title of the novel, which was deliberately suggestive of the first circle of Dante's *Inferno*, was indicative of its moral purposes. As with Dante's poem, *The First Circle* was essentially concerned with the moral nature of man. The novel was a portrait of life at Mavrino, a fictional research institute that was formally part of the labour camp network but where the conditions were generally good. To a considerable extent, the characters of the novel were vehicles for moral ideas. Furthermore, they were designed to be typical. According to Leona Toker, they were 'metafictional' to the extent that they replicated ordinary Soviet attitudes.[60] There were also autobiographical elements in the novel. The hero of the novel, Nerzhin, had much in common with Solzhenitsyn himself. Nerzhin found that imprisonment had helped him to reach a higher, spiritual state; he had come to know that 'only character mattered', and that this was something that everybody had to forge for himself, by constant effort over the years.[61] The novel propagated a spirituality that was similar to that of *The Gulag Archipelago*; both works emphasised the value of spiritual and sometimes material poverty, suggesting a kind of 'non-possessor' spirituality. The narrator concluded the novel with a description of a group of inmates being driven away, observing: 'They were at peace with themselves. They were as fearless as men who have lost everything they ever had – a fearlessness hard to attain but enduring once it is reached.'[62]

It has been noted that the socialist realist novel was a kind of *Bildungsroman* in the sense that its main concern was the formation of character.[63] *The First Circle* was similar. The reader is introduced to the moral consequences of certain kinds of behaviour. Volodin, an official in the Ministry of Foreign Affairs who on a whim warns an old friend that he is about to be arrested, is himself arrested and sentenced to a term in the camps. However, although he 'loses' in a material sense, Volodin is enhanced spiritually. A new moral consciousness is awakened in him: 'Now there matured in him the sense of another truth about himself and the world: that we only have one conscience – and that a crippled conscience is as irretrievable as a lost life.'[64]

Volodin makes the right choice, and the true meaning of life opens itself up to him as a result. However, other figures in the novel are unable to see that truth. The head of research at Mavrino, Yakonov, is locked into a career of compromise following an occasion when he signed an article about the rottenness of Western society that 'wasn't exactly the whole truth', but 'wasn't exactly a lie'. Galakhov, a writer who follows the party line, finds that his work has become 'safe', and that his work is always constructed with the views of the chief reviewer in mind.[65] Yakonov and Galakhov have good careers, but no spiritual life. In this, they are fictional illustrations of a point that Solzhenitsyn made in *The Gulag Archipelago*: 'Only those who decline to scramble up the career ladder are interesting as human beings. Nothing is more boring than a man with a career.'[66] By contrasting the ideas and fate of Nerzhin and Volodin, on the one hand, and Yakonov and Galakhov, on the other, the novel gives moral and spiritual instruction about how readers should approach the crucial moral decisions of their lives.

Grossman's novels also portrayed the consequences of different moral choices. *Life and Fate*, which was originally completed in 1960, but only appeared in a complete version in 1980 long after the author's death in 1964, is renowned for its rich account of Soviet life during the Second World War; however, it was also a novel concerned with the nature of conscience. Of particular interest in this respect were Grossman's descriptions of Viktor Shturm, physicist and member of the Academy of Sciences. One day an article is posted on Shturm's institute notice-board which is critical of those who lack faith in 'Russian science', and implicitly of Shturm himself, who is Jewish. Pressure is put on Shturm to write a letter of repentance, in which he acknowledges the errors of his research. Some of this pressure comes from his colleagues; however, much of it comes from 'an invisible force' and 'hypnotic power' coming from inside himself. Shturm risks his career and all his worldly security and decides not to write a letter of repentance. The effect of this decision on his soul is very strong:

> He felt a sense of lightness and purity. He felt calm and thoughtful. He didn't believe in God, but somehow it was as though God were

> looking at him. Never in his life had he felt such happiness, such humility. Nothing on earth could take away his sense of rightness now.[67]

However, Shturm's new moral strength becomes tangled up in his personal life. He gets drawn into an internal debate about whether or not he should keep a relationship going with a woman, Maria Ivanovna Sokolov, who is not his wife. His emotions override his judgement, and he cannot be honest with himself about the situation. His inability to break out of this circle of confusion then undermines the robustness of his former convictions about not signing the letter. When he is subsequently asked at work to sign a letter from prominent Soviet scientists refuting some accusations that have been made by the *New York Times* against the Soviet government, he finds himself overwhelmed by a sense of impotence and fear, and he signs the letter. His sense of inner freedom and lightness disappear completely:

> His friendship with Chepyzhin, his affection for his daughter, his devotion to his wife, his hopeless love for Maria Ivanovna, his human sins and his human happiness, his work, his beloved science, his love for his mother, his grief for her – everything had vanished away.[68]

As in *The First Circle*, there was an autobiographical element in *Life and Fate*; Grossman himself had signed a letter demanding retribution for the Jewish doctors who were accused in 1952 of involvement in the Doctor's Plot. However, as well as the autobiographical element, Grossman's descriptions of the moral consequences of compromise with Stalinism were such as at least to suggest an awareness of the Orthodox and wider Christian mystical tradition; right moral choices bring light and religious belief into the soul; a refusal to let go of sinful attachments leads on the contrary to moral confusion and instability.

Grossman's *Forever Flowing*, which was completed in 1963 and first published in full by the *émigré* Posev Press in 1974, was also concerned with spiritual issues.[69] It recounts the return to Moscow of a man named Ivan Grigorevich after thirty years in the labour camps. Ivan Grigorevich goes to visit his cousin, Nikolai Andreevich, who has been silent about his cousin's fate and in the meantime has become a famous research scientist in an important academic institute. Initially, Nikolai Andreevich is drawn to repent of his comfortable life while his cousin suffered. The reader is told that, while waiting for Ivan to come and visit, Nikolai considered how 'totally honest' he would be with him, and how he would 'confess to Ivan all his pangs of conscience, set forth abruptly all his vile and bitter weakness'. However, when the cousins meet face to face, all Nikolai's regret and sadness about those who disappeared during the purges vanishes: it becomes 'utterly essential to rid himself of, to repress in himself . . . his bad conscience, his sense of the illegitimacy of the miraculous thing that had happened to him'. In the end he does not wish to 'confess and repent', but only 'to justify and brag'.[70] Grossman thus presents the picture of a man who has lost the capacity to repent; Nikolai Andreevich's conscience, though not absolutely corrupted, cannot function in the right way.

The consequences of moral choices are also examined in Vladimir Maksimov's novel *The Seven Days of Creation*, published in 1971 by Posev Press. The fate of two characters in the novel illustrates some of the moral purposes of the book. In the first and last sections of the novel, Maksimov describes the changing attitudes of Petr Lashkov, a veteran party official living in a town called Uzlovsk. Through a series of minor events, Lashkov is brought to a new level of self-understanding; he comes to appreciate why his life has lacked a real connection with the people around him. Of his family and neighbours he says to himself: 'Instead of going out to them, I always cut myself off. They got no light nor warmth from me, nor did anybody else ... I must begin all over again.' This new beginning eventually leads him to some kind of religious conviction and an affirmation of life.[71] Whereas Lashkov is becoming newly aware of the world around him, the spirit of his son, Vasilii, is changed by a terrible compromise. Vasilii, who lives in Moscow, falls in love with a neighbour, Grusha, but then spurns her because the arrest of her brother makes her a dangerous person to know. The local plumber takes his place in Grusha's life. The consequences for Vasilii's character are devastating. When he parts with Grusha he feels 'some part of himself closing off' and, subsequently, a feeling of 'major, irreparable loss'. Vasilii's spirit is deadened by choosing security over love. As with so many other Russian writers, the themes of moral responsibility, self-giving and self-overcoming are central to Maksimov's vision. A Jewish theatre director, Mark Kreps says to Lashkov's actor-grandson, Vadim, that 'for as long as you are capable of feeling personal guilt toward other people, no one can turn you into a pig'; 'the aim of art ... is to give yourself, not to assert yourself'; 'you want to have your revelations for nothing, but they have to be paid for, often with everything you have'.[72]

How to respond to interrogation was a central theme in another important dissident novel, Yurii Dombrovskii's *The Faculty of Useless Knowledge*, which was published by the YMCA Press in Paris in 1978. *The Faculty of Useless Knowledge* is a novel on the grand scale, comparable in intent to some of Dostoevskii's works. Set in 1937 in Alma-Ata, the novel is built around the arrest and interrogation of an archaeologist from the local museum, Georgii Zybin. Determined to hold on to his peace of mind, and not to allow the regime any psychological hold on his character, Zybin declares to his cell-mate: 'I'll be able to live at peace with myself, not frightened that I've left something in their hands that could at any moment catch me in a steel trap like a rat.'[73] Zybin survives his interrogations without making any false confessions. His fate is contrasted with that of his assistant, Vladimir Kornilov. Kornilov initially believes that he can outwit the NKVD, and he agrees to inform on a priest, Father Andrei, purely to establish Father Andrei's innocence. However, he is drawn into the NKVD's web to the point that he eventually agrees to inform on Zybin. He is a weak rather than a malicious man, who becomes so morally adrift that the narrator says at one point that 'he was already a dead man and saw as a dead man'.[74]

Spiritual life and death are thus central themes of the novel. Zybin, in conversation with the young interrogator, Tamara Dolidze, suggests that some of the investigators have lost their humanity altogether: 'They're not even existence. They're a kind of non-life.'[75] Also, the difference between real and artificial behaviour is explored. The local NKVD chief Yakov Neiman, it is noted, has lost the capacity to know whether his actions are real or not. In commenting on an outburst of anger by Neiman, the narrator states:

> Whether this feeling of instantaneous lashing fury was genuine, or whether he had invented and nurtured it – i.e. whether it was a feeling at all, or some sort of professional adaptation, essential to him in his work – Neiman had never considered and consequently did not know one way or the other.[76]

While the novel warns of the possibilities of spiritual death, it also holds out the possibility of change and even redemption; Dolidze comes to understand the deadly nature of what she is doing; and Neiman also comes to address his spiritual emptiness.[77]

Conscience itself is discussed in the novel. One of Zybin's cell-mates, Georgii Kalandarashvili, a Georgian veteran of the labour camps, asks Zybin: 'What sort of concept is [conscience] anyway? It's virtually Pilate's question: "What is truth?"'. Kalandarashvili is strongly committed to the idea of conscience. He distinguishes at one point between a human and a wolf's conscience. He also notes that people have their own models of conscience, and that some people have a 'demarcation line' in their brains that keeps out morally uncomfortably information.[78]

The novels, then, of Solzhenitsyn, Grossman, Maksimov and Dombrovskii, were partly a literary attempt to explore the phenomenology of conscience, and the nature of spiritual life and death. The reader was presented with the contrasting consequences of different moral choices. In this sense, the works had a specific educative intent; they were training manuals of conscience. They also reflected the importance of the idea of moral law in dissident literature. Peter Doyle notes that Dombrovskii's ethical outlook, like Solzhenitsyn's, was not only liberal humanist, but also 'ethically and philosophically absolutist'.[79] This could be said about all these writers; they all interpreted the mechanism of conscience in the light of a perceived universal moral or natural law. There was something in common here with the socialist realist tradition in the sense that character formation was a central concern. However, the context was of course different; the Soviet project was now the enemy rather than the friend of conscience.

Religious motifs were clearly important in the works of Solzhenitsyn, Dombrovskii and Maksimov. Another writer with similar concerns was Leonid Borodin. Borodin had been a member of the All-Russian Social-Christian Union, and then spent six years in strict regime camps from 1967 until 1973. In his novel *The Third Truth* (1982), Borodin tried to show how suffering could be redemptive. The novel conveyed the idea that there was a religious alternative to the ideologies of the Reds and the Whites. One of the heroes of the novel, the Siberian ranger Ivan Ryabinin, who is sent to the camps for twenty-five years for no particular reason, discovers a faith in God in the camps. He finds that in confinement 'his soul started to be born anew'; he discovers the truth (*istina*) conveyed by people who are in touch with 'another world'; and he learns how to forgive people and finds that the experience of forgiving brings light into his soul, leading to the attainment of a 'new state of still and joyful peace'. Ryabinin's friend Selivanov has a different fate. A wicked person who has killed people, he stays behind while Ryabinin suffers. On Ryabinin's return, he asks himself why God allowed Ryabinin, an innocent religious man, to suffer while he remained free. Following Ryabinin's death, he addresses him in his mind: 'Now I understand why life turned out like it did for you ... It's you who have taken all my sins on yourself ... paid for them ... and died in my place before your time.'[80] The idea that the innocent take upon themselves the sins of the guilty clearly had roots in Christian theology; however, the emphasis on sacrifice and expiation clearly also reflected currents of thought that existed in both religious and secular dissident thinking.

Hope of redemption was not universal. A more pessimistic vision can be found in Georgii Vladimov's novel, *Faithful Ruslan*, which was circulated in samizdat before it was published in the *émigré* journal *Grani* in 1975. Vladimov worked as an editor at *Novyi mir* from 1956 to 1959. He became chairman of the Soviet Amnesty group after Turchin left for the West in October 1977, and later emigrated to West Germany in 1983. *Faithful Ruslan* was the story of a labour camp guard dog that loyally served the authorities and was disoriented by the disbandment of the camps in the mid-1950s. The dog is presented sympathetically: he is faithful to his master; and he bears no grudge against camp inmates, even if he is very aggressive. Yet his outlook is a dependent one in that his master decides what is good and evil.[81] Furthermore, his purpose in life is simply to enforce the rules: 'His tragedy is that, with his strongly ingrained sense of "service", and with his native bravery, vigor, and intelligence, he has not been trained for anything constructive.'[82] After the camp is disbanded, Ruslan continually laments the passing of his days of service, because he then had a sense of belonging and purpose; he finds it hard to adapt to a freer climate. The root of Ruslan's tragedy, however, lies in the fact that he does not understand the true nature of the system. His Instructor observes one day that the weakness of one of his fellow dogs is that he believes that the system is infallible; and he says to Ruslan: 'If you want to survive, understand this: look on the whole business as a game. You're too serious.'[83]

Writers frequently raised ethical issues in relation to other worlds or futuristic scenarios. In Chingiz Aitmatov's novel, *The Day Lasts More than a Hundred Years* (1980), two cosmonauts respond to a signal from an extraterrestrial civilisation. Without consulting their bosses, they choose to act as representatives of all mankind, in accordance with their own 'convictions and conscience'.[84] The episode conveys the idea that to follow personal conviction, even at the risk of public censure, is a good and brave thing to do. In Vladimir Savchenko's science fiction novel, *Self-Discovery* (1979), conscience comes up in relation to the theme of identity. One of the main characters in the novel sees a man approaching him along a pavement, only to discover that it is not a man at all, but 'a living pang of his conscience coming toward him on that street'.[85] In Tarkovskii's space odyssey, *Solaris* (1972), which was based on a science fiction novel by Stanislaw Lem, the hero Chris Kelvin meets his own conscience in a different way. Confronted with the apparition of an old girlfriend, Hari, whom he had treated badly, he is forced to re-examine his own past behaviour. Hari, in conversation with Chris and his fellow space scientists, says of herself: 'We are you, yourselves; your own conscience.'[86]

Issues of conscience were very important to Tarkovskii. In *Sculpting in Time*, he wrote that freedom was inseparable from conscience, and that conscience was an '*a priori* immanent in man' even though its manifestations were often at variance with the demands of biological evolution or the material interests of man.[87] His film *Stalker* (1979) was another work that explored issues of conscience. In the film, a professor and a writer are taken by a guide (known as a stalker) on a journey of self-discovery to a place known as 'the zone', where it is said that people's dreams come true. At the end of the film, the writer, deeply disillusioned by the experience says: 'Conscience, spiritual torment – this is just an intellectual invention.'[88]

Much of this literature and film exhibited an attitude of high seriousness. Yet seriousness was not all-pervasive. Humour, for example, was a feature of Vysotskii's songs. In his 'Parable of Truth and Lie', Vysotskii describes how 'Crude Lie decoyed tender Truth one night into her lair'.[89] There was humour too in some of Galich's poems. In 'A Conjuration of Good and Evil', a policeman, who is described as the agent of 'Good', tells the poet that he must leave his flat because 'to live in our flat Evil hadn't a permit'.[90] Here the Soviet regime's moral world has come to look ridiculous. 'Conscience' itself makes an appearance in some of the comic texts of the period. In Vladimir Voinovich's account of village life on the eve of the war, *The Life and Extraordinary Adventures of Private Ivan Chonkin*, one of the minor characters, Svintsov, suddenly starts experiencing feelings of unease about his previous contempt for human life. The narrator ironically observes:

> These feelings are usually called pangs of conscience, but Svintsov, never having experienced anything of the sort before, was unable to identify them ... Had Svintsov been better educated he would have found the explanation of his life in historical expediency, but he was an ignorant man and his conscience, once awakened, would not go back to sleep.[91]

Rather differently, conscience is treated with irony in Benedict Erofeev's exploration of drunkenness in Moscow, *Moscow-Petushki* (1976). In his inebriated ramblings, Erofeev states that he was shocked to meet a woman with seamless stockings, and that a seam 'might have lifted the burden off [his] soul and conscience'.[92]

Moral seriousness was often most obvious when the authorial voice was at its strongest. In noting the autobiographical nature of some of Solzhenitsyn's writings, Grigorii Svirskii suggested that the real hero of Solzhenitsyn's prose was Solzhenitsyn himself, and that the hero-centred structure of his works was one aspect of a larger 'hero-centered world-view'.[93] There is some truth in this, and it also points to the importance of the authorial voice in Solzhenitsyn's writings. His novels functioned as instruments of moral education in part because he was clearly in control. On the other hand, it might be said that, as with Tolstoi, the final hero of Solzhenitsyn's writings is the moral law itself. Authorial control is less evident in the more complicated structure of Dombrovskii's *Faculty of Unnecessary Things* and even less visible in Maksimov's *Seven Days of Creation*. Clearly, some novelists were exploring ways of promoting a moral vision more discreetly. Sinyavskii and Aksenov were among other writers who were experimenting with new forms.

Grigorii Svirskii characterised post-war Soviet writing as 'the literature of moral resistance'. There is much to be said for this interpretation, for even official writers were often making moral criticisms of the system. Svirskii's own account of late Soviet literature is itself an illustration of this kind of 'moral resistance' literature. In Svirskii's view, Soviet literary history was a battleground, and the readiness of writers to confront the truth in their work was connected with the quality of the writing itself. He stated that some prose writers 'adopted an all-round defence position affording protection to each other', and 'did not surrender'. On the other hand, 'others fell silent of their own accord when they saw the fate of those who had refused to desist'. According to Svirskii, Il'ya Ehrenburg's 'moral fibre stiffened' towards the end of his life; Aleksandr Yashin 'died a victor'; Lydia Chukovskaya became the 'cultural conscience of the country'. On the other hand, Svirskii states that Konstantin Fedin turned into a 'spineless, arrogant and malevolent character' after the death of his first wife; and, contemptuous of the career of Konstantin Simonov, he suggests that the Simonovs of the Soviet Union 'wanted the courageous to be forgotten'.[94]

Svirskii saw literature as a player in the wider struggle between good and evil that was taking place in Soviet society, and judged writers in moral terms. Like Solzhenitsyn, he took the view that artistic and moral truth are interconnected. Svirskii's attitudes also reflected the anti-political tendency of the dissident intellectual milieu. Svirskii assumed that the state was a threat to the integrity of the individual. This view was widely held by writers. In his diary in 1965, David Samoilov wrote down his ten primary moral principles. The second of them was: 'The state is always physically stronger than the individual. Morally a person is stronger and higher than the state.'[95] This anti-statism was evidently widely shared. It illustrates that the anti-political tendencies of some of the human rights activists were replicated in the wider literary intelligentsia.

9 Moral aspects of in-system dissent

As late Soviet literature indicates, it would be a mistake to see the Soviet dissidents in isolation from the rest of Soviet society. The ethical concerns of the dissident movement were in a general sense shared by the Soviet intelligentsia as a whole. This is also evident in the field of philosophy. In the post-war era, the nature of morality became a central concern of philosophers. At a conference in 1947, which was called to discuss G. Aleksandrov's *History of West European Philosophy*, Zhdanov criticised Soviet philosophers for their lack of productivity and a failure to relate Marxism to the problems of Soviet life. This led to the founding of the journal *Voprosy filosofii*. Stalin himself opened the door to new philosophical perspectives; his articles on linguistics in 1950 emphasised that 'the superstructure' of society, of which morality, in Marxist thought, was considered to be a part, was capable of influencing social development, and this gave philosophers a justification for focussing on moral issues.[1] From the late 1940s onwards, there was an enormous increase in the publication of journal articles and books that were devoted to moral issues. From 1961 till 1965 a series of articles on ethics as a theoretical discipline were published in the journal *Filosofskie nauki*; the first of these was an article by L.M. Arkhangel'skii on the fundamental concepts of ethical philosophy.[2] Discussion of value theory was introduced into Soviet ethics with the publication of V.P. Tugarinov's monograph, *On the Values of Life and Culture* (1960).[3] A.F. Shishkin's *The Foundations of Marxist Ethics* (1961) was the first of a series of textbooks on ethics that were widely distributed and that asserted the validity of ethics as a discipline in its own right. The emerging interest in ethics was institutionalised with the founding of the Department of Ethics and Aesthetics at Leningrad University in 1960, and the Department of Marxist-Leninist Ethics at Moscow State University in 1969.[4] Alongside the increased interest in ethics, there was a growth of interest in the nature of individuality; some of the first philosophical and sociological works on individuality began to appear during the Khrushchev era.[5]

The primary concerns of Soviet ethicists included the refutation of bourgeois theories of ethics, and the inculcation of Soviet values in the population. Ethicists sought to establish more firmly the theoretical basis for Soviet ethics. This involved a search to reconcile the tensions that were inherent in the Marxist-Leninist world-view. They had to emphasise the class-based and historically-defined nature of morality while at the same time promoting the objectivity of ethics and communist ideals, and they had to defend a 'scientific' interpretation of history without promulgating a mechanistic or fatalistic outlook. The questions of 'ends' and 'means' thus became an important field of study; philosophers sought to reject the idea that any means were justified if the end was legitimate, while at the same time refusing to endorse the 'abstract humanism' that rejected all means that were apparently immoral in themselves.[6] Since Soviet philosophers denied the validity of Christian, Kantian or natural law theories of morality in which individuals were treated as ends rather than means, the challenge was to find an alternative and humane basis for morality. The very fact that it was being attempted at all indicated that the Soviet regime wanted to give its ethical world-view a sounder theoretical foundation.[7] The concept of conscience itself received considerable attention in books and articles.[8]

The tension between idealism and materialism in the Marxist tradition was a theme that was frequently addressed in the 1960s and 1970s. Notably, a number of thinkers made an attempt to combine elements of idealism or universal values with a Marxist outlook. In 1963, the Georgian philosopher, G.D. Bandzeladze wrote a dissertation in which he argued that all-human and class morality had existed together at certain stages of historical development. Bandzeladze subsequently edited *Current Problems of Marxist Ethics* (1967), a collection of essays in which a number of authors challenged conservative Marxist interpretations. One of them, P.M. Egides, explored the concept of alienation in the works of the young Marx. The early Marx had attracted considerable interest among young intellectuals since the appearance in 1956 of the first complete Russian edition of his *Economic-Philosophical Manuscripts* of 1844; indeed, the very study of the early Marx was a subtle indication of discontent with the regime. Egides suggested that there was a difference between creative Marxists and dogmatists, arguing that the former wanted to create a 'free society of free people' while the latter wanted to turn people into automatons.[9]

Another of the contributors to Bandzeladze's collection was Ya.A. Mil'ner-Irinin. Mil'ner-Irinin's manuscript *Ethics or the Principles of True Humanity* (1963) was one of the most influential texts in late Soviet ethics, even though only sixty or so copies of the work were made available. The first chapter, along with another article on the same subject, was also printed in Bandzeladze's collection. Mil'ner-Irinin's views aroused such interest that many Soviet philosophers informally came to divide themselves into supporters and opponents of his thinking.[10] Mil'ner-Irinin differed from Kant in arguing for the social rather than the rational origins of moral reasoning, but otherwise the strongly idealistic element in his thinking clearly owed much to Kant; he was also much influenced by Hegel, Marx and Spinoza. He also declared in the foreword to his book that he was strongly committed to the Leninist conception of morality. At the same time, he rejected the view that morality was in itself a class phenomenon (*klassovost' morali*), instead taking the view that there was a class dimension to morality (*klassovost' v morali*).[11]

Mil'ner-Irinin argued that ethics was not a science about what is, was or will be, but a science that focussed on what *ought* to be. His philosophical system was rooted in a doctrine of conscience. In his article 'Ethics is the Science of What Ought to Be Done', he stated: 'In essence there is only one moral principle – conscience; in it the moral law of man and mankind is embodied.' He argued that conscience was made up of ten principles of equal worth which together formed a moral law that could never be transgressed in part without breaking the whole; he described these as the principles of conscience, self-perfection, good, social property, labour, freedom, nobility, gratitude, wisdom and action. Mil'ner-Irinin did not dispense completely with the class dimension of morality; he argued that the working class was the carrier of this revolutionary all-human morality. At the same time, he stated that conscience at one and the same time embraced 'all-human, class and intimately-personal dimensions', and that in its final manifestation all-human morality would not have a class dimension. There were some potentially liberal elements in his thinking. In emphasising the importance of freedom of conscience, he stated that

> a man is only spiritually free when he acts out of the necessity of his own nature, according to the promptings of his own conscience – the conscience of all toiling humanity, without being coerced into it by anyone, anything and in any way.[12]

In the first chapter of his book, 'Ethics, or the Principles of True Humanity: The Principle of Conscience', Mil'ner-Irinin provided a 184-point description of the principle of conscience. He called conscience 'the spiritual principle in man, the inner (intimate) source of all the spiritual life of humanity' and the 'light of reason'. Although Mil'ner-Irinin was a convinced atheist, some of these ideas could be likened to medieval concepts of natural law. Likewise, Mil'ner-Irinin's discussion of guilt was sometimes suggestive of traditional religious interpretations, even if his approach was entirely secular. He noted the 'disturbance' (*vozmushchenie*) and 'shame' (*styd*) that people underwent when they did not fulfil the commands of conscience, and explored the nature of the expression 'a clean conscience' (*chistaya sovest'*).[13]

Mil'ner-Irinin's work did not meet with official approval. He was criticised in *Kommunist* for emphasising the absolute nature of morality and departing from the methods of historical materialism.[14] Bandzeladze's collection itself aroused some controversy. Indeed, the authorities convened a special conference specifically to criticise it.[15] Possibly the fact that the book appeared in the same year as the invasion of Czechoslovakia also counted against it, for there were some parallels between the ideas in the collection and the thinking of the Prague Spring.[16]

Another important Soviet ethicist was Oleg Drobnitskii (1933–1973). Drobnitskii wrote a series of articles and books on moral consciousness and the concept of morality, culminating in his posthumously published *The Problems of Morality* (1977) which sought to combine universal values with Marxist moral relativism.[17] In an essay specifically on the problem of conscience in moral philosophy, Drobnitskii sought to find an objective social basis for conscience that contrasted with modern Western subjectivist doctrines, while at the same time not abandoning the personal dimension to moral choice. He concluded by defining conscience in its social dimension:

> [Conscience] is not simply an experience, feeling or conviction, but the relationship [*otnoshenie*] of a person to the world as expressed in one or another psychological form. It is the kind of relationship wherein a person takes upon himself responsibility not only for his own moral condition but for everything that daily happens around him.

He also stated that conscience is not something that is inherent in a person from the beginning, but that 'a person must take possession of his conscience, even if for him it is thereby necessary to change himself'.[18] His use of the word conscience was also interesting. At one point, in a discussion of existentialism, he referred to 'the principle of personal authenticity, of faithfulness to one's "I", i.e. conscience'.[19] Here conscience and the 'I' were interchangeable concepts; it was an idea of conscience similar to Albrekh't's concept of it, as expressed in his *How to Be a Witness.*

The 'golden rule' was another potentially subversive ethical idea. In 1972, Abdusalam Guseinov published an article on the 'golden rule of morality', in which he traced the philosophical history of the golden rule, starting with Confucius. Although he accepted the overall Marxist framework of philosophy, Guseinov was accused of propagandising Biblical values, and the article was only published after quotation marks had been added to the phrase 'golden rule'.[20]

Yurii Davydov, of the Institute of Art History, was another philosopher with new ideas. In his *The Ethics of Love and the Metaphysics of Self-Will* (1982), published in an edition of 50,000 by 'Molodaya gvardiya', Davydov praised the moral values of Tolstoi and Dostoevskii as against those of Schopenhauer, Nietzsche, Sartre and Camus, and emphasised the value of moral absolutes, particular the absolutes of love and self-sacrifice. Natural law and indeed religious conceptions of morality were clearly important to Davydov. Discussing Dostoevskii's understanding of conscience, Davydov observed that the message of *Crime and Punishment* was one of tragedy arising 'not in the presence of a "dead God", but before a *dead* or, better, *a deadened conscience*'. According to Davydov, conscience was in 'an indissoluble union' with what Dostoevskii generally called 'nature'.[21] In response, *Kommunist* criticised Davydov's abandonment of the class approach to morality and what it saw as his inadequate understanding of religious perspectives on morality.[22]

In the 1970s and early 1980s, the party placed great emphasis on moral education. In his report to the 24th Party Congress in 1971, Brezhnev noted that the communist morals of the new Soviet man could only be consolidated through struggle with 'survivals of the past', and declared that the Central Committee had taken steps to create a 'moral atmosphere' that included such qualities as respect for people, honesty, trust and comradeship.[23] There was a lot of talk of the 'management' and 'regulation' of the population, and the idea that occupational groups should have their own codes of professional ethics became very popular in these years.[24] The regime expected philosophers to provide advice on how to achieve its social goals. Most were willing to help. Shishkin, for example, stated that the theory of communist morality had as its basic object of study 'the experience of the education and self-education of the masses under the guidance of the Marxist party'.[25] In general, many philosophers were committed to the goals set for them by the party. The historian of Soviet moral philosophy, Philip Grier, observed that a person could not read very much of the Soviet philosophical literature without becoming convinced of the 'sincerity (if not the persuasiveness) of many of its authors'.[26]

Soviet philosophy, then, was much occupied with ethics, and although official philosophers did not challenge the system directly, they often raised questions that discreetly challenged its ideological foundations. In the sphere of political thought, there was a tighter sense of control, and orthodoxy reigned. Even there, however, the study of the young Marx, for example, could be a way of exploring the ethical dimensions of Soviet politics without arousing the ire of the authorities.

Just as the intellectual interests of the dissidents reflected some of the wider concerns of the Soviet intelligentsia, so also their moral anxieties were part of a wider existential and moral restlessness. It is impossible to understand the behaviour of some of the reform-minded party intellectuals of the 1980s without looking at the processes of moral self-examination and evasion that they went through prior to perestroika. To explore this need not mean to assume a simplistic Orwellian interpretation of Soviet life where everybody thought one thing and did another. Life was more complicated than that. Some members of the party certainly continued to believe in the ideology at a certain level. Moreover, where there was doubt, it was often unrecognised. Indeed, belief and fear or doubt were often mixed up together. Tat'yana Velikanova reported a conversation with an elderly Jewish woman whose enthusiasm for the Soviet system appeared to conceal a layer of anxiety:

> I say to the woman that people are afraid in this system of power. 'No', she says, 'I am not afraid of anything. No one is afraid. People like me have nothing to fear.' And then she sees some book ... on the table, samizdat, and it is enough to look at one page and she takes fright and goes pale.[27]

Aleksandr Tsipko suggested that the Soviet system was rooted in 'a kind of sublimated fear'.[28] There were often layers of repressed fear that were only revealed in certain situations.

Although it is difficult to measure belief, there were certainly many people who continued to believe in the Soviet project, or at least in parts of it, in the late Soviet era. Many party members originally joined the party out of conviction. In recalling the 1930s, Aleksandr Yakovlev stated: 'We believed very strongly and sincerely in what then existed.'[29] Vadim Bakatin 'entered the party with pleasure ... with a certain pride'.[30] Nail' Bikennin recalled that he 'consciously entered the party, and was proud of it, and consciously entered the apparatus of the [Central Committee]'. He was very aware of the fact that he was the only Tatar ever to work in the Central Committee.[31]

Belief and unease sometimes existed at the same time. Tsipko experienced a 'feeling of unease' on joining the party, but he was already by that time a statist (*gosudarstvennik*), and he was strongly attracted by the 'strength of order' (*sila poryadka*) that the party represented.[32] Where there was a restless conformity, an elaborate set of myths was created to justify a refusal to confront the regime directly. According to Vladimir Shlapentokh these could be summarised in certain key phrases: 'I Am a Patriot'; 'Any Politics is Dirty'; 'Only Moral Self-Improvement is Important'; 'Dissidents are Inferior'; 'High Professional Performance Above All'; and 'Don't Tease the Bosses'.[33]

Some doubters believed that a career in the system did not need to affect their inner integrity. Gordievskii entered the KGB with the view that he could remain an 'internal rebel' and an 'opponent in [his] mind'.[34] However, some who initially had doubts about the regime eventually lost them. Boris Belenken recalled how 'people who worked for the regime gradually started to love their work'. Some, it seems, deliberately chose career over conscience. Michael Rozov, who taught philosophy of science at the Institute of Automation and Electrometers at Akademgorodok, recalled that he joined the party in 1965 for career reasons, even though it went against his conscience at the time:

> It was a work permit ... If I had wanted to keep a completely clear conscience, I would not have done it ... This ticket protected me from

> something and at the same time did not demand anything special from me except the carrying out of purely external rituals.[35]

Like Rozov, the future Constitutional Court judge Ernest Amestistov found the question of whether or not to join the party a difficult one. He became a party member in 1967 when he was working at the Institute of the International Labour Movement, at that time a fashionable base for reform-minded party intellectuals such as Merab Mamardashvilli, Yurii Zamoshkin and Yurii Karyakin. Ametistov recalled later that there were two reasons behind his decision to join: first, he wanted to boost his career, and second, he was persuaded that the system could only be changed from within. Yet, Ametistov recalled later, when he looked back on the decision, he wondered whether in fact he had simply used the second argument to justify the first. In spite of the fact that he joined the party, Ametistov was never wholehearted about it. He did not speak in party gatherings, and either refused to vote or absented himself when votes came up. He managed to preserve his reputation, he recalled: 'They did not find quotations which were in favour of their work.' He eventually left the party in 1986, soon after the launch of perestroika; he would have left earlier if had not been for fear of ending up in a psychiatric hospital.[36]

Rozov's suggestion that joining the party was a purely external ritual indicates that people sometimes came to delineate their public and private selves. In doing this, they could take the view that certain external actions had no essential meaning and did not reflect their true selves. Some chose to see their behaviour as a kind of game. Tsipko, who grew up in an anti-Soviet household, began to adapt to the system when he was at school in the 1950s: 'Everyone went into the Komsomol and the instinct of self-preservation appeared; you start to live by those rules of the game.' Boris Belenken recalled of his life in the 1970s: 'I participated in certain rules of the game ... Life was totally divided into two spheres ... I was of course a "man of the kitchen" [*chelovekom kukhni*].'[37] Gordievskii suggested that most of his contemporaries understood the reality of Soviet life when they were 16 or 17, but that they 'accepted it as part of their lives, and decided to play by Soviet rules'.[38] It is less clear if the phrase 'the rules of the game' was itself widely used. Interviewed in 2003, Gordievskii stated that the phrase 'rules of the game' was really a construction of the previous ten years and reflected the desire of people to justify their past conformity; the phrase itself was not used in the previous era.[39]

The tendency for people to divide their lives into public and private spheres, or to distinguish 'ritual' actions from 'genuine' ones, was widespread. 'I wanted to survive, but not at any price', commented one historian,[40] and that was typical. There was much private unease and restlessness as people sought to work out what they might or might not allow themselves to do. Some people sought in their minds to come to what could be termed a private individual 'deal' or 'contract' by which they would agree to do one thing, but not another.[41] For example, they informally tried to set boundaries beyond which they would not permit themselves to go. The TASS journalist, Eduard Rozental', posted to the African state of Mali, recalled that he refused the KGB's request to report on his Soviet colleagues, although he agreed to report to them about Africans. A future historian of church history, Nikolai Shaburov, who went to university in the 1970s, decided that he was willing to quote Marx in his writings, but would avoid making the ritual mention of Lenin. The problem for Shaburov, however, was how to keep the boundary fixed. He noted that it was hard to keep to his decision: 'I cannot say that I always held to that. There were various ritual moments. We had a subject at university, "The History of the Party," and I would memorize something ... assuring oneself that it was a ritual.' Shaburov found that fear of social disapproval made it very hard for him to follow his convictions. With regard to Soviet elections, in which there was only one official candidate to choose from, he said: 'I believed that if I were an honest man, I would ... cross out the candidate that stood there. But I did not do it because I could not endure the glances of people.' The fear of being marginalised kept people within bounds. No one wanted to be a 'white crow' (*belaya vorona*) that would stand out from the crowd.[42]

How to avoid lying was one of the dilemmas. One strategy was to give the impression of saying one thing while in fact saying another. This was the approach adopted by some of the literary figures when they 'recanted' in 1963. The dissident from Odessa and future deputy-leader of the Yabloko Party, Vyacheslav Igrunov, recalled: 'I often thought one thing and was compelled to give the impression that I thought another.' For example, in the exam on the CPSU which Igrunov took as part of the requirements to enter an Economics Institute in 1969, he told the truth, but in such a way that his teacher 'could not understand at all what [he] was saying'.[43] It is notable that Igrunov used the word 'compelled' to explain why he used this strategy; he was effectively saying that his actions were forced upon him by circumstances.

Another related tactic was to give the impression of being a fool. German Andreev noted: 'I gave the impression that I was a fool – up until a certain moment, when I understood that you cannot play such a game if you want to be completely inwardly free.'[44] *Shveikovanie*, a word derived from the main character in Czech novelist Jaroslav Hasek's *The Good Soldier Shveik*, who was very adept at getting out of tricky situations, was a widely used term. The theatre director Yurii Lyubimov, whose productions at the Taganka Theatre pushed at the boundaries of censorship under Brezhnev, recalled that there was 'an element of sport' in his tussles with the authorities, and that 'most of [his] victories came through *shveikovanie*'.[45] A related tactic was 'clowning' (*klounada*). The historian Sergei Podbolotov, who attended school in St Petersburg in the 1970s, recalled that in having to pretend that people like Brezhnev were great heroes, he and his fellows assumed the view that a kind of charade was being acted out:

> There were subjects ... where it was necessary to answer that Brezhnev was a great hero ... Everyone knew that it was a lie ... but we saw what was happening around as a kind of absurdity [*absurd*], as if we had something of a punk [*punkovskii*] approach to it, a kind of clowning. Everyone is playing a role. And we, let us say, become honest with one another when we leave the school.[46]

People used to try to evade certain subjects. Gordievskii became skilled at making positive speeches about other Soviet officials at embassy anniversaries and receptions; however, he would avoid referring to the party or the country, and instead talked about such things as friendship, honesty and people's personal qualities. Ideology was thereby avoided.[47] Aleksandr Yakovlev stated that he did not do anything that he did not have to do, and that when it was necessary to do something, he did it 'in such a way that nothing practically came of it'.[48] Rozov recalled that he 'never said anything unnecessary in the auditorium'.[49] Historians avoided politically sensitive topics.[50] Awkward situations were sometimes avoided altogether. Amalrik knew eminent scientists who went to the countryside to harvest potatoes in order not to have to sign letters condemning Sakharov.[51]

There was also evasion of another kind too. A scientist friend of Sergei Kovalev stated to him that he preferred to remain ignorant of the issues facing the human rights movement:

> Serezha, don't try to convince me of something. All the general issues that you talk about – I understand them and can formulate them no worse than you. But I do not wish to know the details, because if I know the details, I will not be able to do the science and in general live. And I don't want that.[52]

Some thus chose ignorance in order to avoid the discomfort of handling uncomfortable information.

Many tried to express opposition in a safe way. The 'fig in the pocket' – the signal of dissent that was expressed in obscure code – was very common.[53] It was common to use 'Aesopian' terminology. People wrote historical works or novels about other parts of the world that were intended to be understood as attacks on aspects of the Soviet system. Articles that were critical of Soviet policy were deliberately obscured so that their meaning was only apparent to a sensitive and informed reader. Ernest Ametistov went into the law department at Moscow University and eventually chose a career as a scholar rather than as a practical lawyer, because it involved less political interference. Like others he tried to avoid mentioning Marx and Lenin in his publications. He was also critical of communism in his writings, but in such an obscure way that it was difficult to know what he was writing about:

> Many there did not understand what I wrote. I wrote for example about the necessity of the priority of international law . . . I proved the necessity from a theoretical angle . . . In the final analysis this conception worked against communism, against the system.[54]

Nevertheless, it was necessary to be careful with Aesopian phraseology in case its meaning was too obvious. Fedor Burlatskii got into trouble in the late 1960s for writing a series of articles on Spain and the possibilities of democratisation under Franco, which people understood to be about the USSR.[55] Writing in 1983, Thomas Venclova said: 'It is permissible to expose the tyrants of Rome or Byzantium, although here one must avoid expressions and analogies that are too obvious.'[56]

Ametistov's decision to avoid a practical legal career indicates that people sometimes made career choices specifically in order to avoid conflicts with the state. The historian of Russian philosophy Albert Sobolev did this; he chose not to defend his candidate's dissertation on Semyon Frank in order to avoid ideological pressure, and took a job in the reference section of the Institute of Philosophy where he did translations and wrote references, and avoided the requirement to publicly declare his views. Rozov decided to avoid a career in areas of philosophy that were close to politics because of the potential there for ideological conflict, and chose the philosophy of science instead. People thus tried to avoid careers where either their intellectual freedom might be challenged, or they could be required to be dishonest about their true convictions. The cases of Ametistov, Sobolev and Rozov illustrate not only that people made career choices with moral criteria partly in mind, but that there existed in the Soviet system 'niches' or places of safety where a measure of privacy or intellectual freedom was permitted. As Rozov put it: 'There were many, figuratively speaking, ecological niches [*ekologicheskikh nish*] . . . certain social niches.'[57] The cost of this freedom was different in each case: for Ametistov, it was the sacrifice of a practical career; for Sobolev the price was a loss of professional status; for Rozov it meant choosing a particular academic pathway. Yet the price of this relative freedom was also a public silence about the negative features of the regime; a certain measure of intellectual freedom and ease of conscience could sometimes be bought in return for silence.[58]

It was part of the dissident culture to try to avoid doing deals with the authorities altogether. However, even the more well-known dissidents sometimes did deals with the authorities. Most obviously of course, Krasin and Yakir agreed to give information to the KGB in return for their release. However, in other little ways, deals were struck. Natal'ya

Gorbanevskaya promised not to participate further in human rights activities in order to get released from the Kazan psychiatric hospital after she was confined there in 1969, even though she knew her promise was not genuine, and guessed that the doctors knew also. With hindsight, she said, her conscience was at ease over the matter, although there was one moment when she felt as if she and the doctors 'were formulating lies together' which made her feel uncomfortable. It was nevertheless a big issue for her; back in ordinary life, she met the dissident Vladimir Gershuni, who had been in Orlov psychiatric prison and had refused to talk to the doctors, and Gershuni suggested that she had capitulated.[59]

Religious believers adopted a variety of strategies regarding the 'rules of the game' of Soviet life. Party or Komsomol membership was sometimes a dilemma for those who were or became religious. Anatolii Krasikov, Deputy Head of TASS after 1979 and from 1992 till 1996 head of Yeltsin's press office, converted to Orthodoxy in the 1960s when he was TASS representative at the Vatican. In spite of his new religious convictions, he felt no unease at remaining within the party, and thought it would be better to fight for change within the system. Others decided not to confront the issue directly. When the philosopher Oleg Genisaretskii, a member of a positivist philosophical circle associated with G.P. Shchedrovitskii, converted to Orthodoxy, he concluded that his newly-found Orthodox convictions were not in principle compatible with party membership, but that since party membership gave him the freedom to pursue his philosophical work, he would not rescind his membership, but let God and the party resolve the problem for him. On the other hand, Irina Yazykova, a member in the early 1980s of the 'Ecumen' group, became religious during her university studies and later turned down an invitation to join the party, concluding that a person who was 'honest in a little' was 'honest in a lot'.[60]

It is important not to view moral attitudes to the Soviet regime in a static way. Tolerance or benign scepticism as regards the Soviet system was sometimes turned into dissent by particular experiences. Although he had doubts about the Soviet system, Gordievskii became a candidate member of the party in 1963 'without any sensation of unease'. Yet his scepticism about the system turned into dissent with the Soviet invasion of Czechoslovakia; he interpreted this as the 'principal turning-point' of his life. Indeed, he later interpreted his defection in terms of conscience: 'Far from having qualms of conscience [about collaborating with the British], I felt relief and euphoria that I was no longer a dishonest man working for a totalitarian state'; rejecting Soviet communism, he stated that it had been more important to him to be 'honest' to his own conscience and to the West.[61]

For many, the life of deceit was dissatisfying. Brodskii suggested that trying to outsmart the system could easily become a full-time job, and that at the same time it left people dissatisfied with themselves:

> One was constantly aware that the web one had woven was a web of lies, and in spite of the degree of success or your sense of humour, you'd despise yourself. This is the ultimate triumph of the system: whether you beat it or join it, you feel equally guilty.[62]

Amalrik was more severe about it. He suggested that people's lives became 'a kind of game in which their own personalities were gradually lost'.[63] It also sapped people's energy. Venclova observed: 'A person wastes all his strength, all his time, all his inventiveness on this ridiculous game.'[64]

Venclova also noted the existence in Soviet writers not only of the 'inner censor' – something like a Freudian superego – but also a 'seductive demon-jester' that continually rebelled against the censor, and which sought to 'push the limits' of what was acceptable.[65] Here there were two inner voices: a 'seductive demon-jester' and an 'inner censor'. Slightly differently, the film-director, Elem Klimov, whose film *Agony* was widely shown during perestroika, said in an interview in the late 1980s that many people in former days had been subject to an 'inner censor' or 'inner editor' that prevented them acting upon their convictions. He noted the presence of this phenomenon in himself: 'Even I still feel him inside me – a cautious little man sitting behind a small desk somewhere on the right side of the brain saying, "You'd better not do this. Don't take that step." It's torture.' Klimov then suggested that the 'inner censor' had come to supersede what he called a 'moral censor': 'There should be in each of us a moral censor telling us to do the right thing. Instead, there's still this little inner censor implanted there by years of terror and fear.'[66] Klimov's inner censor seems to have been something like Freud's superego, and his 'moral censor' to have been akin to a form of natural conscience. There was also something here of a traditional religious distinction between true and false forms of conscience. Klimov remained a convinced socialist during perestroika, so his 'moral censor' was not 'anti-communist' in its intuitions.

Perestroika was launched 'from above'. The impetus for reform came from within the party itself, and can partly be traced to certain clusters of independent thinking that existed in or on the edge of the party. For example, in 1961 when he was head of the Department for Liaison with Ruling Communist and Workers' Parties, Andropov sought advice from a small group of young intellectuals, who were then still outside the party, including Burlatskii, Georgii Shakhnazarov, who became one of Gorbachev's chief advisors on foreign affairs, Georgii Arbatov, later head of the USA-Canada Institute and the economist Oleg Bogomolov.[67] Arbatov, Shakhnazarov and Bogomolov also worked for a time for the reform-minded, Prague-based journal *Problemy mira i sotsializma*. Elsewhere, the more liberal atmosphere of Novosibirsk gave Abel Agenbegyan's Institute of Economic and Industrial Organisation, set up in 1961, a relative measure of independence. The sociologist Tat'yana Zaslavskaya worked there from 1963. Also in Novosibirsk, the Central Economic-Mathematical Institute was founded in 1963. There were also patrons of reformist thinking in the party; Aleksei Rumyantsev, editor of *Problemy mira i sotsializma* from 1958–1964, was an important protector of liberal-minded party members.[68]

An interesting figure with links to reformist party networks was Len Karpinskii. Karpinskii, who was the son of a famous Bolshevik, became Secretary of the national Komsomol Central Committee in 1959, and then head of the department of Marxism-Leninism at *Pravda* in 1962. However, he was fired from *Pravda* in 1967 after co-authoring with Burlatskii an article in *Komsomol'skaya pravda* calling in a euphemistic way for less censorship.[69] Following the invasion of Czechoslovakia, Karpinskii wrote and circulated a document (under the pseudonym of L. Okunev), entitled 'Words Are Also Deeds', in which he attacked the Soviet clampdown on the Czech reformers and argued for freedom of thought. He suggested that in certain circumstances party intellectuals could form an alliance with the wider intelligentsia, and that such a group of party intellectuals could become a hidden, internal opposition within the bureaucracy. Furthermore, he envisaged the possibility of a 'parliamentary road to socialism'.[70] Karpinskii had links with certain dissident intellectuals. He knew Roy Medvedev well, and had read manuscript copies of all his historical works. However, he got into trouble with the KGB when a copy of 'Words Are Also Deeds' was discovered in Medvedev's apartment. Then, in 1975, he was found to possess another subversive manuscript and charged with starting an activity against the party. This led to him being expelled from the party.[71]

'Conscience' became an increasingly important concept to Karpinskii. During perestroika, he told the American journalist, David Remnick, that the idea of 'intellectual conscience' was a central feature of his thinking. He said of this: 'It's not a natural inborn conscience, yet a conscience that stems from a kind of thinking that links you with a moral attitude to reality.' Faced with a society soaked in blood and heading towards collapse, he said, 'your conscience cannot remain neutral'. Karpinskii recalled that he did not personally take risks, but that he was 'compelled' to take certain steps by his conscience. Karpinskii declared that he had got accustomed to using Aesopian language in his criticisms of the system. Yet he noted that when people never expressed their opinions openly, it damaged them psychologically:

> One can only behave in that split way of thinking for a while, but then you begin to degenerate and start to speak only what is permitted and the rest of the conscience and the soul decays. Many people did not survive to perestroika. We had to create an internal moral system, and not everyone could sustain it indefinitely.

As regards Solzhenitsyn's call for people to desist from lying, Karpinskii stated: 'We tried not to live by lies, but we couldn't always mange it.'[72] The principle of 'intellectual conscience', he said elsewhere, is that if you understand something to be true, you are morally obliged to act upon it. This, however, was 'the most difficult thing for most people'. Following Mamardashvili's description of the USSR as a 'non-society', he described it as an 'anti-economy' and 'anti-world' where it was difficult to know where exactly the lie was located.[73] Karpinskii was also interested in 'repentance', another subject that was much discussed during perestroika. In an interview published in 1989, he suggested that there were some actions before 1965 for which he needed to repent. Yet he said that he had nothing particular to repent of from his years as a 'half-dissident'. He referred to the need for some kind of collective repentance, stating that all of those who lived in the system and did as they were told 'ought to repent'.[74]

Initially, Karpinskii saw no conflict between his moral convictions and his support for perestroika. He later commented that although he was expelled from the party in 1975, he had remained a party member in his soul, and felt 'tied' to the party.[75] During perestroika, he remained committed to a reformed version of socialism, similar to that promoted during Lenin's New Economic Policy, and rejoined the party after a petition for his rehabilitation was presented at the 19th Party Conference by Yurii Afanas'ev, Nikolai Shmelev and Karyakin. He went to work for *Moscow News*. He later noted, however, that although his reasons for rejoining the party had been honourable, he had also been motivated by the desire once again to be a political commentator for a newspaper.[76] At the same time, Karpinskii gradually moved away from socialism during these years towards a liberal world-view. In June 1990 he wrote in *Moscow News* that the concept of socialism had 'no clear boundaries', and he declared that he was himself committed to ideological pluralism and universal human values.[77] Following the attempted clampdown in Lithuania in January 1991, Karpinskii once again left the party – this time voluntarily.

Karpinskii's experience indicates the importance of the idea of conscience and moral values to certain reform-minded party members. It also casts light on the evolution of moral ideas in late Soviet Russia, and the way in which perestroika opened a door for the expression of ideas that were long felt but little articulated. It also shows the influence of dissidents on the younger communist intelligentsia. Through people like Karpinskii, ideas passed from samizdat into party circles. Karpinskii compared himself to Roy Medvedev, although he noted that he was less active than Medvedev. However, he suggested that 'full dissidents' like Medvedev and Sakharov played a more important role in influencing perestroika than timid 'half-dissidents' like himself.[78] This is a matter for debate. According to Burlatskii, dissident intellectuals like Sakharov and Solzhenitsyn did not influence political practice in the Soviet Union so much as public opinion; Burlatskii noted the constructive role that was played by figures like Roy and Zhores Medvedev, but nevertheless remarked that conservative politicians were very wary of dissident ideas, and that made it harder for people like himself to articulate critical views for fear of being labelled dissidents.[79]

In his book, *Lenin's Tomb*, David Remnick included Karpinskii in a chapter entitled 'The Double Thinkers'.[80] It is a good phrase, and one that also applies to another party intellectual who was influential during perestroika, Aleksandr Tsipko. Tsipko read the early Marx while in his first year studying philosophy at Moscow State University in the early 1960s. However, in his second year, he read *Landmarks*, and was drawn in the direction of conservative and metaphysical ideas. He later read and was impressed by *From under the Rubble* and *The Foundation Pit*, and the works of Viktor Astaf'ev.[81] Yet, although unconvinced by Marxism, Tsipko made a career as a party philosopher at Moscow State University. He eventually became Yeltsin's leading statist critic in 1991–1992.[82]

Tsipko said in 2003 that it was 'possible to be cunning [*mozhno skhitrit'*] ... and to use Marxism to move away from Marxism'.[83] There is some evidence that he did indeed try to do this. In 1968, he co-edited a book on moral issues, *Conversations on Morality: A Rough Academic Plan and Methodological Recommendations in a System of the Political Enlightenment of Youth*. Although the book was full of quotations from Lenin and Marx, it posed moral questions in a way that pointed beyond class morality narrowly defined. The book contained lots of references to conscience and a chapter on the subject.[84] It is probably impossible to establish exactly the extent to which books of this kind were indeed an attempt to subvert the system by using its own ideology. There was doubtless room for self-deception here. Tsipko himself commented in an interview that his book *Optimism and History* (1974), which was written under the influence of the younger Marx, was partly the result of a number subconscious impulses: the desire to publish a book, to be famous, and at the same time to work within the framework of the state ideology.[85]

Tsipko's subsequent writings consistently emphasised the non-dogmatic nature of Marxism-Leninism. In *Socialism: The Life of Society and Man* (1980), for example, Tsipko declared that conservative or dogmatic approaches to the world could never last, and noted that Lenin himself had warned against closed systems of thought.[86] Similarly, in *Certain Philosophical Aspects of the Theory of Socialism* (1983), he stated that Marx and Lenin were realists, and that no abstract solutions to the problems of building socialism were to be found in the works of Marx, Engels and Lenin.[87] Doubtless, the call for realism was a coded call for reform. In *Socialism*, some of Tsipko's strongest comments were tucked away in the footnotes; he rejected the use of violence for humanistic ends and lamented the murderous energy unleashed by revolutions. Furthermore, while he noted that the class approach might help one to understand history, it could never turn cruelty and violence into a moral good.[88]

Tsipko's scepticism about the revolutionary tradition came into the open in a ground-breaking series of articles in the journal *Nauka i zhizn'* in 1988–1989. The articles were partly a response to an article by the writer Igor Klyamkin in *Novyi mir* in 1987, in which Klyamkin suggested that the kind of liberalism that *Landmarks* represented was simply not viable in the Russia of 1917 because it lacked a social base, and that the October Revolution had succeeded because it had been a 'social revolution'.[89] Tsipko countered by declaring that Stalin could not be blamed for the betrayal of the revolution, for the whole revolutionary tradition itself was at fault.[90] At the same time, Tsikpo steered clear of criticising Lenin, and did not condemn the Marxist tradition altogether, declaring that the 'real humanism' of Marx and Engels was founded on the principle of the freedom and spiritual autonomy of the individual.[91]

The articles in *Nauka i zhizn'* can partly be seen as moves in a political game. Indeed, Tsipko himself later talked of them in those terms:

> A moment came . . . It was a game. Remember that these essays would never have appeared if I had not been working for the Central Committee. The censor would never have permitted it . . . My text was like lightning in those times. So it was useful for someone.

He declared that this was the case of a man trying to destroy the ideology, while at the same time knowing how to play the game according to the rules of that system.[92] If Tsipko was right in this, the *Nauka i zhizn'* articles should be read not so much as a guide to Tsipko's ideas, but as an indicator of what were then the ideological limits for party intellectuals. Yet, if that is true, it raises a new problem: Tsipko's articles stop being a reliable guide to what Tsipko actually believed.

Tsipko was indeed playing a kind of game, but he was probably also trying to come to terms with his own life and career. The evidence suggests that he was both sceptical of Marxism, while at the same time being disappointed by its failure. In *Moscow News* in 1990, he declared that he had been cured of his enslavement to Marxist dogma when he read *Landmarks* twenty-five years before.[93] However, in another article of 1990, he indicated that he was one of those who became disillusioned with Marxist ideas. He wrote: 'As the pace of ideological changes was quickening, we could see things ever more clearly'; and he said that he was finding it 'ever more difficult to convince himself that he was acting honestly by remaining a CPSU member'.[94] A couple of years later, in a preface to a collection of essays by Aleksandr Yakovlev, he declared that Yakovlev's writings recorded the drama of all Soviet intellectuals who had believed in Marxism, in particular in the vision of the early Marx. He observed: 'In later years we groped for the truth and eventually realized that we had believed in a chimera. For conscientious people it was an unbearably bitter and excruciating experience.'[95] It seems that Tsipko wanted both to signal that he had never really believed in Marxist ideology, certainly in its narrower form, while at the same time suggesting that he was a disillusioned communist. Tsipko's attitude to Lenin was slightly different. In his book *Is Stalinism Really Dead?*, published in the West in 1990, Tsipko stated that the mature Lenin had become more realistic after the end of the Civil War, and gone 'beyond the framework of orthodox Marxism'.[96] Yet even the defence of the later Lenin likely concealed doubts. Tsipko later stated that when people defended the realism of Lenin's later years, it was often because they were afraid of breaking with Marxism altogether.[97]

Like Karpinskii, Tsipko deployed the language of 'conscience'. In *Is Stalinism Really Dead?*, he declared that perestroika was a 'moral revolution' and that its starting-point had been 'the shame' felt by many over their political conformity and subservience in the past. He stated that Stalinism's worst legacy was 'hardened souls', and that 'at no other time in the history of Russia did so many people act against their consciences and violate their souls to save their flesh'. He also said that an intelligentsia should be the bearer of 'critical conscience, of the spirit of doubt and common sense', but that the Russian intelligentsia had lacked the necessary moderation to provide these things. Tsipko's understanding of conscience seems to have contained both materialistic and Christian elements; he endorsed Marx's materialism, while at the same time defending Christian morality and saying that religion had helped people to realise that they had 'souls and consciences'.[98]

Tsipko's writings of the period are best read not as a guide to a defined system of ideas, but as an illustration of how a party intellectual, who was likely never convinced of Soviet ideology, sought to recast his ideas in the new circumstances. Tsipko's ideas were in flux. At the same time, Tsipko's case again raises deeper questions about how to interpret human subjectivity. Like some dissidents, Tsipko was inclined to read his initial doubts about communism as reflective of a more real version of himself than the personality that was revealed when he worked in the party–state apparatus. He evidently believed that by playing a 'game', he could work for the regime as a temporary necessity, while his essential self, which was located elsewhere, remained largely unchanged.

Tsipko's case also raises again the interpretative problem of establishing the reliability of people's memories, especially when it comes to matters of belief. In the late 1980s, it suddenly became highly desirable to have been an oppositionist. In an article in the newspaper *Argumenty i fakty*, for example, Burlatskii presented the 1967 article he co-wrote with Karpinskii for *Komsomol'skaya pravda*, which had got the two of them into trouble, in a very positive light, while the paper's former editor stated that Burlatskii had originally tried to shift responsibility for the article onto Karpinskii.[99] The past itself was now contentious ground in a new way. Burlatskii was certainly a pragmatic figure. He declared during perestroika that the country needed to restore its 'political conscience';[100]

yet one commentator suggested that he was one of the 'complete opportunists'.[101]

The examples of Karpinskii and Tsipko illustrate some of the dilemmas faced by party members who sought to change the system from within, yet who benefited from working for the system at the same time. Their moral and intellectual restlessness was not an isolated phenomenon. It was part of a wider 'critical anti-Stalinist outlook' in the reformist intelligentsia.[102] Yet this restlessness was also semi-repressed; it could only come to the fore when perestroika opened the door for it. Whether the word 'dissent' embraces the attitudes of Karpinskii and Tsipko is questionable. They were 'reform-minded' as much as 'dissent-minded'. Yet the value of using the term 'dissent' in relation to their actions is that it highlights the overlap that often existed between dissidents who tried to exert pressure on the regime from outside, and those who preferred to work from within.

10 The ethics of the party reformers

There was an anecdote of the 1970s that reflected the moral reputation of the party in certain circles: Question: What is black, small and always silent? Answer: the party conscience. It is easy to assume that personal feelings of conscience had to be set aside if a person wanted a successful career in the party. If that was so, it means that the language of conscience, when it was used by the party leadership, is best seen in instrumentalist terms; it was a ploy by people to legitimise themselves or to mobilise the population. Doubtless there is a great deal of truth in this perspective. However, the deeper problem of instrumentalism is that it cannot embrace the complexity of human motivations, and it thus essentially avoids the problem altogether. In the case of perestroika, there is, in fact, considerable evidence to suggest that the moral restlessness that troubled so many members of the intelligentsia also reached into the higher echelons of power. How deep that restlessness was, and how far it influenced government policy are difficult to say, but it certainly existed.

It is important not to be naïve about the party's commitment to ethics. 'Never forget', Khrushchev once said to Arkadii Shevchenko, a high-ranking Soviet diplomat who defected to the USA in 1978, 'the appeal that the idea of disarmament has in the outside world. All you have to do is say, "I'm in favour of it," and that pays big dividends. A seductive slogan is a most powerful political instrument.' At the same time, Khrushchev also said that propaganda and true negotiations should be considered to be complementary to one another.[1] These words encapsulate some of the dilemmas that face the historian of morality. While it would be a mistake to take all statements of moral intent at face value, it would be wrong too to make the assumption that all ethics can be reduced to politics.

Party leaders, of course, did not see their own behaviour in purely cynical terms. Nail' Bikennin, who worked for the Central Committee for twenty-one years, stated that throughout the Soviet era there were people at the top with a 'developed sense of comradeship, courage and conscientiousness'; not everyone lived by the principle, 'What can I get out of this?.'[2] There were certainly some figures in the upper reaches of the party who came to be seen as role models. For example, Vadim Medvedev, the Politburo's ideology chief from September 1988 to July 1990, was influenced by the example of V.S. Tolstikov, First Secretary of the Leningrad Party Obkom in the 1960s; Tolstikov, in Medvedev's view, was 'a very emotional, honest and open man'.[3] At the same time, Medvedev also noted that party morality varied in different regions. From 1968 till 1970 Medvedev was a Secretary of the Leningrad City Party Committee; then in 1970 he moved to Moscow to become Deputy Director of the Propaganda Department of the Central Committee. Moscow, he immediately noticed, had 'a well-developed system of so-called unofficial relationships', involving *blat*, extortion and bribery.[4] The situation in Leningrad was 'simpler and not so refined'.[5]

Much of the source material on the ethical thinking of party leaders is to be found in memoirs, and once again this raises a dilemma. Bikennin noted that after the collapse of communism there were various things that a former member of the Central Committee or the KGB was supposed to say in his memoirs. The person had to declare that 'he had only entered [the institution] in order to break up the "criminal organisation" from within and that within its gloomy walls he always felt himself a dissident'. In regard to his awareness of Soviet terror, the party leader would say either that he knew all about the criminality of the regime from childhood, or alternatively that he only got to know about terror in his old age. 'Choose according to your taste', Bikennin said.[6] On the other hand, it is easy to overstress this point. Some party leaders were well aware that people had a tendency to embellish their pasts. In his memoirs, Vadim Bakatin noted that after the collapse of the USSR many people easily exaggerated the levels of their former dissent: 'Many hurry now, on any suitable occasion, to inform the world that they always kept a "fig in the pocket".' Bakatin insisted instead that he was never anti-communist in his convictions, and that he had no disagreements with the party until the last years of perestroika.[7]

The moral discourse that was a feature of perestroika did not appear suddenly. It was partly rooted in the fact that the Bolshevik project was from its inception a moral one, even though the original vision had largely lost its attraction by the 1980s. However, it also reflected a wider concern about the moral state of the USSR that was already evident on the eve of perestroika. Mobility within the system depended to a large degree on patronage networks, and nepotism was widespread.[8] The black market was booming, and the dividing line in the country between the legal and the illegal was 'indistinct'.[9] Corruption was widespread, and was one of the reasons why the economy was in a bad way. It was also hard to introduce substantial reforms. Kosygin's attempt to introduce managerial incentives into the economy in 1965 as part of a package of economic reforms foundered in bureaucratic inertia, and since then little serious change had been attempted.

There was an underlying problem relating to incentives and motivation. In her 'Novosibirsk Report' (1983), Tat'yana Zaslavskaya suggested that the lack of incentives for workers in the Soviet economy meant that there was a severe motivational crisis in the country. In 1983–1984, Zaslavskaya and Aganbegyan talked with Gorbachev about the widespread evidence of 'rampant cynicism, alcoholism, and ... the catastrophic degeneration of the work ethic'.[10] There was also a sense of social degeneration in the sphere of family life. One raikom First Secretary in Moscow noted in 1985 that family problems were increasingly discussed at party meetings, and he called for the promotion of 'highly-moral behavioural models' and conditions in which the emulation of such models would become an 'inner motivation in the individual'.[11] Life expectancy was falling rapidly. It reached a particularly low point in the early 1980s when the life expectancy for men was 61.4 per cent, and for both men and women in rural Russia 59.3. Both the economic and the social crises were linked to the problem of alcoholism. According to one estimate, there was a total population loss of between 30 and 35 million between 1960 and 1985 as a result of alcohol abuse.[12]

Anecdote has it that Gorbachev and Shevardnadze themselves had a feeling that the country was in a serious malaise. Apparently Shevardnadze said to Gorbachev, 'Everything's rotten', while the two of them were holidaying on the Black Sea in 1984.[13] On being made General Secretary, Gorbachev reportedly said to his wife Raissa: 'We cannot go on like this.'[14] Of course, it is easy to pick comments like these out of context in order to suggest that the new party leadership had a conscious sense that the country was in a fundamentally bad way. In fact, there is no evidence to indicate that Gorbachev, Shevardnadze and Yakovlev believed that the Soviet system itself was flawed.

At the same time, the more conservative communists were also conscious that there was a problem. Brezhnev's successor, Andropov, was a disciplinarian who believed that a stricter regime would produce results. Corruption was targeted. In January 1983, the government increased the penalties for corruption, embezzlement and bribery. The anti-alcohol campaign that was launched soon after Gorbachev came to power reflected the same approach. Essentially, the government saw consumption as the problem itself, rather than as a symptom of a problem, and thought that by clamping down on alcoholism the situation could be improved. In the short term they were successful. The amount of alcohol consumed was reduced considerably. In the Russian republic, for example, it fell from 13.6 to 5.6 litres per head from 1984–1988.[15] However, the accompanying loss of revenue discouraged the government from persisting and the campaign petered out in 1988. The anti-alcohol campaign was largely promoted by Yegor Ligachev and Mikhail Solomentsev within the leadership. Gorbachev happily embraced it, but he was never a convinced abolitionist and later he tried to dissociate himself from the policy.[16]

One of the difficulties in analysing Gorbachev's ideas is to know exactly which ideas were his own, and which came from the small group of people who worked with him. His closest advisers on many issues were his foreign policy advisor Aleksandr Chernyaev, Vadim Medvedev and Aleksandr Yakovlev. Shakhazarov was influential on foreign policy. Others who worked closely with him at different times included Bikennin and Aleksandr Boldin. When Gorbachev worked on a speech, he dictated his ideas to a small group, who then turned his thinking into a text. Occasionally, however, his advisors were able insert their own ideas into the texts. According to Bikennin, Gorbachev's important speech on the 'living creativity of the people' of December 1984 was prepared by Boldin, Bikennin, Medvedev and Yakovlev. Bikennin claimed that he himself added the concepts of 'acceleration' (*uskorenie*) and the 'human factor' into the text. Gorbachev's book, *Perestroika* (1987), which reflected the underlying vision of perestroika in its early years, was in part a fruit of this teamwork. According to Vadim Medvedev, Chernyaev, Yakovlev and Medvedev himself all contributed to the preparation of the text. However, Medvedev also emphasised Gorbachev's central importance to the editorial process, and denied that the book was ultimately the work of others.[17] Ultimately, it may be impossible to clarify who was responsible for which ideas during perestroika. Indeed, the fact that Gorbachev's speeches were often a fruit of collective work is indicative of the way in which political ideas are often shaped by particular social networks rather being the fruit of lone inspiration.

The policy of *glasnost'* was a response to the kinds of problems that had been highlighted by Zaslavskaya and Aganbegyan. Gorbachev first used the phrase '*glasnost*'' at a conference in December 1984 at which he declared that providing workers with open and honest information about life was a sign of 'trust in people'; it raised the level of labour activism, reduced bureaucracy and helped avoid errors in party and state work. *Glasnost'*, he then wrote in *Perestroika*, would help people better understand the Soviet past and present, and consequently help them to participate better in the process of restructuring.[18] Gorbachev's understanding of morality and conscience fitted into this political framework. In a speech in May 1987, he declared that perestroika should be approached with the same 'persistence, good conscience [*dobrosovestnost'yu*] and thoroughness' that were needed for preparing space flights. The speech was entitled 'To be a patriot of one's country, to live and work according to conscience'; it thus specifically linked morality with patriotism and hard work.[19] This was a utilitarian understanding of ethics and conscience, and in this sense Gorbachev was a typical Soviet leader. Contemporary propaganda reinforced the idea that conscientious behaviour reinforced the needs of party and state. Posters were printed in 1986 and 1987 entitled, 'Live and work in truth and good conscience', and, 'To live and work with a clear conscience is the first commandment of a communist'.[20]

Although Gorbachev's ethical utilitarianism matched that of his predecessors, the fact that he recognised that the country faced a serious motivational crisis should not be underestimated. Furthermore, his thinking in the first years of perestroika contained enough references to the need for freedom and universal values to suggest a real shift in the regime's ideology. At the Central Committee Plenum of 27 January 1987, Gorbachev suggested that reform would be based on a 'psychological restructuring' of the Soviet character away from the submissiveness of the past.[21] This was a declaration of the importance of freedom; only free individuals could be fully responsible. In the Soviet Constitution of 1936, freedoms had been granted 'for the purpose of strengthening the socialist system'[22]; and indeed the idea of freedom had always been limited by the Soviet political context. However, Gorbachev believed that a greater measure of pluralism did not need to compromise the power of the state. In *Perestroika* he declared that perestroika united socialism with democracy.[23] A second important feature of Gorbachev's political thinking was his open espousal of universal human values. Although in *Perestroika* Gorbachev stated his commitment to Leninist principles, he said much that suggested a universal rather than a class approach to morality.

Perestroika was in many ways an attempt to re-establish the ethical viability of Soviet socialism. The book was full of moral phraseology, and it included a number of references to conscience. Gorbachev lamented the 'decay in public morals' and the 'symptoms of moral degradation in the country', and stated that the moral aspect of perestroika was 'of tremendous importance'. Without a revival of socialist values, he said, the restructuring drive would not work.[24] He wrote that the ideas of perestroika had been prompted 'not just by pragmatic interests and considerations but also by our troubled conscience'. He noted that 'reason and conscience' were beginning to 'win back ground', observing that letters to the party from people in the country suggested a widespread urge to live and work 'as bid by conscience'. The main task, he stated, was to 'lift the individual spiritually', and 'to mould a socially active person, spiritually rich, just and conscientious'. He declared: 'What is needed is greater order, greater conscientiousness, greater respect for one another and greater honesty. We should follow the dictates of conscience.' Furthermore, Gorbachev suggested that his own way of conducting policy reflected this high-minded approach:

> We have, as a matter of fact, excluded all discrepancy between what we tell our foreign interlocutors behind closed doors and what we declare and do in public . . . There must be more light and more openness in international affairs and less tactical manoeuvring and verbal juggling.[25]

There was unquestionably a straightforward quality in Gorbachev's approach to negotiation that made progress on foreign policy issues possible. In his memoirs, *My Six Years with Gorbachev*, Chernyaev recalled a conversation that took place between Gorbachev and Helmut Köhl on 28 October 1988, which seems to have reflected these qualities:

> We witnessed an amazing metamorphosis that day ... [The two men] talked to each other like ordinary people ... And there was no hint of the 'class approach', there were no ideological assaults or any other clashing viewpoints, not a hint of hostility or distrust, no attempts to trick the opponent or mislead him regarding intentions.

Chernyaev suggested that as a result of the meeting, the trust between Gorbachev and Köhl began growing rapidly, trust that soon turned into 'a real, informal friendship'.[26] Also in his memoirs, Chernyaev cited an occasion when Gorbachev insisted on keeping his promises to the international community. In January and March 1989, he blocked a move by Shevardnadze to use military aid to prop up the Afghan leader Mohammed Najibullah's crumbling regime, which would have meant breaking international agreements. After discussion with key policy-makers, Gorbachev announced: 'I am definitely against all bombings or anything of the kind. While I am general secretary I won't permit anyone to trample the promise we made in front of the whole world.'[27]

Gorbachev certainly saw his own conduct of foreign policy in a positive ethical light. This is evident from his account of the arms control negotiations at the Reykjavik summit of October 1986. In his memoirs, Gorbachev recorded that he arrived at the summit with some bold proposals for arms reductions that even some of his own generals were unwilling to accept. Reagan also did not respond positively, and negotiations broke down. Gorbachev recalled that his first reaction had been to try to exploit the breakdown of negotiations for propaganda advantage. Yet he resisted that: 'My inner intuition was telling me that I should cool off and think it all over thoroughly.' Forty minutes later he gave a press conference in which he declared the summit a breakthrough rather than a failure. According to Gorbachev, the decision involved a choice between acting in anger and manipulating the situation, or following his 'inner intuition'.[28] Gorbachev evidently believed that his stance at the conference was the result of some kind of internal moral victory over himself.

Gorbachev's account of what happened at Reykjavik puts him in such a good light that it is hard not to be sceptical about it. Nevertheless, irrespective of the genuineness of these observations, which it will always be difficult to establish, it is possible to interpret Gorbachev's actions here and elsewhere not so much as reflecting a commitment to moral principle as 'common sense'. Indeed, a number of commentators suggest that common sense was an important feature of Gorbachev's outlook. Chernyaev himself commented that Gorbachev rejected Marxism-Leninism in favour of basic common sense.[29] In a biography of Gorbachev,

Gorbachev's one-time press secretary, Andrei Grachev, stated that Gorbachev's main God was 'common sense'.[30] There were other advocates of common sense among the party reformers. Bakatin was an admirer of 'common sense'.[31] Tsipko once suggested the perestroika was best seen as a 'revolution of common sense'.[32] It may indeed be that in certain circumstances, the words 'conscience' and 'common sense' had a similar meaning. In his book *The Fate of Marxism in Russia*, Yakovlev lamented that there were few in Russia who appealed 'to people's conscience, to their common sense'.[33]

For all his boldness in certain situations, Gorbachev was himself moulded by his experience of Soviet life, and gained power by using the system to his advantage. Perhaps it was for this reason that the more radical democrats thought that he was playing 'a game called democracy', while in reality he was allied with neo-Stalinists like Ligachev.[34] Gorbachev certainly adopted many of the practices typical of his milieu. He tacitly admitted this himself in *Perestroika* when he said: 'We have grown accustomed to many practices where there was no openness.'[35] Of course, adapting to the system was a way of surviving. Yakvolev noted that 'the Byzantinism of those days was not so much a way of conducting politics, but simply a means of survival in the nomenklatura'. 'No one', Yakovlev also said, 'slipped into power in defiance of the System. No one. Gorbachev included.'[36] These men developed the psychological blocking mechanisms necessary to shield themselves from uncomfortable realities. Bakatin stated in his memoirs that 'people became accustomed to such a life, and worked out certain mechanisms of self-defence, including from their own consciences'.[37]

Gorbachev was certainly ready to adapt to the system. It appears, for example, that he was prepared to submit his friendships to its dictates. One of his closest friends from student days, Zdenek Mlynar, was one of the authors of the reformist Czech party programme of 1968. When Gorbachev visited Prague in 1969 with Ligachev, then head of the Tomsk Party, he did not visit Mlynar, and even removed him from his address book.[38] In 1969, the acting head of the Faculty of Philosophy at the Stavropol Agricultural Institute, F.B. Sadykov, published a reformist text entitled *Unity of the People and Contradictions of Socialism*, which provoked an angry response from Moscow, and consequently a reprimand from the local party. Gorbachev recalled: 'We really tore him to pieces ... My speech was highly critical. Sadykov was severely reprimanded and dismissed as faculty head.' Yet Gorbachev also reported that he did not feel fully at ease about the treatment of Sadykov and others: 'I had qualms of conscience about the cruel and undeserved punishment meted out to them.'[39]

'[Gorbachev] acted by the general rules of the game', Grachev noted. However, Grachev also suggested that although Gorbachev was ready to make eulogistic speeches when required, he was unhappy in doing so:

> Although Gorbachev did not ascribe to this linguistic babble [*treskotne*] a serious importance, and saw it as an annoying but inevitable obligation, in the depths of his soul, as with any normal person, there developed a frustration and moreover an anger that, unlike the majority who had only to listen to this flagrant nonsense, he had actively to carry out this bad spectacle.

If Gorbachev accepted the 'rules of the game', he in later years seems to have believed that his personality was modified by doing so. He recalled that in their youth both he and Raissa were by nature 'maximalists', but that his character subsequently underwent a certain change: 'Raissa remained the same, but I, specifically because of my duties and various problems, had to become a "man of compromises".'[40]

In his memoirs, Gorbachev acknowledged the power that the system had over people like him. His grandfather, Pantelei Gopkalo, was arrested during the purges of 1937–1938. However, throughout all his years as Stavropol Party Secretary, Gorbachev never asked to look at the proceedings against his grandfather. Indeed, it was not until after August 1991 that he asked to see them – when Bakatin was head of the KGB. He recalled: 'I never managed to cross that invisible mental barrier to ask for them.'[41]

The most reform-minded of the party leaders was Aleksandr Yakovlev, by reputation the 'architect of perestroika'. Like Gorbachev, Yakovlev found himself in the awkward position of questioning the system while defending it at the same time. As Tsipko wrote, there was 'a combination of the roles of a priest and a detractor of the doctrine in one and the same person'.[42] Yakovlev's reformism became public when he published a long article in *Literaturnaya gazeta* in November 1972, attacking dogmatism and Russian nationalism.[43] He subsequently became Soviet Ambassador in Canada for ten years. A month after Gorbachev became General Secretary, he was made head of the Institute of World Economy and International Relations (IMEMO) in Moscow. As early as December 1985, he sent a memorandum to Gorbachev suggesting that the one-party system be dismantled, arguing that the first step in this would be to divide the Communist Party itself into progressives and conservatives. Gorbachev rejected the idea as too risky.[44] Yakovlev was made a candidate member of the Politburo in January 1987, and a full member in June 1987 when he assumed responsibility for ideology and propaganda.

Like Gorbachev, Yakovlev was strongly committed to the ethical dimensions of perestroika. In an article 'Perestroika and Morality', published in *Sovetskaya kul'tura* in 1987, Yakovlev stated that conscience, morality and responsibility were 'self-regulating qualities' that were greatly needed in society. He also said that it was important to instil in people a sense of their own worth, and this was something that was 'inseparable from conscience'. He also described morality and democracy as inseparable. At the same time, he defended the October Revolution as a 'moral revolution of protest'.[45] In another essay 'The Political Philosophy of Perestroika' (1988), Yakovlev declared that the source of perestroika's vitality was a 'moral feeling' and that 'from the very outset all the problems of perestroika and the developments of its concept were stated and resolved in moral rather than purely pragmatic terms'. He stressed the importance of the ethical dimension of socialism and called for a 'renaissance of the people's spirituality'.[46]

Yakovlev's attitude to Marxism evolved during perestroika in important ways. Like Tsipko, it seems that he had long been sceptical about aspects of Marxism.[47] In an interview given in 2003 he stated that he read Marx while studying at the Academy of Social Sciences in 1956–1960 and concluded that it was a 'kind of nonsense' (*erunda*), and that he realised that Lenin was a 'mediocre publicist' at that time.[48] Yakovlev also promoted the kind of anti-dogmatism that was to be found in the ideas of Tsipko and later Gorbachev; at the beginning of perestroika, he wrote a paper in which he strongly criticised the 'dogmatic interpretation of Marxist-Leninism'.[49] At the same time, in spite of his avowed scepticism of Marxism, Yakovlev continued to defend it publicly. In 'The Political Philosophy of Perestroika', he wrote: 'We have stated the problem of morality in our life, dialectically, in Marxist terms.'[50]

A key moment in the evolution of Yakovlev's ideas was his speech in July 1989 given in honour of the bicentennial of the French Revolution. It was at this point that Yakovlev publicly dissociated himself not only from Stalinism, but also from Leninism. Lenin's 'revolutionary romanticism' that idealised violence, he declared, was at the heart of the problem. More than that, however, he declared that the whole European revolutionary tradition was at fault. The Bolsheviks, believing in violence as a 'cleansing force', had looked to the Jacobin terror of 1793 as a model. The crimes of the Soviet state from Lenin onwards were rooted in an 'idealization of revolutionary violence that [traced] back to the very sources of the European revolutionary tradition'. Yakovlev stated that 'the idea of violence as the midwife of history had exhausted itself'.[51]

This thinking fed into a more substantial theoretical repudiation of Marxism, published in the West as *The Fate of Marxism in Russia*.[52] This was written before and during the summer of 1990, and was shaped by the events of the 28th Party Congress when the position of many of the delegates caused Yakovlev to have grave doubts whether the reforms would turn out well. *The Fate of Marxism in Russia* was an attack on every aspect of Marxism. Yakovlev clearly had lost any intellectual respect for Marxism. 'There is nothing serious or scientific in Marxism, even if there is an Enlightenment and Kantian origin in Marxism', he said. He also attacked the ethical foundations of Marxism, stating that Marxism 'contrasted with the entire spiritual order in Russia', and was 'formulated and developed as an ideology for overcoming and destroying everything that made up the material and spiritual foundations of contemporary civilization'. All Marxist doctrine, he declared, was aimed 'against universal human morality as the ethical basis of civil society'. He condemned the idea that everything could be justified if it served the idea of total revolution, and stated that Bolshevism was an 'anti-human precept'. He also noted Marx's opposition to the idea of the Christian doctrine of the essential spiritual equality of people. One of Marx's great failings, he said, was to suggest that people were not spiritually equal; he assumed that the social worth of a person who was striving to become a 'real essential human being' was not the same as someone who was not struggling and had been deformed by the unreasonableness of social relations. In this, Yakovlev said, there was a 'latent store of revolutionary maximalism'.[53] In other words, Marx's theory opened the door to mass violence.

The concept of conscience came up repeatedly in *The Fate of Marxism in Russia*. He wrote: 'Conscience, solidarity and charity operate along with economic interests'; 'In the end, Marx brought us to the abyss, to stagnation, to the destruction of conscience'; and 'The highest but always knowable form of information, just as its result, is conscience as the measure of morality and justification of the very existence of humanity'.[54] Elsewhere, Yakovlev came to advocate what he termed 'moral democracy'; he noted that democracy alone was not enough, for Hitler had come to power through a referendum. What was needed was 'democracy based on deep-rooted human morality and conscience'.[55] Yakovlev also used the term 'conscience' in relation to specific political issues. Chernyaev reports that in January 1989, on discovering that Shevardnadze wanted to aid Najibullah, Yakovlev rang Chernyaev and declared that he was uneasy about it. 'My conscience is troubling me', he said.[56] Yakovlev also sought to justify his own political moves in terms of conscience. After leaving the party in 1991, Yakovlev stated in an interview that 'one should act morally, that is according to one's conscience', and that in leaving the party, he 'acted in that way'.[57] In a later book, *Striving for Law in a Lawless Land* (1996), Yakovlev suggested that in Russia there was a tragic contradiction between law and conscience; since law was so often associated with tyranny, conscience was contrasted with law. He also endorsed Kistyakovskii's point in *Landmarks*, that Russia lacked a legal consciousness.[58]

Yakovlev stated in his memoirs that Gorbachev's ideas reflected a mixture of idealism and pragmatism, and belief and unbelief.[59] His own outlook certainly contained a strong dose of pragmatism also. He gained a reputation for concealing his views. One party leader called him 'the great silent one' (*velikii mol'chalnik*). Yakovlev later recalled: 'I understood very well that to constantly speak the truth would only bring harm. It would inspire your enemies, and give them an excuse. And that would be it. I was silent, and pursued my own business.'[60] It was possible to interpret this kind of pragmatism as reflecting tactical wisdom. In a comment that likely contained an element of self-justification, Tsipko stated that

Yakovlev's approach allowed him space to pursue his policies more discreetly: 'I don't think we can rebuke him for taking his time and not telling the truth about Marxism when he was in office. He would have given the opponents of reform more pretext to attack the as yet fragile democracy.'[61] Yakovlev's pragmatic sense of what was and what was not possible contributed to the way in which Tengiz Abuladze's film *Repentance* was released in 1986–1987. Yakovlev saw the film privately and suggested that the film be leaked carefully to selected audiences; the number of screenings would then be increased, until there was some inevitability about the film's acceptance.[62]

However, Yakovlev's pragmatism also meant that he had a relatively poor reputation with the intelligentsia. He was asked by Brezhnev's ideology chief Mikhail Suslov to manage the propaganda side of the Sinyavskii–Daniel trial, but replied that he was 'not sufficiently "in the know" to take part', and that the matter should be handled by another department. Yakovlev said of this: 'I wouldn't exactly call that bravery of the highest order.'[63] In fact, Yakovlev later seems to have felt a certain discomfort about the past. In his memoirs he declared:

> For many years, I betrayed myself. I was doubtful and confused about myself, hunting out justifications for what was happening around me in order to silence a querulous conscience [*vorchlivuyu sovest'*]. All of us, especially the nomenklatura, lived this kind of double, or even triple life. We thought one thing, said another, and did a third.

While he was in Canada, he said, he was 'ashamed sometimes' for things that happened in Soviet foreign policy.[64] In *The Fate of Marxism in Russia*, he wrote: 'I also see the contradictions and my inability to shake off completely the burden of the beliefs and errors of many years and the desire to be charitable to the deceptions of the past.'[65]

As well as referring to conscience, Yakovlev emphasised the importance of repentance. In a Presidential decree of 13 August 1990, all the victims of political repressions from the 1920s to the 1950s were rehabilitated. This was followed by another decree by which Soviet citizenship was returned to twenty-three former dissidents, including Chalidze, Kopelev, Orlov, Solzhenitsyn and Voinovich. On 20 August, Yakovlev appeared on the evening news programme *Vremya* to say that the two decrees were acts of 'repentance'. He stated that the second of the decrees was effectively directed against the party leadership itself:

> I think it smells of hypocrisy when we rehabilitate someone and pretend to be graciously pardoning them for their past sins. It is not they whom we are pardoning, it is ourselves. It is we who are guilty for the long years that they have been slandered and repressed. It is ourselves we are rehabilitating.

These people, he said, wanted good and freedom for the country, but the leadership answered with evil, prisons and camps.[66] Yakovlev referred to the earlier period of repressions, noting that the judges of that time were now dead. However, he commented that the judges who had sentenced the later generation of dissidents were still alive. He appealed to people to avoid revenge against these judges, yet at the same time observed: 'People must know their names and actions, in order to judge them by the moral criteria which our society is in so much need of.'[67]

By repentance, Yakovlev meant an acknowledgement of responsibility for past repressions, and in this sense his speech reflected the emphasis on de-Stalinisation and truth-telling that was typical of the time. The statement, 'It is we who are guilty', however, was ambiguous, for it is not clear whether or not Yakovlev was implying a personal sense of guilt for the past. This use of the plural in reference to repentance was widespread. Chernyaev introduced his own memoirs by observing that his country had a difficult history 'for which not "somebody else", but all of us, are to blame.'[68] In the cases of both Yakovlev and Chernyaev, shame and blame are generalised, although a sense of personal responsibility is discreetly implied. Elsewhere, Yakovlev emphasised the personal nature of repentance, although he warned against a 'general national striptease'. In an interview of May 1991, he explained that each person had to take responsibility before his conscience for his involvement in deeds of the past, whether it were for shooting, betraying or informing on someone, or simply for being silent:

> It is necessary to say to oneself: 'It depends on me!' And to act accordingly. That is the meaning of repentance. The inner work of the soul and conscience, and not a general national striptease. Repentance is not a trial of somebody. It is confession – honest and full. And each should decide for himself, whether he should repent and in what way.[69]

The spiritual dimension of perestroika seems to have loomed increasingly large in Yakovlev's mind. Speaking at a Vatican conference in January 1992, he declared that perestroika was not a political revolution in a conventional sense and was not based on class struggle; rather it was 'revolution of conscience' that was connected with what he described as 'a feeling of shame for our life and for our history that the overwhelming majority of people had'.[70] What lay behind these points is not fully clear. Once again, Yakovlev's comments contained a hint of personal shame, but his points were also sufficiently collectivised to distance him from direct responsibility. Doubtless, too, he shaped his message to engage with a Vatican audience. At the same time, his interpretation was consistent with his previous writings. Commenting in 2003 on the speech, Yakovlev stated that what he had said was an 'illusion', but that he remained optimistic about the capacity of people to move beyond barbarism.[71]

Yakovlev's world-view came to reflect the synthesis of Christian and liberal values that was typical of the period. Two commentators noted that Yakovlev's speech of 20 August 1990 was remarkable for its heavy use of moral and particularly Christian phraseology.[72] Yakovlev was respectful of religion. He declared in his book on Marxism that 'the great systems of values were made by religions', and that 'the early Christian concepts, ethics, and moral ideas were not artificially invented'. Some of Dostoevskii's thinking was an inspiration here. Yet Yakovlev was not a religious person himself. His sympathies lay more with Kantian ethics. He opposed Marx's materialistic emphasis on natural necessity, believing instead in the spiritual freedom of man. In this Kant and Hegel were his models: 'The recognition of a spiritual rather than a natural necessity is authentic freedom. This is where ethical socialism originated for the Kantians. In the spirit of Kant, Hegel provides the solution for the antinomy of freedom and necessity.'[73]

Shevardnadze was also a man whose ideas contained a strong ethical dimension. In his recollections, *The Future Belongs to Freedom* (1991), he suggested that moral factors were central to perestroika; 'universal, human values' as an alternative to the 'absolute of class origin' were a central feature of the ideology of perestroika. Asked at the 27th Party Congress how the values of the working class differed from universal human values, he replied that the two were not inherently contradictory: 'The relationship is one of a part to a whole.' Shevardnadze dissociated himself from the doctrines of Machiavelli, and presented himself as an advocate of a moral approach to politics, declaring that 'moral politics' was the 'credo of the pragmatist'.[74] He said that lying was 'always counter-productive', and that high aims could not be realised by low methods, truth by lying, or justice by unjust means. Instead, embracing the philosophy of Abuladze's *Repentance*, he stated that an ethical approach to life, based on self-denial and sacrifice, could become 'a generally accepted norm for human existence': 'Politics has to come to terms with this sooner or later.' Shevardnadze was also in theory committed to non-violence. He stated that many of his generation were deeply affected by a '1956 complex', which involved the rejection of the use of force as a political instrument.[75] In regard to his religious beliefs, Shevardnadze said in 2000 that he was a believer and that he 'probably always believed in God, even in the Politburo', although he also noted, 'You cannot become religious in a day.'[76]

Throughout *The Future Belongs to Freedom*, Shevardnadze referred to his relationship with the regime, and to the moral choices and dilemmas that he faced during his career. He said that he questioned the Stalinist system in his youth, even though he continued to believe in Stalin personally; only later, 'when this machine began to fall apart', did he remember the 'anxious brooding' of his youth. His father-in-law was executed as an enemy of the people, and Shevardnadze was warned by a high-ranking party functionary that his resumé would suffer if he married his wife,

Nanuli; he thus married her, he said, knowing that he could be made a 'pariah' and an 'outcast'. Although he denied that *The Future Belongs to Freedom* was a confessional work, it contained a confessional tone in places. Shevardnadze stated that he originally joined the party with mixed motives:

> Some people were drawn to the Party from an instinct for self-preservation or the realization that there was no other way of finding a place in society worthy of their talents; others, and there were quite a few of them, were prompted by their heart and soul. It would not be truthful for me to claim that in my case only the second motive was at work, without the first.

He also said that he should have protested against the treatment of the dissidents; indeed he was 'obligated to protest', but he was 'not prepared to do so, either inwardly – psychologically – or politically'.[77]

Shevardnadze also interpreted certain events of the perestroika era in moral terms. He stated that the making of the film *Repentance* was a 'question of principle' for him. On hearing of Abuladze's concept for the film, he expressed uncertainty that it would ever get a wide distribution, but encouraged Abuladze to go ahead with it. When he moved to the Ministry of Foreign Affairs in Moscow, the film was put on hold for a while; according to his recollections, his 'conscience pricked [him] now and then' about this.[78] In defending his decision to resign as Minister of Foreign Affairs in December 1990, he declared: 'Although I had said publicly time and again that nothing would keep me from leaving office if I found it impossible to be true to my convictions, few people took me seriously.'[79]

Yet, if *The Future Belongs to Freedom* suggested a man who endorsed many of the moral ideas of the period, Shevardnadze remained a complex and ambiguous figure. According to a recent biography of him, he was 'opportunistic, flexible, pragmatic, and ruthless'.[80] The emphasis on human rights that characterised his tenure at the Foreign Ministry can be seen as the product of sound calculation as much as idealism; it appealed to American leaders like George Schultz, who was a strong advocate of human rights. His leadership style was always autocratic; indeed, he himself stated that perestroika had been carried out by 'sending out directives from above'.[81] As Georgian Party Secretary, he was tough with the dissidents, and had always been ready to indulge in the ritual flattery of Brezhnev that was expected of party leaders. He had a reputation for shifting his ideas according to circumstances; in his memoirs, Ligachev emphasised the 'elasticity' of Shevardnadze's views, and stated that he was ready to adapt himself to whatever policy the leadership adopted.[82] He also had a reputation for cunning. He would apparently speak privately with Gorbachev, encouraging him to make a certain point or state a particular principle in a speech, and then use Gorbachev's subsequent statements to say that this was what Gorbachev wanted. He justified his loyalty to the Soviet regime on two grounds: belief in the system, and later the need to protect his reformist agenda.[83] If there was a confessional element in *The Future Belongs to Freedom*, it was not in the end clear what Shevardnadze was taking responsibility for. He stated that the root of the existing evils was not in individual people, but in 'the system'.[84] If this was the case, then no personal repentance was needed.

Like his fellow party leaders, Boris Yeltsin also used moral rhetoric. However, he used it in a different way. His popularity stemmed partly from the fact that he mobilised the sense of injustice that was latent in the population. He spoke openly of the hypocrisies of the system; for example, at the 27th Party Congress in February 1986, he said: 'We can no longer tolerate the unquestioned authority of rank, the infallibility of the leader, the double moral standards.'[85] At the same time, Yeltsin's political rise was due to the fact that he was willing to challenge the way in which the party's power was enforced. Most notably, at a Central Committee Plenum in October 1987, Yeltsin took the floor at the end of the meeting and declared that perestroika was encountering difficulties, and that the party needed to draw lessons from the 'blank spots' in Soviet history. He claimed that Gorbachev was being eulogised in an excessive way, and stated that he himself wished to retire as First Secretary of the Moscow Party. Yeltsin's intervention was unscripted, and indeed it was unclear whether or not he had planned to make it in advance.

Politburo members reacted with outrage. Ligachev rejected Yeltsin's comments, and stated that he was not pulling his weight in the Politburo. Shevardnadze declared that Yeltsin's speech was 'completely irresponsible', characterised by 'primitivism', and 'at a certain level a betrayal of the party'.[86] Yakovlev stated that the speech was 'politically mistaken' and 'morally unsatisfactory', and that Yeltsin had been carried away by personal ambition. He also said that Yeltsin had confused personal frustrations with the larger political situation, and that his attitude was deeply conservative, rather than revolutionary.[87] The purport of Yakovlev's remarks, he said later, was that Yeltsin's provocative attitude might turn out to be counter-productive to the reform process; and apparently Yeltsin himself approached Yakovlev afterwards and said, 'Perhaps you are right.'[88]

Yeltsin, although unwell, was forced to attend a Party Plenum in Moscow on 13 November attended by Politburo members, where he was formally reprimanded for his outburst. Following a succession of aggressive attacks, Yeltsin admitted that 'ambition' had been one of his main traits of character, and that he had been unable to fight it successfully. He then confessed to his guilt:

> I am very guilty before the Moscow Party organization, very guilty before the Gorkom, before the Buro, before all of you, and of course I

> am very guilty before Mikhail Sergeevich Gorbachev, whose authority is high in our country and in the whole world.[89]

Yeltsin was then formally made First Deputy Commissar of the USSR State Construction Committee, an unexpected appointment which indicated that disgraced party leaders might still maintain a presence in public life. According to his memoirs, Yeltsin then went into a time of severe self-examination. The following spring, he started to re-emerge. He gave an interview for the BBC in May 1988 that showed no signs of repentance. Then in August 1988 he declared in an interview for the Riga edition of *Sovetskaya molodezh'* that socialism was losing his attraction for him; he said that 'people found themselves pressed down by the fraudulent moral standards of the regime', and that the state had 'trained people to be unanimous in suppressing dissent, not united in aspirations'.[90]

At one level, Yeltsin's actions at the October Plenum and after were comparable to the actions of some of the dissidents. Yeltsin essentially challenged the party's internal 'rules of the game'. It was a vital moment in his rise to power, and perhaps did lead to a kind of self-liberation. Certainly, in his autobiography *Against the Grain*, (1990), Yeltsin wrote that he had had to 'screw up [his] courage' in order to speak out at the October Plenum. However, by expressing himself in this way, Yeltsin was also promoting an image of himself as a courageous fighter against oppression.[91] Vadim Medvedev recalled Yeltsin as a 'demagogue', and suggested that Ligachev was a 'much more honest [*poriadochnyi*] person' than Yeltsin in the sense that his views remained consistent from day to day, whereas Yeltsin's convictions were constantly changing.[92] Perhaps, indeed, Yeltsin's actions were the outcome of a certain kind of combative temperament. Whatever the motives, Yeltsin was empowered by his experience; he had gone through a *prorabotka*, confessed his wrong-doing, and then repudiated his recantation.

Yeltsin was quoted by the *Washington Times* in December 1989 as saying that the '"rusty nail" had to be pulled out once and for all, rather than little by little'. He stated: 'We can't achieve something positive by compromising.'[93] Again, it was the kind of uncompromising language that certain of the dissidents used. The more moderate Politburo reformists were essentially gradualists. Bakatin, for example, believed in an evolutionary approach to political change, and came to regret the 'Bolshevik' nature of perestroika.[94] On a trip to London, the democrat Galina Starovoitova joked that Bakatin wanted to cut off the cat's tail bit by bit. Bakatin retorted: 'A cat without a tail is still only a cat without a tail, and we need a tiger and not a cat.' The radical economist Grigorii Yavlinskii stated: 'It is impossible to jump over the abyss in two strides'; Bakatin's view was that the best option was 'to build a bridge and cross the [abyss] gradually'.[95]

The Russian title of *Against the Grain* was *Confession on a Set Theme.* The different titles illustrate the different ways in which political opposition to the Soviet regime was interpreted. The Western publisher chose a title that suggested Yeltsin was a dissenter and that was thus likely to appeal to Western liberal opinion; on the other hand, the Russian version located the book closer to Russia's moral and spiritual traditions. On the one hand, Yeltsin was making his bid for freedom; on the other he was making a personal commitment to truth. Both titles accurately reflected tendencies within the book; indeed, Yeltsin's commitment to both tendencies reflected the dual nature of glasnost. At the same time, the titles pointed to the different ways in which Western and Russian audiences read the process of perestroika.

In terms of the genre, Yeltsin's *Against the Grain* and Shevardnadze's *The Future Belongs to Freedom* had much in common; both works were a mixture of straightforward memoir and moral autobiography. Indeed, they were not unlike the works of dissidents who interpreted their lives as a moral journey: Shevardnadze partly structured his life as a series of moral decisions, where sometimes he chose rightly and at other times wrongly; Yeltsin's confrontation with the party leadership in the autumn of 1987 was presented as the moment when he liberated himself from enslavement to the state through an act of truth-telling. If these men had little contact with dissident ideas at the beginning of perestroika, their memoirs suggest that by the late 1980s, dissident ethics were beginning to permeate their thinking. However, there was another moral tradition at work in these memoirs: the party tradition of self-criticism. Self-criticism was an integral feature of party life. To some extent, then, these memoirs reflected the party's own ethical tradition, as well as that of the dissidents. More generally, both Shevardnadze's and Yeltsin's recollections had political purposes. The confession as political philosophy was very much alive.

It is difficult to measure the influence of the dissident intelligentsia on the party leadership. There was clearly an awareness of dissident thinking. In summer 1978, a speech by Solzhenitsyn at Harvard was videoed and shown to top KGB and party leaders.[96] Bikennin recalled that when Yakovlev was in Canada, the two of them shared Sakharov's ideas about convergence. Also, when he worked at the Central Committee, Bikennin got hold of the books of some of the dissidents from the KGB and from the editorial offices of *Voprosy filosofii*, including *The Gulag Archipelago*.[97] Clearly, some of Gorbachev's key advisers were well informed about the debates that had raged within the intelligentsia over the previous decades. At the same time, there was ignorance too. The relative freedom that existed for party leaders was combined with a measure of isolation. *Glasnost'* started to break down that isolation. Not only was the Soviet intelligentsia and the wider population affected by the policy of *glasnost'*, so too were some of the creators of the policy themselves. The party reformers launched the policy with one set of purposes, and found that the debate itself rebounded back on them to reshape their own thinking. This certainly was the case with Yakovlev, but it happened with Gorbachev too. There is an example of this in Chernyaev's memoirs when he describes talking to Gorbachev in January 1989 about Solzhenitsyn's *Lenin in Zurich*, a work in which Lenin was depicted as a quasi-demonaic figure driven by inner compulsions and rage. Gorbachev was apparently impressed by the book, although he later told Sergei Zalygin that he could not forgive Solzhenitsyn for his view of Lenin.[98] Chernyaev quotes him as saying: 'It's human. Anyone, even a great hero, can be shown as an ordinary person, reduced to a philistine. But this is not caricature. You really recognize Lenin.' Chernyaev goes on to suggest that Gorbachev henceforth began to see Lenin as an 'ordinary person, one who could not only make a mistake…, but who probably made a mistake of "historic proportions"'. Chernyaev then read the book himself, noting that he was 'amazed by the author's relative objectivity, considering his hatred of the revolutionary cause'.[99]

At the same time, it would be a mistake to assume that ideology and politics alone held the key to the attitudes of the party reformers. There were clearly many factors at work. Ordinary relationships and jealousies were important. Bikennin recalled that one of the most dangerous moments of his life was when he was rude to a man whose wife was Brezhnev's sister-in-law. Here ideology was not central at all.[100] Writing about Gorbachev in *Moscow News*, Elena Bonner said that she could discern the love that existed between Gorbachev and his wife Raissa, and that she could see something very similar in Yeltsin's home.[101] To her, the quality of these people's marriages said something about their character. Social and professional background was doubtless vital. Bakatin's background was in capital construction, and the characteristics he most admired in some of the USSR's ministers of heavy industry were 'super-professionalism' and 'human wisdom'.[102] Ethnic background was important. As a young man, Shevardnadze was influenced by the world of the Georgian village.[103] These things are a reminder of how difficult it is to generalise about moral values; each person's outlook is shaped by different influences.

11 Conscience and repentance during *glasnost'*

The policy of *glasnost'* led to a vigorous public debate in the USSR about moral and religious questions. Soon after Gorbachev came to power, there was a change of direction in cultural policy. In 1986 Gorbachev and Yakovlev manoeuvred a number of their supporters into key positions. For example, in May 1986 Klimov became Secretary of the USSR Union of Cinematographers, and in summer 1986 Sergei Zalygin became chief editor of *Novyi mir*. Dmitrii Likhachev was appointed Chairman of the Soviet Cultural Foundation in November 1986. Sakharov was released from internal exile in Gor'kii in December 1986.[1] Also in 1986 Yurii Afanas'ev was made rector of the State Historical Archives. Bikennin became editor of *Kommunist* in May 1987. Journals and newspapers adopted very diverse positions on Gorbachev's reforms: *Kommunist*, *Religiya i nauka* and *Voprosy filosofii* generally promoted reform within a traditional Soviet framework, whereas *Literaturnaya gazeta*, *Novyi mir* and *Ogonek* emphasised universal human and sometimes Christian values. In respect to 'conscience', another important newspaper was the weekly *Moscow News*, although that was in part designed for a foreign readership.[2]

During the first years of perestroika, literary works were at the forefront of the ethical debate. Certain writers supported the official thinking on communist ethics. The plays of Mikhail Shatrov, for example, promoted a strongly neo-Leninist message. Shatrov's *The Dictatorship of Conscience* (1986) implicitly attacked Stalinist and Brezhnevite versions of communism while still advocating revolutionary idealism. Conscience and Leninism were linked. Towards the end of the play, one of the characters solemnly declares to the audience: 'For as long as there are people who, speaking in Leninist words, take no word on trust, say no word against conscience, do not fear any difficulty, do not fear any struggle for a serious purpose, history will not be pointless.'[3] His play *Onward, Onward, Onward!*, written in 1987, addressed the question of ends and means. It was an imaginary dialogue between key Bolshevik leaders, which involved a re-appraisal of the legacy of the revolution. The play was overtly political in the sense that it offered support for Gorbachev's line that the

October Revolution was a very positive event that had only been distorted by Stalinism. The Soviet police chief Feliks Dzerzhinskii, for example, was presented as a man of virtue, his conscience still burdening him over his support for Ordzhonikidze and Stalin during the Georgian affair in 1922. Lenin's ethics were depicted as very different from Stalin's. Marxism, communism, and the October Revolution, Lenin declared, were impossible without 'a specific set of political and moral standards'; and he stated: 'All the truly socialist measures that have been brought about – yes! Stalin's methods – no! Morality à la Stalin – no!'[4]

Another work that created a strong impression was Anatolii Rybakov's *Children of the Arbat*, first published in the journal *Druzhba narodov* in 1986. The novel, which had been written in the 1960s, depicted the lives of young people in Moscow in 1934 at the time of the 17th Party Congress. It was in some ways a typical piece of socialist realism in that it was constructed around a tension between students imbued with a genuine party spirit and others with cynical careerist attitudes. The hero of the novel, Sasha Pankratov, a young engineering student and loyal member of the Komsomol, is unjustly accused of subversion, and arrested and sent into exile. At the end of the novel, Pankratov meets an elderly communist woman, Lydia Grigorievna, who has committed herself to caring for the son of some suppressed kulaks. Her selflessness impresses Pankratov, and he says of her behaviour:

> People are still upholding the highest human values, and one of those values is compassion . . . I don't know much about Christian theology. But I think that what moved Lydia Grigorievna was above religion and ideas, it was the capacity to sacrifice oneself for others . . . human feeling has not been killed in people and it never will be.[5]

This was the kind of humanist spirituality that reform-minded communists could endorse.

Rybakov was in a sense looking for a spiritual foundation for the Soviet project. In this aspiration, he represented a wider tendency. Many writers believed that Russia had lost its way spiritually. It was a feeling that was well expressed by the hero of Viktor Astaf'ev's short story 'The Blind Fisherman', published in *Nash sovremennik* in 1986. Lamenting the loss of moral values and religious belief, he cries: 'Who is there to pray to? Of whom do we ask forgiveness? For we surely once knew and have not yet forgotten how to forgive, to forgive even our enemies.'[6]

The spirituality of the literature of the first years of perestroika was not always orthodox. For example, in 1986 and 1987, *Novyi mir* published two important novels that reflected both enthusiasm and scepticism about Christianity. The hero of Chingiz Aitmatov's *The Place of the Skull* (1986) was a young man, Avdii Kallistratov, who sought to develop an updated form of Christianity, and to sacrifice his life in the struggle against evil.

Kallistratov denied the idea of a transcendent God, stating, 'There is no God outside consciousness', and 'The church is me myself.'[7] The novel included a long dialogue between Christ and Pontius Pilate. In Tendryakov's *An Attempt at Mirages* (1987), a team of researchers explored the role of the individual in history by examining what would happen if an important person was removed from history. Christ was chosen for removal. However, when a physicist feeds data into a computer in order to come up with a contemporary ideal of an Apostle, the computer comes up with a Christ-like leader figure.[8] *An Attempt at Mirages* had been first submitted to *Novyi mir* in 1982, but contained lots of quotations from the Bible and thus had to wait for a more liberal climate before it could appear. The philosophy behind the novels of both Aitmatov and Tendryakov was arguably close to that of the 'God-builders', Lunacharskii and Gor'kii, whose concept of God differed considerably from the traditional Jewish or Christian one.[9] Aitmatov, defending *The Place of the Skull*, still felt the need to affirm his own atheism.[10]

The sense that the country was in a spiritual crisis sometimes led to a focus on apocalyptic themes. The Strugatskiis' novel *The Doomed City* (1988), a work originally completed in 1975, was the story of a journey in the afterlife of a government official, Andrei, who in his previous life had risen to the top through manipulating the system to his advantage. In the novel, which was full of implicit references to Dante's *Divine Comedy*, there was a continual interplay between the temporal world that Andrei came from, and the afterlife that he was now in. They were indeed likened to one another, and depicted as realms of spiritual disorder. The underlying message of the novel was that the Soviet Union was spiritually a kind of hell.[11] Vladimir Dudintsev's novel, *White Clothing* (1988), a portrait of honest scientists struggling against a politicised scientific establishment during the Lysenko era, was full of biblical quotations. It took its title from a verse in the Book of Revelation in which people in 'white clothing' are described as those who have passed through the 'great tribulation'.[12]

The republished works of forgotten writers also reinforced the idea that communism had brought about a terrible spiritual crisis. Vladimir Zazubrin's novella, 'The Chip', written in the post-revolutionary era but only published in early 1989, added to the burgeoning literature on the moral psychology of revolutionary behaviour. The story was a study of the inner state of the head of a Cheka unit during the Civil War, Andrei Srubov. Srubov is responsible for executing enemies, and his actions are depicted as destructive of his true humanity. His mother tells him: 'You have turned into someone else.' Some of those carrying out executions are described in the same way: 'Three of them worked just like machines. Their eyes were empty.'[13] Yet Srubov is also in turmoil over what he is doing: 'Not everything was allowed. Everything had its limits. But how could one prevent oneself from crossing those limits?.'[14]

In regard to moral and religious issues, the most important work of the period was Abuladze's film, *Repentance*. The screenplay of *Repentance* was written in 1981–1982, and the film was itself completed in December 1984. It began to be shown towards the end of 1986 to private audiences at the Writers' Union club, the House of Cinema and the Artists' Union, and it was then released for commercial distribution in 1987. Thirty million tickets were sold, although it was a demanding film and audiences were often depleted by the end of performances.[15] The film was an examination of the life and legacy of a Stalin-like dictator, Varlam, and the moral and religious issues that arose when the state that he ruled started to confront its past. Generational issues were important in the film. Varlam's son and political successor is a weak man who is too much connected to his father's legacy to face the past honestly; indeed, Abuladze stated that he regarded Abel as more dangerous than his father because his split consciousness made him 'more unpredictable'. In attempting to confess his sins, Abel even acknowledges his own moral blindness himself: 'I'm losing my moral principles, I can no longer distinguish good from evil, I can justify any baseness.' Abel's son Tornike eventually brings matters to a head, accusing his father of being responsible for the trial of Keti, the wife of a former artist who died in the labour camps: 'She's not insane and she's not guilty. How can you go on lying forever? All you care about is your own well-being; doesn't your conscience bother you?' Tornike shoots himself, and Abel is confronted fully with the consequences of his behaviour. The film ends on a religious note. An old woman asks: 'What good is [a road] if it doesn't lead to a church?'[16]

A reviewer in *Pravda* interpreted *Repentance* in the light of the politics of the day, suggesting that facing the truth about the past was necessary for the promotion of humanism and democracy, and for a 'genuine socialist revitalisation'. Rather differently, in an article for *Moscow News*, Vladimir Lakshin discussed the theme of repentance itself. He suggested that in the film there were two repentances, one true and one false: Abel's first attempts at self-appraisal are inadequate until his son Tornike's suicide forces him towards a truer reckoning. Lakshin interpreted the suicide as an 'expiatory sacrifice'. The public reacted to the film in a variety of ways, some, for example, welcoming the explicit exploration of Soviet excesses, and others expressing irritation that the past was brought up in that way.[17] The power and popularity of the film were due to the fact that it addressed questions of personal complicity with Stalinism in a direct and provocative way. It was perfectly attuned to the generational conflicts and moral debates of the 1980s, and in offering a spiritual interpretation of Soviet history replicated the concerns of some of the literature and film of the previous decades.

Artistic explorations of moral and religious questions provoked a wider philosophical debate about the sources of morality and religion. Aitmatov's *The Place of the Skull*, for example, was the excuse for a discussion in the popular daily paper, *Komsomol'skaya pravda*, about the relations between culture, morality and religion. In July 1986, one of the country's leading atheists, N. Kryvelev, strongly criticised Aitmatov's novel on the grounds that to reject principled, logical atheism was to reject the 'very foundations of a scientific and materialist world-view'. Kryvelev's article provoked Yevtushenko to a reply in December 1986, in which he complained that Kryvelev had made the mistake of confusing the opinions of the hero of the novel with those of Aitmatov himself. However, he also argued that it was wrong to exclude religion from mankind's experience of morality, and that the Bible was a 'great cultural monument'. He lamented the fact that the state press had published the Koran but not the Bible, and suggested that it was not possible to gain an adequate understanding of the classics of Russian literature without knowing the Bible. Yevtushenko was not writing from a religious point of view. He believed that culture was the source of morality: 'Atheism in and of itself is not the source of morality. Culture is that source. The culture of human behavior. The culture of conscience that has no need of scientific diplomas.'[18] Yevtushenko's article was printed alongside an article by another representative of scientific atheism, Suzen Kaltakhchyan, in which Kaltakhchyan said that the moral standards and artistic works which had been associated with religion over the centuries in fact had nothing in common with religion and were determined by the 'concrete, historical forms of socio-economic life and the class struggle'.[19]

Novyi mir played an important part in fostering discussion about the origins of morality. In an article in 1987, the writer Andrei Nuikin reacted negatively to what he saw as the doctrinaire atheism of Kryvelev and Kaltakhchyan, and stated that it was important for people to learn how to debate matters of religion in a balanced way. He himself defended the atheist position, declaring that atheism could explain the earthly, social nature of the commands of the categorical imperative, and that it taught a person 'to listen to the commands of his own soul, his own conscience' which were the 'most sensitive indicators of morality'.[20] Later in the same year, another writer, Arsenii Gulyga, noted the positive contribution that religion had made to morality over the centuries, and suggested that although the time for religion had passed, its experience remained valid. He criticised the authorities' refusal to publish the Bible in any quantity, and he also called for an appreciation of the ethical teachings of Lessing, Kant, Schopenhauer and Solov'ev. His own position was to call for moral absolutes without the religious dimension: 'There is no God, but that does not mean that everything is permitted ... Truly, in rejecting religion, we must not throw out the idea of the moral absolute, we must not forget about reverence.' He suggested that shame, compassion and reverence were the key elements of morality.[21] In an article on Vladimir Solov'ev in *Literaturnaya gazeta* in 1989, Gulyga raised some of the same themes. Without embracing Solov'ev's religious world-view, he suggested that

Solov'ev had brought to completion Kant's ethical system, and stated that the country's moral state was caused not only by social and economic conditions, but also by the 'predominant, relativistic conceptions of ethics'.[22]

The nature and origins of morality continued to be a concern of Abdusalam Guseinov. Writing in *Kommunist* in 1988, Guseinov called for an emphasis on morality, while also rejecting 'moralism': 'True morality begins where moralism ends.'[23] In an interview with a Kiev journal in 1990, Guseinov went on to lament the academic nature of contemporary ethics, noting that young people wanted an ethics that could help them learn something about 'pangs of conscience, guilt, repentance, etiquette', and to learn how to analyse the 'moral collisions' that abounded in their lives; ethics should be at the service not simply of the academy, but of life. Guseinov himself recommended stoicism as a philosophy that could help people face death, or deal with tragedies like Chernobyl.[24]

Another man whose writings about moral issues provoked widespread discussion was the novelist and journalist, Daniil Granin. In particular, Granin's article, 'On Charity', which appeared in *Literaturnaya gazeta* in March 1987, provoked a lot of debate about the moral state of the country. Granin lamented the loss of the culture of mutual self-help that had existed in the war years, and the widespread use of bribery among the medical profession. He attributed these things to the fact that 'social injustice, the lie, window-dressing and selfishness' had gone unpunished in Soviet life, and more specifically to the mass repressions of the collectivisation period when people were prevented from helping their neighbours. He also noted that epithets like 'sister of charity' or 'brother of charity' had been entered in dictionaries as dated. Taking some of Pushkin's stories as a model, he called for literature that would depict the suffering and sadness of many people's lives.[25]

Historians also raised moral issues. Indeed, the past became something of a battleground over which moral debates took place. The regime of Ivan the Terrible, for example, provoked heated discussion about ethics and about the role of historians. In 1987, the specialist on sixteenth-century Russian history V.B. Kobrin published an article in the journal *Znanie-sila* in which he noted that Soviet historians had generally justified Ivan the Terrible's cruelty as necessary for the consolidation of state power. However, Kobrin criticised the terroristic methods used by Ivan, and argued that a more gradualist path of reform had been available in the sixteenth century. Moreover, he suggested that historians should not avoid making moral judgements, for to do so meant in effect to advocate the philosophy that the ends justify the means. In saying this, Kobrin clearly had in mind certain aspects of Soviet history, as well as the story of Ivan the Terrible.[26]

Dmitrii Volkogonov was another historian with moral concerns. In his biography of Stalin, which caused a major stir when it appeared in 1989, Volkogonov suggested that Soviet power had been built upon lies. He observed: 'If lies are repeated often enough . . . they come to seem like the truth.' He also made repeated references to the theme of 'conscience': 'The individual consciences of those Bolsheviks . . . who did realize that Lenin's Testament required close scrutiny, were silenced by the slogan of "unity"': 'No one in the Central Committee leadership made any attempt to exercise their conscience when they had the chance, however late in the day'; 'Anyone with a conscience could not survive in the NKVD'; and 'People allowed their own consciences to be driven into a reservation'.[27] Volkogonov's thinking was clearly informed by his own experience. He was quoted in 1991 as saying that his break with Soviet communism in the 1980s was a moment of personal liberation:

> History has literally led me to a complete denial of all that I had been praying for my whole life. The only thing I can be proud of – the greatest merit of my life – is that I was able to alter fundamentally my views. I feel very happy that by the end of my life I have freed myself from this horrible nightmare, this primitivism.[28]

There were a number of historians who did not like the new emphasis on morality. In *Kommunist*, the party theorists G. Bordyugov, V. Kozlov and V. Loginov complained that in recent historiography, 'the mythology of the "purity" (*neporochnosti*) of the revolution' had been exchanged for another mythology – 'the mythology of the "original sin" of the revolution'; the real drama of the history had been turned into a 'terrible, didactic fairy tale'. As to the violence of the revolution, they declared that the Bolsheviks had been forced to use violence by peculiar historical circumstances.[29] Such views provoked strong reactions. Disputing their ideas in a roundtable discussion in *Literaturnaya gazeta* in 1990, Tsipko challenged the view that cruelty, retribution and violence were necessarily embedded in the march of Soviet history. It was wrong, he said, to argue that the people of the 1920s and 1930s lived by entirely different values from those of their own day.[30]

Much of the debate about the moral and spiritual state of the country was engendered from within the country, and was sparked by people who were effectively 'in-system' dissenters. The boldness of some of the discussion should not be underestimated. In an editorial in *Referendum*, which was launched in 1987, one writer observed that dissidents who had said in the past what was being said now, had been put in jail for it.[31] However, in 1988–1989 the intellectual revolution took a new turn. A host of important works that were previously considered anti-Soviet appeared, including Dombrovskii's *The Faculty of Useless Knowledge* (*Novyi mir*, Nos 8–11, 1988), Grossman's *Life and Fate* (*Oktyabr'*, Nos 1–4, 1988) and *Forever Flowing* (*Oktyabr'*, No. 6, 1989) and Pasternak's *Doctor Zhivago* (*Novyi mir*, Nos 1–4, 1988). There was particular controversy over the publication of Solzhenitsyn's writings. An initial announcement by *Novyi mir* in

October 1988 that it would serialise *The Gulag Archipelago* the following year was rescinded, and the following month Vadim Medvedev announced that Solzhenitsyn's works would not be republished. However, the leadership changed its mind the following year. 'Live Not by the Lie' came out in *Dvadtsatyi vek i mir* (No. 2, 1989), 'Matryona's House' in *Ogonek* (Nos 23 and 24, 1989), and *The Gulag Archipelago* started to appear in *Novyi mir* in August 1989.[32] However, by the time that Solzhenitsyn's works appeared, many intellectuals had already read them in samizdat or *tamizdat* editions, and his work provoked less discussion than might have been expected.[33]

The publication of many previously forbidden works permitted the absorption of the dissident intellectual heritage into the country's public culture. It also gave added impetus to the re-evaluation not only of Stalinism but the revolutionary tradition itself. In this, *glasnost'* was effectively taken over by dissident ideas. At the same time, the impetus for this change came in a sense 'from below', from reform-minded intellectuals who already knew dissident ideas from their reading of samizdat and sought to make them mainstream. This was a point that was emphasised by Orlov. He asserted that after years of secretly reading and discussing the ideas of Sakharov and Solzhenitsyn, Soviet citizens began to emerge from their '*samizdat*-filled kitchens' to push the boundaries of *glasnost'* 'towards the dissidents' conception of it'; freedom of expression in the Western sense as a fundamental human right became the accepted doctrine of the time. According to Orlov, it was the people themselves who created *glasnost'*.[34] At the same time, dissident ideas helped to influence the party reformers themselves. There is considerable evidence to suggest that Gorbachev borrowed the term *glasnost'* itself from the dissidents.[35] More generally, the dissidents left behind 'a corpus of writings and an example of personal heroism' that inspired the reformers of the Gorbachev era.[36]

It was not just the dissident tradition that became accessible, however. Russian Orthodox culture and teachings became available. There was a renewed interest in pre-revolutionary political traditions. *Landmarks* was arguably one of the canonical texts of the period; both liberal and conservatives found inspiration in it, and it reflected the religious humanist tendencies of the period. At the same time, Western popular culture was very influential with the younger generation. Mikhail Epstein suggested that the 'sixtyish' conception of literature as a 'social tribune' and a 'moral homily' was foreign to the younger generation of people who were reaching maturity in the 1980s.[37] The outlook of the younger generation, which was strongly shaped by the values of Western consumerism and pop music, had more individualistic and environmental concerns.

Not everyone approved of the moral ideas of the reform-minded intelligentsia. There were powerful conservative forces that saw things differently. Valentin Rasputin wrote in 1988 that although truth depended on morality, it was not the same thing as morality.[38] Many conservatives were worried that the emphasis on truth-telling and repentance was damaging to the interests of the state and nation. There were in effect three groups in the conservative opposition to Gorbachev's reforms: neo-Stalinists, national Bolsheviks and conservative nationalists. These groups in effect formed an unlikely alliance from 1987 onwards.[39] Through newspapers and journals such as the newspaper, *Sovetskaya Rossiya*, the weekly *Literaturnaya Rossiya*, the monthly journals, *Nash sovremennik, Moskva*, and *Molodaya gvardiya*, they were able to present a strong alternative to Gorbachev's reforms.

The neo-Stalinist view of the past was cogently articulated in Nina Andreeva's article in *Sovetskaya Rossiya* in 1988, 'I Cannot Forego My Principles', which was seen by many as part of a campaign by Ligachev to halt the process of perestroika. Andreeva stated that with too much focus on the negative sides of Soviet history, 'nihilistic views' were intensifying among some students, and she called for a renewed emphasis on the 'class vision' of the world.[40] She asserted that contemporary views of the Stalin era were one-sidedly negative, and she complained about the 'left-liberal dilettantish socialism' that rejected proletarian collectivism in favour of the 'intrinsic worth' of individuals, and the substitution of 'scholastic ethical categories' for social and political criteria.[41] National Bolsheviks like the novelist Yurii Bondarev were also concerned that Soviet history was being wrongly maligned. Speaking at the 19th Party Conference Bondarev expressed concern about what he saw as the nihilistic and extremist tendencies that had taken hold during perestroika: 'Confidence in history, in all the past, in the older generation, in inner human honour which is called conscience, in justice, in objective *glasnost'* – these things have been broken.' He declared that *glasnost'* and democracy should involve a high level of moral and civic discipline.[42]

Conservative nationalism was different. Valentin Rasputin was a good example of this tendency. Rasputin was never a member of the Communist Party, and he was strongly critical of the destruction of traditional Russian culture that had taken place during Soviet rule. Yet he was also worried by the values of the West. In an interview published in 1988, entitled 'If by Conscience', Rasputin declared that no young man who knew Glinka, Mussorgskii and Chaikovskii, and who had read Pushkin, Dostoevskii and Tolstoi, could get totally absorbed in rock music. He added: 'In brief, our enemy will quickly take over the hearts of those that are not occupied with what is ours.'[43] At the Congress of People's Deputies in 1989, Rasputin regretted the fact that perestroika seemed to be accompanied by open attacks on traditional morality. He drew attention to what he called the 'open propaganda of sex, violence and liberation from moral norms' that was taking place in the country, and condemned the use of explicit sex education in schools. He declared: 'Our youth senselessly perished in Afghanistan, but just as senselessly is it being crippled by the undeclared war against morality.'[44] Later, Rasputin, along with Bondarev, was among the group of twelve conservative nationalists and communists who signed a letter to the Soviet people that was printed in *Sovetskaya Rossiya* on 23 July 1991, which regretted the decline in love for the fatherland that had motivated their forebears. The signatories suggested that the 'most sacred things in life' for their grandfathers and fathers had been the homeland and the state.[45]

Although literature was at the forefront of *glasnost'*, it became less influential as the media became more independent and alternative political parties emerged. It lost the lure of 'forbidden fruit'.[46] Moreover, the history of literature in the Soviet era itself became a matter of considerable controversy. Questions were asked about the extent to which writers were themselves responsible for advocating social utopias. One article in *Literaturnaya gazeta* in 1991 raised the question of whether literature itself was not partly responsible for the bloodshed of the twentieth century.[47] More generally, the call to repentance, while at one level promising some kind of national healing on the basis of truth-telling, was also a source of enmity between liberals and conservatives as battles raged over who was guilty for the excesses of the past.[48]

During *glasnost'*, 'conscience' itself was a widely used term, a concept onto which people could project their concern about the moral state of the country, and their desire for some kind of moral and spiritual renewal. In his article in *Komsomol'skaya pravda* in 1986 Yevtushenko referred to what he called the 'culture of conscience'.[49] There was a widespread aspiration to create something like a 'culture of conscience', if that is understood to mean a culture that was founded on respect for human life. For many intellectuals, this kind of culture was understood to be a high culture. The idea that the arts had an ethical purpose, so beloved of the Russian literary tradition, was widely held during perestroika. Klimov, for example, declared that he had a 'messianic conception' of perestroika and *glasnost'*. He stated that film could help to restore morality and justice, and not only in the USSR; furthermore, he said that the world was moving towards 'a precipice of moral and spiritual emptiness' and that perestroika could 'improve the moral and spiritual atmosphere around the world'.[50]

A central figure in seeking to reformulate Soviet culture, and establish it on ethical foundations, was Dmitrii Likhachev. Likhachev's position as the head of the Soviet Cultural Fund, and his own academic expertise, made him an obvious focus for this ethical and cultural concern. Furthermore, although he was reform-minded, he was not a threat to the system. Some of his essays prior to perestroika included harmless quotations from Lenin that suggested an acceptance of the rituals of Soviet publishing.[51] During perestroika, this continued; Likhachev used references to Lenin to justify calls for less censorship and the opening up of Russia's cultural heritage.[52]

For Likhachev, culture and morality were closely linked. Writing on what he called the 'ecology of culture' in 1979, Likhachev stated that there were two kinds of ecology, a 'biological ecology, and a cultural or moral ecology', but he also noted that there was no separation between these two ecologies in the same way that there was no sharp separation between nature and culture.[53] Likhachev also drew attention to the two kinds of ecology in his *Letters on Goodness and Beauty* (1985), stating that the cultural sphere was essential for the moral and spiritual life of man. He saw great value in the public dimension of culture, noting that through streets, squares, canals, homes and parks people were reminded of the past, indeed they had a responsibility to people in the past and the future.[54] In an interview for *Literaturnaya gazeta* in 1988, Likhachev stated that technical knowledge was only a means to an end, and argued that culture itself was the purpose of the development of mankind. He clearly understood culture to mean high culture, endorsing the idea that there should be a Ministry of Culture, and rejecting the notion that culture should be subject to self-financing. There should be no free market in culture.[55] The Cultural Fund that he headed, he said, was then working out models of cultural life for small cities and villages. Earlier, in an article in *Literaturnaya gazeta* in January 1987 entitled 'Pangs of Conscience', Likhachev wrote that works of high culture contained 'exacting moral and ethical content', and he described literature as the 'conscience of a society'.[56]

In 'Pangs of Conscience', Likhachev condemned what he called the 'moral colour blindness' that meant that people could not distinguish between right and wrong. He regretted that petty dishonesties, such as forgetting to return books to their owners and not paying fares on the tram, were widespread, and stated: 'He who is true in small things is true in large things.'[57] He also said that the absence of conscientiousness in people caused material damage to the economy, suggesting that there had been a 'lack of civic conscience' in Soviet society in recent years. There was much in these points that the Gorbachev regime could endorse. However, Likhachev's article was also daring for its time. Likhachev called for an open society, and criticised fraud, arbitrary decisions and the anonymous writing of denunciations. He also stated that only those who had learned to think for themselves would be able to resist evil and live according to their consciences. Likhachev also said that satirical literature was beneficial to society, and called for the publication of works by Akhmatova, Bulgakov, Platonov and Zoshchenko.[58]

Likhachev distinguished conscience from honour. He wrote: 'Conscience always arises from the depths of the soul, and a person is always cleansed to a greater or lesser degree by his conscience. Conscience nags. Conscience is never false. It can be muffled or exaggerated (extremely rarely).' Honour, on the other hand, was often false. Likhachev particularly criticised the kind of 'honour of the uniform' that led people to defend false or faulty projects. True honour, he said, was in harmony with conscience. Likhachev recommended that as well as playing a central role in personal relationships, honour and conscience should be adopted at the state level.[59] There was no theoretical explanation of conscience here. However, the fact that Likhachev believed that conscience arose in the soul and had a cleansing power suggests that he had something of an Orthodox understanding of it. In an earlier essay of reflections on Russia, Likhachev wrote that the hesychast tradition had played an important role in forming the ethical ideals of ancient Rus' and in helping the Russian people to endure hardship and to approach the world with an attitude of love, kindness and non-violence; Likhachev's concept of conscience was not dissimilar to a hesychast version of it, although there were no specific religious references in the article.[60]

'Pangs of Conscience' provoked such a large reader response that a follow-up interview, 'From Repentance to Deed', appeared in *Literaturnaya gazeta* in September 1987. It opened with a quotation from a reader who said that all his attempts to live by his conscience had ended in a 'crushing defeat'. In response, Likhachev noted that 'civic conscience' demanded courage and sacrifice. In an implicit reference to 'hostage-taking', Likhachev agreed with the view that it was difficult to follow the dictates of conscience when it meant that others would thereby suffer. He noted that in professional situations people easily found themselves in a serf-like dependence on their employers: '[A person] cannot leave his "boss" [*barina*], even though the "boss" has got angry with him, and wants to take revenge.' Yet Likhachev emphasised that it was very important to resist and not to give way; he suggested that the hardships that a person went through in trying to be true to his conscience were nothing compared with the spiritual and soulful torments that would occur if he acted against his principles. His answer was an implicit recognition that appeals to conscience were often a challenge to the accepted patronage networks of Soviet society.

Likhachev's world-view contained an element of providentialism. He stated that he had managed to preserve his spiritual health in the Soviet system because he had not become embittered by his experiences on Solovki and on the White Sea Canal; he had accepted these experiences as 'something that had to be, as fate'. He also assumed the existence of a universal moral law, rooted in human nature: 'Morality is in human nature. Its norms are steadfast and eternal.' At the same time, Likhachev clearly wanted to see the emergence of a public sense of conscience. In the sphere of literature he said to readers: 'Do not be reconciled to bad books. Manifest your civic activity. Let the shop and the publisher know whom you are voting against.' Likhachev also stated that even more than *glasnost'*, the country needed democracy, and that people needed to learn to tolerate the opinions of others.[61] However, while evidently endorsing certain religious perspectives, Likhachev was also anxious to avoid any element of Orthodox nationalism. Writing in *Ogonek* in 1988 prior to the millennium celebrations, he praised the church's role in creating Russian culture, and emphasised Christianity's contribution to Russian ethical life. However, he also came out strongly against the unification of church and state, and warned that many Russians were only becoming interested in Christianity because it was fashionable.[62]

Likhachev was also interested in the theme of repentance. In 'From Repentance to Deed', he wrote: 'We are all guilty for what has happened in the decades gone by. I say it again: everyone, with no exceptions.' The refusal by people to acknowledge their own guilt led some, according to Likhachev, to seek revenge for past wrongs, and to seek to use *glasnost'* to attack those people they did not like. He believed this was wrong; to return evil for evil simply doubled the evil.[63] Writing in *Moscow News* in 1991, he stated that the lack of repentance at the government level was having a detrimental effect on policy. He called on the CPSU to repent of its crimes, and suggested that the political dynamics of 1991 had a spiritual element to them. He declared that Gorbachev was surrounded by those who had little knowledge of the people and who lacked good judgement, and said that these people were motivated by fear because they had not repented.[64] In this case, Likhachev's assumptions were similar to those of the dissidents who took the view that without a measure of self-overcoming, proper understanding of the world was impossible.

Likhachev was promoted as a role model for the intelligentsia in the early years of perestroika. He combined Russian patriotism, moral universalism, and support for the Soviet regime in a way that suited the party reformers. His 80th birthday in 1986 was celebrated with great enthusiasm in the press. The writers of a lengthy biographical article in *Literaturnaya gazeta* suggested that in a country where there was a lack of people who reflected the best moral principles, Likhachev had the quality of refinement (*intelligentnost'*); and this refinement was made up of 'unselfishness and benevolent accessibility'. There was 'not a drop of vanity, self-interest or complacency' in his behaviour, relationships and business dealings. There was in him a 'natural, organic quality from the cultural depths, from that living soil out of which our remarkable Russian intelligentsia arose, carrying from one generation to another the great tradition of democratism, honour and conscientiousness [*sovestlivosti*]'.[65]

Another figure who became a role model for the intelligentsia during perestroika was the Georgian philosopher, Merab Mamardashvili. Mamardashvili, who studied philosophy at Moscow University in the late 1940s, worked for a time as an editor for *Voprosy filosofii* and *Problemy mira i sotsializma* (1961–1966). He then became widely known for giving lectures, or what he called *besedy* (conversations). Always more of a performer than a writer, Mamardashvili had a marked ability to inspire audiences. Tape-recordings of his lectures provided the basis for a number of key works that were only published after his death.[66] According to one observer, his lectures on Descartes, given in Moscow in 1981, marked the birth of 'the professional philosophical spirit' in the country.[67] In these meditations, Mamardashvili emphasised the themes of faith, the possibility of God within a rationalist universe, the 'miracle of individual thought', and the centrality of epistemology to any primary philosophy. In general, he was always interested in the nature of philosophy, the experience of consciousness and individual autonomy.[68] Mamardarshvili was more interested in epistemology than ethics. However, he believed that conscience was essential to human identity. He took the view that the human being existed in 'the field of conscience and understanding', conscience being in the soul and understanding in the mind.[69]

For many intellectuals, Mamardarshvili came to represent an ideal of intellectual integrity. When he died in 1990, Nelli Motroshilova of the Institute of Philosophy observed that he spoke to hundreds of thousands of people as 'an aristocrat of the spirit, a Philosopher, a Wise Man', and that the Soviet regime had forgotten how important real philosophy was for a people's spirit, culture and conscience.[70] *Moscow News* printed a series of articles emphasising his greatness as a thinker, and his moral worth as a person. Aleksandr Yakovlev stated that his life had been one of 'honest service to knowledge and moral life', and that he had been 'inconvenient' to many people. Mamardashvili's archivist, Yurii Senokosov, stated that Mamardashvili saw the world in the 'dazzling light' of 'good and evil', and that he had been a person with 'a sense of absolute personal guilt and, at the same time, responsibility'. The sociologist Boris Grushin praised Mamardashvili for his refusal to adapt to and become infected by the evils of Soviet life. He commented that like Andrei Sakharov, Mamardashvili had kept himself 'untainted' by this influence, thereby demonstrating great 'non-conformism', and this proved that a man could be stronger than 'outward circumstances'. Karyakin praised Mamardashvili as a man who had remained true to his conscience. Karyakin observed that Mamardashvili had '[refused] to accept any compromises of philosophical conscience for the sake of politics'. He maintained in himself 'the organic combination of the culture of thinking with the culture of conscience', and he was one of those who had contributed to 'saving the honour, dignity and conscience of our sinful generation'.[71]

As an iconographic figure, Mamardashvili appealed to a more liberal and philosophical constituency than Likhachev. In addition, it is notable that the moral qualities that people saw in him partly corresponded to dissident ethics; Mamardashvili was admired for his refusal to compromise on his principles. At the same time, in a more general sense the articles that greeted Mamardashvili's death illustrated the intelligentsia's hunger to find new ethical role models, and its enduring commitment to the idea of personal integrity and virtue.

The interest in issues of conscience during perestroika was not just a matter of theoretical debate. The late 1980s were a time of soul-searching.

The semi-dissident historian, Mikhail Gefter, who had been involved with the journal *Poiski*, noted that even the best people had troubled consciences about the past. In an essay of 1988, he stated: 'Conscience is surely a great enigma – how it came to a person and how it was retained, and how it is maintained in spite of everything?' Quoting Albert Schweitzer's observation that 'a clean conscience is an invention of the devil', Gefter noted that some of the best people were morally troubled about their lives: 'In my youth and later, I knew people who had not done even a small base thing, but who today refuse to consider themselves innocent on the largest global account.'[72]

Daniil Granin noted that calls for repentance and truth-telling sometimes reflected an attitude of extremism. In an interview in 1987, he stated that '[to live] life according to the truth demands daily courage, the constant work of conscience'; yet he also observed that he sometimes had to work with people who were 'possessed fanatics of truth', and that this was very difficult. 'Ordinary human life', he argued, 'cannot be cruel in its demand for absolute truth.' This provoked the objection of a number of readers who believed that people should never compromise with truth. One respondent wrote: 'Truth is truth. The more merciless it is the better; we've had enough of compromises with the truth; we're fed up with half-truths, we're disillusioned with your position; what kind of morality is collaboration?' Granin commented that on meeting such 'extremists of truth', he found that they did not listen to any arguments, and stated only that people should have spoken out:

> The youngest of them say that it was necessary to speak out under Khrushchev and Brezhnev, without any consideration. And under Stalin! Their short memory or complete ignorance amazes me – surely they are aware of the all-powerful censors, the fears of editors, the panic demands on the radio and television.

At the same time, Granin also conceded the rightness of some of the questions. For himself, he noted: 'Constant battles with the censor led me to the point where the censor made a nest within me.' He warned against trying to judge the past at a judicial level: 'To replace the work of conscience with the work of criminal courts is impossible.' Nevertheless, he also noted that the lack of a system of retribution made matters of repentance very difficult: 'First of all elementary justice must triumph; only then can the conscience of people be addressed.'[73]

At a personal level, people were often preoccupied with whether or not they should have spoken out publicly against the regime. For some, the past suddenly looked morally tainted. One of Stalin's senior intelligence chiefs, Pavel Sudoplatov, recalled that he had been so committed to the Soviet Union that he had 'averted [his] eyes' from every brutality, finding justification in the transformation of the country from a backward nation into a superpower.[74] David Samoilov wrote about how his conscience had been dulled. In one of his last poems, written in 1989, which carried echoes of Tyutchev's 'Silentium', he wrote: 'One does not believe in public acts of repentance. / It would be better to be silent [*promolchat'*] and conceal [*utait'*].' Yet he went on to say that a new kind of moral reckoning was now needed: 'Now it is necessary to speak severely with oneself, and not to act as it was before – / Do you remember? – when conscience was dulled. / Oh, what a misfortune took place!'[75]

Oleg Bogomolov, Director of the Institute of International Economy and Political Studies, concluded that his past life had been full of self-deception. In 1990, he wrote that during the previous era he and like-minded colleagues had wondered which was more honourable: to prolong the life of the leadership by 'inserting into their speeches sensible ideas' or 'to renounce any participation in all this'. Unfortunately, he said, he and his friends chose the former option, and deceived themselves into believing that their academic notes sent to the leadership were somehow progressive. Bogomolov suggested that the greatest thing that he and some of his colleagues did was to heed Solzhenitsyn's call to refuse to participate in lies, but even that had not been very resolute. He went on to express regret that he and his contemporaries had lacked Sakharov's courage: 'We should have protested openly against deception, untruth and violence ... the main root of evil was cowardice and slavish submission to fate.' He then added: 'Repentance is necessary, not for the sake of punishment, as a ritual, but for self-purification, so that all our souls can finally awaken.'[76]

Repentance took various forms, both personal and collective. The philosopher Yurii Zamoshkin, dying of cancer in autumn 1991, expressed sorrow for signing an Academy of Sciences document attacking Sakharov, saying: 'Now I realize I was wrong. I need to repent ... I do repent.'[77] During a visit to the offices of *Literaturnaya gazeta* in 1992 by Natal'ya Solzhenitsyn, a representative of the paper, speaking in the name of everyone who had worked for the paper in the 1970s, 'asked forgiveness' of Solzhenitsyn for all that had been written about him in the paper.[78] At a conference in Switzerland, the Russian religious philosopher, Vladimir Zelinskii asked forgiveness of people from Poland, Czechoslovakia and other East European countries for all the evil, fear, suffering and lies caused at the hands of his country.[79] Yet Zelinskii's statement was unusual. Repentance on behalf of the nation raised the problematic question of whether it was the USSR or Russia that was morally guilty for the crimes of the Soviet era.

Clearly for some people, feelings of moral unease already existed prior to perestroika. For such people, *glasnost'* opened the door to a public articulation of these sentiments. For others, the public discourse of the time encouraged them to ask questions about their lives that they had not considered before. At the same time, it should be remembered that repentance became a fashionable theme during perestroika. In terms of the public gaze in the late 1980s and early 1990s, what might once have looked like a successful career in the party bureaucracy or the KGB now easily appeared immoral and punctuated by compromises. In this context, while many expressions of regret for the past were certainly heartfelt, some statements of repentance were likely also made in a ritualistic sense; they were the expected response to the situation. Such statements were a new form of self-criticism, *glasnost'*-style. The rules of the game were changing.

12 The democratic movement and its dilemmas

Calls to repentance were at one level calls to social reconciliation. The presidential decrees on rehabilitation of August 1990, which were described by Yakovlev as an act of 'repentance', facilitated the re-integration of some of the former dissidents into the life of the country, and made possible a sense of shared national memory. At another level, however, the idea of repentance threatened the security of some people. Who should repent, and for what, was a big issue, and it was one that affected many parties and organisations. It was clearly a major challenge to the CPSU, for it threatened to undermine its legitimacy in many areas. The Moscow Patriarchate was another body that found it an awkward subject.

It was a notable feature of the repentance discourse of the perestroika era that it was fuelled by members of the intelligentsia and religious dissidents rather than the church hierarchy. Many members of the Moscow Patriarchate had links to the party or the KGB, and as an institution it had long pursued a policy of cautious conformism. Indeed, the Moscow Patriarchate was arguably the only all-union organisation apart from the KGB not to undergo restructuring during perestroika.[1] Between 1986 and 1988, official attitudes to the church changed. In November 1986, Gorbachev told a meeting of party functionaries in Tashkent that religious affiliation and party membership were incompatible.[2] However, in April 1988 at a meeting with Patriarch Pimen at the Kremlin prior to the millennium celebrations, Gorbachev described believers as 'Soviet people, working people, [and] patriots', and stressed that the state's legislation on religion would be revised in line with Leninist principles. In July 1989, Konstantin Kharchev, who had recently retired as Chairman of the Council for Religious Affairs, stated that he had gone through a 'crisis of conscience' during the period 1985–1986 when 'personal experiences' led him to reject the old doctrine of the incompatibility between the church and communism. He stated that perestroika had led him out of the crisis and changed the climate so that the church was no longer incompatible with the regime.[3]

In response to the regime's apparent change of heart, the Moscow Patriarchate emphasised its loyalty to the state and support for perestroika. At the meeting with Gorbachev in April 1988, Patriarch Pimen noted the role that the church played in promoting universal human norms, and stated that the church had encouraged 'the moral education of the faithful, the assertion of the dignity of the human personality, the strengthening of the sanctity of the family home and a conscientious attitude towards labour'.[4] At the same time, as well as building bridges with the state, the Patriarchate also sought to establish its relative independence. On 27 December 1988, Pimen informed the Synod that he considered it necessary to study the issue of the rehabilitation of Russian Orthodox Church clergy and laymen.[5] In January 1989, the church announced the setting up of a commission to gather material on priests and believers who had been persecuted. Importantly, also, Patriarch Tikhon, who had led the church from 1918–1925 during some of the worst persecutions, was canonised.[6]

This was a signal that the church was ready to distance itself from aspects of Soviet rule. This was important, because the church was increasingly required to compete with the Russian Orthodox Church Abroad (ROCA). In the first nine months of 1990, the Moscow Patriarchate opened 1,830 new churches.[7] However, in June 1990, ROCA, known in the USSR itself as the Free Russian Orthodox Church, opened its first parish in Suzdal'. It quickly expanded, attracting adherents of the True Orthodox Church, who had for years pursued a catacomb-like existence.

The Moscow Patriarchate was engaged in a delicate balancing act: it wished to maintain its dialogue with the state while establishing its independence. In elevating Tikhon to sainthood, the church highlighted the balancing act that Tikhon himself had been engaged in. In a paper that was delivered at a conference in September 1989, and subsequently published in the *Journal of the Moscow Patriarchate*, Archbishop Simon of Ryazan and Kasimov read out an extract from one of the speeches at Tikhon's burial service in 1925 in which it was stated that Tikhon had had to try to find a 'common language' in order to keep the church afloat, and that 'much tact and wisdom, much patience and discernment, much love for his work and desire for peace' had been needed for him to do this work. According to Archbishop Simon, Tikhon had 'consistently and effectively' sought to maintain the church's independence on the basis of 'peaceful coexistence' with the new system.[8] Loyalty to the church and personal courage were among the qualities in Tikhon that were highlighted by the Moscow Patriarchate's formal statement on his canonisation in October 1989.[9]

The mixture of support for the Soviet leadership along with assertions of independence meant that although the church was increasingly popular, it was not entirely trusted by the intelligentsia.[10] Indeed, as perestroika progressed, the Moscow Patriarchate came under increasing scrutiny as questions were asked about the extent to which clerics had collaborated with the KGB. In November 1989, Gleb Yakunin was the opening speaker at the founding conference of a group set up to promote perestroika within the church itself.[11] Patriarch Aleksei, who succeeded Pimen, addressed the issue himself at a speech at Georgetown University in November 1991. He talked of how 'one had to struggle to remain oneself' in Soviet life, and declared that he had faced a 'dreadful choice'. He could have spoken out publicly against anti-religious persecution, but he would probably have been retired to a monastery as a result. He declared that God had made him responsible for his flock of believers, and that by speaking out he would have deprived them of the Eucharist and the chance to attend church: 'I would have committed a great, indelible sin, and out of concern for my own moral reputation I would have left the running of my diocese and betrayed my flock.'[12]

At the same time as justifying his past failure to stand up to the regime, the Patriarch distanced the church from Metropolitian Sergei's declaration of 1927. He stated that Sergei was told that if he did not sign the declaration, hundreds of bishops who were then under arrest would be shot. The declaration was not voluntary, and 'falsehood' ran throughout it, he said. He noted that to say this did not mean to attack the state, but simply to say that the state could be mistaken:

> We think perhaps the state can be mistaken, very badly mistaken, sometimes even criminally mistaken, and that when this happens, we have the right and the duty to bear witness before God, before our consciences, before the whole world to this infringement of God's truth.[13]

There was certainly a shift of thinking about conscience and the state here. If in earlier decades, obedience to state authority had been promoted both for the church itself and for the individual believer, the Patriarch's statement hinted that in certain circumstances, obedience to ecclesiastic authority or personal conscience might take precedence over obedience to authorities.

Although the church largely succeeded in establishing itself as a new source of moral authority during perestroika, the churchman who most captured the imagination of the intelligentsia, Father Aleksandr Men', did not represent the church hierarchy at all. This was partly because he had a reputation for holiness. It was also due to the fact that his perspective on Christianity fitted in well with the main Christian humanist currents of the time. His vision of Christianity was ecumenical and open-minded. At the same time, he was regarded with suspicion in conservative Orthodox circles, partly because his father was Jewish and many of his parishioners were converted Jews.

In an interview Men' gave four days before his death on 9 September 1990, he noted that many people who had sought to find in the church an alternative to Soviet ideology had been disappointed to find instead a 'new version of a closed society'.[14] In a posthumously published interview, he associated himself with the humanist tradition of Pico della Mirandola, Savonarola and Erasmus that did not reject the Christian gospel, but sought a rebirth of it. He distinguished between the kind of religion associated with the thinkers Berdyaev, Solov'ev and Mikhail Tareev[15], which he described as 'free and humane', and a 'closed one' that was 'life-denying' and debased the individual.[16] Elsewhere, he stated that the *Philokalia* had been compiled mainly for those who lived apart from the world, and that its special place in Orthodoxy had mistakenly led to a widespread belief that the Church Fathers preached a rejection of culture. Men' contested this, calling for the return of Christianity to an open model, and what Berdyaev had called 'the churching of the world'. Like Likhachev, Men' also called for repentance. He regretted that during the millennium celebrations of 1988, there had been 'not a single word of repentance' or reference to the tragedy of the Russian Church, but only 'triumphalism and self-congratulation'. Anti-Semitism, he said, remained a problem in the church. He subsequently stated that civilisations that repented could recover, citing Nineveh's positive response to Jonah's warning in the Book of Jonah as an example.[17]

Men's thinking and personality were very popular. He was once described as a missionary to the 'tribe' of the Russian intelligentsia.[18] The response to his death in the liberal press illustrated the way in which he had come to capture the imagination of the liberal Christian intelligentsia. In an article in *Ogonek*, 'Do Not Weep for Me', it was suggested that there were similarities between Men's death and Christ's; both were executed by the representatives of an empire.[19] In *Literaturnaya gazeta*, a group of Men's friends noted that just as John the Baptist had prepared people for the coming of Christ, so Men' had prepared people for accepting Christ in their hearts.[20] An article in *Demokraticheskaya Rossiya* suggested that Men' had been 'a spiritual pastor of the intelligentsia', just as the intelligentsia was called to be a pastor to the people; and it emphasised Men's universality, noting that he was open to truth in other branches of Christianity and other religions.[21]

The social anthropologist Ernest Gellner argued that the collapse of the Soviet system involved the end of a moral order and its replacement with civil society as an 'a-moral order'; the Soviet system was designed to enforce a particular version of truth, whereas the liberal democratic polity that took its place involved the endorsement of pluralism and the management of difference. Civil society meant 'the breaking of the circle between faith, power and society'; in the new dispensation, inquiry into truth and commitment to the maintenance of social order were separated.[22] Gellner's argument reflected the tendency of scholars to interpret the collapse of the USSR from a Western liberal perspective, and it has much validity to it. At the same time, an exploration of the uses of the word conscience by democrats and democratic groups during perestroika suggests that a concern for establishing a moral as well as a free society was part of their agenda.

The right to 'freedom of conscience' was an important element in the democratic ideology of the 1980s. The Soviet Constitution of 1977 guaranteed Soviet citizens 'freedom of conscience', interpreting it to mean the right to confess or not to confess any religion, and to perform religious worship or to propagate atheism.[23] However, since in the USSR anti-religious propagandists differentiated between bourgeois and Marxist-Leninist conceptions of freedom of conscience,[24] this commitment to freedom of conscience was clearly ambiguous.

Policy on freedom of conscience became a controversial issue during perestroika, and indeed became a matter of competition between the Soviet state under Gorbachev and the Russian Federation under Yeltsin. A new Law on the Press and Mass Media was passed in June 1990 that outlawed censorship and created a new registration process that freed the press from party supervision.[25] A few months later on 1 October 1990, a new Soviet law on Freedom of Conscience and Religious Organisations was passed that reaffirmed the previous commitments to freedom of conscience.[26] The law permitted evangelism, teaching religion to children and Sunday Schools. All educational establishments were obliged to acknowledge freedom of conscience. Religious citizens and organisations were guaranteed equality in all areas of public life, including access to the media. Students training in theological institutions were permitted to defer military service, making them the same as students in secular education, and soldiers were permitted to attend religious services in their free time.[27] Controversy nevertheless remained over the fact that religious organisations remained subject to the Council for Religious Affairs.[28] On 25 October 1990, the Russian Federation passed a more liberal Law on the Freedom of Religious Denominations, which included the right to perform religious instruction in school premises outside school hours, and the right to refuse to perform military service on religious grounds. The question of how to deal with conscientious objectors was not dealt with in the Soviet version of the law.[29] Although it was not yet clear how much power Russian laws had as against All-Union laws, the Russian version of the new law was clearly more liberal in emphasis. The struggle for greater freedom of conscience was thus part of the institutional struggles of the time.

The new Soviet law was clearly a liberalising development. However, it was also assumed that it would have a positive effect on the moral life of the country. In *Pravda vostoka*, TASS observer L. Ermakova stated that millions of people regarded the law on freedom of conscience as the basis for a moral revival.[30] If this is accurate, it suggests that what was essentially a liberalising measure was widely interpreted in moral terms. The combined desire to promote liberal policies alongside a universal morality was evident in the programme of the Christian Democratic Union (CDU), set up in Moscow in August 1989, and headed by the former dissident Aleksandr Ogorodnikov. The CDU programme stated that the basis of state law should be the Universal Declaration on the Rights of Man and the International Pact on Civil and Political Rights. In the section on 'freedom of conscience', it stated: 'Conscience, thought and faith make up the inalienable, free property [*dostoyanie*] of the individual and are not subject to state power, which is directed only at the actions of individuals.' Conscience was here understood as a kind of inherent category, giving a person moral worth and identity. However, freedom of conscience was certainly not understood as a recipe for radical individualism. In the section on foreign policy, the CDU stated that policy should be made on the basis of the principles of all-human morality, and not expediency, and there was a reference to the 'norms of international law and morality'.[31] Freedom of conscience and universal morality were here brought together.

The Russian Christian-Democratic Party (RCDU), which was founded in May 1990 after a split in the CDU, also promoted freedom of conscience in a liberal sense; it guaranteed clearly defined political and civil rights and 'freedom of expression, assembly, conscience, the press, demonstration, and unions', and declared that the basis for the Russian constitution would be the Universal Declaration on the Rights of Man. However, the section on freedom of conscience in the RCDU programme also contained a call for property that had historically belonged to the church to be returned.[32] Here, freedom of conscience was understood as something that would protect the church and rectify historical injustice. It was a moral as well as a liberal idea.

While it is not surprising to find this combination of liberal and moral features in a party committed to a mixture of Christianity and democracy, it was in fact a combination that was present in much of the reformist thinking of the period. For example, the Ukrainian nationalist organisation Rukh included among its fundamental guidelines both the 'protection of human rights and freedoms and national rights, [and] the moral healing of the individual and society'.[33] In the economic sphere, too, arguments for liberalisation during perestroika were not articulated as arguments against a moral order. The alternative to the enforced moralism of the centrally-planned economy was not necessarily understood as amoral. This is evident in the thinking of the economist, Nikolai Shmelev. Shmelev, who had once worked in the Central Committee under Yakovlev, published a widely discussed article on the Soviet economy in *Novyi mir* in 1987, in which he called for the opening up of a Soviet market. He declared that Soviet attempts to circumvent the objective laws of economic life and to suppress work incentives that for centuries had 'answered the nature of man' had led to the opposite outcomes from those that had been intended.[34] Shmelev's reference to the 'nature of man' suggests that he assumed the existence of a human nature that was not purely plastic. In a subsequent interview, Shmelev suggested that efficiency and morality could go together: 'It is very simple. Everything that is economically inefficient is immoral and everything that is economically efficient is moral.' He stated, indeed, that it was 'common sense' to approach things in that way, and that the economic theories that had been invented in offices had ended up 'violating economic law and life itself'.[35] Principles, he was saying, should arise from life, and not the other way around.

From their inception, the informal social and political movements of the late 1980s were concerned with ethical questions. An important vehicle for the politics of conscience was the environmental movement. Environmental concerns brought together both nationalists and democrats. Nationalist environmentalists believed in the importance of preserving Russian culture and morality. Their emphasis was on rural life, and they promoted the restoration of churches and monasteries. The Anti-Nuclear Society led by M.Ya. Lemeshev, and the Fund for the Restoration of the Cathedral of Christ the Saviour led by the writer V.A. Soloukhin were expressions of this tendency. Valentin Rasputin was involved in the Baikal Fund. Sergei Zalygin's organisation Ecology and Peace brought together many of those who had been involved in the campaigns to prevent the diversion of rivers.[36]

One movement that did not flourish in the perestroika years was the brigades (*druzhiny*) for nature protection. In 1960 the Moscow Society of Naturalists was central to the formation of the first of these student brigades, which was set up in the Biological Faculty of Moscow State University. In the pre-perestroika period, these groups were an important means for developing civic activism. However, as political life became more diverse in the late 1980s, many students were attracted into politics itself. However, out of the brigades there emerged the Social-Ecological Union founded in August 1987. Its first major conference took place in December 1988, and on February 1989 it organised a rally protesting against the construction of the Volga-Chograi Canal that took place in 100 cities. It was 'the first truly nationwide protest in Soviet history'.[37] In this campaign, calls for environmental protection were combined with a concern for personal moral renewal. The authors of an article in *Sovetskaya Rossiya* on the environmental situation in the lower Volga regretted the crudity of people in the Volga area and the lax morals of younger people. Noting that ecology had to be 'moral', they referred to the science of protecting against the erosion of the soil, but warned that there was no science against the 'erosion of conscience'.[38] The same combination of environmental and moral concern existed elsewhere. In a demonstration in Vingis Park in Lithuania in July 1988, there was a banner with the statement, 'Clean up our consciences and our rivers.'[39]

Calls for the extension of *glasnost'* were a central part of the dissident strategy in these years. Lev Timofeev, Larisa Bogoraz and Sergei Kovalev founded Press-Club *Glasnost'* in July 1987. Following his release from prison in 1987, a former editor of *Bulletin V*, Sergei Grigoryants, launched the journal *Glasnost'* which soon established itself as the most important example of the new samizdat. These calls for *glasnost'* reflected the general emphasis on openness and truth-telling that had been so important in the dissident movement. In these early years of perestroika, the dissident understanding of *glasnost'* clearly differed from that of the party reformers, for there were attempts to intimidate *Glasnost'* into silence. After 1991, Gorbachev suggested that the dissident movement and perestroika were 'stages in one process' but that was certainly not his view in 1987. Moreover, although at the beginning Gorbachev's concept of *glasnost'* had considerable support, organisations like the Memorial Society, Moscow Tribune and the Interregional Group played an important role in encouraging the reformist intelligentsia to switch support away from the official concept of *glasnost'* towards *glasnost'* as freedom of expression.[40]

The ethical vision of the dissident and reformist intelligentsia found its fullest expression in the Memorial Society. Two informal opposition groups emerged in the early 1987: the Club for Social Initiatives and the Club Perestroika. For a period in the Spring of 1987, the two groups worked together under the auspices of Club Perestroika. In June 1987 at a meeting of the Club for Social Initiatives, the geologist Yurii Samodurov suggested that a monument be erected to all the victims of Stalin's terror, an idea that had originally been proposed by Khrushchev. Vyacheslav Igrunov then suggested that the monument should be dedicated to all the victims of Soviet repressions. The idea attracted widespread support when it was put before a conference sponsored by the Club and the Moscow City Council in August. In subsequent months, a group called To Keep Alive the Memory of Victims of Repressions emerged, which later became the Memorial Society.

Memorial had a very high profile. At a large outdoor Moscow meeting of Memorial in June 1988, a petition with many thousands of signatures was handed over to Afanas'ev and Klimov for them to present at the 19th Party Conference. In the summer of 1988, backed by *Literaturnaya gazeta*, the Memorial Society successfully attracted the sponsorship of the Artists', Filmmakers', Theatre Workers', Architects' and Designers' Unions, and also the journal *Ogonek.* Following a public poll, those who agreed to participate in the Social Council of the organisation included Afanas'ev, Karyakin, Roy Medvedev, Okudzhava, Lev Razgon, Anatolii Rybakov, Sakharov, Mikhail Shatrov, Yeltsin and Yevtushenko. It was an impressive list.[41] However, keeping this diverse group of people together was difficult. The question of whether or not the society's objectives should be political was a matter of considerable debate in the group. Eventually, the Memorial Society became the equivalent of a civil rights movement.[42]

'Conscience' was a central idea in the Memorial Society and for the liberal press that supported it. Yevtushenko wrote the manifesto for the society, and stated that the purpose of the society was 'to cleanse the nation's conscience and to be clean in the eyes of our children'.[43] Afanas'ev interpreted Memorial as a 'movement of conscience', suggesting that it had a role in the formation of civil society in the country.[44] In November 1988, *Ogonek* and *Moscow News* were sponsors of a 'Week of Conscience'. The purpose of the week was to bring to people's awareness the criminality and suffering of the Stalin period. Here the stress on 'conscience' was designed to provoke remembrance of the past. However, it was also designed to prompt feelings of guilt and repentance in the population. A journalist for *Moscow News* commented:

> By perpetuating the memory of the victims of the people's tragedy we commit an act of nationwide repentance. We admit our guilt to them. The law does not know this guilt. Conscience alone knows it. We are to blame for the fact that they fell victim. Memory helps us save our soul.[45]

At the same time, *Ogonek* called for a 'Memorial of Conscience' suggesting that a memorial was a warning as well as a monument, and that it was necessary 'for moral cleansing', so that consciousness became 'active' and actions 'decisive'.[46] The Week of Conscience took place in the Palace of Culture of the Moscow Electric Lightbulb Factory. Thousands of people came to the event. People laid flowers on a labour camp barrow in front of a brick wall depicting a map of the Gulag, and made contributions to the fund that was created to support Memorial.[47]

At the founding conference of Memorial on 29–30 October 1988, delegates confronted a very difficult question: how to distinguish between perpetrators and victims? In her remarks, Larisa Bogoraz objected to attempts to provide chronological parameters to the repression – to suggest definitively that the process had began in 1918, 1921 or 1927. Moreover, she suggested that the people, while in part victim of the repression, were also responsible for it in that they had not been ready to resist. It was not possible to distinguish clearly between victims, executioners and accomplices: 'To say that these people are guilty and these not guilty is impossible.' Likewise, in an article in *The Memorial Gazette*, Lev Razgon noted that people working for the system were not always comparable; Yezhov and Beria were not morally equivalent to the intelligence agents who tried to warn the country about the Nazi invasion. For this reason, he endorsed the idea that any monument raised to the victims of terror should be given the simple and very general inscription: 'To those who were innocently killed.'[48] The question of how to commemorate the victims in fact became a prolonged and complicated process.[49]

Memorial played a unifying role in the reform movement in that it brought together both former dissidents and reform-minded party members. Indeed, one of the reasons for the success of the democratic movement was that there was a unity between the former dissident intelligentsia and the reformist wing of the party. Sakharov, especially, played an important role in transmitting the ideas and values of the dissidents to reform-minded party members.[50] The alliance of these two groups was exemplified in the formation in 1989 of a club that was organised to monitor the progress of perestroika, Moscow Tribune. It included among its members Afanas'ev, Batkin, Karpinskii, Karyakin and Sakharov. Whereas Sakharov was a former dissident and Karpinskii was then outside the party, Afanas'ev was a convinced neo-Leninist and supporter of Gorbachev until as late as October 1988. Indeed, he was one of the leaders of the reform movement, and editor of an important collection of essays on perestroika, *There Is No Alternative* (1988), which reflected the growing convergence between party reformers, semi-dissidents and some former dissidents. Afanas'ev certainly adopted the moral language of the time. In his own article in *There Is No Alternative* he called for an overcoming of the past, and 'something like a collective moral cleansing'.[51] In an interview published in 1989, he said: 'It is absolutely necessary to tell the whole truth. We cannot ensure the success of perestroika without it . . . A society cannot live or develop normally without knowing where it came from and what it is . . . History is self-awareness.' He went on to say: 'Half-truths about the past will lead to half measures today.'[52] Self-censorship was not the only problem faced by historians, he noted; it was also 'fear, inertia, lack of resolve', and 'habits bred by having led comfortable lives too long'.[53]

Afanas'ev was the most outspoken of the democratic faction at the Congress of People's Deputies in May–June 1989 that was formalised in July 1989 as the Interregional Group. The Interregional Group contained the same combination of dissident and party figures as Moscow Tribune. The five co-chairmen of the group were Afanas'ev, Sakharov, Yeltsin, the economist Gavril Popov, and the Estonian academician Viktor Pal'm. The umbrella group Democratic Russia, which was set up in January 1990, grew out of the Interregional Group. On 2 February 1990, there was a large demonstration in Moscow that was supported by Democratic Russia, the Interregional Group, Memorial and Shield, a reformist group created by young army officers. In his address to the crowd, Yeltsin called for the end of Article 6 of the Constitution that guaranteed the party's leading role in the country and outlawed opposition political parties. Gorbachev decided to rescind Article 6 later in the month.[54]

The alliance between reformist communists and some former dissidents was controversial. The whole question of whether it was appropriate for former dissidents to work with the Soviet regime remained a divisive one. When Sakharov came out in support of perestroika after his return from Gor'kii, he was widely criticised by former dissidents and *émigrés*. Sakharov was upset, for example, by a critical article by Mal'va Landa – a dissident whom he greatly admired[55] – in which she accused him of collaboration with the authorities.[56] The newspaper *Ekspress-khronika*, edited by Aleksandr Podrabinek, spoke of the 'dissident nomenklatura'.[57] Sakharov and Kovalev were accused of 'going out' (*ukhod*) into parliamentary activity and of 'collaboration' (*sotrudnichestvo*) with the state.[58]

There were also continuing tensions between Sakharov and Solzhenitsyn on matters of principle. Hostility to Stalinism was the unifying idea behind Memorial.[59] However, this was too moderate for Solzhenitsyn, who turned down an invitation to be on Memorial's Council. In a telephone conversation with Sakharov in 1988, Solzhenitsyn stated that he could not endorse Memorial's ideological line on the grounds that he was against limiting criticism to Stalin alone; Lenin was the cause of the problem, and while Lenin's crimes were still a taboo subject in the USSR, he would not be a part of Memorial. In his memoirs, Sakharov explained why his own attitude to the matter was more pragmatic. Memorial, he said, was a mass organisation and thus 'mutual tolerance' had to be the rule. It also had to function in the conditions of 'Soviet reality'; thus the cautious formulation in the bylaws of Memorial that spoke of 'the victims of Stalinist repressions and other victims of state terrorism and illegal government acts' was more appropriate. The very fact that the Central Committee tried hard to prevent the registration of Memorial, Sakharov said, itself indicated that it had not succumbed to conformity.[60] Sakharov clearly felt that Solzhenitsyn lacked flexibility. He seems to have seen Maksimov in a similar way. After meeting Maksimov in Paris in 1989, he recalled that 'he was, as usual, battling "rhinoceroses" and their accomplices and the accomplices of their accomplices'.[61]

Many dissidents certainly found it difficult to know whether uncompromising hostility to the Soviet state was appropriate during perestroika. Differences in the dissident movement were very evident in early 1987 when Gorbachev offered the country's political prisoners a pardon. The question was whether or not it was permissible to accept this pardon and, if so, how to phrase the application for release in such a way that it was not in itself another subtle compromise with the regime. Sakharov and Kovalev were among those who encouraged prisoners to accept the offer of pardon. Others, however, saw this as yet another example of an attempt to undermine the integrity of people.

A variety of strategies were adopted in the phrasing of applications. Al'brekht was released after he stated his commitment to Soviet legality: 'I have always respected and observed Soviet laws. I intend in future to go on doing so.' Similarly, Timofeev wrote in his application that he had never had any intention of bringing harm to the Soviet system. This, he recalled later, was a compromise, because he believed that what the authorities wanted was in itself unlawful. Although he interpreted this as a 'compromise' on his part, he saw it as a justifiable one because it did not concern fundamental principles. He said: 'Without compromises with the system you can only communicate in a radical language.'[62]

Others sought to distance themselves from the concept of pardon; Grigoryants phrased his application for release so that it contained no reference to the idea of 'pardon', and likewise the young dissident, Kirill Popov, inserted into his application a statement that he did not consider his application a request for pardon. Ogorodnikov wrote that he supported the programme of reforms, but also drew attention to the fact that he was 'a son of the Orthodox Church and a prisoner of conscience'.[63] Tat'yana Velikanova tried hard to refuse her 'pardon'. She recalled: 'There was a decree of the Presidium of the Supreme Soviet about my pardon ... I said I do not want your pardon and I will not leave here.' Eventually, however, she was forced to take her passport, and returned to Moscow.[64] In late 1983, Podrabinek had been offered freedom on the basis of certain promises, and he refused. He was released anyway.[65]

It is interesting that unlike in their protest to the Soviet government on hostage-taking in 1972, when they were united, Kovalev and Velikanova were now on different sides. It reflects the fact that the ideological cleavages of the perestroika era did not necessarily replicate those of the earlier time. Although he backed Gorbachev's proposal, Sakharov seems to have recognised the strength of some of the dissident concerns. He subsequently wrote: 'The demand in 1987 that prisoners of conscience appeal for pardon was of course illegal from a moral and judicial point of view.'[66]

Clearly, some dissidents continued to be guided by the uncompromising ethical system that was formed in the previous decades. In standing firm or only compromising on non-essentials, people felt that they could maintain their self-respect. However, people also faced pressure to preserve their moral reputations as well as their self-respect, for one of the key questions in the emerging democratic movement was how people had behaved in the previous era. Did they stand out against the regime, or did they play by the 'rules of the game'? This became an important issue for some of the political parties that were founded at the end of perestroika. It was, for example, an important question for the Social Democratic Party of Russia (SPDR), which was founded in May 1990, and which in turn grew out of the Social Democratic Association that arose in 1987–1988. Although roughly 20 per cent of the members of the SPDR were former party members, its leaders Aleksandr Obolenskii, Pavel Kudyukin and Oleg Rumyantsev were not, and a number of its members had suffered political persecution. In discussions as to whether the SPDR should unite with the Republican Party of Russia (RPR), where many of the members had formerly belonged to the CPSU, the issue of party membership became a big issue. In an interview of 1991, Obolenskii stated that anyone who had joined the Communist Party had stepped over an 'invisible, internal boundary' within himself that had meant subjugation to the party; however, members of the SPDR had chosen not to 'violate' their own individuality by joining the party. Obolenskii and others clearly saw party membership as essentially immoral or evil; past participation made a person guilty. However, it was not just a question of assigning guilt. People who had refused to join the party were aware that their career prospects might have suffered as a result. Obolenskii noted:

> For many of us refusal to join began the erection of obstacles that prevented us from realizing our own personal and career goals. Even now, it's hard, before it was impossible, fully to realize oneself without joining the party. The Republicans are all formers; things changed, and then they left.[67]

Conversely, it seems, members of the Republican Party of Russia were generally proud of the fact that they had tried to introduce reform from within the party.

Another opposition group, Democratic Union, adopted a particularly radical line. Democratic Union, which was originally associated with Club Perestroika, was set up in May 1988 as an opposition political party.[68] It was the most radical of the democratic groups, and it regarded the other democratic groups as insufficiently bold; indeed, it refused to join Democratic Russia, when it was founded in October 1990. Some of those in Democratic Union described themselves as 'liberal revolutionaries'.[69] Democratic Union regarded the very essence of the Soviet system of government as 'fallacious' (*porochnoi*), and sought a transformation rather than a modification of the system.[70] According to one of its leaders, Valeriya Novodvorskaya, they looked at communists who were starting to embrace democratic ideas 'as do grown-ups [who] are looking at the efforts of a child who is trying to take his first steps – with condescension'. Their refusal to participate in the system meant that they were uncorrupted: 'We never made any compromises.'[71] Democratic Union encouraged civil disobedience as a means of breaking with Soviet patterns of complicity and enslavement, and through a campaign of demonstrations and protest it played a significant role in expanding the space for political action in the country.[72]

Radical members of Democratic Russia were also wary of becoming contaminated by working for the communist regime. In a lengthy article in *Demokraticheskaya Rossiya* in the autumn of 1990, Il'ya Zaslavskii saw the situation in terms of two irreconcilable systems: totalitarian and democratic. The key primary objective, he suggested, was to move from the first of these to the second. In achieving this, he said, there could be no compromise with the communists:

> There can be no compromise with the communists, for the ideology of communism brooks no compromise. Compromise with them is as impossible as compromise with the devil; for a compromise is always a bargain, and everyone knows the price of a bargain with the devil.[73]

Some, of course, adopted a more pragmatic line. Democratic Russia itself was in fact an umbrella movement for a very diverse range of people. The Democratic Party of Russia, which was established in May 1990 under the leadership of Nikolai Travkin was also more conciliatory; it stated in its programme: 'While rejecting communist ideology, we have never called for the persecution of specific people – of the representatives of that ideology.'[74] Kovalev was ready to work with former opponents. In an interview with *Referendum* in 1990, Kovalev was asked what it felt like to be sitting alongside people who had serviced the mechanisms of oppression under the old system. He replied: 'I don't like it, but it has to be done. That is the nature of democracy. These people represent someone, and express certain interests.' He also suggested that the tactics that had worked in the days of the human rights movement needed to be modified. Whereas for the dissidents, moral opposition was primary, and they had thought little about the possible consequences of their actions, it was now vital for people to evaluate the consequences of their behaviour. The destruction of the old system was in itself not sufficient: 'If we achieve one thing alone – the final collapse of the system – then nothing except chaos will result from it.'[75]

It is interesting, however, to note that Yeltsin's rise to power did not resolve the intelligentsia's age-old dilemma over whether to work with the government or not. For some, collaboration with the emerging state structures as well as collaboration with the Soviet state was something to be avoided. This is illustrated by the discussions that took place during a meeting of Moscow Tribune on 16 October 1991, when a number of prominent intellectuals and politicians gathered to discuss whether they should support Yeltsin unconditionally or only monitor his activities from a position of opposition. As the discussants themselves noted, the issues were very similar to the questions that had exercised the intelligentsia after 1905, and that were raised in *Landmarks*. In her opening paper, the literary critic and political activist, Marietta Chudakova stated that the intelligentsia had become so accustomed to its role as an opponent of power, that at a moment when it should have been supporting the regime, it could only criticise it; she had the press and television particularly in mind. Following the example of *Landmarks*, she proposed that the intelligentsia should embrace a new role: 'Not opposition, but co-operation with power; and even more than co-operation, defence and participation.' Chudakova stated that the democratic forces should be ready 'to unite on any, even a very average rather than optimum platform', to unite among themselves and to rally round the Russian President. Chudakova was strongly backed by Karyakin, who emphasised that the state and population were now united: 'You and we are now the power.'

By contrast, Leonid Batkin noted that Sakharov had only offered conditional support for Gorbachev, and he suggested the same approach be adopted towards Yeltsin. According to Batkin, the intelligentsia could not but be critical of Yeltsin's ties with industrial leaders like Arkadii Volskii and the former party elites. Likewise Yurii Boldyrev, later a co-founder of the Yabloko Party in 1993, lamented that the actions of the new leaders were little different from those of the old, and feared that reform from above would in the end be for the interests of a monopolistic, capitalistic class. The philosopher L. Bibler suggested that the idea of a common platform was a 'path to authoritarianism'.[76]

How to deal with the communist legacy also continued to be a problem for democrats after the collapse of the USSR. After the August coup, Bukovskii suggested to some of Yeltsin's advisors that there should be a commission for exploring the crimes of communism, suggesting that the trial of the coup-leaders should be turned into a trial of the party. It was important, he said later, to 'kill off the wounded beast before it recovered from shock'. Bukovskii had in mind something akin to the Nuremberg trials after the Second World War. Bukovskii met and discussed what was needed in a TV conversation with Bakatin, who had been made head of the KGB after the coup with the brief to reform it. Bukovskii wanted to show viewers that the dissidents were not out for revenge, and he argued against the public exposure of informers; in his view, the dividing line between those who were members of the party and those who were not and between informers and simply conformists was not very precise. It was not 'mass hysteria, reprisals, denunciations and suicides that such a court examination would necessarily call for, but *repentance*'. Bakatin agreed with many of Bukovskii's ideas, but he baulked at the suggestion that there should be an international commission to explore the Soviet archives.[77] Yeltsin too would not back Bukovskii's ideas. The window of opportunity, if it had been there at all, quickly passed.

Less radically, a trial about the legality of the Community Party did occur. Between 23 August and 6 November 1991, Yeltsin issued a series of decrees banning the CPSU in Russia. The legality of this was challenged by a group of thirty-six Russian communist deputies, and this was followed by a counter-petition filed by a group of fifty-two deputies led by Oleg Rumyantsev, who argued that the party was an unconstitutional organisation. The matter came before the Constitutional Court in July 1992 in a trial that amounted to an examination of the constitutionality of the party's activities since 1917.[78] The first witnesses called by the prosecution were Bukovskii, Razgon and Yakunin.[79] The court eventually found the ruling organs of the party to be illegal, but declared that its local branches were not. However, the trial was never allowed to go beyond the issue of constitutionality to address the question of criminality.

It was certainly in Yeltsin's interests to emphasise the evils of his enemies. In his speech at the White House on 19 August 1991, Yeltsin referred to the 'arbitrary rule and lawlessness of these putschists' and described them as 'men with neither shame nor conscience'.[80] This moral discourse remained an important feature of Yeltsin's rhetoric well after

1991. A few years later, speaking at the burial ceremony for Nicholas II in July 1998, Yeltsin said: 'We are all guilty ... Burying the victims of the Ekaterinburg tragedy is an act of human justice, a symbol of unification in Russia and a redemption of common guilt.' He went on to say: 'We must end the century which has been an age of blood and violence in Russia with repentance and peace.'[81] Yeltsin's call for repentance in 1998 reflected the continuing bitterness that many people felt towards the legacy of communism, and the desire for moral and spiritual renewal. Doubtless, too, the country desperately needed a renewed sense of national unity. At the same time, by 1998 Russian politics had changed a lot. It was not clear to everyone that the Yeltsin regime marked a moral advance on what had gone on before. The Russian Communist Party under Zyuganov still attracted a lot of support. For many people, too much freedom rather than too little was now the problem. Consequently, Yeltsin's calls for repentance were perhaps also a way of him defending the new system he was creating.

As icons of the perestroika era, both Solzhenitsyn and Sakharov were very important. Solzhenitsyn's influence on the political arena was less immediate than Sakharov's. The fact that he remained in Vermont, USA, until 1994 distanced him from events. Moreover, although he published a widely discussed essay on Russian politics in 1990, *How to Rebuild Russia*, Solzhenitsyn generally steered clear of political involvement. Yet his books helped to shape the culture of the era. 1990 was heralded as the 'year of Solzhenitsyn'.[82] Moreover, his ideas were sometimes implicit in the rhetoric of the democratic movement. For example, during the attempted clampdown in Lithuania in January 1991, *Moscow News* called on people to refrain from lies: 'We appeal to reporters and journalists: If you lack courage or opportunity to tell the truth, at least abstain from telling lies! Lies will fool no one anymore.'[83] Solzhenitsyn's authority endured well beyond 1991, especially among those who sought to promote a combination of national and liberal ideas. Putin evidently wanted to be associated with him, for on his eighty-fifth birthday in 2003, he sent him a card with the message: 'You never accepted compromise.'[84]

Sakharov, always a more political and pragmatic figure than Solzhenitysn, was effectively the moral leader of the democratic movement during perestroika.[85] This moral leadership continued even after his death in December 1989. One of the stated aims of Democratic Russia was to defend the ideas of Andrei Sakharov; and this was said to mean the promotion of freedom, democracy, the rights of man, a multiparty system, free elections, and a market economy.[86] Sakharov's political philosophy was a liberal democratic one, and he was essentially a Westerniser. At the same time, as well as advocating freedom and pluralism, he endorsed the moral concerns that were typical of the time. Writing in *There Is No Alternative*, he referred to the 'moral degradation' of Soviet society and the pervasiveness of 'hypocrisy and lies'. He said: 'The corrupting lie, failure to speak out and hypocrisy must depart forever from our life.'[87] This was stronger language than Sakharov had employed twenty years earlier. Sakharov thus promoted the combination of liberal and moral ideas that was a hallmark of so many of his contemporaries.

Sakharov was appealing because he represented an appealing combination of great scientist and secular saint.[88] He was certainly perceived as a saintly figure. Indeed, twice in interviews during 1990, Brodskii called for the Russian Orthodox Church to canonise Sakharov.[89] Following his death in December 1989, Sakharov's stature as a moral role model increased dramatically. At the Congress of People's Deputies, Il'ya Zaslavskii unsuccessfully called for a day of mourning for Sakharov, commenting later that he felt obliged to do this because Sakharov was the 'conscience' of the country.[90] A special section of *Moscow News* was devoted to his memory, headed 'Andrei Sakharov, Our Bitter Conscience'.[91] In *Izvestiya*, Gorbachev headed the list of top party leaders who signed an article about Sakharov that concluded with the sentence: 'Everything that Andrei Dmitrievich did was dictated by his conscience, by deep humanistic convictions.'[92]

There was something of a cult of Sakharov. Even a poster was produced by 'Plakat', the state publishing house for posters, presenting Sakharov as the 'torch of conscience'.[93] There is no reason to doubt the genuine affection in which Sakharov was held. He was not a 'manufactured' icon in the way that some of the Soviet role models had been. However, there was more to it than that. As with Likhachev and Mamardashvili, some people saw in him an incarnation of some of the best values of the older Russian intelligentsia.[94] Yet he was also attractive because he represented some of the political tendencies of the time. Sakharov was a unifying figure. In *Moscow News*, Gavril Popov, then deputy mayor of Moscow, observed that Sakharov had come to symbolise the compromise between socialism and capitalism.[95] It was a good point. The attempt to pursue a middle course between ideologies of the left and right was one of the central tendencies of perestroika. Sakharov gave that tendency a moral authority. Furthermore, Sakharov modelled a path of constructive engagement with the regime. Mikhail Gefter wrote in *Referendum* in 1990 that there was no more painful or nagging question for people than that of when to hold back and when to co-operate. Sakharov's example, he said, was instructive: 'In asking ourselves this, we can happily turn to the memory, spiritual experience and achievement (*podvig*) of Andrei Sakharov. Who did more than he in recent years, last year especially, to bring together a non-violent civic opposition and civic concord?'[96]

Sakharov gave people a different vision of politics. In *Literaturnaya gazeta*, the writer of a long article on Sakharov, Yurii Rost, stated that he found it hard to do justice to a man who stood before 'God and Conscience' in world history, and alongside Mahatma Gandhi and Albert

Schweitzer. Sakharov, he said, 'carried a religious temple [*khram*] within himself, without realising it'. Rost also stated that 'bargaining as a form of political communication' was 'completely unacceptable' to Sakharov.[97] Rost's attitude to politics suggests that among the wider intelligentsia politics itself continued to be treated with suspicion. Yevtushenko praised Sakharov for bringing ethics into politics. In an article in *Ogonek*, Yevtushenko noted that although Sakharov was not a political animal, he found himself at the epicentre of politics because 'in a conscience-less administrative system, an active conscience [was] a political phenomenon'. He observed that the example of Sakharov suggested that 'political dilettantism with a clean conscience' was much more effective than 'professional politicking where conscience [was] not clean'.[98]

Sakharov was thus seen as a man who brought an ethical dimension into politics. It was a vision that democrats felt the need to hold onto in the 1990s. Writing in *Izvestiya* in 1998, Kovalev wrote that Sakharov's moral philosophy was rooted in 'intellectual responsibility' or the 'responsibility of the scholar'. He stated that he represented a purer stream of democratic values than many of his colleagues. He differed from men like Yeltsin, Popov, Anatolii Sobchak and Sergei Stankevich in the sense that these others had learned to be 'politicians'; they had learned 'to lie, to stay silent, to justify the means by the ends – what [had] forever defined the professional level of politics'. In Kovalev's opinion, Sakharov's death was something of a relief for people with this perspective; the subsequent attempt to turn Sakharov into an 'icon' reflected the traditional strategy of 'spiritually killing' an uncomfortable figure. Kovalev's statement reflected his own suspicion of 'politics', as well as the wider need of democrats to dissociate themselves from the grubbier version of liberal democracy that seemed to have flourished in Russia.[99]

Sakharov, Solzhenitsyn, Men', Likhachev and Mamardashvili appealed to a variety of constituencies in the reformist intelligentsia, and their iconic status reflected a society that was hungry for new role models. There were others too, normally former dissidents. Since the dissidents represented such a diversity of views, most political parties were able to claim moral authority through association with one or another dissident. In 1990, for example, the CPSU had Roy Medvedev as a role model, Democratic Russia had Gleb Yakunin as well as the Leningrad-based artist Yulii Rybakov and the former political prisoner Mikhail Molostvov, and the nationalists had Vladimir Osipov. After the collapse of the USSR, Democratic Choice had Kovalev and Boris Zolotukhin, Yabloko had Igrunov, and some of the nationalist groupings in the new Duma had Zinoviev.[100] Throughout the late 1980s and early 1990s, Shafarevich gave added authority to extreme nationalism and anti-Semitism.[101]

Being fashionable brought a new set of problems. Fame was not always easy to deal with. The human rights activist, Andrei Mironov, who was tortured and jailed for eighteen months under Gorbachev, noted that having a dissident past became something of a badge of honour for him; he became a 'holy cow . . . having a false feeling of euphoria'.[102] Sakharov was uncomfortable with some of the adulation. In his memoirs he criticised Solzhenitsyn for exaggerating his [Sakharov's] moral stature,[103] and he once said that his fate had proved greater than his personality.[104] It was perhaps Sakharov's very modesty that attracted so many people to him.

13 Conclusion

There are dangers in focussing exclusively on moral issues. In emphasising 'conscience' it is possible to see Soviet history solely from this one point of view. The possibility of distorted perspective, however, is a problem for any scholar focussing on one theme. Another potential danger lies in taking words too much at their face value. In discussing Soviet dissent, Vail' and Genis rightly noted that appeals to conscience suffered strongly from repetition.[1] Certainly, the word 'conscience' became so widely used in late Soviet Russia that it was sometimes used as a substitute for serious thought. In this sense, its importance as a guide to experience can be exaggerated. On the other hand, for the historian even the superficial use of a word can illustrate the concerns of a society.

In a recent study, Catriona Kelly has argued that the Soviet public's interest in advice literature and general assertion of values pointed not to a moral vacuum at the end of the Soviet era, but to the survival of ethical traditions.[2] There remained in the post-Soviet population a 'resilience and a residual sense of duty'.[3] This is an important point. The widespread interest in conscience in late Soviet Russia reflected the continuing strength and influence of Russian moral traditions in the late Soviet period. Yet, if older traditions remained influential, there was also a strong sense of moral decline. According to the camp veteran and memoirist Oleg Volkov, 'the decades-long propaganda to root out the principles and norms founded on conscience could not but destroy in the people the very idea of Good and Evil'.[4] On the eve of perestroika, there was a feeling of moral malaise that went far beyond the political elites. The hunger for new role models during perestroika pointed to a society that was morally dissatisfied. In this context, the idea of 'conscience' hinted at a lost moral normality or stability that many people hankered after.

The sense of moral crisis that existed at the end of the Soviet era played an important part in bringing down the Soviet system. Soviet ideology, and the moral vision on which it was sustained, could no longer engage a population that had become disappointed with the material achievements of socialism, and was cynical about the realities of Soviet life. The regime had lost the ability to appeal to the 'human factor'. In its early days, the party's moral energy had stemmed partly from its capacity to mobilise a mixture of enthusiasm and grievance. However, by the late 1980s enthusiasm had dissipated and grievance was turned against the party itself. At a global level, Soviet communism continued to attract support in the 1970s and 1980s in Asia, Africa and Central America. However, the invasions of Czechoslovakia and Afghanistan were a shock to some of its more idealistic supporters, and disillusionment was growing. At home, the failure of the Soviet model to compete with Western consumer-orientated economies undermined its credibility. The system was tired.

At the very top of the Soviet system, there was a lack of confidence in the communist project. This was most evident in the refusal of the elite from the Khrushchev era onwards to use the kind of terror that earlier Soviet leaders had employed. Khrushchev's Secret Speech was not only important politically, it was also important in terms of ethics. Even if the speech did not involve the staunch confrontation with Stalinism that Khrushchev suggested, it still conveyed the idea that certain kinds of behaviour were unacceptable. Khrushchev reintroduced ethics into politics. In spite of its renewed conservatism, the Brezhnev regime never fully reversed this. With the rise of Gorbachev, the interest in ethics was renewed. Those moments when violence was used, such as the clampdown in Lithuania in January 1991, were few, and they were not sustained.

At another level, however, the hesitant turn towards universal values that took place under Khrushchev was influenced by the fact that, from its inception, the Bolshevik project was self-consciously moral. Conflicts between idealism and realism in Soviet ethics were never resolved. Even Lenin could only justify his realism by appealing to a future ideal. The mature Soviet system was always emphasising morality, even if only in an instrumental sense, as a means of serving the state. In addition, the regime's official philosophers showed a growing interest in ethics from the late 1950s onwards. There were increasing attempts to combine class morality with universal values. Thus, the emphasis on ethics that was typical of perestroika also grew out of the party's own search to find an adequate moral foundation for the building of socialism.

At the same time, the very consolidation of the Soviet regime and its institutions under Stalin was productive of an emphasis on conscience. For the state, the school and the family to function adequately, people had to behave in a responsible way. Revolutionary ethics were only really helpful as a means of destroying what came before. To make the system function properly, the Soviet regime increasingly turned to more traditional forms of morality to the point where in its last decades it was promoting a moral framework that had much in common with Judaeo-Christian ethics. Honesty, conscience, truthfulness and faithfulness were all emphasised. Dissidents, as well as party reformers, were shaped by these official ethics: 'The dissidents did what they were taught in the Soviet school: to be honest, principled, unselfish and ready for self-sacrifice.'[5]

However, late Soviet and Judaeo-Christian ethics had obvious differences. Most obviously, there was no place in the former for a Creator God. Furthermore, for all its universalism, late Soviet ethics contained a strong utilitarian component. Like his predecessors, Gorbachev promoted honesty and conscience to the extent that they would strengthen the power of the state. Sometimes, especially among a younger generation that was increasingly enamoured of Western popular culture, the state's ethical teachings created great cynicism. On the other hand, they also gave people a framework that they could either accept or reject, and doubtless affected them in subconscious ways.

There is much here for the philosopher of history as well as for the more traditional historian. Soviet history arguably points to a kind of natural law explanation of the human condition: there is a moral law embedded in the world, and societies that try to get away from it must in the end be accountable to it. Initially hostile to eternal moral principles or universal values, the Soviet regime found that the institutions that it created could not function without them. In fact, the party was always parasitical on the idea of universal values since it could only reject absolutes by appealing to an absolute. However, the emphasis on truth and conscience was dangerous to the regime. In the 1980s, desirous to promote a more humane and honest society, the regime found that it could only do so by putting into question the very revolution that had brought it to birth. The Soviet Union was a house divided against itself; it was 'self-subversive'.[6] In a certain sense, then, the Soviet regime stumbled against the moral law itself. In this connection, the regime was always constrained by the Russian language. It was not able to alter fundamentally the meanings of the concepts of conscience, truth, lies and freedom, and was in a sense answerable to them. The ethical staying power of the Russian language was an obstacle to its more utopian dreams.

Pre-revolutionary cultures also helped to shape dissident and reformist ethics. Some of these had long-term roots. The language and spirituality of Byzantium played a certain role. There were European as well as Russian influences. In 'Humanism and the Present' (1923), Osip Mandelstam stated that humanistic values were like gold currency that had been taken out of circulation, and predicted that there would be a day when the gold coinage of the European humanistic tradition would re-emerge.[7] It is an attractive image. In all sorts of ways, classical, Christian and Enlightenment ethical traditions provided sustenance to dissidents and party reformers. The moral concerns of pre-revolutionary Russian literature also played an important role in this respect, and during the Soviet era literature continued to play a vital role in the moral formation of people.

Moral resistance, of course, did not inevitably grow out of these larger tendencies. Dissident and reformist ethics were shaped not only by impersonal traditions and social forces, but also by personal choices. Perestroika was launched by a small group of young party leaders. The dissident movement also owed its direction and energy to certain key personalities. The moral direction and debates of the late Soviet era were shaped by Khrushchev, Pasternak, Yesenin-Vol'pin, Bukovskii, Solzhenitsyn, Sakharov, Gorbachev, Yakovlev and Yeltsin, as well as by larger cultural tendencies. These individuals reinforced or redirected the moral traditions that were already at work in the country, and put their own stamp upon them.

Moral restlessness was one of the characteristic features of late Soviet Russia. According to memoirs and oral histories, many intellectuals were troubled about the way in which they tacitly gave their support to the regime, and sought ways of demarcating what they would and would not do. In-system dissenters generally felt that it was possible to be pragmatic about moral choices, and they sometimes argued that certain of their actions were ritualistic and did not fundamentally affect their personalities. However, dissident ethics were the fruit of a more radical way of dealing with this moral restlessness. The idea emerged that people who spoke their minds honestly and courageously would become inwardly free personalities. Some dissidents came to believe that people who worked for the regime lost touch with their true selves. To compromise with the regime, or to give way during interrogation, meant to become a divided and lesser personality. No one wanted that, and dissident novels and memoirs often presented strategies of self-defence to prevent it. Moral absolutes were often emphasised in these strategies, for the slightest chink in a person's armour might give the state its chance. For reasons of self-preservation, it became imperative to speak out against oppression or to refuse to live by lies. The struggle with the state was in this sense a matter of spiritual life and death. This dissident ethic primarily related to relations with the state. Dissident writings contained little on honesty in the workplace, the utilisation of property or the ethics of family life.

The experience of struggling against the state led some dissidents, although not all, to adopt a hostile attitude to politics itself. Whereas the dissent of the Khrushchev era often involved political idealism, members of the human rights movement sometimes exhibited anti-political attitudes. These people assumed that politics by its very nature was a dirty business. The non-political outlook of some of the human rights activists reflected the fact that the dissident movement was primarily an intellectual movement. It attracted more than the average number of scientists and writers, and never acquired the broader social and political base that, for example, the Solidarity movement in Poland was able to. The dissident suspicion of politics may also have been one of the reasons why relatively few Soviet dissidents went on to make successful political careers. In this respect, Sakharov and Kovalev were exceptional.

At the same time, there were differences among dissidents in types of moral opposition. In emigration in 1922–1923, Struve and Frank had argued over whether it was better to oppose Bolshevism actively or to wait for a spiritual transformation in the country.[8] Oppositionists of the late Soviet era faced the same dilemmas. Solzhenitsyn and Pomerants, for example, differed over how far it was right to oppose evil actively. Solzhenitsyn, who believed that in men like Tvardovskii it was possible to see the spiritual effects of a life of compromise, promoted a robust moral confrontation with the state and with evil generally. His strong views doubtless often made people feel morally uncomfortable, and for this reason it is never easy to interpret people's attacks on him; some who criticised him may have been simply defending themselves from their own moral unease. Yet some people, like Pomerants, felt that he was too strident, and he alienated some of his contemporaries. Those who disagreed with his ideology, or sought a more moderate form of dissidence, generally preferred Sakharov's example.

In 1984 Mamardashvili suggested in a lecture that the destruction of the foundations of civilisation in the twentieth century had led to an 'anthropological catastrophe'.[9] This kind of thinking appealed to intellectuals who believed that the USSR was in a spiritual crisis, and it reflected a general tendency in the intelligentsia to see the world in moral and spiritual terms. Brodskii wrote of Nadezhda Mandelstam's memoirs that that they were 'a view of history in the light of conscience and culture'.[10] Moral interpretations of history were common among dissidents and reformers. They were sometimes the outcome of religious conviction, as was the case, for example, with the contributors to *From under the Rubble*. However, secular as well as religious thinkers sometimes saw the world in moral terms. Writing from the West in the mid-1980s, Bukovskii stated that he normally sought to avoid the moralising tendency inherent in using labels like 'good' and 'evil', but that in order to give a clear and succinct account of the present world situation, he had ended up by doing just that.[11] This prophetic tendency was also evident in reform-minded party intellectuals and leaders like Volkogonov, Yakovlev and Shevardnadze, and it was even present to some degree in Yeltsin's thinking.

The spiritual interests of the Soviet dissidents both shaped and reflected a wider interest in metaphysical and moral issues across Eastern Europe. The experience of communism prompted intellectuals in a number of countries to ask questions about the nature of good and evil, and to assume the reality of a moral universe. This was a point that was made by Milosz in *Newsweek* in 1983: 'The basic difference between [Eastern and Western] societies is that we who are "Easterners" believe in the primitive notions of good and evil.'[12] In response to a morally chaotic world, religious and secular thinkers alike were drawn to the idea of a natural conscience. Solzhenitsyn, who rejected much of the Enlightenment world-view, and Havel, who endorsed it, both adhered to a morality that was shaped by ideas of natural conscience and Christianity.[13] Some western religious thinkers interpreted the Soviet collapse from a spiritual point of view. For example, the Catholic writer, George Weigel, described the fall of communism as a 'revolution of the spirit'.[14] However, this was not the language of secular western historians.

Although it had roots in Russian history, the dissident movement had distinctive ideological and sociological features. The liberal emphasis on human rights and non-violence was clearly stronger among the dissidents than it was in the pre-revolutionary era. In discussing this, Amalrik argued that the pre-revolutionary social movement had called on people to 'sacrifice [their] "I" for the sake of the general public', whereas the dissidents had sought to replace that kind of 'senseless sacrifice' not with selfishness, but with the idea of one's 'I' in 'the universal sense'.[15] This is an important point. The idea of the uniqueness of the individual was clearly more important to the dissidents than it was to the earlier revolutionary intelligentsia. Dissidents were also more ecumenical in outlook. As Aleksandr Daniel said, the dissident movement was broader than its nineteenth-century counterpart in that it did not divide up into clearly defined ideological and political groups, but embraced a wide range of forms of dissent.[16]

With regard to legal norms, there were diverse attitudes among dissidents and reformers. Chalidze, Litvinov and Aleksandr Yakovlev all endorsed Kistyakovskii's thesis that Russians had traditionally lacked a legal consciousness. However, Solzhenitsyn's conviction that conscience and justice were overlapping ideas reflected a more conservative emphasis. He believed Russia's problems were more spiritual than legal or political, and a suspicion of Western legalism continued among some patriotic thinkers. Yet traditional Russian divisions between secular and religious traditions were blurred in these decades. The presence in the human rights movement of Orthodox believers like Gorbanevskaya and Khodorovich indicated a certain convergence of liberal and Christian thinking on this issue.

There was indeed a dialogue of traditions at the heart of the human rights movement and more generally in dissident and reformist culture. Christians and humanists, liberals and conservatives, and moderate socialists and Marxist-Leninists all found a place there. Although not completely new in Russian history, this ecumenical spirit now became a mainstream tendency in the Russian intelligentsia. The two underlying ideas at the heart of this alliance of traditions were the idea of universal or absolute moral values on the one hand, and the freedom of the individual on the other. At the same time, moral discourses often concealed a negative rather than a positive agenda. It has been noted that the Soviet state was often given the epithet 'totalitarian' because it removed the need for a deeper and more sophisticated analysis.[17] The word 'conscience' was sometimes used in the same way; it was used to evade thought as well as to encourage it. Conscience was regarded as the answer to all that was wrong in Russia, but to describe exactly what it constituted was altogether more difficult. Len Karpinskii observed in 1991 that a philosophy of destruction was not sufficient: a positive programme was also needed.[18] This was always a problem for the dissidents and party reformers. In opposing communism, socialists, liberals, nationalists and Christians could unite around a common programme of opposition to repression and lies. However, when it came to finding a common understanding of conscience or the creation of a positive programme, it was much more difficult. The prevailing discourse of conscience may also have trapped some people into believing that complex political issues could be easily reduced to matters of right and wrong.[19] This might account for some of the disillusionment felt by Russian intellectuals after 1991, when they found that democratic processes did not automatically create a more moral society.

The emphasis on moral absolutes and liberal values had a Protestant quality to it. In the Soviet era, people often had their religious experiences outside the framework of the church, in flats and labour camps. Arguably a kind of 'Reformation' was taking place. Luther's combined emphasis on obedience to God and the individual conscience was being replicated here. Indeed, a kind of Christian liberalism was not unusual in dissident circles. At the same time, this kind of liberalism had very varied manifestations. Solzhenitsyn, for example, represented a more patriotic or conservative strain of it in that he saw the nation as well as the individual as a moral entity.[20] His national liberal attitudes clearly differed markedly from the opinions of people in the centre or on the left of the human rights movement. There were also conservative critics of Soviet ethics who were not liberal at all. Some of the village writers, for example, assumed a collective form of conscience. Rasputin emphasised loyalty to nation, soil and ancestry, and his authoritarianism was particularly evident in his support for conservative forces during the summer of 1991. Shafarevich was another whose moral opposition to communism did not lead in a liberal direction. The Russian Orthodox Church was also conservative on matters of conscience. It preached the importance of obedience to ecclesiastical and state authorities, and in this generally prioritised the collective over the individual. However, many clerics, both before and during perestroika, found the dual loyalty to church authority and personal conscience hard to maintain.

In one sense, perestroika was a moral revolution, or at least the result of one. In the decades after Stalin's death, an ethical paradigm shift took place, and this helped to shape the debates unleashed by *glasnost'*. There was a turning away from the materialist and utilitarian ethics that had been central to Bolshevism. This paradigm shift partly owed something to the French revolutionary tradition. Ideas about human rights and popular sovereignty, associated with the French Revolution, finally began to assert themselves in the USSR.[21] However, Russian oppositionists of the late Soviet era differed from their French revolutionary predecessors, and indeed from the late nineteenth-century Russian revolutionaries, in having an interest in spiritual and metaphysical issues. In this regard, they had something in common with the English revolutionaries of the seventeenth century. Their interest in issues of spiritual self-defence, and in the nature of good and evil, placed them closer to thinkers with a religious outlook. More generally, their tendency to invoke a higher moral authority, for example by using the term 'conscience', suggests that intellectual traditions that had their sources in a pre-Enlightenment age were strongly at work in late Soviet society. It is easy to interpret modern European history in terms of the growing centrality of ideas of rationality and human rights in politics. However, along with these Enlightenment concerns, the focus on natural conscience was testimony to the influence of other ethical and religious traditions.

One of the reasons for the ethical paradigm shift was undoubtedly the influence of the dissidents. Prior to perestroika, dissident ideas permeated party structures by way of academic institutes and samizdat. They sometimes created a sense of moral unease. There is evidence, albeit not very extensive, that some of the party reformers had struggles of conscience that were not so different from some of the dissidents; and this moral dissatisfaction was surely partly engendered by the dissidents. Of course, dissident culture was just part of a range of influences on the leadership, and its importance should not be exaggerated. Western political ideas, as well as the party's own political philosophers and advisors, clearly influenced the leadership in important ways too. Yet the dissidents contributed to the regime's growing lack of ideological self-confidence. Furthermore, during perestroika itself, as the space for public debate expanded, dissident ideas became increasingly mainstream. Leading oppositionists, most notably Sakharov and Solzhenitsyn but also others, suddenly became iconic figures not only in the intelligentsia but also with the wider public. In a variety of senses, then, the dissidents played an important role in undermining the moral legitimacy of the Soviet state and ideology. To a degree, perhaps, they also contributed to the comparative lack of violence that accompanied the Soviet collapse.[22]

At the same time, the idea that there was a 'revolution of conscience' during perestroika, as Yakovlev suggested in 1992, is problematic. Yakovlev himself admitted that it was not so simple. With the collapse of the USSR, it was briefly possible to believe that a new dawn was breaking in Russian life. However, the optimistic mood did not last long. While one set of problems had apparently been dealt with, a new one suddenly emerged. The democratic 'free-for-all', and the corruption associated with it, left some people nostalgic for an older world. To know how to create and consolidate a free and pluralistic society was not easy. Whereas the ethics of the dissidents and party reformers were often well adjusted to the problems of late Soviet Russia, something new was needed to deal with the dilemmas of pluralism and the free market. It was not easy to know what kind of idea could hold together such a diverse and complicated country.

There was a paradigm shift, but it did not immediately transfer into a change of mentality and practices. Even after an authoritarian political system falls, the mental habits engendered by it continue to be influential. In Russia after 1991, authoritarian patterns of behaviour remained common. There was always the possibility that the country would seek to go back to the kinds of comforting certainties that had characterised the previous era. The fact that people were still so divided over the Soviet legacy, and that so many of those in power owed their positions to the previous regime, meant that it was hard for the country to really move forward. Yet history is like that. One of the lessons of the Bolshevik Revolution was that a change of political system and ideology does not necessarily lead to a change in human nature and motivation. Russia after 1991 discovered the same thing.

Appendix

List of interviews

All interviews are in Russian unless stated. Note: (tr.) = transcript available from author.

Alekseeva, Ludmilla, Moscow, April 2003.
Ametistov, Ernest, Caux-sur-Montreux, August 1994 (tr.).
Andreev, German, Paris, March 1997.
Bakatin, Vadim, Moscow, March 2003 (tr.).
Belenken, Boris, Moscow, April 1996.
Bikennin, Nail', Moscow, April 2003 (tr.).
Bogoraz, Larisa, Moscow, April 1996 (tr.).
Bolshakova, Natal'ya, Riga, March 2003.
Borisov, Fr. Aleksandr, Moscow, March 2003.
Bukovskii, Vladimir, Cambridge, October 1995.
Chugrov, Sergei, Caux-sur-Montreux, July 1995.
Genisaretskii, Oleg, Moscow, April 1996.
Ginzburg, Aleksandr, Paris, March 1997.
Gorbanevskaya, Natal'ya, Paris, March 1997 (tr.).
Gordievskii, Oleg, United Kingdom, February 2003 (English).
Guseinov, Abdusalam, Moscow, March 2003.
Daniel, Aleksandr, Moscow, April 2003.
Igrunov, Vyacheslav, Copenhagen, May 1995.
Karyakin, Yurii, Moscow, April 1999.
Khakhaev, Sergei, St Petersburg, April 2003.
Khodorovich, Tat'yana, Paris, March 1997 (tr.).
Kochetkov, Fr. Georgii, Moscow, April 1996.
Kolerov, Modest, Moscow, April 1996.
Kovalev, Sergei, Moscow, April 1999.
Krasikov, Anatolii, Moscow, April 1998.
Kruglyi, Lev, Paris, March 1997.
Landa, Mal'va, Moscow, April 1998.
Lashkova, Vera, Cambridge, October 1995.
Lyubimov, Yurii, Moscow, April 2003.
Mamontov, Arch. Viktor, Karsava, March 2003.

Maslenikova, Zoya, Moscow, April 1996.
Medvedev, Vadim, Moscow, April 2003 (tr.).
Medvedev, Zhores, London, January 1996.
Mironov, Andrei, Caux-sur-Montreux, July 1995.
Murinson, Aleksandr, London, June 1995 (English).
Plyushch, Leonid, Paris, March 1997.
Podbolotov, Sergei, St Petersburg, March 1996.
Pomerants, Grigorii, Moscow, April 1998.
Poresh, Vladimir, St Petersburg, March 1996.
Pustintsev, Boris, St Petersburg, April 2003.
Ratushinskaya, Irina, London, November 1995 (English).
Rozental', Eduard, Caux-sur-Montreux, August 1994.
Rozov, Mikhail, Moscow, April 1996.
Shaburov, Nikolai, Caux-sur-Montreux, July 1995.
Shreider, Yulii, Moscow, April 1996.
Sobolev, Albert, Moscow, April 1996.
Solovei, Valerii, London, May 1995.
Trusova, Tat'yana, Moscow, April 2003.
Tsipko, Aleksandr, Moscow, January 1998 and March 2003 (tr.).
Velikanova, Tat'yana, Moscow, January 1998 (tr.).
Yakovlev, Aleksandr, Moscow, March 2003 (tr.).
Yazykova, Irina, Moscow, April 1996 (tr.).
Yoffe, Venyamin, St Petersburg, March 1996.
Yudin, Aleksei, Moscow, April, 1996.
Zubov, Andrei, Moscow, April 1996.

Notes

Introduction

1 See on this William C. Wholforth, 'Realism and the End of the Cold War', *International Security*, 19, 3, 1994–1995, pp. 91–129.
2 See on this, Moshe Lewin, *The Gorbachev Phenomenon* (London: Radius, 1988), pp. 6–8.
3 Robert English, *Russia and the Idea of the West: Gorbachev, Intellectuals and the End of the Cold War* (New York: Columbia University Press, 2000), pp. 7, 89, 194.
4 David Caute, *The Dancer Defects: The Struggle for Cultural Supremacy during the Cold War* (Oxford: Oxford University Press, 2003), pp. 1–2.
5 Aleksandr Solzhenitsyn, 'Zhit' ne po lzhi!', *Publitsistika: stat'i i rechi* (Vermont/Paris: YMCA Press, 1981), pp. 168–172.
6 A.Y. Shtromas, 'Dissent and Political Change in the Soviet Union', *Studies in Comparative Communism*, XII, 1979, pp. 212, 237.
7 Mikhail Gorbachev, *Perestroika* (New York: Harper and Row Publishers, 1987) p. 25.
8 Alexander Yakovlev, 'The Political Philosophy of Perestroika', in *Perestroika Annual* (London: Futura, 1988), p. 63.
9 See on this, Robert Horvath, 'The Dissident Roots of *Glasnost'*', in Stephen Wheatcroft (ed.), *Challenging Traditional Roots of Russian History* (Basingstoke: Palgrave Macmillan, 2002), p. 174.
10 This is a phrase used by John Keep in *The Last of the Empires* (Oxford: Oxford University Press, 1995), Chapter 6.
11 Quoted in James Billington, *The Icon and the Axe* (New York: Vintage Books, 1970), p. 569.
12 Billington, *The Icon and the Axe*, p. viii.
13 G.P. Fedotov (ed.), *A Treasury of Russian Spirituality* (London: Sheed and Ward, 1989), p. 1.
14 See Isaiah Berlin, 'Two Concepts of Liberty', in *Four Essays on Liberty* (Oxford: Oxford University Press, 1990), pp. 120–121.
15 See also on this O.G. Drobnitskii, *Problemy nravstvennosti* (Moscow: Nauka, 1977).
16 C.S. Lewis, 'Conscience and Conscious', in *Studies in Words* (Cambridge: Cambridge University Press, 1967), p. 183.
17 Nicholas Dent, 'Conscience', in E. Craig (ed.) *The Routledge Encyclopedia of Philosophy*, vol. 2 (London: Routledge, 1988), pp. 579–581.
18 Oleg Kharkhordin, *The Collective and the Individual in Russia* (Berkeley, CA: University of California Press, 1999), p. 57; Kharkhordin translates *soznatel'nost'* as 'Conscience' (using the upper case). I have not followed this

practice, retaining the more traditional translation of consciousness, and thus leaving conscience exclusively for *sovest'*.

19 Stephen Thomas, 'Conscience in Orthodox Thought', in Jayne Hoose (ed.) *Conscience in World Religions* (Leominster: Gracewing, 1999), p. 99.

20 Robert Hodge, *What's Conscience For?* (Slough: St Paul's, 1995), p. 224.

21 See Edward G. Andrew, *Conscience and its Critics* (Toronto: University of Toronto Press, 2001), pp. 19–23.

22 Hayden White, *Metahistory* (Baltimore, MD: The Johns Hopkins University Press, 1973), p. 365.

23 Paul Lehmann, 'The Decline and Fall of Conscience', in C.E. Nelson (ed.) *Conscience: Theological and Psychological Perspectives* (New York: Newman Press, 1975), p. 31; John Macquarrie, 'The Struggle of the Conscience for Authentic Selfhood', in C.E. Nelson (ed.) *Conscience*, p. 157.

24 Vera Dunham, *In Stalin's Time* (Cambridge: Cambridge University Press, 1976), p. 4.

25 Richard Stites, *The Women's Liberation Movement in Russia* (Princeton, NJ: Princeton University Press, 1978), p. 390.

26 Igal Halfin, *From Darkness to Light: Class, Consciousness and Salvation in Revolutionary Russia* (Pittsburgh: Pittsburgh University Press, 2000), p. 39.

27 Martin Malia, *The Soviet Tragedy* (New York: The Free Press, 1994), pp. 3, 64.

28 Leonard Schapiro, *The Origin of the Communist Autocracy* (London: Macmillan, 1977), p. xix.

29 Robert Service, 'Joseph Stalin: The Making of a Stalinist', in John Channon (ed.) *Politics, Society and Stalinism in the USSR* (Basingstoke: Macmillan, 1998), p. 29.

30 See Philip Boobbyer, 'Moral Judgements and Moral Realism in History', *Totalitarian Movements and Political Religions*, 3, 2 (2002), pp. 83–112.

1 Russian moral traditions before 1917

1 Joseph Brodsky, *Less Than One* (London: Penguin, 1987), p. 165.

2 P. Ia. Chernykh, *Istoriko-etimologicheskii slovar' sovremennogo Russkogo yazyka*, vol. 2 (Moscow: Russkii yazyk, 1993), p. 184.

3 Stephen Thomas, 'Conscience in Orthodox Thought', in Jayne Hoose (ed.) *Conscience in World Religions* (Leominster: Gracewing, 1999), p. 99.

4 See Pavel Florensky, *The Pillar and the Ground of Truth* (Princeton, NJ: Princeton University Press, 1997), pp. 16–20.

5 Nikolai Berdyaev, 'Philosophical Truth and the Moral Truth of the Intelligentsia', in N.A. Berdyaev *et al.*, *Landmarks*, trans. M. Schwartz (New York: Karz Howard, 1977), p. 21.

6 Aleksandr Solzhenitsyn, 'Zhit' ne po lzhi!', *Publitsistika: stat'i i rechi* (Vermont/Paris: YMCA Press, 1981), p. 172.

7 Leonid Andreev, 'Vserossisskoe vran'e', *Polnoe sobranie sochinenii*, vol. 5, 1913, quoted in Ronald Hingley, 'That's No Lie, Comrade', *Problems of Communism*, XI, 2, 1962, p. 48.

8 Fyodor Dostoevsky, *The Diary of a Writer* (Haslemere: Ianmead Ltd, 1984), pp. 133–136.

9 See on this Philip T. Grier, *Marxist Ethical Theory in the Soviet Union* (Dordrecht: D. Reidel Publishing Company, 1978), p. 86.

10 Daniel Rancour-Laferriere, *The Slave Soul of Russia* (New York: New York University Press, 1995), p. 18.

11 Fedotov (ed.), *A Treasury of Russian Spirituality* (London: Sheed and Ward, 1989), p. 5.

12 'Lord Jesus Christ, Son of the Living God, Have Mercy on Me, a Sinner'.

13 John Meyendorff, *Byzantium and the Rise of Russia* (Cambridge: Cambridge University Press, 1981), p. 96.
14 Fedotov (ed.), *A Treasury of Russian Spirituality*, pp. 5–6.
15 Billington, *The Icon and the Axe* (New York: Vintage Books, 1970), p. 51.
16 Ken Parry *et al.* (eds), *The Blackwell Dictionary of Eastern Christianity* (Oxford: Blackwell, 1999), pp. 378–379.
17 Thomas, 'Conscience in Orthodox Thought', pp. 104–105.
18 Ibid., pp. 110–111.
19 *The Philokalia*, vol. 1, translated and edited by G. Palmer, P. Sherrard and K. Ware (London: Faber, 1979), pp. 186, 198.
20 Ibid., vol. 1, p. 3.
21 Thomas, 'Conscience in Orthodox Thought', p. 112.
22 Geoffrey Hosking, *Russia and the Russians* (London: Penguin Books, 2001), p. 174.
23 'The Life of Archpriest Avvakum by Himself', in Fedotov (ed.), *A Treasury of Russian Spirituality*, p. 181.
24 See on this Michael Epstein, 'After the Future: On the New Consciousness in Literature', in T. Lahusen with G. Kuperman (eds) *Late Soviet Culture* (Durham, NC: Duke University Press, 1993), p. 269.
25 Aleksandr Pushkin, quoted in Dimitri Obolensky (ed.) *A Heritage of Russian Verse* (Bloomington, IN: Indiana University Press, 1976), p. 93.
26 See Pamela Davidson, 'The Moral Dimension of the Prophetic Ideal: Pushkin and His Readers', *Slavic Review*, 61, 3, 2002, p. 514.
27 A.S. Pushkin, *Sochineniya v trekh tomakh*, vol. 1 (Moscow, 1978), p. 206.
28 *The Works of Alexander Pushkin*, selected and edited by A. Yarmolinsky (London: Nonesuch Press, 1939), p. 353.
29 A.S. Pushkin, *Sochineniya v trekh tomakh*, vol. 2 (Moscow: Khudozhestvennaya literatura, 1978), p. 347.
30 Orlando Figes, *Natasha's Dance* (London: Allen Lane, 2002), p. 316.
31 Vladimir Lenin, 'Lev Tolstoy as the Mirror of the Russian Revolution' (1908) in V.I. Lenin, *Collected Works*, 47 vols (Moscow-Leningrad, 1960–1970), vol. 15 (London: Lawrence and Wishart, 1963), p. 205.
32 See Figes, *Natasha's Dance*, pp. 329–331.
33 See in particular 'Stavrogin's Confession', not included in the original text; Fyodor Dostoevsky, *The Devils* (London: Penguin Books, 1983), pp. 671–704.
34 Isaiah Berlin, *Russian Thinkers* (London: Hogarth Press, 1978), p. 247.
35 See Leo Tolstoy, *Anna Karenina*, trans. C. Garnett (London: Heinemann, 1977), p. 3.
36 Nikolai Leskov, *Lady Macbeth of Mtsensk and Other Stories*, trans D. Macduff (London: Penguin Books, 1987), p. 170; N.S. Leskov, *Povesti i rasskazy* (Moscow: Khudozhestvennaya literatura, 1966), p. 72.
37 Leo Tolstoy, *A Confession and Other Religious Writings* (London: Penguin Books, 1987), p. 20.
38 Aleksandr Izgoev, 'On Educated Youth', in *Landmarks*, p. 91.
39 Sergei Bulgakov, quoted in P.C. Boobbyer, *S.L. Frank* (Athens, OH: Ohio University Press, 1995), p. 6.
40 Donald Fanger, 'The Peasant in Literature', in W.S. Vucinich (ed.) *The Peasant in Nineteenth Century Russia* (Stanford, CA: Stanford University Press, 1968), p. 239.
41 Billington, *The Icon and the Axe*, p. 374.
42 Ibid., p. 416; see also Sarah Hudspith, *Dostoevsky and the Idea of Russianness* (London: RoutledgeCurzon, 2004), pp. 38–39, 41.
43 M.E.. Saltykov-Shchedrin, *Skazki* (Tver': Tverskoi gosudarstvennyi universitet, 1996), pp. 41–50.

44 S.A. Askol'dov, 'Religioznyi smysl russkoi revolyutsii', in S.A. Askol'dov *et al.*, *Iz glubiny* (Paris: YMCA Press, 1967), p. 50.
45 David Saunders, *Russia in the Age of Reaction and Reform 1801–1881* (London: Longman, 1992), p. 148.
46 Ibid., pp. 157–158, 152, 149.
47 Quoted in Hosking, *Russia and the Russians*, p. 274.
48 Nikolai Berdyaev, *The Origin of Russian Communism* (Ann Arbor, MI: The University of Michigan Press, 1983), pp. 49–50.
49 Ibid., p. 40.
50 Quoted in Saunders, *Russia in the Age of Reaction and Reform*, p. 161.
51 V.G. Belinsky, *Selected Philosophical Works* (Moscow: Foreign Languages Publishing House, 1948), p. 158.
52 Berlin, *Russian Thinkers*, pp. 86–87.
53 *My Past and Thoughts: The Memoirs of Alexander Herzen*, vol. 4, trans. C. Garnett and revised H. Higgins (London: Chatto and Windus, 1968), p. 1728.
54 See Martin Malia, *Alexander Herzen and the Birth of Russian Socialism* (Cambridge, MA: Harvard University Press, 1961), p. 399.
55 Berlin, *Russian Thinkers*, p. 150.
56 Marshall Shatz, *Soviet Dissent in Historical Perspective* (Cambridge: Cambridge University Press, 1980), p. 69.
57 N.G. Chernyshevsky, *What Is to be Done?*, trans. L. Turkevich (New York: Vintage Books, 1961), p. 234.
58 Lavrov quoted by James P. Scanlan, in his 'Introduction' to Peter Lavrov, *Historical Letters* (Berkeley, CA: University of California Press, 1967), p. 24.
59 Franco Venturi, *Roots of Revolution* (New York: The Universal Library, 1960), p. 503.
60 For a discussion of the intelligentsia's radicalism, see Richard Pipes, *The Russian Revolution, 1899–1919* (London: Collins Harvill, 1990), Chapter 4.
61 Bogdan Kistyakovsky, 'In Defense of Law', in *Landmarks*, pp. 118, 128.
62 Sergei Bulgakov, 'Heroism and Asceticism: Reflections on the Religious Nature of the Russian Intelligentsia', in *Landmarks*, p. 36.
63 S.L. Frank, 'The Ethic of Nihilism', in *Landmarks*, pp. 163, 166.
64 Ibid., pp. 160, 184 (emphasis in original).
65 Richard Sakwa, 'The Struggle for the Constitution in Russia and the Triumph of Ethical Individualism', *Studies in East European Thought*, 48, 1996, p. 116; Pipes, *The Russian Revolution, 1899–1919*, p. 158.
66 Mikhail Meerson-Aksenov, 'Rozhdenie novoi intelligentsii', in P. Litvinov *et al.* (eds) *Samosoznanie* (New York: Khronika, 1976), p. 93; quote taken from *Nastavlenie dlya prepodavatelei v voenno-uchebnykh zavedeniyakh*, 1848.
67 See Hosking, *Russia and the Russians*, p. 216.
68 Interview with Tat'yana Khodorovich, Paris, March 1997.
69 See on these practices and values, David Moon, *The Russian Peasantry, 1600–1930* (London: Longman, 1999), pp. 132, 192, 234, 271, 278.
70 Ibid., p. 338.
71 Berdyaev, *The Origin of Russian Communism*, p. 8.
72 Samuel C. Ramer, 'Traditional Healers and Peasant Culture in Russia, 1861–1917', in E. Kingston-Mann *et al.* (eds) *Peasant Economy, Culture, and Politics of European Russia, 1800–1921* (Princeton, NJ: Princeton University Press, 1991), pp. 216, 220.
73 These points on patronage are derived from Geoffrey Hosking, 'Patronage and the Russian State', *The Slavonic and East European Review*, 78, 2, 2000, pp. 307–308.
74 Fyodor Dostoevsky, *The Brothers Karamazov*, trans D. Macduff (London: Penguin Books, 1993), p. 277.

75 Hugh Seton-Watson, *The Russian Empire* (Oxford: Clarendon Press, 1990), pp. 256–257.
76 Maurice Hindus, *Red Bread* (Bloomington, IN: Indiana University Press, 1988), p. 191.
77 Lynne Viola, 'The Second Coming: Class Enemies in the Soviet Countryside, 1927–1935', in J. Arch Getty and Roberta T. Manning (eds) *Stalinist Terror* (Cambridge: Cambridge University Press, 1993), pp. 97–98.
78 Quoted in Philip Boobbyer, 'Truth-telling, Conscience and Dissent in Late Soviet Russia: Evidence from Oral Histories', *European History Quarterly*, 30, 4, 2000, p. 560.

2 Tension and change in revolutionary ethics

1 For more on this tension in Soviet ideology, see Philip T. Grier, *Marxist Ethical Theory in the Soviet Union* (Dordrecht: D. Reidel Publishing Company, 1978), pp. x, 109, 167, 219.
2 James Scanlan, *Marxism in the USSR* (Ithaca, NY: Cornell University Press, 1985), p. 266.
3 Boobbyer, *S.L. Frank* (Athens, OH: Ohio University Press, 1995), pp. 103–104.
4 V.I. Lenin, *Selected Works*, vol. 2 (London: Lawrence and Wishart, 1947), pp. 155, 197.
5 N. Bukharin and E. Preobrazhensky, *The ABC of Communism* (London: Penguin Books, 1970), p. 127.
6 A.A. Guseinov, 'Nravstvennye al'ternativy perestroiki', in *Yazyk i sovest'* (Moscow: Rossiiskaya Akademiya Nauk, Institut Filosofii, 1996), p. 31; article first published in *Filosofskaya i sotsiologicheskaya mysl'* (Kiev), No. 7, 1990, pp. 3–15.
7 Bernice Glatzer Rosenthal, *New Myth, New World: From Nietzsche to Stalinism* (University Park, PA: Pennsylvania State University Press, 2002), pp. 3, 124.
8 Ibid., p. 81.
9 V.I. Lenin, *Selected Works*, vol. 1 (Moscow, 1947), pp. 265–266.
10 Quoted in Grier, *Marxist Ethical Theory in the Soviet Union*, p. 107.
11 Lenin, *Selected Works*, vol. 2, pp. 667, 670.
12 Quoted in Richard Pipes (ed.) *The Unknown Lenin* (New Haven, CT: Yale University Press, 1996), p. 153; for more on Machiavelli in the USSR, see E.A. Rees, *Political Thought from Machiavelli to Stalin: Revolutionary Machiavellism* (Basingstoke: Palgrave Macmillan, 2004).
13 Lenin, 'O rabochem edinstve', *Polnoe sobranie sochinenii*, vol. 24 (Moscow: Gos. izd. politicheskoi literatury, 1961), p. 192; cited in Zoya Berbeshkina, *Problema sovesti v Marksistsko-Leninskoi etike* (Moscow: Izd. VPSh i AON pri TSK KPSS, 1963), p. 56.
14 Yurii Annenkov, *Dnevnik moikh vstrech*, vol. 2 (New York: Inter-Language Literary Associates, 1966), p. 269.
15 See Pipes, *The Unknown Lenin*, p. 50.
16 See, for example, Operational Order 00447 in J. Arch Getty and Oleg V. Naumov (eds) *The Road to Terror* (New Haven, CT: Yale University Press, 1999), p. 477.
17 Quoted in Alexander Yakovlev, *Striving for Law in a Lawless Land* (Armonk, NY: M.E. Sharpe, 1995), p. 16.
18 'Sovest'', *Bol'shaya sovetskaya entsiklopediya* (1949–1958), gen. ed. S.I. Vavilov (Moscow: Gosudarstennoe nauchnoe izdatel'stvo), vol. 39, p. 472.
19 V.I. Lenin, *Izbrannye proizvedeniya v dvukh tomakh* (OGIZ: Gos. Izd. politicheskoi literatury, 1943), pp. 147–149.

20 Oleg Kharkhordin, *The Collective and the Individual in Russia* (Berkeley, CA: University of California Press, 1999), p. 60.
21 Ibid., p. 167; from Emelyan Yaroslavskii, 'O partetike', in A. Guseinov *et al.* (eds) *Partiinaya etika: dokumenty i materialy 20-kh godov* (Moscow: Izd. politicheskoi literatury, 1989), p. 167.
22 See Bohdan R. Bociurkiw, 'Lenin and Religion', in Leonard Schapiro and Peter Reddaway (eds), *Lenin: The Man, the Theorist, the Leader* (London: Pall Mall Press, 1967), p. 108.
23 Quoted in Dimitry Pospielovsky, *A History of Marxist-Leninist Atheism and Soviet Anti-Religious Policies* (London: Macmillan, 1987) pp. 3–4.
24 Bociurkiw, 'Lenin and Religion', p. 128.
25 As described in Andrzej Walicki, *Marxism and the Leap to the Kingdom of Freedom* (Stanford, CA: Stanford University Press, 1995), pp. 305–306.
26 Guseinov, 'Nravstvennye al'ternativy perestroiki', p. 31.
27 Quoted in Khrushchev's Secret Speech, *Khrushchev Remembers*, trans. S. Talbot (London: Sphere Books Ltd, 1971), p. 520.
28 See on this Billington, *The Icon and the Axe* (New York: Vintage Books, 1970), p. 531.
29 See Lars H. Lih *et al.* (eds) *Stalin's Letters to Molotov* (New Haven, CT: Yale University Press, 1995), pp. 241–242.
30 Leon Trotsky, 'Their Morals and Ours', in Irving Howe (ed.) *The Basic Writings of Trotsky* (London: Mercury Books, 1964), pp. 378, 396.
31 Ibid., pp. 378, 395.
32 Guseinov, 'Etika Trotskogo', *Yazyk i sovest'*, p. 61; article first published in *Eticheskaya mysl'. Naucho-publitsisticheskie chteniya, 1991* (Moscow: Respublika, 1992), pp. 264–285.
33 Trotsky, 'Their Morals and Ours', pp. 380–381, 373, 384.
34 Viktor Kravchenko, *I Chose Freedom* (London: Readers Union Ltd, 1949), pp. 421–422.
35 Ignazio Silone in Arthur Koestler *et al.*, *The God that Failed* (London: Hamish Hamilton, 1950), p. 210.
36 'The letter of an Old Bolshevik', in Boris Nicolaevsky (ed.) *Power and the Soviet Elite* (New York: Praeger, 1965), p. 55.
37 P.H. Solomon, *Soviet Criminal Justice under Stalin* (Cambridge: Cambridge University Press, 1996), pp. 156–173.
38 Ian Kershaw and Moshe Lewin, 'Afterthoughts', in I. Kershaw and M. Lewin (eds) *Stalinism and Nazism* (Cambridge: Cambridge University Press, 1999), p. 356.
39 Philip Boobbyer, *The Stalin Era* (London: Routledge, 2000), p. 89.
40 Alexandra Kollontai, 'Make Way for the Winged Eros!', in Alix Holt (ed.) *Selected Writings of Alexandra Kollontai* (London: Allison and Busby, 1977), pp. 290–292.
41 Jeffrey Brooks, 'Public Identities in *Pravda* during the 1920s', in Stephen White (ed.) *New Directions in Soviet History* (Cambridge: Cambridge University Press, 1992), pp. 32–36.
42 Interview with Natal'ya Gorbanevskaya.
43 Boobbyer, *The Stalin Era*, p. 157.
44 Interview with Aleksandr Yakovlev.
45 Interview with Ludmilla Alekseeva.
46 Interview with Vadim Bakatin; Bakatin was Interior Minister from October 1988 to December 1990.
47 Mikhail Gorbachev, *Memoirs* (London: Bantam, 1997), p. 29.
48 Quoted in Philip Boobbyer, 'Truth-telling, Conscience and Dissent in Late Soviet Russia', *European History Quarterly*, 30, 4, 2000, p. 559.

49 See Boobbyer, *The Stalin Era*, pp. 158–159.
50 See on this D.J. Richards, *Soviet Chess* (Oxford: Clarendon Press, 1965), pp. 62–63.
51 See V. Volkov, 'The Concept of *kul'turnost'*: Notes on the Stalinist Civilizing Process', in S. Fitzpatrick (ed.) *Stalinism* (London: Routledge, 2000), p. 217 ff.
52 Jeffrey Brooks, *Thank You, Comrade Stalin!* (Princeton, NJ: Princeton University Press, 2000), p. 126.
53 See John Dunstan, *Soviet Schooling in the Second World War* (Basingstoke: Macmillan, 1997), pp. 150–152.
54 Quoted in Boobbyer, 'Truth-telling, Conscience and Dissent', p. 559.
55 Gorbachev, *Memoirs*, p. 56.
56 Maxim Gorky, *My Universities* (London: Penguin Books, 1991), p. 113.
57 Mikhail Sholokhov, *Virgin Soil Upturned* (London: Putnam, 1966), p. 458.
58 See Katerina Clark, *The Soviet Novel: History as Ritual* (Bloomington, IN: Indiana University Press, 2000), p. xii.
59 Stephen Lovell, *The Russian Reading Revolution* (Basingstoke: Macmillan, 2000), p. 61.
60 Maureen Perrie, *The Cult of Ivan the Terrible in Stalin's Russia* (Basingstoke: Palgrave, 2001), p. 85 ff.
61 David Brandenberger, *National Bolshevism* (Cambridge, MA: Harvard University Press, 2002), p. 44.
62 Ibid., pp. 43–62.
63 See Paul Debreczeny, '"*Zhitie Aleksandra Boldinskogo*": Pushkin's Elevation to Sainthood in Soviet Culture', in T. Lahusen and G. Kuperman (eds), *Late Soviet Culture* (Durham, NC: Duke University Press, 1993), p. 47 ff.
64 See *Great Soviet Encyclopedia*, third edition, vol. 13 (Moscow, 1973), p. 433.
65 L. Kosmodemyanskaya, *The Story of Zoya and Shura* (Moscow: Foreign Languages Publishing House, 1953), pp. 92–93.
66 Ibid., pp. 220–223.
67 Ibid., p. 76.
68 Igal Halfin, 'Looking into the Oppositionists' Souls', *The Russian Review*, 60, 3, 2001, pp. 319, 325, 335.
69 Kharkhordin, *The Collective and the Individual in Russia*, pp. 73, 212–226, 227, 262.
70 See Kharkhordin, ibid., p. 262.
71 Igal Halfin, *Terror in My Soul* (Cambridge, MA: Harvard University Press, 2003), p. 42.
72 See *Report of Court Proceedings in the Case of the Anti-Soviet "Bloc of Rights and Trotskyites"* (Moscow: People's Commissariat of Justice of the USSR, 1938), pp. 625–626.
73 Evgenia Ginzburg, *Into the Whirlwind*, trans. P. Stevenson and M. Harari (London: Collins and Harvill, 1967), p. 17.
74 Dmitry S. Likhachev, *Reflections on the Russian Soul: A Memoir*, trans. B. Adams (Budapest: Central European University Press, 2000), pp. 267–270.
75 Hannah Arendt, *The Origins of Totalitarianism* (San Diego: Harcourt Brace Jovanovich, 1979), p. 452.
76 See on this Stefan Rossbach, *Gnostic Wars* (Edinburgh: Edinburgh University Press, 1999), p. 209.
77 Steven Merritt Miner, *Stalin's Holy War* (Chapel Hill, NC: University of North Carolina Press, 2003), p. 167.
78 Quoted in Michael Burleigh, *The Third Reich: A New History* (London: Pan Books, 2001), p. 499.
79 Halfin, *Terror in My Soul*, pp. 39–41.

3 Moral experience under Stalin

1 Jochen Hellbeck, 'The Diary of Stepan Podlyubnyi, 1931–1939', *Jahrbücher für Geschichte Osteuropas*, 44, 4, 1996, pp. 359, 354.
2 Vasily Aksenov, *Ozhog* (1980), quoted in Geoffrey Hosking, *A History of the Soviet Union* (London: Collins, 1990), pp. 312–313.
3 See Philip Boobbyer, 'Truth-telling, Conscience and Dissent in Late Soviet Russia', *European History Quarterly* 30, 4, 2000, p. 563.
4 F. Beck and W. Godin, *Russian Purge and the Extraction of Confession*, trans. from German by E. Mosbacher and D. Porter (London: Hurst and Blackett Ltd, 1951), p. 194; the authors of the book were themselves victims of arrest.
5 Maurice Hindus, *Red Bread* (Bloomington, IN: Indiana University Press, 1988), pp. 295–296.
6 Pyatakov's words as reported by N. Valentinov, 'Sut' bol'shevizma v izobrazhenii Yu. Pyatakova', *Novyi zhurnal*, no. 52, 1958, pp. 151–153.
7 Lewis Siegelbaum and Andrei Sokolov, *Stalinism as a Way of Life* (New Haven, CT: Yale University Press, 2000), p. 103.
8 *Izvestiya*, 2 September 1992; quoted in Igal Halfin, *Terror in My Soul* (Cambridge, MA: Harvard University Press, 2003), p. 279.
9 Quoted in Albert Leong, *Centaur: The Life and Art of Ernst Neizvestnyi* (Lanham, MD: Rowman and Littlefield Publishers, Inc., 2002), p. 4.
10 See Oleg Khlevniuk, *In Stalin's Shadow: The Career of 'Sergo' Ordzhonikidze* (Armonk, NY: M.E. Sharpe, 1995), pp. 175–178.
11 Angelica Balabanoff, *Impressions of Lenin*, trans. I. Cesari (Ann Arbor, MI: University of Michigan Press, 1964), p. 144.
12 Ibid., p. 138.
13 Quoted in Roy Medvedev, *Let History Judge* (Oxford: Oxford University Press, 1989), pp. 429–430.
14 Evgenia Ginzburg, *Into the Whirlwind* (London: Collins/Harvill, 1967), pp. 32–33; *Krutoi marshrut* (Milan: Arnoldo Mondadori, 1967), pp. 42–43.
15 Ginzburg, *Krutoi marshrut*, p. 27.
16 See Philip Boobbyer, 'The Moral Lessons of Soviet History: The Experience of Opposition to Evil', *Religion, State and Society*, 21, 3 & 4, 1993, p. 361.
17 Balabanoff, *Impressions of Lenin*, p. 143.
18 Vaclav Havel, 'The Power of the Powerless', *Living in Truth* (London: Faber, 1987), p. 42.
19 Nadezhda Mandelstam, *Hope Abandoned*, trans. M. Hayward (Harmondsworth: Penguin Books, 1976), pp. 191, 202.
20 Dmitri Panin, *The Notebooks of Sologdin*, trans. J. Moore (London: Hutchinson, 1976), p. 174.
21 Quoted in Boobbyer, 'The Moral Lessons of Soviet History', p. 357.
22 Vitaly Shentalinsky, *The KGB's Literary Archive* (London: Harvill Press, 1995), pp. 61–62, 66–67.
23 Quoted in R.W. Davies, *Soviet History in the Yeltsin Era* (Basingstoke: Macmillan, 1997), p. 176.
24 Quoted in Boris Starkov, 'Narkom Yezhov', in J.A. Getty and R.T. Manning (eds) *Stalinist Terror* (Cambridge: Cambridge University Press, 1993), p. 33.
25 Vyacheslav Polosin, 'Vechnyi rab ChK', *Izvestiya*, 22 January 1992, p. 3.
26 Robert Tucker, *Stalin in Power: The Revolution from Above, 1928–1941* (New York: W.W. Norton and Company, 1990), p. 448.
27 Dmitri Volkogonov, *Stalin: Triumph and Tragedy*, trans. H. Shukman (London: Weidenfeld and Nicolson, 1991), pp. xxiv, 220.
28 Quoted in J.A. Getty and O. Naumov (eds) *The Road to Terror* (New Haven, CT: Yale University Press, 1999), p. 558.

29 Sheila Fitzpatrick, *Stalin's Peasants* (New York: Oxford University Press, 1994), pp. 8–9.
30 Stephen Kotkin, *Magnetic Mountain* (Berkeley, CA: University of California Press, 1995), pp. 154, 220.
31 Grigorii Pomerants, *Zapiski gadkogo utenka* (Moscow: Moskovskii rabochii, 1998), p. 45.
32 Anna Krylova, 'The Tenacious Liberal Subject in Soviet Studies', *Kritika*, 1, 1, 2000, p. 128.
33 Quoted in Leonid Kozlov, 'The Artist and the Shadow of Ivan', in R. Taylor and D. Spring (eds) *Stalinism and Soviet Cinema* (London: Routledge, 1993), p. 130.
34 Dmitry Shostakovich, *My Testimony*, ed. S. Volkov (London: Hamish Hamilton, 1979), p. 140.
35 Leong, *Centaur*, p. 182.
36 Viktor Kravchenko, *I Chose Freedom* (London: Readers Union Ltd, 1949), p. 304; Robert Conquest, *The Great Terror: A Reassessment* (London: Pimlico, 1990), p. 293.
37 See Boobbyer, *The Stalin Era*, p. 140.
38 Kravchenko, *I Chose Freedom*, pp. 41, 52, 108, 288.
39 Ibid., pp. 132, 201, 199, 320, 309.
40 Ibid., pp. 473, 474, 479, 365, 407.
41 Petro Grigorenko, *Memoirs*, trans. P. Whitney (London: Harvill Press, 1983), p. 36.
42 Lev Kopelev, *The Education of a True Believer*, trans. G. Kern (London: Wildhood House, 1981), pp. 234–235.
43 G.A. Tokaev, *Betrayal of an Ideal* (London: Harvill Press, 1954), p. 33.
44 Czeslaw Milosz, *The Captive Mind* (New York: Vintage Books, 1981), p. 55.
45 Halfin, *Terror in My Soul*, p. ix.
46 Svetlana Alliluyeva, *Twenty Letters to a Friend*, trans. P. Johnson (London: Hutchinson, 1967), p. 193.
47 Hannah Arendt, *The Origins of Totalitarianism* (San Diego: Harcourt Brace Jovanovich, 1979), p. 475.
48 Quoted in Geoffrey Hosking, 'The Second World War and Russian National Consciousness', *Past and Present*, no. 175, May 2002, p. 173.
49 Quoted in ibid., pp. 173–174.
50 Vera Inber, *Leningrad Diary*, trans. S. Wolff and R. Grieve (London: Hutchinson, 1971), pp. 73–74.
51 N. Mandelstam, *Hope Abandoned* (Harmondsworth: Penguin Books, 1976), p. 391.
52 Varlam Shalamov, *Kolyma Tales*, trans J. Glad (Harmondsworth: Penguin Books, 1994), pp. 411–412.
53 Ibid., pp. 428–429.
54 D.S. Baldaev *et al.* (eds) *Slovar' tyuremno-lagerno-blatnogo zhargona* (Moscow: Kraya Moskvy, 1992), p. 229.
55 Boris Chichibabin, 'Poka sushchestvuet sovest'', http://www.mtu-net.ru/rayner/avtorskaja/poes_katorgi10.htm. Accessed 18 August 2004.
56 Evgenia Ginzburg, *Into the Whirlwind*, p. 156.
57 Alexander Solzhenitsyn, *The Gulag Archipelago*, vols iii–iv, trans T. Whitney (London: Collins and Harvill Press, 1975), p. 617.
58 Solzhenitsyn, *The Gulag Archipelago*, vols iii–iv, pp. 598, 615; A.S. Solzhenitsyn, *Arkhipelag GULag*, iii–iv (Paris: YMCA Press, 1974), p. 586.
59 Alexander Solzhenitsyn, *The Gulag Archipelago*, vol. 3, trans. H. Willetts (London: Collins and Harvill, 1978), p. 98.
60 D.S. Likhachev, *Reflections on the Russian Soul* (Budapest: Central European University Press, 2000), pp. 119, 102.

61 Panin, *The Notebooks of Sologdin*, pp. 167, 240.
62 See Father Walter J. Ciszek with D.L. Flaherty, *He Leadeth Me* (New York: Doubleday, 1973).
63 For an example, see Vladimir and Evdokia Petrov, *Empire of Fear* (London: André Deutsch, 1956), pp. 109–110.
64 Quoted in W.C. Fletcher, *A Study in Survival* (London: SPCK, 1965), pp. 29–30; Epistle to the Romans, 13.5.
65 S.M. Miner, *Stalin's Holy War* (Chapel Hill, NC: University of North Carolina Press, 2003), pp. 327, 86.
66 Vera Vasilevskaya, *Katakomby XX veka* (Moscow: Fond imeni Aleksandra Menya, 2001), p. 101.
67 Il'ya Basin, 'Skhiigumen'ya Mariya i podpol'nyi zhenskii monastyr'', *Christianos*, vol. 7 (Riga, 1998), p. 148.
68 Miner, *Stalin's Holy War*, p. 144.

4 The rebirth of conscience under Khrushchev

1 Robert Service, *A History of Twentieth Century Russia* (Cambridge, MA: Harvard University Press, 1998), p. 293.
2 Larisa Bogoraz and Aleksandr Daniel, 'V poiskakh sesushchestvuyushchei nauki (Dissidentstvo kak istoricheskaya problema)', *Problemy Vostochnoi Evropy*, nos 37–38 (Washington, DC, 1990), pp. 159–160.
3 See Philip Boobbyer, 'Truth-telling, Conscience and Dissent in Late Soviet Russia', *European History Quarterly*, 30, 4, 2000, p. 559.
4 Interview with Larisa Bogoraz.
5 Joshua Rubenstein, *Soviet Dissidents* (Boston: Beacon Press, 1980) p. 3.
6 Ernst Neizvestnyi, *Govorit Neizvestnyi* (Frankfurt: Posev, 1984), p. 37; see also Albert Leong, *Centaur: The Life and Art of Ernst Neizvestnyi* (Lanham, MD: Rowman and Littlefield), pp. 73–77.
7 Fyodor Burlatskii, 'Democratization is a Long March', in Stephen F. Cohen and Katrina van den Heuvel, *Voices of Glasnost*' (New York: W.W. Norton and Company, 1989), p. 176.
8 Boobbyer, 'Truth-telling, Conscience and Dissent', p. 562; Vera Pashennaya (1887–1962) was from 1941 Professor at the Shchepkin Theatrical School.
9 See A. Ledeneva, *Russia's Economy of Favours* (Cambridge: Cambridge University Press, 1998), p. 40.
10 Abraham Rothberg, *The Heirs of Stalin* (London: Cornell University Press, 1972), pp. 344–345.
11 See Andrei Sakharov, *Memoirs* (London: Hutchinson, 1990), p. 216.
12 See C.P. Snow, *The Two Cultures* (New York: Cambridge University Press, 1959), p. 4.
13 Leonid Plyushch, *History's Carnival*, ed. and trans. M. Carynnyk (London: Collins and Harvill Press, 1979), p. 70.
14 Joseph Brodsky, *Less Than One* (London: Penguin, 1987), p. 7.
15 Boobbyer, 'Truth-telling, Conscience and Dissent', p. 560.
16 Interview with Boris Pustintsev.
17 Grigori Svirski, *A History of Post-War Soviet Writing: The Literature of Moral Opposition* (Ann Arbor, MI: Ardis, 1979), pp. 61–66.
18 Mikhail Meerson-Aksenov, 'The Dissident Movement and *Samizdat*', in M. Meerson-Aksenov and B. Shragin (eds) *The Political, Social and Religious Thought of Russian 'Samizdat'* (Belmont, CA: Nordland, 1997), pp. 28–29.
19 Mikhail Meerson-Aksenov, 'Rozhdenie novoi intelligentsii', in P. Litvinov *et al.* (eds) *Samosoznanie* (New York: Khronika, 1976), pp. 107–108.
20 Rubenstein, *Soviet Dissidents*, p. 18.

21 Robert Horvath, 'The Dissident Roots of *Glasnost*'', in Stephen Wheatcroft (ed.) *Challenging Traditional Roots of Russian History* (Basingstoke: Palgrave Macmillan, 2002), p. 186.
22 Bukovsky, quoted in Rubenstein, *Soviet Dissidents*, p. 2.
23 Vladimir Bukovsky, *To Build a Castle*, trans. M. Scammell (London: André Deutsch, 1978), pp. 80, 90–91, 94, 104.
24 Ibid., p. 120.
25 Rubenstein, *Soviet Dissidents*, pp. 20–21.
26 See Rubinstein, *Soviet Dissidents*, p. 21.
27 A.S. Esenin-Vol'pin, *A Leaf of Spring* (London: Thames and Hudson, 1961), p. 49.
28 Ibid., pp. 135, 139.
29 Horvath, 'The Dissident Roots of *Glasnost*'', pp. 177, 179.
30 Bukovsky, *To Build a Castle*, p. 192.
31 Rubenstein, *Soviet Dissidents*, p. 22
32 Marshall Shatz, *Soviet Dissent in Historical Perspective* (Cambridge: Cambridge University Press, 1980), p. 151.
33 D. Volkogonov, *Stalin: Triumph and Tragedy* (London: Weidenfeld and Nicolson, 1991), p. 577.
34 N. Khrushchev, *Khrushchev Remembers* (London: Sphere Books, 1971) pp. 520–521.
35 Ibid., pp. 511, 510.
36 Ibid., p. 509.
37 Nail' Bikennin, 'Kak pisat' memuary, ili dvoinoi avtoportret', *Svobodnaya mysl'*, XXI, 6, 2000, p. 105.
38 M. Heller and A. Nekrich quoted in A. Walicki, *Marxism and the Leap to the Kingdom of Freedom* (Stanford, CA: Stanford University Press, 1995), p. 512.
39 Ronald Hingley, 'That's No Lie, Comrade', *Problems of Communism*, XI, 2, 1962, p. 50.
40 Interview with Aleksandr Tsipko, 1998.
41 Meerson-Aksenov, 'The Dissident Movement and *Samizdat*', p. 27.
42 Quoted in P.T. Grier, *Marxist Ethical Theory in the Soviet Union* (Dordrecht: D. Reidel, 1978), p. 108.
43 Priscilla Johnson and Leopold Labedz (eds) *Khrushchev and the Arts: The Politics of Soviet Culture, 1962–1964* (Boston: MIT Press, 1965), p. 68.
44 Richard T. De George, *Soviet Ethics and Morality* (Ann Arbor, MI: University of Michigan Press, 1969), p. 111.
45 James Scanlan, *Marxism in the USSR* (Ithaca, NY: Cornell University Press, 1985), p. 268.
46 De George, *Soviet Ethics and Morality*, p. 111.
47 Catriona Kelly, *Refining Russia* (Oxford: Oxford University Press, 2001), p. 315.
48 Nikita Khrushchev, *Za dal'neishii pod'em proizvoditel'nykh sil, za tekhnicheskii progress vo vsekh otraslyakh narodnogo khozyaistva* (Moscow: Gospolitizdat, 1959), p. 46; cited in Berbeshkina, *Problema sovesti*, p. 105.
49 Cited in Z. Berbeshkina, *Problema sovesti v Marksisto-Leninskoi etike* (Moscow: Izd. VPShi AON pri TSK KPSS, 1963), p. 88.
50 *Izvestiya*, 15 January, 1962; cited in Berbeshkina, *Problema sovesti*, p. 103.
51 Berbeshkina, *Problema sovesti*, p. 57.
52 Nina Baburina (ed.) *The Soviet Political Poster* (London: Penguin Books, 1985), no. 156. See also http://www.poster.s.cz/listy/russ6.htm. Accessed, 21 August 2004.
53 Andrei Amalrik, *Notes of a Revolutionary*, trans. G. Daniels (London: Weidenfeld and Nicolson, 1982), p. 105.

54 Irina Ratushinskaya, *Grey Is the Colour of Hope*, trans. A. Kojevnikov (Sevenoaks: Sceptre, 1989), pp. 28–29.
55 Bukovsky, *To Build a Castle*, p. 152.
56 See Nathaniel Davies, *A Long Walk to Church* (Boulder, CO: Westview Press, 1995), pp. 35, 43, 41.
57 See Nikita Khrushchev, *Vospominaniya* (Moscow: Vagrius, 1997), between pages 416 and 417.
58 Quoted by Catherine Andreyev in *The Times Higher Educational Supplement*, 5 December 2003, p. 31.
59 Khrushchev, *Khrushchev Remembers*, p. 309.
60 Bukovsky, *To Build a Castle*, pp. 112–113.
61 Vladimir Shlapentokh, *Soviet Intellectuals and Political Power* (London: I.B. Tauris and Co. Publishers Ltd, 1990), p. 162.
62 John Keep, *The Last of the Empires* (Oxford: Oxford University Press, 1995), Chapter 6.
63 Olga Berggol'ts, *Literaturnaya gazeta*, 16 April 1953; cited in Keep, *Last of the Empires*, p. 121.
64 Vladimir Pomerantsev, 'Ob iskrennosti v literature', *Novyi mir*, XXIX, 12, 1953, pp. 218, 220.
65 Ludmilla Alexeyeva and Paul Goldberg, *The Thaw Generation* (Boston: Little, Brown and Company, 1990), pp. 72–73.
66 Fedor Abramov, 'Lyudi kolkhoznoi derevni v poslevoennoi prozy (Literaturnye zametki)', *Novyi mir*, XXX, 4, 1954, p. 231.
67 Konstantin Simonov, 'Literaturnye zametki', *Novyi mir*, XXXII, 12, 1956, p. 242.
68 Dina Spechler, *Permitted Dissent in the USSR* (New York: Praeger, 1982), p. 49.
69 Vladimir Dudintsev, *Not by Bread Alone*, trans. E. Bone (London: Hutchinson, 1957), pp. 174, 438.
70 Ibid., pp. 216, 101.
71 Ibid., p. 447.
72 Boris Pasternak, *Doctor Zhivago*, trans. M. Hayward and M. Harari (London: Flamingo, 1984), pp. 18–19.
73 Ibid., pp. 257, 573.
74 Ibid., pp. 444, 274, 289.
75 James Billington, *The Icon and the Axe* (New York: Vintage Books, 1970), p. 556.
76 Keep, *Last of the Empires*, p. 128.
77 Yevgeny Yevtushenko, 'A Time for Summing Up', in S. Cohen and K. van den Heuvel, *Voices of Glasnost'* (New York: W.W. Norton, 1989), pp. 264–265.
78 Svirski, *A History of Post-War Soviet Writing*, 319.
79 Yevgeny Yevtushenko, *Collected Poems, 1952–1990* (Edinburgh: Mainstream, 1991), pp. 114, 115–116.
80 P. Johnson and L. Labedz (eds) *Khrushchev and the Arts* (Boston: MIT Press, 1965), pp. 156, 168–169.
81 Ibid., pp. 209, 204–206.
82 Ibid., p. 208.
83 Shlapentokh, *Soviet Intellectuals and Political Power*, p. 151.
84 Tvardovsky, 'Tyorkin in the Other World', in Johnson and Labedz (eds) *Khrushchev and the Arts*, p. 271.
85 Aleksandr Solzhenitysn, *The Oak and the Calf*, trans. H. Willetts (London: Collins and Harvill Press, 1980), p. 50.
86 Ibid., pp. 66, 211.
87 Ibid., pp. 56, 178, 242.

88 Feliks Svetov, *Opyt biografii* (Paris: YMCA Press, 1985), p. 241.
89 Thomas Venclova, 'On the Art of Writing in the USSR', in *Forms of Hope* (Riverdale-on-Hudson: Sheep Meadow Press, 1999), pp. 228–229.
90 Vladimir Lakshin, *Solzhenitsyn, Tvardovsky and Novy Mir* (Cambridge, MA: MIT Press, 1980), pp. 10, 18, 20, 21, 22; Lakshin's essay was first published in *The Twentieth Century: A Socio-Political Digest and Literary Magazine*, vol. 2 (1977).

5 The ethics of the human rights movement

1 Ludmilla Alexeyeva uses *inakomyslie* for the concept of dissent in her book, *Soviet Dissent* (Middletown, PA: Wesleyan University Press, 1987).
2 Petr Vail' and Aleksandr Genis, *60-e: Mir sovetskogo cheloveka* (Moscow: Novoe literaturnoe obozrenie, 1998), pp. 176–177.
3 Nina Komarova, *Kniga lyubvi i gneva* (Paris, 1994), p. 289.
4 Pavel Litvinov, 'O dvizhenii prava cheloveka v SSSR', in P. Litvinov *et al.* (eds) *Samosoznanie* (New York: Khronika, 1976), pp. 78–79; see also Larisa Bogoraz and Aleksandr Daniel, 'V poiskakh sesushchestvuyushchei nauki', *Problemy Vostochnoi Evropy*, nos 37–38 (Washington, DC, 1990), pp. 152–153.
5 Andrei Amalrik, *Notes of a Revolutionary* (London: Weidenfeld and Nicolson, 1982), p. 21.
6 Andrei Sinyavskii, 'Dissidentstvo kak lichnyi opyt', *Russkaya mysl'*, 25 February 1982, p. 10.
7 Interview with Sergei Kovalev, 'Dissident s parlamentskim mandatom', *Referendum*, no. 35, 1990, in Lev Timofeev (ed.) *Referendum, zhurnal nezavisimykh mnenii: izbrannye materialy* (Paris, n.d. publisher's foreword dated 3 October 1992), p. 175.
8 Emma Gilligan, 'Sergei Kovalyov and the Defence of Human Rights in Russia', PhD thesis, University of Melbourne, 2001, p. 32; see Sergei Kovalev, second chapter of Russian version of memoirs, pp. 1–2 (henceforth 'Memoirs'); this is electronically stored at the Memorial Society, Moscow; the Russian version is a slightly longer version of the German edition: S. Kowaljow, *Der Flug des Weissen Raben* (Berlin: Rowholt, 1997).
9 Philip Boobbyer, 'Truth-telling, Conscience and Dissent in Late Soviet Russia', *European History Quarterly*, 30, 4, 2000, p. 567.
10 Larisa Bogoraz, 'This Is Just the Start', *Moscow News*, 49, 8–15 December 1991, p. 7.
11 Interview with Vyacheslav Bakhmin, 'Samizdat byl v kazhdom intelligentskom dome', *Segodnya*, 11 December 1999, p. 4.
12 Amalrik, *Notes of a Revolutionary*, p. 48.
13 Andrei Amalrik, 'Will the Soviet Union Survive until 1984?', in Andrei Amalrik, *Will the Soviet Union Survive until 1984?*, ed. Hilary Steinberg (New York: Harper Colophon Books, 1970), pp. 20–21.
14 See also on this, Emma Gilligan, 'Sergei Kovalyov and the Defence of Human Rights in Russia', PhD thesis, University of Melbourne, 2001, p. 3.
15 For a transcript of the trial, see 'Trial of a Young Poet', *Encounter*, XXIII, 3, September 1964, pp. 84–91.
16 See Max Hayward, 'Introduction', in Abram Tertz (Andrei Sinyavsky), *A Voice from the Chorus*, trans. K. Fitzlyon and M. Hayward (London: Collins and Harvill Press, 1976), pp. viii–ix.
17 Quoted in Leopold Labedz and Max Hayward (eds), *On Trial: The Case of Sinyavsky (Tertz) and Daniel (Arzhak)* (London: Collins and Harvill Press, 1967), pp. 192–193.
18 Abram Tertz, *On Socialist Realism* (New York: Pantheon Books, 1960), p. 38.

19 Labedz and Hayward (eds), *On Trial*, pp. 203–204.
20 Boris Shragin, 'Iskuplenie Yuliya Danielya', in *Mysl' i deistvie* (Moscow, 2000), p. 338; Daniel's pseudonym was Nikolai Arzhak.
21 Leopold Labedz, 'Preface', *On Trial*, p. 13.
22 Labedz and Hayward (eds), *On Trial*, p. 290.
23 Joshua Rubenstein, *Soviet Dissidents* (Boston: Beacon Press, 1980), pp. 43–45.
24 Ibid., pp. 22, 64–66.
25 Vladimir Bukovsky, *To Build a Castle* (London: Andre Deutsch, 1978), p. 239; Rubenstein, *Soviet Dissidents*, p. 65.
26 Details in Rubenstein, *Soviet Dissidents*, p. 72.
27 For details, see Pavel Litvinov (compiler) and P. Reddaway (ed.) *The Trial of the Four* (New York: Viking Press, 1972), pp. 228–283, 399–406.
28 Peter Reddaway, 'Introduction', in *The Trial of the Four*, p. ix; see Pavel Litvinov (ed.) *The Demonstration in Pushkin Square*, trans. M. Harari (London: Harvill Press, 1969).
29 Rubenstein, *Soviet Dissidents*, p. 52.
30 Anatoly Marchenko, *My Testimony*, trans. M. Scammell (London: Sceptre, 1987), pp. 411, 415.
31 Litvinov, *The Trial of the Four*, pp. 225–227.
32 Aleksandr Daniel, 'Dissidentstvo: kul'tura, uskol'zayushchaya ot opredelenii?' in K. Yu. Rogov (ed.) *Rossiya-Russia. Novaya Seriya. Vyp 1 (9): Semidesyatie kak predmet istorii russkoi kul'tury* (Moscow, 1998), pp. 5–7.
33 Meerson-Aksenov, 'The Dissident Movement and *Samizdat*', in M. Meerson-Aksenov and B. Shragin (eds) *The Political, Social and Religious Thought of Russian 'Samizdat'* (Belmont, CA, Nordland, 1997), p. 32.
34 Kovalev, 'Memoirs', pp. 1–2.
35 Andrei Sakharov, *Memoirs*, trans. R. Lourie (London: Hutchinson, 1990), pp. 275, 365.
36 Amalrik, *Notes of a Revolutionary*, pp. 24, 26.
37 L.I. Bogoraz, 'Iz vospominanii', *Minuvshee*, 2, 1986, pp. 82, 84; Vadim Delone, *Portrety v kolyuchei rame* (London: Overseas Publications Interchange, 1984), p. 23.
38 Kovalev, 'Memoirs', p. 8.
39 Quoted in Natalia Gorbanevskaya, *Red Square at Noon*, trans. A. Lieven (London: André Deutsch, 1972), pp. 213–214.
40 Ibid., pp. 281–282.
41 Natal'ya Gorbanevskaya, 'Mozhesh' Vyiti na Ploshchad', Smeesh' Vyiti na Ploshchad'', 25 August 1983, *Russkaya mysl'*, p. 10.
42 Rubenstein, *Soviet Dissidents*, p. 130.
43 Yuri Orlov, *Dangerous Thoughts*, trans. T. Whitney (New York: W. Morrow, 1991), p. 192.
44 Amalrik, *Notes of a Revolutionary*, p. 60.
45 Gorbanevskaya, *Russkaya mysl'*, 25 August 1983, p. 10.
46 Gorbanevskaya, *Red Square at Noon*, p. 284.
47 Vail' and Genis, *60-e: Mir sovetskogo cheloveka*, p. 183.
48 K. Zhitnikov, 'The Decline of the "Democratic Movement",' in Meerson-Aksenov and Shragin, *The Political, Social and Religious Thought of Russian 'Samizdat'*, p. 255; this article was distributed in samizdat and then published in the Paris-based journal *Vestnik RSKhd*, no. 106, 1972.
49 Aleksandr Galich, 'Staratel'skii val'sok', *Pesnya ob Otchem Dome* (Moscow: Lokid-Press, 2003), pp. 242–243.
50 Gorbanevskaya, *Russkaya mysl'*, 25 August 1983, p. 10.
51 Vladimir Pimonov, *Govoryat "osobo opasnye": sbornik interv'yu* (Moscow: Detektiv Press, 1999), p. 51.

52 Delone, *Portrety v kolyuchei rame*, p. 20.
53 Vail' and Genis, *60-e: Mir sovetskogo cheloveka* p. 180.
54 Rubenstein, *Soviet Dissidents*, pp. 98, 100–102.
55 Interview with Natal'ya Gorbanevskaya.
56 Interview with Larisa Bogoraz.
57 Peter Reddaway (ed.) *Uncensored Russia: The Human Rights Movement in the Soviet Union* (London: Jonathan Cape, 1972), pp. 39, 21, 23.
58 Andrei Sakharov, *Memoirs* (London: Hutchinson, 1990), p. 361.
59 The appeal can be found in George Saunders (ed.) *Samizdat: Voices of the Soviet Opposition* (New York: Monad Press, 1974), pp. 365–369; the other signatories were G. Altunyan, V. Borisov, M. Dzhemilev, A. Lavut, A. Levitin-Krasnov, Y. Maltsev and G. Pod'yapolskii.
60 Rubenstein, *Soviet Dissidents*, pp. 144, 166.
61 T. Velikanova, S. Kovalev, T. Khodorovich, 'Otkrytoe pis'mo', *Initsiativnaya gruppa po zashchite prav cheloveka v SSSR: sbornik dokumentov* (New York: Khronika, 1976), p. 39.
62 Kovalev, 'Memoirs', pp. 39, 17, 28.
63 Boobbyer, 'Truth-telling, Conscience and Dissent', p. 571.
64 Rubenstein, *Soviet Dissidents*, p. 268.
65 Sakharov, *Memoirs*, p. 499.
66 Interview with Boris Belenken.
67 *Informatsionnyi bulletin*, no. 1, 12 December 1979, AC No. 3873, Komitet zashchity Tat'yany Velikanovy, Memorial Society Archives, pp. 19, 25, 23.
68 Boobbyer, 'Truth-Telling, Conscience and Dissent', p. 569.
69 See on this Sof'iya Chuikina, 'Uchastie zhenshchin v dissidentskom dvizhenii (1956–1986)', http://ngo.org.ru/ngoss/get/cid11564/id12678.html. Accessed 19 August 2004.
70 Interview with Ludmilla Alekseeva.
71 Rubenstein, *Soviet Dissidents*, pp. 131, 133.
72 Orlov, *Dangerous Thoughts*, p. 192.
73 Rubenstein, *Soviet Dissidents*, pp. 218–219.
74 Orlov, *Dangerous Thoughts*, pp. 333–334.
75 Ibid., pp. 189–190.
76 Quoted in Paul Goldberg, *The Final Act: The Dramatic, Revealing Story of the Moscow Helsinki Watch Group* (New York: Morrow, 1988), p. 39.
77 Aleksandr Solzhenitsyn, 'Zhit' ne po lzhi!', *Publitsistika: stat'i i rechi* (Vermont/Paris: *YMCA Press*, 1981), pp. 168, 170–172.
78 Alexander Solzhenitsyn, 'The Smatterers', in Alexander Solzhenitsyn *et al.*, *From under the Rubble* (London: Collins, 1976), p. 275.
79 Vaclav Havel, 'The Power of the Powerless', in *Living in Truth*, p. 55; see also J. Goldfarb, *Beyond Glasnost'* (Chicago: University of Chicago Press, 1989), pp. 104–105.
80 Amalrik, *Notes of a Revolutionary*, p. 278.
81 Pavel Litvinov, 'Otkrytoe pis'mo A.I. Solzhenitsynu', *Vestnik RSKhD*, 114, IV, 1974, pp. 258–259; Sergei Bulgakov, 'Heroism and Asceticism', in *Landmarks*, pp. 23–63.
82 A.I. Solzhenitsyn, 'Otvet A. Solzhenitsyna P. Litvinovu', *Vestnik RSKhD*, 114, IV, 1974, pp. 261.
83 K. Burzhuademov, 'Aktivno dumat', uspeshno rabotat', smelo zhit'', in '"Ne zhit' po lzhi"/sbornik otklikov-sporov na stat'yu A.I. Solzhenitsyna', 1977–1979, Memorial Archives (Moscow), f. 130, op. 1, delo 28, pp. 8–11.
84 Grigorii Pomerants, in '"Ne zhit' po lzhi"/sbornik otklikov-sporov', p. 133.
85 See Aleksandr Daniel, 'Dissidentstvo: kul'tura, uskol'zayushchaya ot opredelenii?', p. 8.

86 Gorbanevskaya, *Red Square at Noon*, p. 284.
87 Interview with Aleksandr Daniel.
88 Quoted in M. Shatz, *Soviet Dissent in Historical Perspective* (Cambridge: Cambridge University Press, 1980), p. 151.
89 Fedor Tyutchev, 'Silentium', in *The Heritage of Russian Verse* (Bloomington, IN: Indiana University Press, 1965), p. 132.
90 Vail' and Genis, *60-e: Mir sovetskogo cheloveka*, p. 181.
91 Galich, *Pesnya ob Otchem Dome*, pp. 78–79, 242–243.
92 Tat'yana Velikanova, 'Vozrazheniya', '"Ne zhit' po lzhi"/sbornik otklikov-sporov', p. 21.
93 Interview with Aleksandr Daniel.
94 Vail' and Genis, *60-e: Mir sovetskogo cheloveka*, p. 183.
95 Tat'yana Khodorovich, 'Otkrytoe pis'mo Leonidu Plyushchu', *Kontinent*, vol. 9, 1976, p. 239.
96 Kovalev, 'Memoirs', pp. 19, 11.
97 See, T. Trusova, 'Khranyu s lyubovyu v pamyati svoei', in E.E. Pechuro (ed.) *Zastupnitsa: Advokat S.V. Kallistratova* (Moscow: Zven'ya, 1997), p. 187.
98 Interview with Tat'yana Trusova.
99 V. Sokirko, '"Pravda i beda dissidentov"– pis'mo v izdatel'stvo *Moskovskii rabochii*', Tri pis'ma 1982–1983, Semeinyi arkhiv V. Sokirko, Memorial Archives, fond 130, op. 1, delo 25.
100 Vladimir Voinovich, *Portret na fone mifa* (Moscow: Eksmo, 2002), p. 148.
101 Ibid., pp. 150, 146, 166, 100.
102 Interview with Natal'ya Gorbanevskaya.
103 David Samoilov, *Podennye zapisi*, vol. 2 (Moscow: Vremya, 2002), pp. 300–301.
104 Vail' and Genis, *60-e: Mir sovetskogo cheloveka*, p. 178.
105 Aleksandr Daniel, 'Dissidentstvo: kul'tura, uskol'zayushchaya ot opredelenii?', p. 10.

6 In search of inner freedom

1 Gorbanevskaya, *Russkaya mysl'*, 25 August 1983, p. 10.
2 Andrei Amalrik, 'An Open Letter to Kuznetsov', in Andrei Amalrik, *Will the Soviet Union Survive until 1984?* (New York: Harper Colophon Books, 1970), p. 65.
3 Andrei Amalrik, *Notes of a Revolutionary* (London: Weidenfeld and Nicolson, 1982), p. 26.
4 Dmitri Nelidov, 'Ideocratic Consciousness and Personality', in Mikhail Meerson-Aksenov and B. Shagrin, *The Political, Social and Religious Thought of Russian 'Samizdat'* (Belmont, CA: Nordland, 1997), pp. 271, 276, 277, 290.
5 Quoted in L. Alexeyeva and P. Goldberg, *The Thaw Generation* (Boston: Little, Brown and Company, 1990), p. 125.
6 Vladimir Al'brecht, *Kak vesti sebya na obyske* (Moscow: Krovopolitprosvet, 1976; Frankfurt: Posev, 1977), p. 8.
7 Vladimir Al'brekht, *Kak byt' svidetelem* (Paris: Izd. zhurnala 'A – Ya', 1983), pp. 9, 19, 70, 17, 136. These references are taken from the second edition of the book, which was corrected and expanded by Al'brekht.
8 Al'brekht, *Kak byt' svidetelem*, pp. 61–62, 72.
9 Quoted in Joshua Rubinstein, *Soviet Dissidents* (Boston: Beacon Press, 1980), pp. 253–254.
10 Svetlana Alliluyeva, *Twenty Letters to a Friend* (London: Hutchinson, 1967), p. 245.
11 See Philip Boobbyer, 'Truth-telling, Conscience and Dissent in Late Soviet Russia', *European History Quarterly*, 30, 4, 2000, p. 577.

12 Vail' and Genis *60-e: Mir sovetskogo cheloveka* (Moscow: Novoe Literaturnoe obozrenie, 1998), p. 179.
13 See Boobbyer, 'Truth-telling, Conscience and Dissent', p. 575.
14 Vladimir, Pimonov, *Govoryat 'osobo opasnye'* (Moscow: Detektiv Press, 1999), p. 223.
15 Komarova, *Kniga lyubvi i gneva*, p. 452.
16 Amalrik, *Notes of a Revolutionary*, pp. 80–81.
17 Pimonov, *Govoryat 'osobo opasnye'*, p. 160.
18 Interview with Ludmilla Alekseeva.
19 Pimonov, *Govoryat 'osobo opasnye'*, p. 126.
20 Interview with Ludmilla Alekseeva.
21 Pechuro (ed.) *Zastupnitsa: Advokat S.V. Kallistratova*, pp. 77, 112, 116.
22 T. Trusova, 'Khranyu s lyubov'yu v pamyati svoei', in Pechuro (ed.) *Zastupnitsa: Advokat S.V. Kallistratova*, p. 189.
23 Interview with Oleg Gordievskii.
24 These insights are taken from Barbara Walker, 'On Reading Soviet Memoirs: A History of the "Contemporaries" Genre as an Institution of Russian Intelligentsia Culture from the 1790s to the 1970s', *Russian Review*, 59, 3, 2000, pp. 341, 344, 347.
25 Leona Toker, *Return from the Gulag: Narratives of Gulag Survivors* (Bloomington, IN: Indiana University Press, 2000), pp. 74, 94–95.
26 Andrei Sakharov, *Memoirs* (London: Hutchinson, 1990), pp. 15–16.
27 See Philippe Lejeune, 'The Autobiographical Pact', *On Autobiography*, ed. P.J. Eakin (Minneapolis: University of Minnesota Press, 1989), p. 5.
28 V. Bukovsky, *To Build a Castle* (London: André Deutsch, 1978), pp. 123, 136–139, 227, 336, 279.
29 Boobbyer, 'Truth-telling, Conscience and Dissent', p. 576.
30 Interview with Vladimir Bukovskii.
31 Interview with Vladimir Bukovskii.
32 Interview with Natal'ya Gorbanevskaya.
33 Vladimir Maksimov, 'Interv'yu Vladimira Maksimova Bi-Bi-Si', *Kontinent*, 122, 1, 1977, p. 278.
34 See George Weigel, *The Final Revolution* (New York: Oxford University Press, 1992), p. 52.
35 Natan Sharansky, *Fear No Evil*, trans. S. Hoffman (London: Weidenfeld and Nicolson, 1988), pp. 43, 16.
36 Bukovsky, *To Build a Castle*, p. 24.
37 Sharansky, *Fear No Evil*, p. 122 ff.
38 Viktor Krasin, *Sud* (New York: Chalidze Publications, 1983), pp. 131, 51, 45.
39 Sharansky, *Fear No Evil*, p. 367.
40 Ibid., pp. 367, 360–361.
41 Ibid., pp. 360–362.
42 Krasin, *Sud*, pp. 6, 97.
43 Krasin, *Sud*, following title page (Matthew, 10.28), and 97.
44 Krasin, *Sud*, p. 7.
45 Ibid., pp. 10, 25.
46 Ibid., pp. 14, 27, 29, 30, 32.
47 Ratushinskaya, *Grey is the Colour of Hope* (Sevenoaks: Sceptre, 1989), pp. 295–296, 278.
48 Interview with Larisa Bogoraz.
49 Vladimir Maksimov, *Kontinent*, 122, 1, 1977, p. 279.
50 Tatiana Goricheva (ed.), *Cry of the Spirit*, trans. Susan Cupitt (London: Fount Paperbacks, 1989), p. 8.
51 Obituary of Feliks Svetov, *The Times*, 18 September 2002, p. 30.

52 Matthew, 5.26; Zoya Krakhmalnikova, *Listen, Prison!*, trans. O. Koshansky (Redding: Nikodemus Orthodox Publication Society, 1993), p. 9.
53 Ibid., p. 105.
54 Ibid., pp. 82–83, 79.
55 Jay Bergman, 'Was the Soviet Union Totalitarian? The View of Soviet Dissidents and the Reformers of the Gorbachev Era', *Studies in East European Thought*, 50, 4, 1998, p. 259.
56 *Listen, Prison!*, pp. 19, 129–130, 35.
57 Tatiana Goricheva, *Talking about God is Dangerous* (London: SCM Press, 1984), pp. 10, 5.
58 Ibid., pp. 10, 13, 45, 16–17.
59 Ibid., p. 45, 98.
60 See on this Philip Boobbyer, 'Religious Experiences of the Soviet Dissidents', *Religion, State and Society*, 27, 3/4, 1999, p. 377.
61 Venclova, 'Prison as Communicative Phenomenon', in *Forms of Hope* (Riverdale-on-Hudson: Sheep Meadow Press, 1999), p. 178.
62 Goricheva, *Talking about God is Dangerous*, p. 11.
63 David Remnick, *Lenin's Tomb* (London: Viking, 1993), p. 269.
64 Quoted in Boobbyer, 'Truth-telling, Conscience and Dissent', p. 567.
65 See Avraam Shifrin, *Chetvertoe izmerenie* (Frankfurt: Posev, 1973).
66 Mikhailo Mikhailov, 'Misticheskii opyt nevoli', *Kontinent*, 5, 1975, pp. 228, 224–225; translated as 'Mystical Experiences of the Labour Camps', in *Kontinent2* (London: Hodder and Stoughton/Coronet Books, 1978), pp. 103–131.
67 Alexander Solzhenitsyn, *The Oak and the Calf* (London: Collins and Harvill Press, 1980), pp. 4, 204.
68 Aleksandr Solzhenitsyn, *Invisible Allies*, trans. A. Klimoff and M. Nicholson (London: Harvill Press, 1997), p. 269.
69 Evgenia Ginzburg, *Into the Whirlwind* (London: Collins and Harvill, 1967), pp. 70, 316, 311.
70 Abram Tertz (Andrei Sinyavsky), *A Voice from the Chorus*, trans. K. Fitzlyon and M. Hayward (London: Collins and Harvill, 1976), p. 69.
71 Andrei Sinyavsky, *Unguarded Thoughts*, trans. M. Harari (London: Collins and Harvill Press, 1965), p. 79.
72 *Vsya zhizn' – Paskha Khristova. Arkhimandrit Tavrion (Batozskii), zhizneopisanie, vospominaniya dukhovnykh chad, propovedi* (Moscow: Otchii dom, 2001), p. 27; Archimandrite Viktor Mamontov, *Serdtse pustyni* (Moscow: Svyato-filaretovskaya moskovskaya vysshaya pravoslavnaya khristianskaya shkola, 2002), p. 42.
73 Mamontov, *Serdtse pustyni*, p. 42.
74 See Sviashchennik Vladimir Vil'gert, 'Vospominaniya ob ottse Tavrione', *Vsya zhizn'*, p. 84; also interview with Archimandrite Viktor Mamontov.
75 Interview with Archimandrite Viktor Mamontov.
76 Interview with Natal'ya Bolshakova.
77 Natal'ya Grigorenko *et al.* (eds), *Umnoe nebo: perepiska protoiereya Aleksandra Menya s monakhinei Ioannoi (Yu. N. Reitlinger)* (Moscow: Fond imeni Aleksandra Menya, 2002), p. 323.
78 *Velikie russkie startsy XX veka* (Moscow: Trifonov Pechengskii monastyr 'Kovcheg', 2002), p. 77.
79 Sv. D. Dudko, 'Pokayanie v Rusi', *Vestnik RSKhD*, 119, iii–iv, 1976, pp. 256, 257, 259, 278, 260, 275, 277, 261, 272, 258.
80 Interview with Archimandrite Viktor Mamontov; for an account of the repressions at the Pochaev monastery in the early 1960s, see Michael Bordeaux, *Patriarchs and Prophets* (London: Mowbrays, 1975), pp. 97–115.

81 Amalrik, *Notes of a Revolutionary* (London: Weidenfeld and Nicolson, 1982), pp. 35, 301.
82 Zoya Maslenikova, *Zhizn' Otsa Aleksandra Menya* (Moscow: Pristsel's/Russlit, 1995), p. 70; for details of Men''s links with the intelligentsia, see pp. 201–219.
83 Ibid., pp. 203–204.
84 Bordeaux, *Patriarchs and Prophets*, pp. 194–195, 218, 228.
85 Ibid., pp. 318–319, 327–329.
86 Dmitry Pospielovsky, *Religion in Communist Lands*, 6, 4, 1978, p. 230; cited in Jane Ellis, *The Russian Orthodox Church* (London: Croom Helm, 1986), p. 275.
87 O. Vsevolod Shpiller, *Stranitsy zhizni v sokhranivshikhsya pis'makh* (Krasnoyarsk: Eniseiskii blagovest', 2002), pp. 436–437, 441.
88 Quoted in Ellis, *The Russian Orthodox Church*, p. 279.
89 Ellis, *The Russian Orthodox Church*, p. 324.
90 Shpiller, *Stranitsy zhizni*, pp. 448, 456–457, 457–458.
91 D. Dudko, 'Zapad ishchet sensatsii', *Izvestiya*, 21 June 1980, p. 6.
92 See also Ellis, *The Russian Orthodox Church*, pp. 430–439.
93 Sharansky, *Fear No Evil*, pp. 295–296.
94 Ibid., pp. 295, 297.
95 I.B. Semenenko-Basin, 'Kanonizatsiya svyatykh v russkoi pravoslavnoi tserkvi v kontekste evolyutsii sovetskoi i postsovetskoi kul'tury (1917–2000)', PhD thesis, Moscow, 2002, p. 43.
96 Ibid., pp. 72, 74.
97 Ellis, *The Russian Orthodox Church*, pp. 401–402.
98 Semenenko-Basin, 'Kanonizatsiya svyatykh', pp. 61–64, 66.

7 Dialogue and division in the dissident movement

1 Alexander Solzhenitsyn, *Invisible Allies*, pp. 111, 113, 115.
2 See David Saunders, *Russia in the Age of Reaction and Reform, 1801–1881* (London: Longman, 1992), pp. 167–168.
3 'The Funeral of Alexei Kosterin', in George Saunders (ed.) *Samizdat: Voices of the Soviet Opposition*, pp. 289, 285; also on Kosterin's funeral, see Andrei Amalrik, *Notes of a Revolutionary* (London: Weidenfeld and Nicolson, 1982), pp. 69–70.
4 'The Funeral of Alexei Kosterin', pp. 310–311.
5 Ibid., pp. 302–306.
6 Ibid., pp. 284, 293.
7 Petro Grigorenko, *Memoirs* (London: Harvill Press, 1983), p. 267.
8 'The Funeral of Alexei Kosterin', p. 323.
9 Sergei Zheludkov, 'Khristianstvo i ateizm', in *Kronid* (Moscow: Rossiiskii gosudarstvennyi gumanitarnyi universitet, 2001), pp. 451, 455.
10 Ibid., pp. 472, 477.
11 Kronid Lyubarskii, 'Khristianstvo i ateizm', p. 464.
12 Ibid., pp. 463, 465, 466, 501.
13 Zheludkov, 'Khristianstvo i ateizm', p. 488.
14 Lyubarskii, 'Khristianstvo i ateizm', pp. 497, 537, 565.
15 Tat'yana Khodorovich, *The Case of Leonid Plyushch* (London: Hurst, 1976).
16 Tat'yana Khodorovich, 'Otkrytoe pis'mo Leonidu Plyushchu', *Kontinent*, 9, 1976, pp. 227–231, 235, 242–243.
17 Leonid Plyushch, 'Dorogaya Tat'yana Sergeevna', *Kontinent*, 9, 1976, p. 246.
18 Ibid., pp. 247–250, 259, 261.
19 Ibid., pp. 250, 251, 253, 249.
20 Peter Duncan, *Russian Messianism* (London: Routledge, 2000), p. 86.

21 *Smenovekhovism* ('Change of Landmarks') was a national Bolshevik tendency popular after the revolution.
22 O. Altaev, 'The Dual Consciousness of the Intelligentsia and Pseudo-Culture', in M. Meerson-Aksenov and B. Shragin (eds) *The Political, Social and Religious Thought of Russian 'Samizdat"* (Belmont, CA: Nordland, 1997), pp. 116, 130–131, 134, 140–145.
23 V. Gorskii, 'Russian Messianism and the New National Consciousness', in Meerson-Aksenov and Shragin (eds) *The Political, Social and Religious Thought of Russian 'Samizdat'*, p. 375.
24 N. Mandelstam, *Hope Abandoned* (Harmondsworth: Penguin, 1976), p. 690.
25 Duncan, *Russian Messianism*, p. 87.
26 Alexander Solzhenitsyn, 'Repentance and Self-Limitation in the Life of Nations', in Alexander Solzhenitysn *et al.*, *From under the Rubble*, pp. 125, 121–122.
27 Ibid., pp. 107, 109, 110–111, 113–114.
28 Ibid., pp. 119–120, 129–133, 135.
29 Ibid., pp. 114–116, 110, 141–142; see also Alexander Solzhenitsyn, *Letter to Soviet Leaders*, trans. H. Sternberg (London: Collins and Harvill Press, 1974).
30 Vadim Borisov, 'Personality and National Awareness', in A. Solzhenitsyn *et al.*, *From under the Rubble*, pp. 204.
31 Ibid., pp. 225–226.
32 F. Korsakov, 'Russian Destinies', in A. Solzhenitsyn *et al.*, *From under the Rubble*, pp. 162, 164; see also on *From under the Rubble*, William van den Bercken, *Christian Thinking and the End of Communism in Russia* (Utrecht and Leiden: Interuniversity Institute of Missiological and Ecumenical Research, 1993), pp. 64–76.
33 Ibid., pp. 162, 165.
34 Igor Shafarevich, 'Does Russia Have a Future?', in A. Solzhenitsyn *et al.*, *From under the Rubble*, pp. 293–294.
35 See Robert Horvath, 'The Specter of Russophobia', *The Soviet and Post-Soviet Review*, 25, 2, 1998, pp. 199–222.
36 Duncan, *Russian Messianism*, pp. 97, 99.
37 P. Litvinov *et al.* (eds) *Samosoznanie* (New York: Khronika, 1976); Vadim Belotserkovskii (ed.) *Demokraticheskie al'ternativy: Sbornik statei i dokumentov* (FRG: Achberg, 1976).
38 The idea of 'religious renaissance' was associated with some of the authors of *Landmarks*. See Nicolas Zernov, *The Russian Religious Renaissance of the Twentieth Century* (London: Darton, Longman & Todd, 1963).
39 P. Litvinov *et al.* (eds) 'Ot sostavitelei', in *Samosoznanie*, pp. 5–9.
40 Evgenii Barabanov, 'Pravda gumanizma', in P. Litvinov *et al.* (eds) *Samosoznanie*, pp. 13–15.
41 Ibid., pp. 24–25.
42 Ibid., pp. 16, 18–20.
43 Mikhail Meerson-Aksenov, 'Rozhdenie novoi intelligentsii', in P. Litvinov *et al.* (eds) *Samosoznanie* pp. 96–98.
44 Ibid., pp. 105–110, 115.
45 Alexander Solzhenitsyn, 'As Breathing and Consciousness Return', in *From under the Rubble*, p. 18.
46 Philip Boobbyer, *S.L. Frank* (Athens, OH: Ohio University Press, 1995), p. 143.
47 Pavel Litvinov, 'O dvizhenii prava cheloveka v SSSR', in P. Litvinov *et al.* (eds) *Samosoznanie*, p. 74.
48 Vadim Belotserkovskii, 'Kontory sinteza', in *Democraticheskie al'ternativy*, (1976), pp. 69–70, 74–75.

49 Ibid., pp. 86, 90, 94.
50 Alexander Solzhenitsyn, 'The Smatterers', in *From under the Rubble*, pp. 260–264.
51 Grigorii Pomerants, 'Son o spravedlivom vozmezdii', in *Sny zemli* (Paris: Izd 'Poiski', 1984), pp. 277–278.
52 Grigorii Pomerants, 'Vozmozhna li chistaya sovest'', manuscript version in possession of Philip Boobbyer, p. 8.
53 Grigory Pomerants, 'The Moral Aspect of Historical Personality', in M. Meerson-Aksenov and B. Shragin (eds) *The Political, Social and Religious Thought of Russian 'Samizdat'* (Belmont, CA: Nordland, 1997), pp. 99, 112–115.
54 Boris Shragin, *The Challenge of the Spirit*, trans. P. Falla (New York: Knopf, 1978), p. 184.
55 See Philip Boobbyer, 'Russian Liberal Conservatism', in G. Hosking and R. Service (eds) *Russian Nationalism Past and Present* (Basingstoke: Macmillan, 1998), pp. 42–43.
56 A. Sakharov, *Memoirs* (London: Hutchinson, 1990), p. 305.
57 Leopold Labedz (ed.) *Solzhenitsyn: A Documentary Record* (Harmondsworth: Penguin Books, 1970), pp. 151–152.
58 Cited in Rudolf Tokes, *Dissent in the USSR* (Baltimore, MD: Johns Hopkins University Press, 1975), p. 173.
59 Valery Chalidze, *The Soviet Human Rights Movement: A Memoir* (New York: The Jacob Blaustein Institute for the Advancement of Human Rights/The American Jewish Committee, 1984), p. 6.
60 Valery Chalidze, *To Defend These Rights*, trans. G. Daniels (London: Collins and Harvill Press, 1975), p. 65.
61 Edward Kuznetsov, *Prison Diaries*, trans. H. Spier (New York: Stein and Day, 1975), pp. 29, 52, 71, 144.
62 Alexander Zinoviev, *The Reality of Communism*, trans. C. Janson (London: Victor Gollancz Ltd, 1984), pp. 234–237.
63 Alexander Zinoviev, *Homo Sovieticus*, trans. C. Janson (London: Victor Gollancz Ltd, 1985), pp. 5, 11
64 Ibid., p. 55.
65 Zinoviev, *The Reality of Communism*, pp. 236–237.
66 Joseph Brodsky, *Less Than One* (London: Penguin, 1987), p. 385.
67 Zinoviev, *The Reality of Communism*, p. 238.
68 Richard Lourie, *Sakharov: A Biography* (Hanover: Brandeis University Press, 2002), p. 27.
69 Sakharov, *Memoirs*, pp. 305, 284, 483.
70 Solzhenitsyn, *The Oak and the Calf*, pp. 371, 373.
71 Sakharov, *Memoirs*, pp. 270–272, 404.
72 Amalrik, *Notes of a Revolutionary*, p. 301.
73 Kovalev, 'Memoirs', p. 5.
74 Andrei Sakharov, *Sakharov Speaks* (London: Collins, 1974), p. 54; Joshua Rubenstein, *Soviet Dissidents* (Boston: Beacon Press, 1980), pp. 86, 54.
75 Andrei Sakharov, 'The View from Red Square', *Saturday Review/World*, 24 August 1974, pp. 52, 110.
76 Andrei Sakharov, *Sakharov Speaks* (New York: Alfred A. Knopf, 1974), p. 172; Andrei D. Sakharov, *My Country and the World*, trans. G. Daniels (New York: Alfred A. Knopf, 1975), pp. 91–92.
77 Andrei Sakharov, 'The Human Rights Movement in the USSR and Eastern Europe: Its Goals, Significance and Difficulties' (8 November 1978) in A. Babyonyshev (ed.), *On Sakharov* (New York: Alfred A. Knopf, 1982), p. 245.
78 Andrei Sakharov, *Alarm and Hope* (New York: Alfred A. Knopf, 1978), pp. 9, 15.

79 Sakharov, *My Country and the World*, p. 40.
80 See Jay Bergman, 'Was the Soviet Union Totalitarian?', pp. 247–248.
81 Sakharov, *Alarm and Hope*, pp. 23, 60.
82 Sakharov, *My Country and the World*, p. 102.
83 Andrei Sakharov, *Memoirs*, p. 4.
84 Quoted in Belotserkovskii (ed.), *Democraticheskie al'ternativy*, p. 325.
85 Interview with Tat'yana Khodorovich.
86 Email from Elena Bonner to Philip Boobbyer, 17 June 2003.
87 Roy Medvedev, *Let History Judge* (Oxford: Oxford University Press, 1989), pp. 672–673, 667.
88 Zhores Medvedev, *Soviet Science* (New York: W.W. Norton and Company, 1978), p. 169.
89 Zhores Medvedev, *The Medvedev Papers*, trans. Vera Rich (London: St Martin's Press, 1971), pp. 257, 250.
90 Ibid., p. 170; Boobbyer, 'Truth-Telling, Conscience and Dissent', p. 567.

8 Conscience in literature

1 Svirski, *A History of Post-War Soviet Writing* (Ann Arbor, MI: Ardis, 1979), p. 48.
2 Joseph Brodsky, *Less Than One* (London: Penguin, 1987), pp. 29, 28.
3 Svirski, *A History of Post-War Soviet Writing*, p. 12.
4 A. Amalrik, *Notes of a Revolutionary* (London: Weidenfeld and Nicolson, 1982), p. 26.
5 Boobbyer, 'Truth-Telling, Conscience and Dissent in Late Soviet Russia', *European History Quarterly*, 30, 4, 2000, p. 558.
6 Yuri Orlov, *Dangerous Thoughts* (New York: W. Morrow, 1991), p. 62.
7 Grigorii Pomerants, *Otkrytost' bezdne: Vstrechi s Dostoevskim* (Moscow: ROSSPEN, 2003), p. 9.
8 Gennadii Shimanov, 'Pered smert'yu', Moscow, 1974, p. 9; samizdat text, Keston Institute Archive.
9 Andrei Tarkovsky, *Sculpting in Time*, trans. Kitty Hunter-Blair (Austin, TX: University of Texas Press, 1987), p. 42.
10 Frank Ellis, *Vasiliy Grossman: The Genesis and Evolution of a Russian Heretic* (Oxford: Berg, 1994), p. 209.
11 Interview with Natal'ya Bolshakova.
12 Sergei Kovalev, 'Memoirs', p. 23.
13 Komarova, *Kniga lyubvi i gneva*, p. 317.
14 Mark Le Fanu, quoted in John Dunlop, 'Religious Themes in Soviet Cinema', *Religion in Communist Lands*, 16, 3, 1988, p. 211.
15 Alexander Yakovlev, *Striving for Law in a Lawless Land* (Armonk, NY: M.E. Sharpe, 1995), p. 55.
16 Eduard Shevardnadze, *The Future Belongs to Freedom*, trans. C. Fitzpatrick (London: Sinclair-Stevenson, 1991), pp. 6–10.
17 Stephen Lovell, *The Russian Reading Revolution* (Basingstoke: Macmillan, 2000), p. 58.
18 Andrei Sakharov, *Memoirs* (London: Hutchinson, 1990), pp. 26–27.
19 Interview with Oleg Gordievskii.
20 Interview with Boris Belenken.
21 Boobbyer, 'Truth-Telling, Conscience and Dissent', p. 560.
22 Religious philosopher Oleg Genisareteskii, quoted in Boobbyer, 'Religious Experiences of the Soviet Dissidents', p. 377.
23 Alexeyeva, *Soviet Dissent*, p. 270.
24 Natal'ya Eksler, *Referendum*, No. 21, November 1988 in *Referendum: Izbrannye materialy*, p. 207.

25 Andrei Sinyavskii, 'Dissidentstvo kak lichnyi opyt', *Russkaya mysl'*, 18 February 1982, p. 14; Sinyavskii specifically refers to Akhmatova, Mandelstam and Pasternak.
26 Marina Tsvetaeva, *Stikhotvoreniya i poemy*, vol. 3 (New York: Russica Publishers, Inc., 1983), p. 79.
27 This is a point made by Geoffrey Hosking in 'The Twentieth-Century: In Search of New Ways, 1953–1980', *The Cambridge History of Russian Literature* (Cambridge: Cambridge University Press, 1989), p. 522.
28 Leonid Batkin, 'Vozobnovlenie istorii', in Yu. Afanas'ev (ed.) *Inogo ne dano* (Moscow: Progress, 1989), p. 162.
29 Mikhail Bulgakov, *The Master and Margerita*, trans. M. Glenny (London: HarperCollins, 1985), p. 7.
30 Ibid., pp. 271–273.
31 Quoted by Robert Chandler in 'Introduction', to Andrei Platonov, *The Foundation Pit*, trans. R. Chandler and G. Smith (London: Harvill Press, 1987), p. xiii.
32 Brodskii quoted in Chandler, 'Introduction', p. xv.
33 Andrei Platonov, 'The Seventh Man', in *Russian Writing Today* (Harmondsworth: Penguin Books, 1977), p. 20.
34 David Gillespie, 'Russian Literature, 1953–1991', in Neil Cornwell (ed.) *The Routledge Companion to Russian Literature* (London: Routledge, 2001), p. 231.
35 See on this Katerina Clark, 'Socialist Realism in Soviet Literature', in Cornwell (ed.) *The Routledge Companion to Russian Literature*, pp. 175, 182.
36 Mikhail Epstein, 'After the Future: On the New Consciousness in Literature', in T. Lahusen and G. Kuperman (eds) *Late Soviet Culture* (Durham, NC: Duke University Press, 1993), pp. 271–272, 276.
37 Boris Thomson, *The Art of Compromise* (Toronto: Toronto University Press, 2001), pp. 294, 216, 218.
38 Leonid Leonov, *The Russian Forest* (Moscow: Progress, 1966), pp. 63, 189, 126.
39 Vladimir Soloukhin, 'Dorogoi sovesti k pravde', in A.Ya. Yashin, *Zemlyaki* (Moscow: Sovremennik, 1989), p. 7.
40 A.Ya.Yashin, 'Rychagi', *Zemlyaki*, pp. 313, 305–306.
41 Aleksandr Yashin, *Izbrannye proizvedeniya*, vol. 1 (Moscow: Khudozhestvennaya literatura, 1972), p. 290.
42 Vladimir Tendryakov, 'The Trial', *A Topsy-Turvy Spring* (Moscow: Progress Publishers, 1978), p. 147.
43 Peter Doyle, 'Introduction', in V. Tendryakov, *The Trial* (Oxford: Basil Blackwell, 1990), p. xxi.
44 Tendryakov, 'The Trial', pp. 185–186.
45 Valentin Rasputin, *Farewell to Matyora*, trans. A. Bouis (Evanston, IL: Northwestern University Press, 1991), pp. 32–33.
46 Ibid., pp. 176–179.
47 Vasily Belov, 'Carpenter Yarns', in *Morning Rendez-Vous* (Moscow: Raduga Publishers, 1983), pp. 49–50.
48 Vasily Shukshin, 'I Believe', in *Snowball Berry Red and Other Stories*, ed. D.M. Fiene (Ann Arbor, MI: Ardis, 1979), pp. 87–95.
49 Geoffrey Hosking, 'The Fiction of Vasily Shukshin', in *Snowball Berry Red and Other Stories*, p. 14.
50 Ellendea Proffer and Ronald Meyer, 'Introduction', in Yuri Trifonov, *The Exchange and Other Stories* (Evanston, IL: Northwestern University Press, 1991), p. 9.
51 Yuri Trifonov, *The House on the Embankment*, trans. Michael Glenny (London: Abacus, 1985), pp. 129, 103, 132, 141, 147.
52 Shragin, 'Iskuplenie Yuliya Danielya', in *Mysli deistvie* (Moscow, 2000), pp. 331, 339.

53 Alexander Solzhenitsyn, *One Word of Truth* (London: The Bodley Head, 1972), pp. 14–15, 4.
54 Tarkovsky, *Sculpting in Time*, p. 234.
55 Ibid., pp. 38–39.
56 Marina Tsvetaeva, *Art in the Light of Conscience* (London: Bristol Classical Press, 1992), p. 166.
57 Alexander Solzhenitsyn, 'Matryona's House', in R. Milner-Gulland and M. Dewhirst (eds) *Russian Writing Today*, pp. 495, 480; A. Solzhenitsyn, *Odin den' Ivana Denisovicha. Matrenin dvor* (Paris: YMCA Press, 1973), p. 148.
58 Duncan, *Russian Messianism*, p. 63.
59 Daniel Mahoney, *Aleksandr Solzhenitsyn* (Lanham, MD: Rowman and Littlefield Publishers, Inc., 2001), p. 53.
60 Toker, *Voices from the Gulag*, p. 188.
61 Alexander Solzhenitsyn, *The First Circle*, trans. M. Guybon (London: Collins and the Harvill Press, 1969), pp. 38–39, 254, 389.
62 Solzhenitsyn, *The First Circle*, p. 581.
63 Katerina Clark, 'Socialist Realism in Soviet Literature', p. 179.
64 Solzhenitsyn, *The First Circle*, p. 348.
65 Ibid., pp. 133, 363.
66 Solzhenitsyn, *The Gulag Archipelago*, vol. 3 (London: Collins and Harvill Press, 1975), p. 455.
67 Vasily Grossman, *Life and Fate*, trans. Robert Chandler (London: Harvill Press, 1985), pp. 672, 697.
68 Ibid., pp. 837, 840.
69 For publishing details, see Ellis, *Vasiliy Grossman*, p. 222.
70 Vasily Grossman, *Forever Flowing*, trans. T. Whitney (Evanston, IL: Northwestern University Press, 1997), pp. 44, 47.
71 Vladimir Maksimov, *The Seven Days of Creation* (London: Weidenfeld and Nicolson, 1975), pp. 23, 63, 71.
72 Ibid., pp. 175, 182, 188, 241, 242.
73 Yury Dombrovsky, *The Faculty of Useless Knowledge*, trans. A. Myers (London: Harvill Press, 1978), p. 213. Originally published as *Fakul'tet nenuzhnykh veshchei* (Paris: YMCA Press, 1978).
74 Ibid., p. 314.
75 Ibid., p. 466.
76 Ibid., p. 356.
77 Peter Doyle, *Iurii Dombrovskii: Freedom under Totalitarianism* (Amsterdam: Harwood Academic, 2000), pp. 162–163.
78 Dombrovsky, *The Faculty of Useless Knowledge*, pp. 396, 475.
79 Doyle, *Iurii Dombrovskii*, p. 196.
80 Leonid Borodin, *The Third Truth*, trans. C. Kelly (London: Harvill Press, 1989), pp. 130–132, 175.
81 Georgi Vladimov, *Faithful Ruslan*, trans. M. Glenny (London: Jonathan Cape, 1979), p. 4.
82 D.B. Brown, *Soviet Russian Literature Since Stalin* (Cambridge: Cambridge University Press, 1978), pp. 367–368.
83 Vladimov, *Faithful Ruslan*, p. 109.
84 Chingiz Aitmatov, *The Day Lasts More than a Hundred Years* (London: Futura, 1984), p. 61.
85 Vladimir Savchenko, *Self-Discovery*, trans. A.W. Bouis (New York: Collier Books, 1979), p. 48.
86 Andrei Tarkovsky, *Collected Screenplays*, trans. W. Powell and N. Synessios (London: Faber and Faber, 1999), p. 174.
87 Tarkovsky, *Sculpting in Time*, p. 234.

88 Tarkovsky, *Collected Screenplays*, p. 413.
89 Yuri Andreyev *et al.* (eds), *Vladimir Vysotsky: Hamlet with a Guitar* (Moscow: Progress Publishers, 1990), p. 161.
90 Alexander Galich, 'A Cycle of Poems', *Kontinentl* (London: André Deutsch, 1976), p. 43.
91 Vladimir Voinovich, *The Life and Extraordinary Adventure of Private Ivan Chonkin*, trans. R. Lourie (London: Jonathan Cape, 1977), pp. 248–249.
92 Benedict Erofeev, *Moscow Circles*, trans. J. Dorrell (London: Writers and Readers Publishing Cooperative, 1981), p. 16.
93 Svirski, *A History of Post-War Soviet Writing*, p. 176.
94 Ibid., pp. 11, 325, 49, 115, 219, 246, 59.
95 David Samoilov, 7 January 1965, *Podennyie zapisi*, vol. 2 (Moscow: Vremya, 2002), pp. 7–8.

9 Moral aspects of in-system dissent

1 Richard T. De George, *Soviet Ethics and Morality* (Ann Arbor, MI: University of Michigan Press, 1969), pp. 4–5.
2 See James Scanlan, *Marxism in the USSR* (Ithaca, NY: Cornell University Press, 1985), p. 268.
3 See James J. O'Rourke, 'The Value Theory of V.P. Tugarinov', *Studies in Soviet Thought*, 28, 1984, pp. 109–116.
4 I.Y. Shchipanov (ed.), *Istoriya filosofskoi mysli v moskovskom universitete* (Moscow: Izd. Moskovskogo universiteta, 1982), p. 183.
5 Kharkhordin, *The Collective and the Individual in Russia* (Berkeley, CA: University of California Press, 1999), p. 338.
6 Scanlan, *Marxism in the USSR*, pp. 283–284.
7 See De George, *Soviet Ethics and Morality*, p. 121.
8 See, for example, Z.A. Berbeshkina, *Problema sovesti v Marksistsko-Leninskoi etike* (Moscow: Izd. VPShi ADN pri TSK KPSS, 1963); L.B. Volchenko, 'Marksistsko-Leninskaya etika o sovesti', *Voprosy filosofii*, 2, 1962, pp. 134–144; L.M. Arkhangel'skii, 'Dobro, dolg, sovest'', *Voprosy filosofii*, 6, 1964, pp. 69–79; I.I. Rezvitskii, 'O sushchnosti kategorii sovesti', *Filosofskie nauki*, 2, 1967, pp. 65–70.
9 P.M. Egides, 'Osnovnoi vopros etiki kak filosofskoi nauki i problema nravstvennogo otchuzhdeniya', in G.D. Bandzeladze (ed.) *Aktual'nye problemy Marksistkoi etiki* (Tbilisi: Izd. Tbilisskogo gosudarstvennogo universiteta, 1967), p. 106.
10 See N.A. Golovko and V.S. Markov, 'Za nauchnost' i konkretnost' v razrabotke problem etiki', *Voprosy filosofii*, 8, 1968, pp. 148–155.
11 Ya.A. Mil'ner-Irinin, *Etika, ili Printsipy istinnoi chelovechnosti* (Moscow: Nauka, 1999), p. 8.
12 Ya.A. Mil'ner-Irinin, 'Etika – nauka o dolzhnom', in G.D. Bandzeladze (ed.), *Aktual'nye problemy Marksistkoi etiki*, pp. 54, 43–53, 27, 36–37, 39, 49; P. Grier, *Marxist Ethical Theory in the Soviet Union* (Dordrecht: D. Reidel, 1978), p. 188.
13 Ya.A. Mil'ner-Irinin, 'Etika, ili Printsipy istinnoi chelovechnosti, printsip sovesti', reprinted in G.D. Bandzeladze (ed.), *Aktual'nye problemy Marksistkoi etiki*, pp. 254, 260, 281, 262, 260.
14 V. Kolbanovskii and V. Efimov, *Kommunist*, 14, 1968, pp. 121–122.
15 See N.A. Golovko and V.S. Markov, 'Za nauchnost' i konkretnost' v razrabotke problem etiki', *Voprosy filosofii*, 8, 1968, pp. 148–155; see also Kolbanovskii and Efimov, *Kommunist*, 14, 1968, pp. 119–126.
16 Scanlan, *Marxism in the USSR*, p. 272.

17 Shlapentokh, *Soviet Intellectuals and Political Power* (London: I.B. Tauris and Co. Publishers Ltd, 1990), p. 164.
18 Drobnitskii, *Problemy nravstvennosti*, p. 181; on Drobnitskii, see Scanlan, *Marxism in the USSR*, pp. 287–291.
19 Drobnitskii, *Problemy nravstvennosti*, p. 170.
20 A.A. Guseinov, '"Zolotoe pravilo" nravstvennosti', in A.A. Guseinov, *Yazyk i sovest'*; originally published in *Vestnik Moskovskogo universiteta: Filosofiya*, 4, 1972, pp. 53–63.
21 Yu. Davydov, *Etika lyubvi i metafizika svoevoliya* (Moscow: Molodaya gvardiya, 1982); Part 1, Chapter 4, 'Smysl utrata pri svete sovesti', and Part 2, Chapter 3, 'Sovest' i ego opponenty.'
22 R. Petropavlovskii, 'Po povody odnoi knigi', *Kommunist*, 8, 1983, pp. 102–114; cited in Scanlan, *Marxism in the USSR*, p. 278.
23 *Report of the Central Committee of the Communist Party of the Soviet Union* (Moscow: Novosti Press Agency Publishing House, 1971), p. 99.
24 This summary is taken from Scanlan, *Marxism in the USSR*, pp. 274, 276.
25 Quoted in Philip Grier, *Marxist Ethical Theory in the Soviet Union*, p. 105.
26 Grier, *Marxist Ethical Theory in the Soviet Union*, p. 214.
27 Boobbyer, 'Truth-telling, Conscience and Dissent', p. 566.
28 Interview with Aleksandr Tsipko, 2003.
29 Aleksandr Yakovlev, 'Perestroika or the "Death of Socialism"', in S. Cohen and K. van den Heuvel, *Voices of Glasnost'* (New York: W.W. Norton, 1989), p. 36.
30 Interview with Vadim Bakatin.
31 Bikennin, "Kak pisat' memuary', p. 105; interview with Nail' Bikennin.
32 Interview with Aleksandr Tsipko, 2003.
33 Shlapentokh, *Soviet Intellectuals and Political Power*, pp. 93–98.
34 Oleg Gordievsky, *Next Stop Execution* (London: Macmillan, 1984), p. 100.
35 Boobbyer, 'Truth-telling, Conscience and Dissent', pp. 579, 564.
36 Ibid, p. 564.
37 Ibid., p. 569.
38 Gordievsky, *Next Stop Execution*, p. 63.
39 Interview with Oleg Gordievskii.
40 Alter L. Litvin, *Writing History in Twentieth-Century Russia*, trans. J. Keep (Basingstoke: Palgrave, 2001), p. ix.
41 Boobbyer, 'Truth-telling, Conscience and Dissent', p. 579.
42 Ibid., pp. 573, 575, 565.
43 Ibid., pp. 572–573.
44 Ibid., p. 572.
45 Interview with Yurii Lyubimov, Moscow; see also Boobbyer, 'Truth-telling, Conscience and Dissent', p. 572.
46 Boobbyer, 'Truth-telling, Conscience and Dissent', pp. 569–570.
47 Interview with Oleg Gordievskii.
48 Interview with Aleksandr Yakovlev.
49 Boobbyer, 'Truth-telling, Conscience and Dissent', p. 572.
50 Litvin, *Writing History in Twentieth-Century Russia*, p. 19.
51 A. Amalrik, *Notes of a Revolutionary* (London: Weidenfeld and Nicolson, 1982), p. 81.
52 Kovalev, 'Memoirs', p. 20.
53 Boobbyer, 'Truth-telling, Conscience and Dissent', p. 573.
54 Ibid., p. 575.
55 Fyodor Burlatskii, '"Democratization is a Long March"', in Cohen and van den Heuvel, *Voices of Glasnost'*, p. 178; see also F. Burlatskii, *Ispaniya: Korrida i Kaudil'o* (Moscow: Pravda, 1967), p. 46.

56 Venclova, 'The Game of the Soviet Censor', in *Forms of Hope* (Riverdale-on-Hudson: Sheep Meadow Press, 1999), p. 188.
57 Boobbyer, 'Truth-telling, Conscience and Dissent', p. 574.
58 On 'niches', see also Amalrik, *Notes of a Revolutionary*, p. 5.
59 Interview with Natal'ya Gorbanevskaya.
60 Boobbyer, 'Truth-telling, Conscience and Dissent', p. 574.
61 Gordievsky, *Next Stop Execution*, pp. 127, 200, 210, 391.
62 Brodsky, *Less Than One* (London: Penguin, 1987), pp. 9–10.
63 Amalrik, *Notes of a Revolutionary*, p. 18.
64 Venclova, 'The Game of the Soviet Censor', *Forms of Hope*, p. 191.
65 Ibid., p. 186.
66 Elem Klimov, '"Learning Democracy": The Filmmakers' Rebellion', in Cohen and van den Heuvel, *Voices of Glasnost'*, p. 244.
67 Fedor Burlatskii, *Khrushchev and the First Russian Spring*, trans. Daphne Skillen (London: Weidenfeld and Nicolson, 1991), p. 191.
68 Robert English, *Russia and the Idea of the West* (New York: Columbia Press, 2000), pp. 70–71, 88, 270 n.26.
69 Karpinskii, 'The Autobiography of a Half-Dissident', in Cohen and van den Heuvel, *Voices of Glasnost'*, pp. 285, 291; David Remnick, *Lenin's Tomb* (London: Viking, 1983), p. 174; F. Burlatskii and L. Karpinskii, 'Na puti k prem'ere', *Komsomol'skaya pravda*, 30 June 1967, p. 4.
70 L. Okunev (Len Karpinskii), 'Words are Also Deeds', in S.F. Cohen (ed.) *An End to Silence* (New York: W.W. Norton and Company, 1982), pp. 308–309.
71 For details, see Karpinskii, 'The Autobiography of a Half-Dissident', in Cohen and van den Heuvel, *Voices of Glasnost'*, pp. 292–293.
72 Remnick, *Lenin's Tomb*, pp. 174, 176–177.
73 Quoted in Boobbyer, 'The Moral Lessons of Soviet History', p. 360.
74 Karpinskii, 'The Autobiography of a Half-Dissident', p. 306.
75 Ibid., pp. 294, 300.
76 Boobbyer, 'The Moral Lessons of Soviet History', p. 360.
77 Len Karpinskii, '"Socialism" Awry', *Moscow News*, 21, 3–10 June 1990, p. 7.
78 Karpinskii, 'The Autobiography of a Half-Dissident', pp. 294, 300.
79 Burlatskii, '"Democratization is a Long March"', p. 179.
80 Remnick, *Lenin's Tomb*, pp. 162–179.
81 Interview with Aleksandr Tsipko, 1998.
82 John Dunlop, *The Rise of Russia and the Fall of the Soviet Empire* (Princeton, NJ: Princeton University Press, 1993), p. 61.
83 Interview with Aleksandr Tsipko, 2003.
84 See V.K. Skopura and A.S. Tsipko, *Besedy o nravstvennosti: primernyi uchebnyi plan i metodicheskie rekomendatsii v sisteme politicheskogo prosveshcheniya molodezhi* (Moscow: Molodaya gvardiya, 1968); chapter on conscience, pp. 58–62.
85 Interview with Aleksandr Tsipko, 1998.
86 A.S. Tsipko, *Sotsializm: zhizn' obshchestva i cheloveka* (Moscow: Molodaya gvardiya, 1980), pp. 9, 13.
87 A.S. Tsipko, *Nekotorye filosofskie aspekty teorii sotsializma* (Moscow: Nauka, 1983), pp. 115, 213.
88 Tsipko, *Sotsializm: zhizn' obshchestva i cheloveka*, p. 275.
89 Igor Klyamkin, 'Kakaya ulitsa vedet k khramu?' *Novyi mir*, 11, 1987, pp. 166, 170.
90 Aleksandr Tsipko, 'Istoki Stalinizma, Ocherk 3: Egoizm mechtatelei', *Nauka i zhizn'*, 1, 1989, pp. 49, 50.
91 Aleksandr Tsipko, 'Istoki Stalinizma, Ocherk 4: Ne nado boyat'sya pravdy', *Nauka i zhizn'*, 2, 1989, p. 54.
92 Interview with Aleksandr Tsipko, 1998; Boobbyer, 'Truth-telling, Conscience and Dissent', p. 568.

93 Alexander Tsipko, 'Awakening Russia', *Moscow News*, 26, 8–15 July 1990, p. 3.
94 Alexander Tsipko, 'Someone Must Quit', *Moscow News*, 22, 10–17 June 1990, p. 3.
95 Alexander Tsipko, 'The Truth is Never Late', in Alexander Yakovlev, *The Fate of Marxism in Russia*, trans. Catherine Fitzpatrick (New Haven, CT: Yale University Press, 1993), p. xvi.
96 Alexander Tsipko, *Is Stalinism Really Dead?* (New York: HarperSanFrancisco, 1990), pp. 90, 96.
97 Interview with Aleksandr Tsipko, 2003.
98 Tsipko, *Is Stalinism Really Dead?*, pp. x, 221–223, 133, 139, 27, 197, 212.
99 Quoted in Dunlop, *The Rise of Russia and the Fall of the Soviet Union*, p. 71.
100 Burlatskii, '"Democratization is a Long March",' p. 191.
101 Quoted in Dunlop, *The Rise of Russia and the Fall of the Soviet Union*, p. 71.
102 Mark Sandle, 'A Triumph of Ideological Hairdressing? Intellectual Life in the Brezhnev Era Reconsidered', in Edwin Bacon and Mark Sandle (eds) *Brezhnev Reconsidered* (Basingstoke: Palgrave Macmillan, 2002), p. 158.

10 The ethics of the party reformers

1 Arkady N. Shevchenko, *Breaking with Moscow* (New York: Alfred A. Knopf, 1985), p. 101.
2 Bikennin, 'Kak pisat' memuary', pp. 97, 100.
3 Interview with Vadim Medvedev; Vasilii Sergeevich Tolstikov was First Secretary of the Leningrad Party Obkom from May 1962 to January 1963 and from December 1964 to September 1970.
4 V.A. Medvedev, *Prozrenie, mif ili predatel'stvo* (Moscow, 1998), p. 48.
5 Interview with Vadim Medvedev.
6 Bikennin, 'Kak pisat' memuary', p. 104.
7 Vadim Bakatin, *Doroga v proshedshem vremeni* (Moscow: Dom, 1999), p. 74.
8 Keep, *The Last of the Empires* (Oxford: Oxford University Press, 1995), p. 210.
9 Zhores Medvedev, *Andropov* (Oxford: Basil Blackwell, 1983), p. 138.
10 Quoted in John Dunlop, *The Rise of Russia and the Fall of the Soviet Empire* (Princeton, NJ: Princeton University Press, 1993), p. 6.
11 Ya.A. Asoskov, *Sotsiologicheskie issledovaniya*, 2, 1985, pp. 50–55; *JPRS*, USS-85-005, 23 December, 1985, pp. 38, 36.
12 Stephen White, *Russia Goes Dry* (Cambridge: Cambridge University Press, 1996), p. 44.
13 C.M. Ekedahl and M.A. Goodman, *The Wars of Eduard Shevardnadze* (University Park, PA: Pennsylvania State University Press, 1997), p. xi.
14 Mikhail Gorbachev, *Memoirs* (London: Doubleday, 1996), p. 165.
15 Keep, *Last of the Empires*, p. 341.
16 White, *Russia Goes Dry*, p. 183.
17 Bikennin, 'Kak pisat' memuary', p. 102; interview with Vadim Medvedev.
18 Stephen White, *After Gorbachev* (Cambridge: Cambridge University Press, 1993), p. 75; Richard Sakwa, *Gorbachev and His Reforms, 1985–1990* (New York: Prentice Hall, 1990), p. 6.
19 M.S. Gorbachev, 'Byt' patriotom svoei rodiny, zhit' i rabotat' po sovesti', *Komsomol'skaya pravda*, 15 May 1987, p. 1.
20 See posters 225 and 512 at http://www.poster.s.cz/listy/russ6.htm. Accessed, 21 August 2004. The second of these by Yurii Zarev was published by the 'Plakat' publishing house in 1987.
21 Sakwa, *Gorbachev and His Reforms*, p. 10.
22 P. Boobbyer, *The Stalin Era* (London: Routledge, 2000), p. 90.

23 Mikhail Gorbachev, *Perestroika: New Thinking for Our Country and the World* (New York: Harper and Row, 1987), p. 35.
24 Ibid., pp. 22, 24, 103.
25 Ibid., pp. 25, 76, 72, 30, 105, 158.
26 Anatoly Chernyaev, *My Six Years with Gorbachev* (University Park, PA: Pennsylvania State University Press, 2000), pp. 199–200.
27 Ibid., p. 208.
28 Gorbachev, *Memoirs*, pp. 539–540.
29 Chernyaev, *My Six Years with Gorbachev*, p. 199.
30 Andrei Grachev, *Gorbachev* (Moscow: Vagrius, 2001), p. 248.
31 Vadim Bakatin, *Doroga v proshedshem vremeni*, p. 247.
32 'Istoriya, revolyutsiya, literatura', *Literaturnaya gazeta*, 7 January 1990, p 3.
33 Alexander Yakovlev, *The Fate of Marxism in Russia* (New Haven, CT: Yale University Press, 1993), p. 5.
34 Chernyaev, *My Six Years with Gorbachev*, p. 263.
35 Gorbachev, *Perestroika*, p. 55.
36 Quoted in Grachev, *Gorbachev*, pp. 148, 66.
37 Vadim Bakatin, *Izbavlenie ot KGB* (Moscow: Novosti, 1992), p. 36.
38 Grachev, *Gorbachev*, pp. 58–59; Gorbachev, *Memoirs*, pp. 64–65, 104–105.
39 Gorbachev, *Memoirs*, p. 105.
40 Grachev, *Gorbachev*, pp. 52, 48, 28.
41 Gorbachev, *Memoirs*, p. 30.
42 Tsipko, 'The Truth is Never Late', in Yakovlev, *The Fate of Marxism in Russia*, p. xvi.
43 A. Yakovlev, 'Protiv Antiiztorizma', *Literaturnaya gazeta*, 15 November 1972, pp. 4–5.
44 Remnick, *Lenin's Tomb*, pp. 298–299.
45 A.N. Yakovlev, 'Perestroika i nravstvennost'', *Sovetskaya kul'tura*, 21 July 1987, p. 2.
46 Alexander Yakovlev, 'The Political Philosophy of Perestroika', in A. Aganbegyan (ed.) *Perestroika Annual*, pp. 58, 63.
47 Chernyaev, *My Six Years with Gorbachev*, p. 38; Aleksandr Yakovlev, *Omut pamyati* (Moscow: Vagrius, 2001), p. 220.
48 Interview with Aleksandr Yakovlev.
49 Yakovlev, *Omut pamyati*, p. 242.
50 Yakovlev, 'The Political Philosophy of Perestroika', p. 59.
51 Quoted in Remnick, *Lenin's Tomb*, pp. 299–300.
52 This was originally published as *Predislovie, obval, posleslovie* (Moscow: Novosti, 1992).
53 Yakovlev, *The Fate of Marxism in Russia*, pp. 2, 37, 6, 16–17, 29, 70, 54.
54 Ibid., pp. 15, 40, 35.
55 Alexander Yakovlev, 'Only Moral Democracy Can Overcome Our Tragic Past', *Moscow News*, 7 June 1990, p. 7.
56 Anatolii Chernyaev, *Shest' let s Gorbachevym* (Moscow: Izd. gruppa 'Progress' 'Kul'tura', 1993), p. 269.
57 A.N. Yakovlev in *Kuranty*, 24 August 1991; reprinted in A.N. Yakovlev, *Muki prochteniya bytiya* (Moscow: Novosti, 1991), p. 361.
58 Alexander Yakovlev, *Striving for Law in a Lawless Land* (Armonk, NY: M.E. Sharpe, 1995), pp. 34, 35.
59 Yakovlev, *Omut pamyati*, pp. 456, 462.
60 Interview with Aleksandr Yakovlev.
61 Tsipko, 'The Truth is Never Late', p. 18.
62 Remnick, *Lenin's Tomb*, p. 45.
63 Ibid., p. 293.

64 Yakovlev, *Omut pamyati*, pp. 16, 218.
65 Yakovlev, *The Fate of Marxism in Russia*, p. 2.
66 Julia Wishnevsky and Elizabeth Teague, 'Aleksandr Yakovlev Speaks of "Acts of Repentance"', *Radio Liberty: Report on the USSR*, 21 September 1990, p. 8; Remnick, *Lenin's Tomb*, p. 304.
67 Aleksandr Yakovlev, 'Akty spravedlivosti i pokayaniya', 20 August 1990; printed in *Muki prochteniya bytiya*, p. 261.
68 Chernyaev, *My Six Years with Gorbachev*, p. 1.
69 Aleksandr Yakovlev, 'Rasproshchat'sya s illyuziyami', *Zerkalo*, 28 May 1991; reprinted in *Muki prochteniya bytiya*, p. 25.
70 Yakovlev, *The Fate of Marxism in Russia*, p. 230.
71 Interview with Aleksandr Yakovlev.
72 Wishnevsky and Teague, 'Aleksandr Yakovlev Speaks of "Acts of Repentance",' p. 9.
73 Yakovlev, *The Fate of Marxism in Russia*, pp. 42, 55, 38, 32.
74 E. Shevardnadze, *The Future Belongs to Freedom* (London: Sinclair-Stevenson, 1991), pp. 62, 57, 64, 176.
75 Ibid., pp. 72, 200, 21.
76 Simon Sebag-Montefiore, *The Spectator*, 22 July 2000, p. 19.
77 Shevardnadze, *The Future Belongs to Freedom*, pp. 17–19, 11–12, xx, 14, 36–37.
78 Ibid., p. 172.
79 Eduard Shevardnadze, *Moi vybor* (Moscow, 1991), p. 17.
80 Ekedahl and Goodman, *The Wars of Eduard Shevardnadze*, p. xii, xxii.
81 Shevardnadze, *The Future Belongs to Freedom*, p. 190.
82 Quoted in Egor Ligachev, *Inside Gorbachev's Kremlin*, trans. C. Fitzpatrick (Boulder, CO: Westview Press, 1996), p. 168.
83 Ekedahl and Goodman, *The Wars of Eduard Shevardnadze*, pp. 42, 15.
84 Shevardnadze, *The Future Belongs to Freedom*, p. 37.
85 Quoted in Leon Aron, *Boris Yeltsin: A Revolutionary Life* (London: HarperCollins, 2001), p. 140.
86 Plenum of the Central Committee of the CPSU, October 1987, *Izvestiya TsK KPSS*, 2, 1989, pp. 242, 265–267.
87 *Izvestiya TsK KPSS*, 2, 1989, pp. 262–263; also see Aron, *Boris Yeltsin*, pp. 209–210.
88 Interview with Aleksandr Yakovlev.
89 Quoted in Aron, *Boris Yeltsin*, pp. 209–210; see *Pravda*, 13 November 1987, p. 3.
90 Aron, *Boris Yeltsin*, pp. 234, 250.
91 Boris Yeltsin, *Against the Grain*, trans. M. Glenny (London: Jonathon Cape, 1990), p. 144. This was published in Russian as *Ispoved' na zadannuyu temu* (Leningrad: Sovetskii pisatel', 1990).
92 Quoted in Aron, *Boris Yeltsin*, p. 341; interview with Vadim Bakatin.
93 Quoted in Aron, *Boris Yeltsin*, p. 341.
94 Bakatin, *Izbavlenie ot KGB*, p. 252.
95 Interview with Vadim Bakatin.
96 Christopher Andrew and Vasili Mitrokhin, *The Mitrokhin Archive* (London: Allen Lane, The Penguin Press, 1999), p. 418.
97 Bikennin, 'Kak pisat' memuary', p. 104; interview with Nail' Bikennin.
98 Dunlop, *The Rise of Russia and the Fall of the Soviet Empire*, p. 79.
99 Chernyaev, *My Six Years with Gorbachev*, pp. 212–213.
100 Interview with Nail' Bikennin.
101 Yelena Bonner, 'Stop, thief!?', *Moscow News* 36, 8–15 September 1991, p. 4.
102 Interview with Vadim Bakatin.
103 Shevardnadze, *The Future Belongs to Freedom*, pp. 6–10.

11 Conscience and repentance during *glasnost'*

1 Details taken from John Dunlop, *The Rise of Russia and the Fall of the Soviet Empire*, pp. 70–71.
2 William van den Bercken, 'The Rehabilitation of Christian Ethical Values in the Soviet Media', *Religion in Communist Lands*, 17, 1, 1989, pp. 6–7.
3 Mikhail Shatrov, 'Diktatura sovesti', *Teatr*, 6, 1986, p. 36; Dunlop, *The Rise of Russia and the Fall of the Soviet Empire*, p. 69.
4 Mikhail Shatrov, *The Bolsheviks and Other Plays*, trans. Michael Glenny (London: Nick Hern Books, 1990), pp. 169, 247.
5 Anatoli Rybakov, *Children of the Arbat*, trans. H. Shukman (London: Hutchinson, 1988), p. 730.
6 Andrei Melville and Gail Lapidus (eds) *The Glasnost Papers* (Boulder CO: Westview Press, 1990), p. 122.
7 Chingiz Aitmatov, 'Plakha', *Novyi mir*, No. 6, 1986, pp. 50, 53.
8 See Mary Seton-Watson, 'Religious Themes in Recent Soviet Literature', *Religions in Communist Lands*, 16, 2, 1988, pp. 117–119; for more in Tendryakov's novel, see Richard Chapple, 'Begrudging Testament: The Christ Who Wouldn't Go Away (On Tendryakov's 'An Attempt at Mirages')', *Australian Slavonic and East European Studies*, 2, 1, 1988, pp. 55–67.
9 Irena Maryniak quoted in Jane Ellis, *The Russian Orthodox Church: Triumphalism and Defensiveness* (Basingstoke: Macmillan, 1996), p. 22.
10 Seton-Watson, 'Religious Themes in Recent Soviet Literature', pp. 121–122, 117.
11 Yvonne Howell, *Apocalyptic Realism: The Science Fiction of Arkady and Boris Strugatsky* (New York: Peter Lang, 1994), pp. 76–77.
12 Revelation 7.13–14. See Richard Chapple, 'Vladimir Dudintsev as Innovator and Barometer of his Time', *Australian Slavonic and East European Studies*, 6, 2, 1992, pp. 1–19.
13 Vladimir Zazubrin (Vladimir Zubtsov, 1895–1938), 'The Chip', in Oleg Chukhontsev (ed.) *Dissonant Voices* (London: Harvill Press, 1991), p. 35.
14 Ibid., p. 63.
15 See J. Woll and D. Youngblood, 'The History That is History', in J. Woll and D. Youngblood, *Repentance* (London: I.B. Tauris Publishers, 2001), p. 91.
16 Woll and Youngblood, *Repentance*, pp. 67, 72, 73.
17 Ibid., pp. 92–93, 94.
18 Yevtushenko quoted in Melville and Lapidus (eds), *The Glasnost Papers*, pp. 123–125.
19 Quoted in Melville and Lapidus (eds), *The Glasnost Papers*, p. 125.
20 Andrei Nuikin, 'Novoe bogoiskatel'stvo i starye dogmy', *Novyi mir*, 4, 1987, p. 259.
21 Arsenii Gulyga, 'Poiski absolyuta', *Novyi mir*, 10, 1987, p. 251.
22 Arsenii Gulyga, 'Vladimir Sergeevich Solov'ev', *Literaturnaya gazeta*, 18 January 1989, p. 5.
23 A.A. Guseinov, 'Moral' bez moralizatorstva', *Kommunist*, 13, 1988, p. 90.
24 A.A. Guseinov, 'Nravstvennye al'ternativy perestroiki', *Yazyk i sovest'*, pp. 49, 43; originally published in *Filosofskaya i sotsiologicheskaya mysl'*, 7, 1990, pp. 3–15.
25 Daniil Granin, 'O miloserdii', *Literaturnaya gazeta*, 18 March 1987, p. 13.
26 Maureen Perrie, *The Cult of Ivan the Terrible in Stalin's Russia* (London: Palgrave, 2001), pp. 189–190.
27 D. Volkogonov, *Stalin* (London: Weidenfeld and Nicolson, 1991), pp. xxiv, 93, 220, 315, 580–581.
28 *The Times*, 7 Dec 1995, p. 15.

29 G. Bordyugov, V. Kozlov and V. Loginov, 'Poslushnaya istoriya, ili novyi publitsisticheskii rai', *Kommunist*, 14, 1989, pp. 74–75.
30 'Istoriya, revolyutsiya, literatura', *Literaturnaya gazeta*, 7 January 1990, p. 4.
31 *Referendum*, No. 3, p. 1; referred to by Irena Maryniak, '*Samizdat* Today – a Review', *Religion, State and Society*, 17, 1, 1989, p. 114.
32 Details from Julian Graffy, 'The Arts', in Martin McCauley (ed.) *Gorbachev and Perestroika* (Basingstoke: Macmillan Press, 1990), pp. 192, 195.
33 Rosalind Marsh, 'The Death of Soviet Literature: Can Russian Literature Survive?' *Europe-Asia Studies*, 45, 1, 1993, p. 119.
34 Y. Orlov, *Dangerous Thoughts* (New York: W. Morrow, 1991), p. 351.
35 Robert Horvath, 'The Dissident Roots of *Glasnost*'', in S. Wheatcroft (ed.) *Challenging Traditional Roots of Russian History* (Basingstoke: Macmillan, 2002), p. 174.
36 Bergman, 'Was the Soviet Union Totalitarian?', p. 261.
37 Epstein, 'After the Future: On the New Consciousness in Literature', p. 262.
38 Valentin Rasputin, Ch. Aitmatov *et al.*, *Esli po sovesti* (Moscow: Khudozhestvennaya literatura, 1988), p. 226.
39 John Dunlop, 'Russia's Surprising Reactionary Alliance', *Orbis*, Summer 1991, p. 423.
40 Nina Andreyeva, 'I Cannot Forgo My Principles', in A. Dallin and G. Lapidus (eds) *The Soviet System in Crisis* (Boulder, CO: Westview Press, 1991), p. 339.
41 Ibid., pp. 343–344.
42 Yurii Bondarev quoted in *XIX vsesoyuznaya konferentsiya Kommunisticheskoi Partii Sovetskogo Soyuza, 28 iyunya – 1 iyulya: Stenograficheskii otchet* (Moscow: izd. politicheskoi literatury, 1988), p. 225.
43 Valentin Rasputin, 'Esli po sovesti', in Ch. Aitmatov *et al.*, *Esli po sovesti*, p. 234.
44 Valentin Rasputin, 'Vam ne nuzhny velikie potryaseniya, nam nuzhna velikaya strana', *Molodaya gvardiya*, 8, 1989, pp. 4–5.
45 From *Korichnevyi putch krasnykh, Avgust 1991* (Moscow: Tekst, 1991), p. 16.
46 Marsh, 'The Death of Soviet Literature', p. 119.
47 'Korv' XX veka: vinovna li slovesnost'?' *Literaturnaya gazeta*, 19 June 1991, p 11.
48 Marsh, 'The Death of Soviet Literature', p. 116.
49 E. Evtushenko, *Komsomol'skaya pravda*, 10 December 1986, p. 2.
50 Elem Klimov, '"Learning Democracy": The Filmmakers' Rebellion', in S. Cohen and K. van den Heuvel, *Voices of Glasnost'* (New York: W.W. Norton, 1989), p. 234.
51 See Dmitrii Likhachev, *Proshloe – budushchemu: stat'i i ocherki* (Leningrad: Nauka, 1985), pp. 74, 194.
52 Dmitrii Likhachev, 'Pangs of Conscience', *Reflections on Russia*, trans. C. Sever (Boulder, CO: Westview Press, 1991), pp. 147, 153.
53 Dmitrii Likhachev, 'Ekologiya kul'tury', *Moskva*, 1979, No. 7; cited in *Proshloe – budushchemu: stat'i i ocherki*, p. 51.
54 Dmitrii Likhachev, *Pis'ma o dobrom i prekrasnom* (Moscow: Detskaya literatura, 1988), pp. 205–208.
55 Dmitrii Likhachev, 'Kul'tura: programma na sto let', *Literaturnaya gazeta*, 7 January 1988, p. 3; for the same point on self-financing, see Likhachev's speech at the Congress of People's Deputies in May 1989, reproduced in *Izvestiya*, 1 June 1989, p. 4.
56 Likhachev, 'Pangs of Conscience', pp. 147, 150; 'Trevogi sovesti', *Literaturnaya gazeta*, 1 Jan. 1987, p. 11.
57 Likhachev, 'Pangs of Conscience', pp. 139–140.
58 Ibid., p. 153.

59 Ibid., p. 145; see also Likhachev, *Pis'ma o dobrom i prekrasnom*, p. 48.
60 Likhachev, 'Reflections on Russia', *Reflections on Russia*, p. 50.
61 Dmitrii Likhachev, 'Ot pokayaniya k deistviyu', *Literaturnaya gazeta*, 9 September 1987, p. 2.
62 Van den Bercken, 'The Rehabilitation of Christian Ethical Values in the Soviet Media', p. 9; see also Dmitrii Likhachev, 'Ot pokayaniya k deistviyu', p. 2.
63 Likhachev, 'Ot pokayaniya k deistviyu', p. 2.
64 Dmitrii Likhachev, 'Coal Isn't Worth Even a Drop of Blood', *Moscow News*, No. 17, 28 April–5 May 1991, p. 1.
65 Svetlana Selivanova, 'Akademik Likhachev', *Literaturnaya gazeta*, 26 November 1986, p. 5.
66 See Merab Mamardashvili, *Kartezianskie razmyshleniya* (Moscow: Izd. gruppa 'Progress' 'Kul'tura', 1993) and *Lektsii o Pruste* (Moscow: Ad Marginem, 1995).
67 Yurii Senokosov, quoted in introduction to *Kartezianskie razmyshleniya*, p. 5.
68 Caryl Emerson, 'Mamardashvili, Merab Konstantinovich', in E. Craig (ed.) *Routledge Encyclopedia of Philosophy*, vol. 6, pp. 66–71.
69 Merab Mamardashvili, 'O dobre i zle' (interview of 1984), published in the collection of his writings, *Moi opyt netipichen* (St Petersburg: Azbuka, 2000), pp. 280–281.
70 N. Motroshilova, 'Byt' filosofom – eto sud'ba', *Literaturnaya gazeta*, 12 December 1990, p. 12.
71 *Moscow News*, 49, 16–23 December, p. 7.
72 Mikhail Gefter, 'Stalin umer vchera', in Yu. Afanas'ev (ed.) *Inogo ne dano*, p. 304.
73 D. Granin, 'Kogo my priachem? Zachem?', in Yu. Afanas'ev (ed.) *Inogo ne dano*, pp. 343–344, 348.
74 Pavel and Anatoli Sudoplatov, *Special Tasks* (London: Little, Brown and Company, 1994), p. 431.
75 David Samoilov, *'Mne vypalo vse . . .'* (Moscow: Vremya, 2000), p. 313.
76 Oleg T. Bogomolov, 'I Can't Absolve Myself of Guilt', in Alexander Dallin and Gail Lapidus (eds), *The Soviet System in Crisis* (Boulder, CO: Westview Press, 1992), pp. 352–354.
77 Michael Henderson, *The Forgiveness Factor* (Salem, OR: Grosvenor Books USA, 1996), p. 115.
78 *Literaturnaya gazeta*, 1 July 1992, p. 3.
79 Cited in *For a Change* (London), October 1989, p. 11.

12 The democratic movement and its dilemmas

1 Vladimir Moss, 'Russian Orthodoxy and the Future of the Soviet Union', *Radio Liberty: Report on the USSR*, 14 June 1991, p. 4.
2 Oxana Antic, 'Developments in Church Life', *Radio Liberty: Report on the USSR*, 14 June 1991, p. 2.
3 Mark Beeching, 'Kharchev Discusses Draft Law on Religious Freedom', *Radio Liberty: Report on the USSR*, 4 August 1989, p. 3.
4 Jane Ellis, *The Russian Orthodox Church: Triumphalism and Defensiveness* (Basingstoke: Macmillan, in association with St Anthony's College, Oxford, 1996), p. 44.
5 Oxana Antic, 'The Gradual Rehabilitation of Orthodox Priests', *Radio Liberty: Report on the USSR*, 8 September 1989, p. 19.
6 Oxana Antic, 'The Russian Orthodox Church Moves Towards Coming to Terms with Its Past', *Radio Liberty: Report on the USSR*, 8 March 1991, p. 4.

7 Oxana Antic, *Radio Liberty: Report on the USSR*, 4 January 1991, p. 15.
8 Arkhiepiskop Ryazanskii i Kasimovskii Simon, 'Svyateishii Patriarkh Tikhon i ego sluzhenie Russkoi tserkvi', *Zhurnal Moskovskoi Patriarkhii*, No. 4, 1990, p. 66.
9 *Zhurnal Moskovskoi patriarkhii*, No. 1, 1990, p. 6.
10 See Irena Maryniak, '*Samizdat* Today – a Review', p. 125.
11 Antic, 'The Russian Orthodox Church Moves Towards Coming to Terms with Its Past', p. 4.
12 Ellis, *The Russian Orthodox Church: Triumphalism and Defensiveness*, 1996, p. 118.
13 *Religion, State and Society*, 20, 2, 1992, pp. 241–242; Ellis, *The Russian Orthodox Church: Triumphalism and Defensiveness*, 1996, p. 128.
14 Alexander Men', *Christianity for the Twenty-First Century: The Life and Work of Alexander Men'*, ed. E. Roberts and A. Shukman (London: SCM Press Ltd., 1996), pp. 165, 166–67, 169.
15 Mikhail Tareev, Russian theologian (1866–1934).
16 Men', *Christianity for the Twenty-First Century*, p. 145; see also Zoya Maslenikova, *Zhizn' Otsa Aleksandra Menya* (Moscow: Pristsel's/Russlit, 1995), pp. 140–141.
17 Men', *Christianity for the Twenty-First Century*, pp. 160, 165, 166–167, 169, 145; see also Maslenikova, *Zhizn' otsa Aleksandra Menya*, pp. 140–141.
18 Sergei Averintsev, 'Missioner dlya plemeni intelligentov', *I bylo utro* (Moscow: AO 'Bvita-Tsentr', 1992), pp. 326–327.
19 Aleksandr Minkin, 'Ne rydaite obo mne', *Ogonek*, 39, 1990, p. 32.
20 *Literaturnaya gazeta*, 12 September 1990, p. 3.
21 Aleksandr Belavin, "Pamyati Aleksandra Menya', *Demokraticheskaya Rossiya*, 4, October 1990, p. 15.
22 Ernest Gellner, *Conditions of Liberty: Civil Society and its Rivals* (London: Hamish Hamilton, 1994), pp. 137, 141, 142.
23 *Konstitutsiya (Osnovnoi zakon) Soyuza Sovetskikh Sotsialisticheskikh Respublik* (Moscow, 1977), p. 7.
24 David Powell, *Antireligious Propaganda in the Soviet Union* (Cambridge, MA: MIT Press, 1975), p. 168.
25 See R. Horvath, 'The Dissident Roots of *Glasnost*", p. 196.
26 See *Sovetskaya Rossiya*, 9 October 1990, p. 2.
27 Michael Rowe, *Keston News Service*, 25 October 1990; ARC newsletter, winter 1990.
28 Oxana Antic, 'Draft Law on Freedom of Conscience Criticized', *Radio Liberty: Report on the USSR*, 28 September 1990, p. 13.
29 Oxana Antic, 'Developments in Church Life', *Radio Liberty: Report on the USSR*, 4 January 1991, p. 16.
30 *Pravda vostoka*, 4 September 1990; cited in Oxana Antic, 'Draft Law on Freedom of Conscience Criticized', *Radio Liberty: Report on the USSR*, 28 September 1990, p. 14.
31 S.D. Baranov *et al.* (eds), *Politecheskie partii sovremennoi Rossii* (Moscow: ROSSPEN, 1993), pp. 163, 165.
32 Ibid., pp. 33, 38.
33 Program of the Popular Movement for the Restructuring of Ukraine, in Ralph Lindheim and George S.N. Luckyj (eds), *Towards an Intellectual History of Ukraine* (Toronto: Toronto University Press, 1996), p. 344.
34 Nikolai Shmelev, 'Avansy i dolgy', *Novyi mir*, 6, 1987, pp. 142, 144.
35 Nikolai Shmelev, 'The Rebirth of Common Sense', in S. Cohen and K. van den Heuvel, *Voices of Glasnost* (New York: W.W. Norton, 1989), p. 151.

36 Douglas Weiner, *A Little Corner of Freedom* (Berkeley, CA: University of California Press 1999), p. 430.
37 Ibid., pp. 431, 434.
38 V. Drobotov and V. Cherkasov, 'Oseni sebya sovest'yu', *Sovetskaya Rossiya*, 1 November 1989, p. 4.
39 A.E. Senn, *Lithuania Awakening* (Berkeley, CA: University of California Press, 1990), p. 87.
40 Horvath, 'The Dissident Roots of *Glasnost*", pp. 191–192, 198, 195.
41 Kathleen Smith, *Remembering Stalin's Victims* (Ithaca, NY: Cornell University Press, 1996), p. 92.
42 Ibid., pp. 97, 100.
43 Yevgeny Yevtushenko, '"A Time for Summing Up"', in Cohen and van den Heuvel, *Voices of Glasnost*, p. 271.
44 Yurii Afanas'ev, *Vedemosti Memoriala*, 28 January 1989, p. 5.
45 Dmitry Kazutin, 'To the Fallen Victims', *Moscow News*, 48, 27 November 1988, p. 11.
46 *Ogonek*, 47, 19–26 November 1988, p. 7.
47 Vitaly Korotich (ed.), *The Best of Ogonyok: The New Journalism of Glasnost'*, trans. C. Porter (London: Heinemann, 1990), pp. 162–167.
48 Lev Razgon, *Vedemosti Memoriala*, 28 January 1989, pp. 3, 4.
49 Smith, *Remembering Stalin's Victims*, pp. 153–160.
50 Jay Bergman, 'Was the Soviet Union Totalitarian?', *Studies in East European Thought*, 50, 4, 1998, p. 261.
51 Yurii Afanas'ev, 'Perestroika i istorichesko znanie', in Yu. Afanas'ev (ed.), *Inogo ne dano*, pp. 496–497.
52 Yuri Afanasyev, '"The Agony of the Stalinist System"', in Cohen and van den Heuvel, *Voices of Glasnost*, pp. 101, 102.
53 Ibid., p. 105.
54 Dunlop, *The Rise of Russia and the Fall of the Soviet Empire*, pp. 93–94.
55 Andrei Sakharov, *Memoirs*, p. 461.
56 Andrei Sakharov, *Moscow and Beyond 1986–1989*, trans A. Bouis (London: Hutchinson, 1990), p. 12.
57 Quoted in Gilligan, 'Sergei Kovalyov and the Defence of Human Rights in Russia', p. 72.
58 Pechuro (ed.) *Zastupnitsa: Advokat S.V. Kallistratova*, p. 6.
59 Smith, *Remembering Stalin's Victims*, p. 103.
60 Sakharov, *Moscow and Beyond*, pp. 58–59.
61 Ibid., p. 75.
62 Pimonov, *Govoryat 'osobo opasnye'*, pp. 28–29, 199.
63 Ibid., pp. 97, 143, 115.
64 Boobbyer, 'Truth-telling, Conscience and Dissent', *European History Quarterly*, 30, 4, 2000, p. 576.
65 Pimonov, *Govoryat 'osobo opasnye'*, p. 128.
66 Andrei Sakharov, 'Neizbezhnost' perestroika', in Yu. Afanas'ev (ed.), *Inogo ne dano*, p. 129.
67 Quoted in M. Steven Fish, *Democracy from Scratch: Opposition and Regime in the New Russian Revolution* (Princeton, NJ: Princeton University Press, 1995), pp. 91–92.
68 For details, see Smith, *Remembering Stalin's Victims*, pp. 80–84.
69 Interview with Valeriya Novodvorskaya.
70 Baranov *et al.* (eds) *Politicheskie partii sovremennoi Rossii*, p. 115.
71 Interview with Valeriya Novodvorskaya.
72 Fish, *Democracy from Scratch*, pp. 108–109.
73 Il'ya Zaslavskii, *Demokraticheskaya Rossiya*, 4, October 1990, p. 3.

74 Baranov *et al.* (ed.), *Politicheskie partii sovremennoi Rossii*, p. 88.
75 Interview with Sergei Kovalev, 'Dissident s parlamentskim mandatom', *Referendum*, No. 35, 1990, in Timofeev (ed.) *Referendum*, p. 175.
76 Galina Koval'skaya, *Demokraticheskaya Rossiya*, 3, November 1991, p. 5.
77 Vladimir Bukovskii, *Moskovskii protsess* (Paris: Russkaya mysl', 1996), pp. 43–47.
78 Richard Sakwa, *Russian Politics and Society* (London: Routledge, 1993), p. 136.
79 Remnick, *Lenin's Tomb*, p. 509.
80 Sakwa, *The Rise and Fall of the Soviet Union*, p. 484.
81 L. Aron, *Boris Yeltsin* (London: HarperCollins, 2001), p. 683.
82 Rosalind Marsh, 'The Death of Soviet Literature: Can Russian Literature Survive?', *Europe-Asia Studies*, 45, 1, 1993, p. 119.
83 Remnick, *Lenin's Tomb*, p. 392.
84 *The Times*, 12 December 2003, p. 19.
85 See Dunlop, *The Rise of Russia and the Fall of the Soviet Empire*, p. 88.
86 Ibid., p. 93.
87 Andrei Sakharov, 'Neizbezhnost' perestroiki', in Yu. Afanas'ev (ed.) *Inogo ne dano*, pp. 123, 127, 124.
88 Dunlop, *The Rise of Russia and the Fall of the Soviet Empire*, p. 89.
89 I. Brodskii, *Bol'shaya kniga interv'yu* (Moscow: Zakharov, 2000), pp. 465, 470.
90 Remnick, *Lenin's Tomb*, p. 284.
91 *Moscow News*, 52, 31 December 1989, pp. 7–10.
92 *Izvestiya*, 16 December 1989, p. 11.
93 The poster was designed by A. Vaganov (Moscow, 1990). See: http://www.poster.s.cz/listy/russ6.htm. Accessed, 21 August 2004.
94 The view of Lev Kopelev and Raissa Orlova, cited in Kelly, *Refining Russia*, p. 328.
95 *Moscow News*, 52, 31 December 1989, pp. 7–10.
96 Mikhail Gefter, *Referendum*, 37, August 1990, in Lev Timofeev (ed.) *Referendum*, p. 177.
97 Yurii Rost, 'Ushel chelovek', *Literaturnaya gazeta*, 20 December 1989, p. 10.
98 Yevgenii Yevtushenko, 'Pechal'no i tverdo', *Ogonek*, December 1989, 52, p. 2; for Yevtushenko's poem on Sakharov, see his *Collected Poems, 1952–1990* (Edinburgh: Mainstream, 1991), pp. 632–634.
99 Sergei Kovalev, 'Andrei Sakharov: Otvetstvennost' pered razumom', *Izvestiya*, 21 May 1998, p. 5.
100 Aleksei Makarkin and Ol'ga Pashkova, *Segodnya*, 11 December 1999, p. 4.
101 See R. Horvath, 'The Specter of Russophobia', *The Soviet and Post-Soviet Review*, 25, 2, 1998, p. 207 ff.
102 Quoted in P. Boobbyer, 'Religious Experiences of the Soviet Dissidents', p. 387.
103 Sakharov, *Memoirs*, p. 399.
104 R. Lourie, *Sakharov* (Hanover: Brandeis University Press, 2002), p. ix.

13 Conclusion

1 P. Vail' and A. Genis, *60-e: Mir sovetskogo cheloveka* (Moscow: Novoe literaturnoe obozrenie, 1998), p. 185.
2 C. Kelly, *Refining Russia* (Oxford: Oxford University Press, 2001), p. 397.
3 Anatole Lieven, *Chechnya: Tombstone of Russian Power* (New Haven, CT: Yale University Press, 1999), p. 21; cited in Kelly, *Refining Russia*, p. 397.
4 Oleg Volkov, quoted in Yurii Sokhryakov, 'Nravstvennye uroki "lagernoi prozy",' *Moskva*, No. 1, 1993, p. 176. For Volkov's memoirs, see *Pogruzhenie*

vo t'mu (Moscow: Pravoslavnaoe bratstvo svyatogo apostola Ioanna Bogoslova, 2002).

5 Vail' and Genis, *60-e: Mir sovetskogo cheloveka*, p. 180.

6 See A. Ledeneva, *Russia's Economy of Favours* (Cambridge: Cambridge University Press, 1998), p. 3.

7 Osip Mandelstam, *The Complete Critical Prose and Letters* (Ann Arbor, MI: Ardis, 1979), p. 183.

8 P. Boobbyer, *S.L. Frank* (Athens, OH: Ohio University Press, 1995), p. 137.

9 Merab Mamardashvili, 'Soznanie i tsivilizatsiya', *Kak ya ponimayu filosofiyu* (Moscow: Izd. gruppa 'Progress' 'Kul'tura', 1992), p. 107.

10 J. Brodsky, *Less Than One* (London: Penguin, 1987), p. 154.

11 Vladimir Bukovsky, *To Choose Freedom* (Stanford, CA: Hoover Institution Press, 1987), p. 30.

12 Cited in T. Venclova, 'Poetry as Atonement', in *Forms of Hope* (Riverdale-on-Hudson: Sheep Meadow Press, 1999), p. 130.

13 Mahoney, *Aleksandr Solzhenitsyn*, p. 43.

14 G. Weigel, *The Final Revolution* (New York: Oxford University Press, 1992), pp. 14, 42.

15 A. Amalrik, *Notes of a Revolutionary* (London: Weidenfeld and Nicolson, 1982), p. 26.

16 Aleksandr Daniel, 'Dissidentstvo: kul'tura, uskol'zayushchaya ot opredelenii?', p. 3.

17 Bergman, 'Was the Soviet Union Totalitarian?', p. 255.

18 Len Karpinsky, *Moscow News*, 45, 10–17 November 1991, p. 3.

19 A version of this idea was suggested to me by Professor Hugh Cunningham.

20 See Boobbyer, 'Russian Liberal Conservatism', pp. 35–54.

21 On these and related issues, see the articles by Richard Sakwa and Krishan Kumar in *Reinterpreting Revolution in Twentieth-Century Europe* (Basingstoke: Macmillan, 2001), pp. 159–197.

22 A point made by Vladimir Bukovskii, speaking at the University of Kent, 10 February 2004.

Index